A CENTURY OF NEWS

First published 2003 by Contender Books
Contender Books is a division of
The Contender Entertainment Group
48 Margaret Street
London W1W 8SE

This edition published 2003

1 3 5 7 9 10 8 6 4 2

ISBN 1 84357 084 X

With many thanks to David Seymour, Emily Seymour, Duncan
Lovett, Lewis Jones, Andrea Henry and Nigel Stoneman.

All images supplied by MGN Ltd

Printed in the UK by Bath Press, Bath and Glasgow
Design by Judith Ash
Repro by Digicol, Kent

Production: Sasha Morton

A CENTURY OF NEWS

A JOURNEY THROUGH HISTORY WITH THE DAILY MIRROR

Edited by David Seymour and Emily Seymour

INTRODUCTION

by David Seymour
Daily Mirror Readers' Editor

This is not a history book. Nor is it simply a history of the *Daily Mirror*, which celebrates its centenary on November 2, 2003. It is a book of the stories and events which have gripped and fascinated, shocked and amused, horrified and touched the ordinary British people over the past hundred years. The *Daily Mirror* was the first tabloid newspaper and those of us who have worked on it will forever claim it is the greatest. At one time it sold 5 million copies a day, the highest circulation of any daily newspaper in the free world and not one that will ever be overtaken. To look in the *Mirror* down the past century is, as its name suggests, to see reflected an image of the highs and lows, triumphs and failures, pageantry and wars, happiness and misery. It was the first paper of the working man and woman in an era when universal education was creating a mass readership. But to attract huge numbers of readers day after day needed something special. It required a mixture of entertainment and fun along with the serious news. Even in the darkest hours of wartime, it was necessary to provide a bit of light relief and frivolity. Those who criticise today's media for 'dumbing down' should look at some of the old *Daily Mirror*s. Even at its height it rarely took itself too seriously. This book provides a social commentary on how the British people and their country have changed. You will find the great wars fully reported and the enormous changes in society – the development of broadcasting, in particular, and the blossoming of that creature alien to former generations, the teenager. Newspapers sadly tend to be dominated by stories of tragedy and some of those in these pages can still evoke pain. Forty years on, it remains hard to read about Aberfan, when a generation of children was wiped out by a moving mountain of coal waste. Great achievements are also recorded here, not least the moment when man first set foot on the Moon. Yet scientific advances often fail to make news and certainly their significance is usually not immediately recognised. The invention of the Pill, which has revolutionised life for countless millions of women, made it into the paper, but only on page 20. Every great newspaper at some time makes news itself. Certainly the *Daily Mirror* has, and not always positively. But it can look back with pride on the part it played in launching the World Wildlife Fund, in protecting baby seals from hunters and

Lord, now lettest thou thy servant depart in peace

These are the opening words of Nunc dimittis — sung in churches during Evening Praise

ELVIS PRESLEY IS DEAD

From JEFFREY IRELAND in New York

ELVIS Presley, the country boy who became the King of Rock, is dead.

Was King of Rock killed by drugs?

One of the latest pictures of Elvis. He died from "respiratory failure" aged 42

LORD LOUIS MOUNTBATTEN Captain of HMS Kelly, Admiral of the Fleet, Viceroy of India, hero of Burma..

Murdered by the IRA

15 SOLDIERS MASSACRED—Back Page

making public the plight of children who are victims of abuse by brutal parents. The *Mirror* has never been shy about promoting itself or its journalists. Anyone who thinks today's paper is immodest should look back at what came decades ago. The pages devoted to launching the column of the '3am girls' in 2000 were mirrored by the space given to introducing in trivial detail the photographers sent out to cover the Balkans war of 1912 – though at least they weren't asked to name their most embarrassing moment and which star they fancied. Much of the *Mirror*'s self-puffery came from a pride in technological and journalistic advances. In the days before electronic wizardry, particularly digital cameras, getting photos back to London fast was often a remarkable feat of organisation which the paper delighted in sharing with its readers. Quite often the real story became how the *Mirror* had got the story. There have been almost 31,000 editions of the *Daily Mirror*, so a huge amount has had to be left out of this book. Some of the selection will be considered quirky, but that reflects the nature of a tabloid newspaper. My thanks to the team involved in producing it – Edith Ash, the designer; *Mirror* sub-editors Pat Welland and

Sean Garnett; Duncan Lovett and Derek Momodu from the picture desk; George McPhee from the picture library; and, especially, Emily Seymour, who created the structure for this book as well as researching it to her usual brilliant standard. But most of all, this book could not have been produced without the work of hundreds of *Mirror* journalists over the century. Editors, reporters, photographers, writers, sub-editors, artists – they have been the *Daily Mirror*. This is their story.

THURSDAY, MAY 13, 1937

Daily Mirror

No. 10434   Registered at the G.P.O. as a Newspaper   ONE PENNY

LONDON ED.

THE CROWNING OF GEORGE VI
KING AND EMPEROR

The moment of Majesty: '' The Archbishop, taking the crown from the Dean of Westminster, places it reverently upon the King's head. At the sight whereof the people, with loud and repeated shouts, cry,
GOD SAVE THE KING.''

FOREWORD

by Alfred Harmsworth,
founder of the *Daily Mirror*

Yesterday marked an epoch in the history of newspaper production. England has now a daily illustrated halfpenny newspaper – the first in the world – and has greeted its appearance enthusiastically. From the first thing in the morning, newsagents arrived from all parts of London to say that they wished to double, treble and quadruple their orders. At the same time telegrams poured in from every town in the provinces. In the publishing office the rush of orders exceeded the most sanguine expectations, and though the already large staff of men had been increased, it was found necessary, as telegrams and orders continued to pour in, to seek hurriedly further assistance. Extra machines have been engaged to prevent any repetition of the shortage. One of our readers yesterday informed us that his application for a *Daily Illustrated Mirror* was greeted with 'sold out' at five newsagents and six bookstalls. He eventually procured a copy, much damaged by the rain, which had been hanging outside a newsagent's shop. He was comparatively lucky. Many people, after just as many inquiries for the paper, were unable to get a copy – even a soaked one. Someone in a small town in the North of England spent 7d in a telegram ordering a single copy of the paper.

But though the rush for yesterday's number was phenomenal, it was less remarkable than the unanimous chorus of approval with which the first halfpenny daily illustrated paper was greeted. 'How is it done at the price?' was the question everywhere. The *Daily Illustrated Mirror* is not only a success; it is a revolution. It upsets every tradition of daily newspaper illustration. Till our appearance the occasional illustrations which were to be found in a daily newspaper were only a kind of 'makeshift' and were only used when it was found necessary to supplement verbal explanation. The *Daily Illustrated Mirror* has altogether altered this point of view. Our illustrations are themselves 'news'. They give news which was formerly only told in words. What has hitherto omly been given to the public weekly we are now giving daily. Every day the camera and the artist's pencil will produce for our readers the news of the day, and that, too, in a perfection which has never before been attained or even attempted. The position of the *Daily Illustrated Mirror* is already unique in the world of journalism. Its possibilities for the future are infinite.

This article first appeared in the Daily Mirror *on January 29, 1904*

1903

November 2, 1903: Britain's Empire is at its height, the Edwardian age has dawned and in a grimy press room in London a legend is born – to press baron Alfred Harmsworth a baby girl called the *Daily Mirror*. A baby girl because from the very start the paper that was to become a cherished national icon was a trailblazer, starting life as the first newspaper produced by women for women. And it was the first with a woman editor – Mary Howarth, who had been appointed to oversee the fledgling paper take its first brave steps. Mary Howarth can never have dreamed that 60 years later her baby would be selling an all time record of five million copies a day. Harmsworth, soon to become Lord Northcliffe, was always brimming with ideas for new projects and had hit on the plan for a newspaper for gentlewomen because, as he wrote in the first edition, 'the freedom, the education, the aims of women have only recently become wide enough to demand serious provision on so large a

The first newspaper produced by women for women

scale'. He wanted the *Mirror* to cover everything from the 'arrangement of flowers on the dinner table to the disposition of forces in the Far East', a revolutionary idea in those far-off days. Equally importantly, he laid down that the paper should be 'entertaining without being frivolous and serious without being dull'. It would be hard to find a better description of the qualities that define the *Mirror* throughout its history. Mary Howarth took her employer's instruction to heart. In a way that would be instantly recognisable today she entertained her readers with articles on 'Dress of the Day', the 'Cult of Beauty' and the 'Jewel Box' as well as pages of fashion and shopping. There was a feature on 'What Shall I Eat?' And a gossip column called 'Social Chit-Chat.' Amid the domestic froth that first twenty-page copy of the *Mirror* – costing just one old penny (about half a penny today) – contained highly topical stories on issues like 'Women's Employment.' Even more radically the paper also featured a full page of foreign news and a report on the planned reorganisation of the armed forces. At a time when women were actively discouraged from taking a wider interest in the world, and 15 years before they got the vote, this was a startling move. The *Daily Mirror* was starting as it would go on - breaking new ground, setting new standards and getting itself talked about.

To-Day's News At a Glance.

Important plans for securing efficient national defence are announced on this page.

Professor Mommsen, the famous German historian, died yesterday.

Lady Spencer died at Spencer House, St. James's-place, on Saturday.

M. Sagouni, the murdered Armenian revolutionary, has been buried at Forest Hill.

Vice-Admiral Hugo Lewis Pearson has been selected as Commander-in-Chief at the Nore.

Reuter says the miners' strike at Bilbao, which caused riot and bloodshed last week, is at an end.

Fifteen persons have been killed and fifty injured in a railway accident near Indianapolis, U.S.A.

Miss Joyce Howard, second daughter of Lady Audrey Buller, was married on Saturday to Colonel Arthur Doyle.

Forty-eight persons, passengers and crew of the Japanese steamer Tokai-Maru have been drowned in collision with a Russian steamer.

The King has given Staff-Captain Rawson, of Portsmouth Dockyard, the Royal Victorian Order for smartness in docking the Victory after her recent collision.

The London Chamber of Commerce has issued a letter showing how inexpensive furs are "doctored" so as to resemble much more valuable skins.

At Manchester on Saturday Sir William Harcourt declared that the gospel of universal dearness was contrary to common sense. At Paisley Mr. Asquith described Mr. Chamberlain's policy as one of lop-sided preference.

The skating season at Prince's opened on Saturday.

The entire Chilian Cabinet has resigned, says Reuter.

Paris newspapers say M. Lepine, Prefect of Police, has resigned.

Between 1,300 and 1,400 borough councillors are to be elected in London to-day.

Miss Lilian Dorothea Devitt was married on Saturday to Mr. H. S. Pendlebury, F.R.C.S.

At Maidenhead the floods are so deep that many inhabitants can only leave their houses in punts.

1,900 London shops will devote a percentage of their receipts to-morrow to the King's Hospital Fund.

Miss Dorothy Grimston, youngest daughter of Mr. and Mrs. Kendal, was married on Saturday to Mr. Robert Meyer.

M. Papazoglu, reputed the wealthiest man in Bulgaria, has (says Laffan) fatally shot himself in the presence of his parents.

Two men and a woman, who are suspected of robbing and defrauding servants all over London, have been remanded at Southwark

The evidence in a divorce petition by Mr Arthur Douglas, of Manchester, showed that the husband forgave his wife three separate times.

An electric disturbance, felt only beneath the surface, seriously interrupted telegraphic communication between England, France, and America.

By the breaking of a lift-rope a workman fell eighty feet and was killed, on Saturday at the Savoy Hotel extension, which is being carried out by American methods.

Page 3 of the first edition - the first news page

1 January Edward VII is crowned Emperor of India

3 March An historic anti-immigration bill is passed by the American Congress

16 June Henry Ford forms a new motor company

19 August At the 6th Zionist Congress, Britain suggests a Jewish state is established in Uganda

8 September In Bulgaria, 50,000 men, women and children are massacred by Turks following a Balkan rebellion

The Daily Mirror.

No. 1. MONDAY, NOVEMBER 2, 1903. One Penny.

READ PAGE THREE FIRST. ☞

17 September Colonial Secretary J. Chamberlain resigns from the Cabinet to campaign for Empire trade tariffs

21 September *Kit Carson*, the first 'wild west' movie is released

10 October The Woman's Social and Political Union is formed by Mrs Emmeline Pankhurst

17 November Meeting in London, Russia's exiled Socialist Democrats split into two groups, the Bolsheviks and the Mensheviks

18 November America and Panama sign a treaty to construct the Panama Canal

1904

It quickly became obvious that the world wasn't ready for a women's newspaper. Sales crashed. As Harmsworth later admitted 'Women do not want daily newspapers designed specially and solely for themselves.' But he had another bright idea. To produce the first daily picture newspaper. So he sacked all the women, amid many tears, and brought in a gang of hard-nosed Fleet Street men. On January 11 1904 the *Daily Mirror* became the first newspaper to print a photograph – of junks taking in stones for the Russian fleet at Newshwang on the Liao river, and on January 25 the paper's name was changed to the *Daily Illustrated Mirror*, with the cost of the paper being halved to one halfpenny

JONES BROTHERS' Prices for
The Celebrated
ROYAL WORCESTER
KIDFITTING
CORSETS

MILITARY CURVE, which gives the erect poise without discomfort.
ROYAL WORCESTER
Kidfitting Corsets.
JONES BROS. (HOLLOWAY), LTD. Holloway Road, N.

– the first example of newspaper price-cutting. There was more to come – on January 28 the *Daily Illustrated Mirror* dramatically lived up to its name by scoring yet another first, a picture on the front page and one guaranteed to tickle the Edwardian fancy. There, staring out from the news-stands was a drawing of the infamous financier Whitaker

Marvellously meaty material for a public hooked on melodrama

SITUATIONS VACANT.

Domestic.

BETWEENMAID wanted at once; £10-£12.—Write Y. B., Bond Street Bureau, 45, New Bond-st, W.

CHILDREN'S Maid wanted; for town; £22-£28.—Write Y. C., Bond Street Bureau, 45, New Bond-st, W.

HOUSEMAID wanted; must be able to wait at table; wages £18 annually.—Apply Matron, Northumberland House, Finsbury Park, N.

HOUSE-PARLOURMAIDS wanted at once.—Call Bond-street Bureau, 45, New Bond-st, W.; wages £26.

KITCHENMAID (young) wanted immediately; £12-£16.—Write Y. K., Bond Street Bureau, 45, New Bond-st. W.

REFLECTIONS

The new Bakerloo Line – the first on the London Underground - was not an immediate success, as the *Mirror* rather churlishly reported. A team of intrepid investigators toured stations and counted the passengers: 'In one carriage four men, one in a top hat, one in a soft black felt and the other two in bowlers. At Trafalgar Square station at 1.32pm a single passenger came down in the lift smoking a cigar. Two women and a man in a blue cloth cap got out at Piccadilly Circus. At Oxford Circus all but four got out and four entered, two of them women, one in red with a brown fur toque trimmed with white flowers at the back, the other dressed in brown with brown hat and brown feathers. 'These figures', the Mirror concluded triumphantly, 'are facts.'

Wright lighting the cigar with which he had poisoned himself after being found guilty of fraud. An inset drawing showed fascinated readers how a cyanide capsule was secreted in the cigar. For a public hooked on the melodrama of the Edwardian stage this was marvellously meaty material and soon the winning formula of low price, riveting stories and innovative pictures began to send the circulation up. The start of the Russian-Japanese conflict a couple of months later was trumpeted with the dramatic headline 'War!' and a picture of gunners preparing to fire at a ship. Never afraid to make a stand, the *Mirror* was firmly on the side of the Japanese. On March 23 the first front page photos appeared, showing the coffin of the Duke of Cambridge being pulled through the streets on a gun carriage – an unprecedented image for the time. A month later, on April 28 the paper reverted to its original title, the *Daily Mirror*, with the slogan 'An Illustrated Paper For Men And Women'. The change of name was marked with a full-page photo of King Edward receiving an enthusiastic welcome at Punchestown races in Ireland, the first of countless thousands of images of the Royal Family to appear in the popular press. The *Mirror* noted slyly that the presence of the legendary ladies' man attracted a much larger crowd of attractive young women than usual.

1903

17 December American inventors Orville and Wilbur Wright take off for a few minutes in the first ever flight

December Charles Booth's *Survey of Life and Labour* condemns the extent of poverty and squalor in London

1904

11 February The British and American governments declare their neutrality in the Russo-Japanese war

31 March 300 Tibetans are killed while trying to halt a British Mission. The Dalai Lama is forced to flee

8 April Britain and France sign a pact resolving historic differences

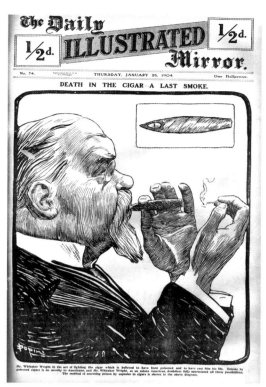

The Daily ILLUSTRATED Mirror.

½d. ½d.

No. 74. THURSDAY, JANUARY 28, 1904. One Halfpenny.

DEATH IN THE CIGAR—A LAST SMOKE.

Mr. Whitaker Wright in the act of lighting the cigar which is believed to have been poisoned, and to have cost him his life. Suicide by poisoned cigars is no novelty to American, and Mr. Whitaker Wright, as an astute American, doubtless fully appreciated all these possibilities. The method of secreting poison by capsules in cigars is shown in the above diagram.

THE WAR IN PICTURES ON PAGES 8 AND 9.

The Daily ILLUSTRATED Mirror.

½d. ½d.

A Paper for Men and Women.

No. 83. MONDAY, FEBRUARY 8, 1904. One Halfpenny.

WAR!

Japan says "No More Negotiations," and Recalls Her Minister in St. Petersburg.

FIGHTING EXPECTED ANY MOMENT.

Tsar Goes to Moscow to Pray for Russian Success.

READY TO FIRE THE FIRST SHOT.

The Japanese sailors on their fast-steaming torpedo-boat destroyers are spotting over the Eastern seas in search of the enemy's ships.

OUR SMALL ADVERTISEMENTS PRODUCE RESULTS. TRY

The Daily ILLUSTRATED Mirror.

½d. ½d.

SMALL ADS. 1d. PER WORD, MINIMUM 1s.

A Paper for Men and Women.

No. 121. WEDNESDAY, MARCH 23, 1904. One Halfpenny.

BURIAL OF THE VETERAN DUKE OF CAMBRIDGE.

½d. Daily Mirror

All the News by Telegraph, Photograph, and Paragraph.

An Illustrated Paper for Men and Women.

No. 151. THURSDAY, APRIL 28, 1904. One Halfpenny.

IRISH ENTHUSIASM AND THE KING.

THE ARRIVAL OF THE KING AT THE ROYAL STAND, PUNCHESTOWN RACECOURSE.—(Photograph by LaFayette, Dublin.)

WARM IRISH LOYALTY.

The King and Queen Alexandra Find Their Way to the Hearts of the People.

18 July In Tehran, a cholera epidemic claims 900 victims a day

21 July The 4,607 mile-long Trans-Siberian railway is completed after thirteen years

10 December Russian physiologist Ivan Pavlov wins the Nobel prize for his work on nerve messages to the brain

22 January A revolution in Russia is crushed when the Tsar's troops fire on striking workers in St Petersburg, leaving 500 dead

17 May A typhus epidemic breaks out in the East End of London

1906

REFLECTIONS

From Our Own Correspondent, New York, Sunday night: Quiet And Simple: The Goelet – Roxburghe Wedding Arrangements. The invitation cards for the marriage of Miss May Goelet with the Duke of Roxburghe have been issued by the mother of the bride. President Roosevelt and family, and the best-known American society people, are expected to attend. The bride's magnificent gifts of jewels from her millionaire friends and relatives beggar description, some of the most valuable being diamond tiaras and collarettes from Mr and Mrs Cornelius Vanderbilt. Miss Goelet has also been the recipient of clocks galore, Sevres china, interesting pieces of furniture, and bric-a-brac collected in all parts of the world. The Duke bought the massive gold wedding ring in London. The Duke of Roxburghe's solicitors have already arrived in America to draw up the marriage settlements and are receiving the handsome fee of £500 for their trouble. The bride will be presented at Court during the spring when she will wear her wedding gown with her diamond gifts.

Fears about immigration are not a modern phenomenon and early in the century a Royal Commission on Alien Immigration recommended placing harsh restrictions on people wishing to enter Britain. This led to the Aliens Act targeting 'undesirables' – paupers, lunatics, vagrants and prostitutes - who should be refused entry. Similarly, anyone who was diseased or had a criminal record was also barred. But genuine asylum seekers were exempt. As ever, the issue raised strong emotions and on January 3, 1906, the *Mirror* ran a series of photos on its front page to explain to readers how the Act was working. In an early foretaste of today's raids by Customs and Immigration, there were pictures of officials keeping watch for suspect ships and an 'aliens' officer' boarding the vessel *Sylvia* from Hamburg, which was carrying Russian and Chinese passengers. One photo showed the *Sylvia*'s saloon passengers rather smugly 'awaiting the arrival of the inspectors with confidence, as they are exempted from inspection under the Act'. Also pictured was the MP for Stepney in the East End of London, Sir William Evans Gordon, who claimed to have a special interest as he represented a constituency in which consid-

erable numbers of Jews from Eastern Europe had settled. Violence linked to immigration flared in the early years of the First World War but in the emotional atmosphere of the times it was more political than racist. Mobs – mainly in the East End – attacked and looted shops and offices belonging to Germans and Austrians. In

Paupers, lunatics, vagrants and prostitutes should be refused entry

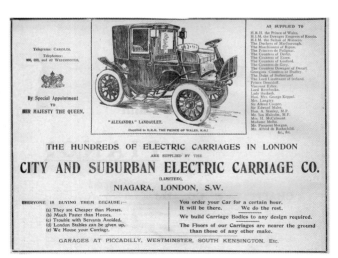

Poplar, a crowd of angry women chased the wives of aliens through the streets, flinging their belongings in the gutter. In Stepney, a crowd of youngsters seized a German baker, bundled him out of his shop and set it on fire. In Startford, to cries of 'Down with the Germans', a 3,000-strong mob attacked premises owned by Germans even though most of the owners had taken British citizenship. A barber's shop in Harlesden was completely wrecked by an angry crowd including soldiers. The Daily Mirror warned: 'Acts of vengeance on Germans in our midst help us in no way and discredit us abroad.' It then had a few words of patriotic advice for the inflamed populace: 'The surest way to obtain a righteous vengeance on the Germans is to serve in the Army and kill German soldiers.'

27 June Russian sailors on the battleship *Potemkin* mutiny against their officers

July The first ever non-British player, American May Sutton, becomes Wimbledon champion

1 July Albert Einstein produces his theory of relativity

14 October Russia and Japan agree peace terms

8 November Encouraged by the authorities, Odessan peasants murder hundreds of Jews

The Daily Mirror

THE MORNING JOURNAL WITH THE SECOND LARGEST SALE.

No. 678. | Registered at the G.P.O. as a Newspaper. | WEDNESDAY, JANUARY 3, 1906. | One Halfpenny.

KEEPING THE UNDESIRABLES OUT OF ENGLAND.

This interesting series of snapshots shows how the Aliens Act is worked at Gravesend. (1) A pilot in the pilot's office at Gravesend watching for incoming vessels; (2) the Sylvia from Hamburg, the first vessel to arrive under the new Act, dropping anchor to await examination; (3) the Customs launch Cerberus conveying the aliens' officers and the medical and port sanitary officers to the Sylvia; (4) Chinamen on board the Sylvia awaiting the arrival of the inspectors; (5) another group of aliens— Russians—on the Sylvia waiting to know their fate, whether they will be allowed to land; (6) Saloon passengers on the Sylvia who await the arrival of the inspectors with confidence, as they are exempted from inspection under the Act; (7) sanitary authorities' hulk at Gravesend, on which the medical officers and port inspectors have their meals and sleep while on duty. Inset is a photograph of Major Sir William Evans Gordon, M.P., for Stepney, the father of the Act.

1906

7 February The Liberal Party gains power in a landslide General Election victory

8 March The British Empire currently reaches across one-fifth of the world's land surface

7 April Mount Vesuvius in Italy erupts

19 April An earthquake in San Francisco devastates the city

17 June The largest, fastest passenger liner, the *Lusitania*, is launched in America

1906

REFLECTIONS

Although the *Mirror* seemed more interested in those days in the rich it also looked out for the downtrodden and sought a better deal for the underprivileged. A 1908 article highlighted the plight of the poor. It said: 'Vagrancy, it is not surprising to learn by an official report, is on the increase. Interesting figures concerning the method of living of the very poor and the inmates of common lodge houses are given. Here is the daily menu of a dock worker of 51. Breakfast – tea 1/2d. Toasted bread, 1d. No dinner. Tea – five fresh herrings, 2d. Potatoes, 2d. Tea, 1/2d. Supper – fried fish, 1d. Potatoes, 1d."

That traditional English fruit, the strawberry, is in short supply. And it's all down to the growth of the motor car. 'This year's strawberries will be a month late, and it is feared the supply will not be plentiful. The cold snap is partly responsible, but another cause is permanent in character. Motor cars are to blame. The strawberry is a delicate plant that refuses to yield good fruit if covered in dust and acres given up to growing it are in the proximity of highways frequented by motor cars. Growers are badly complaining. One told the *Daily Mirror* it is "hopeless to grow strawberries within half a mile of any main road"'.

Suffragette leader Emmeline Pankhurst, left

The fight by suffragettes for women to have the right to vote produced some of the most dramatic events of the first decade of the century. These brave pioneers took their fight to wherever they could get publicity, with no thought for their safety. One, Emily Davison, died after hurling herself under the king's horse at the Derby in 1913. Fittingly for a newspaper originally run by and for women, the *Daily Mirror* supported the unfashionable cause, though it did condemn the suffragettes' resort to violence. It said in an editorial of April, 26, 1906: 'To make things uncomfortable, to create a disturbance, to hold up men's institutions to ridicule – these are the weapons women have to fall back on to compensate for their inferior physical strength.' That day, the *Mirror* reported '*Amazing Scenes in the House*: Suffragettes Interrupt The Women's Vote Debate'. The paper's parliamentary correspondent said: 'Extraordinary scenes were witnessed in the House of Commons last night during the debate on Mr Keir Hardie's resolution in favour of woman suffrage. Mr W. Redmond held that any of God's creatures who were denied the right of a voice in the affairs of the country in which they lived were more or less slaves. Men had no right to assume that they were so infinitely superior to women that they alone should guide the destinies of the country.' But Mr Redmond was in a tiny minority. Certainly one Mr Bottomly gave him no support: 'Mr Bottomly urged that women

God's creatures denied a voice are no more than slaves

should be given a more intelligent interest in political questions. He, however, ridiculed the idea that women should sit in Parliament. Parliament must always be the married man's sanctuary.' No support, either from a Mr Cremer, who made an offensive and patronising speech: 'Mr Cremer declared that if they once opened the door to enfranchise only a small number of women it would ultimately lead to adult suffrage. "Are we prepared," asked Mr Cremer, "to hand over the government of this country to women, who are not breadwinners, and have not to bear the burdens and the responsibilities of life? No, no, Mr Deputy Speaker, I am too fond of them to wish to drag them into the political arena and ask them to discharge duties that they neither understand nor care for." This was too much for the suffragettes who packed the Ladies' Gallery. They unfurled a banner bearing the words "Vote For Women" and frantically waved it, accompanied by cries of "Justice for women!" To their indignation, they were thrown out.'

The Daily Mirror

THE MORNING JOURNAL WITH THE SECOND LARGEST NET SALE.

No. 776.   Registered at the G. P. O. as a Newspaper.   FRIDAY, APRIL 27, 1906.   One Halfpenny.

SUFFRAGETTES WHO RIOTED IN THE COMMONS AND WERE EXPELLED.

The Ladies' Gallery at the House of Commons was the scene of a spirited disturbance on Wednesday night. When Mr. Evans was speaking on the motion for women's suffrage, shrill cries of "Divide!" and "Justice for women!" re-echoed through the House. A white banner, bearing the words "Votes for Women," was thrust through the grille. Finally the Ladies' Gallery was cleared by the police. Reading from left to right, the photograph shows Miss Kenney, Miss Billington, and Mrs. Roe. The two former took an active part in the demonstration in the House, and were forcibly ejected.—(Specially taken by the *Daily Mirror*.)

1910

Here it is – the first great royal tabloid scandal. This then shocking front page picture, taken by an official court photographer, shows King Edward VII lying on his death bed ten days earlier. In a storm of criticism that will be familiar to any modern editor the *Mirror* was unjustly accused not only of stealing the picture but of insensitivity and lack of respect towards the Royal Family. Then, to the horror of the pious and pompous, it was disclosed that the King's widow, Queen Alexandra, had

The first great royal tabloid scandal. Edward VII on his death bed.

asked for the photo to be given to the *Mirror* because it was her favourite newspaper. She would have liked the report accompanying the picture: 'The utmost simplicity characterised King Edward's death chamber. He lay on the single mahogany bedstead where a thousand times he had slumbered almost as peacefully, for his life and the universal love and loyalty of his people gave him rest and gentle dreams'. The writer, warming to his theme, finished with evident relish: 'The manliness and lofty dignity of King Edward's features have never been more evident than when chiselled by the arch-sculptor Death.'

The death of the King, his funeral and the coronation of King George V set a new standard in the amount of space given to any event. A special 24-page edition was produced for the funeral and *Mirror* reporters toured the streets to gauge the mood of the nation. The solemn procession in which the King's coffin was taken to Westminster Hall was reported in splendid detail, including the snippet that the gun carriage was followed by the King's favourite charger and his dog, who was 'inconsolable that he could not find his master'. The writer added sombrely: 'Even in her supreme sorrow the Queen did not forget the grief of these dumb creatures and, ere setting out on the sad journey, found a moment to comfort the masterless dog.'

REFLECTIONS

The death of King Edward VII unleashed huge public grief as illustrated by the *Mirror* headline 'The Nation in Mourning - Shops Besieged by Purchasers of Black Apparel.' The report declared: 'Everything black was eagerly purchased by sad and sombre women in whose eyes it was easy to read the deep grief that had stirred all when the dread news of the beloved monarch's death was made known.. The City warehouses were sent to for their black materials and the ready-made black coat and skirt costumes. Pincushions stacked with hatpins were carefully searched for pins with black jet heads. No one looked at colours in any form.' It was war at the shop counter, for the report added: 'A moment lost in deciding was enough: someone else was ready to seize the coveted garment - for the needs of those who mourned were insistent.'

What to wear for mourning the King

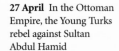

27 April In the Ottoman Empire, the Young Turks rebel against Sultan Abdul Hamid

29 April Lloyd George announces a 'People's Budget', raising taxes to fund the first pensions for the over-seventies

28 September The House of Commons confirms that nine Suffragette prisoners are being force-fed

7 December The self-governing Union of South Africa is created by royal proclamation

1910

10 January Figures show that British Empire trade is booming, and has doubled in the last fifteen years

The Daily Mirror

THE MORNING JOURNAL WITH THE SECOND LARGEST NET SALE

No. 2,044.   Registered at the G. P. O. as a Newspaper.   MONDAY, MAY 16, 1910   One Halfpenny.

EDWARD THE PEACEMAKER AT PEACE : THE LATE KING PHOTOGRAPHED ON HIS DEATH-BED AT BUCKINGHAM PALACE.

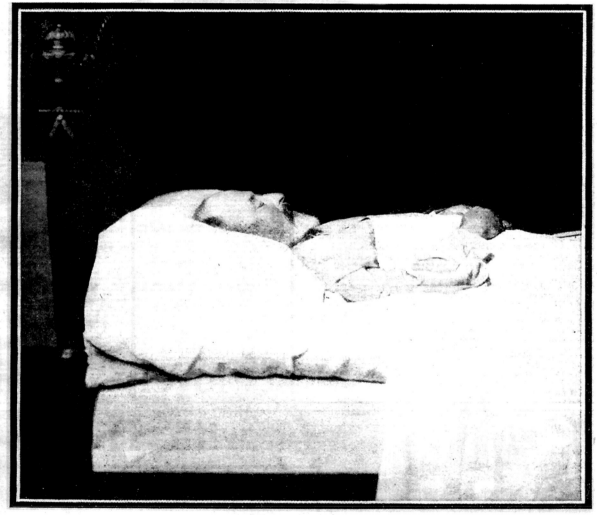

" He looked splendid—I use the word in its regal significance —and as he lay dead his features seemed to reveal the majesty of kingship more than at any moment I remember." These are the words of Sir Luke Fildes, the eminent painter, and were spoken by him after he had left the death-chamber at Buckingham Palace, whither he had been summoned to make a sketch of King Edward the Peacemaker lying on his deathbed. The photograph, which was taken by command of Queen Alexandra by Messrs. W. and D. Downey, of 57, Ebury-street, S.W., May 7, 1910, shows his Majesty after death.

26 January Record floods in Paris devastate the city

1 February The government opens the first eighty labour exchanges to aid the unemployed

10 March The first film to be produced in Hollywood, DW Griffith's *In Old California*, is released

14 April Plans to abolish the House of Lords' veto on government legislation is passed by MPs

1 May The National Association for the Advancement of Coloured People is founded in America

1910

Crippen and le Neve photographed in the dock

We have become used to newspapers and TV programmes like Crimewatch being a vital aid in criminal investigations – but it was the *Mirror* which set the ball rolling more than 90 years ago by helping to nail one of Britain's most notorious killers, the chilling Dr Crippen. Readers were gripped from the moment it became known that the headless body of the doctor's wife Cora had been found in the coal cellar of the home they shared in

'Crippen, I want you,' said Inspector Dew, placing a hand on his shoulder

London. There was no sign of Hawley Harvey Crippen nor of his secretary Ethel Le Neve. As Cora had been a music-hall artiste called Belle Elmore there were plenty of pictures of her for the papers to use. But the *Mirror* scooped the opposition by obtaining the only photograph in existence of Ethel and, having published it with a fanfare, handing over copies to Chief Inspector Dew of Scotland Yard, who was leading the hunt for the missing couple. He was delighted. 'That is a splendid photograph,' he enthused. 'The portrait is so good you can almost imagine she is talking to you.' It was not long before eager members of the public who recognised Ethel, and had seen her with Crippen since their disappearance, came forward. It emerged that the doctor and his lover had boarded a boat, the *Montrose*, for Canada under the names of Mr and Master Robinson. Ethel was dressed as a boy pretending to be Crippen's teenage son. The indomitable Dew of the Yard boarded another steamer, the *Laurentic*, and the transatlantic race was

Cora Crippen in music-hall dress

REFLECTIONS

September 27, 1910: From Our Special Correspondent, War Office Flying Ground, Salisbury Plain: The Daily *Mirror* this morning carried out important and highly successful wireless telegraph experiments with an aeroplane. Mr Robert Loraine, the actor-airman, came down specially from London and made a flight in the course of which he sent wireless signals from the aeroplane. The transmitting apparatus was specially designed by Mr Thorne Baker, the *Daily Mirror* scientific expert and inventor of the telectograph, the machine by which photoraphs are telegraphed from Paris and Manchester to London. It is not too much to say that the brilliant success of the experiment marks a signal step forward in the science of warfare as it is now established that an airman can rapidly and accurately locate the enemy's position.

on to reach Montreal first. But after being traced by the novelty of a picture in the press, Crippen was now doomed by a further stroke of new technology. The captain of the *Montrose* was told the identity of his seemingly innocuous passenger by Marconi's radio telegraph and dutifully hid all copies of English newspapers on board. Meanwhile Crippen, whose harmless bespectacled appearance belied his savage character, was relaxing, spending his time reading a book called *Four Just Men* about a murder in London. He was, however, taking a great interest in how long it would be before the boat reached land. He never set foot on shore as a free man. When the *Montrose* anchored outside Quebec, a rowing boat came out carrying three 'pilots' to navigate the ship into harbour. As Crippen stood by the rail looking out, one of the 'pilots' placed a hand on his shoulder. 'Crippen, I want you,' said Inspector Dew. He, and the *Mirror*, had got their man.

20 May Halley's Comet passes within 13 million miles of the earth

28 May In Kiev, thousands of Jews are ordered to flee by the Russian government

15 June Captain Scott sets out on his expedition to the Antarctic

1910

The Daily Mirror

THE MORNING JOURNAL WITH THE SECOND LARGEST NET SALE

No. 2,110. | Registered at the G.P.O. as a Newspaper. | MONDAY, AUGUST 1, 1910 | One Halfpenny.

END OF THE ATLANTIC CHASE: "DR." CRIPPEN, WHO WAS ARRESTED AT FATHER POINT, CANADA, YESTERDAY.

Yesterday "Dr." H. H. Crippen and Miss Le Neve were arrested at Father Point, Canada, thus bringing to an end the great chase across the ocean, which has provided a detective romance more amazing and more dramatic than ever came from the pen of a Gaboriau. Their capture is a great triumph for wireless telegraphy, which has demonstrated in a new direction its wonderful utility in the service of man. Whatever the outcome of the present case, it has proved the immense potentialities of the invention, which in future will undoubtedly prove a powerful weapon in the armoury of the detective, and a terror to the fugitive from justice. Above is a recent photograph of Crippen, who is alleged to have murdered his wife, Belle Elmore, at 39, Hilldrop-crescent, Holloway.

---

24 August Japan announces the formal annexation of Korea

27 August American Thomas Edison demonstrates the first talking motion pictures

September Sarah Bernhardt is the new star of the music hall

7 September Marie Curie isolates the first pure sample of radium

18 November Suffragettes storm the Houses of Parliament

1910

1910

It was curious that a woman who epitomised the 19th century should be lionised in death by a tabloid of the 20th century. But if anyone deserved a full front page photo it was Florence Nightingale, the legendary 'Lady with the lamp' who was credited with single-handedly creating the profession of nursing. Florence died at 90 having lived for the first decade of the new century and was pictured surrounded by the nurses who owed their livelihood to her and would no doubt have agreed with her claim that 'nurses are born, not made'. Extolling this paragon the *Mirror*, always alert to the human touch, reported that as a child Florence delighted in bandaging her dolls when she growing up on her father's estates in Hampshire and Derbyshire. From there, it was a small step to treating her first patient – a sheepdog with a bad foot which she tended night and day. As a young woman, still fired by the desire to help the sick, she read about the plight of wounded British forces in the Crimean War and 'like a flash realised that here lay her life's work'. Florence, accompanied by a band of 38 devoted helpers, set out at once for Scutari where 5,000 sick and wounded languished in appalling conditions in

Florence Nightingale

Men rose up on their beds to touch her garments as she went by

what passed for hospitals. The *Mirror* reported: 'For 20 hours at a stretch she would stand to see the wounded accommmodated; she was constantly in the operating-rooms; and at nights, an oft-blest figure with lantern in hand, she would go from ward to ward comforting and encouraging the sick and dying. Men would rise up on their beds to touch the garments of "The lady with the lamp" as she went by, and her name was on the lips of the dying.' Florence cut the hospital death rate of forty-two a day to two. Returning to Britain she was awarded £50,000 which she used to set up a home for training nurses. But the strain of her heroism in the Crimea had taken its toll. She became an invalid and could only move around with difficulty. 'I am chained to my room by illness,' she wrote - but she never stopped encouraging others. The *Mirror* commented: 'A serene and resolute courage upheld her to the last.'

The Daily Mirror

THE MORNING JOURNAL WITH THE SECOND LARGEST NET SALE

No. 2,122. | Registered at the G.P.O. as a Newspaper. | MONDAY, AUGUST 15, 1910 | One Halfpenny.

MISS FLORENCE NIGHTINGALE, "THE ANGEL OF THE CRIMEA," WHOSE DEATH IS ANNOUNCED, WITH SOME OF THE NURSES WHOSE PROFESSION SHE CREATED.

The whole civilised world is mourning to-day the loss of Miss Florence Nightingale, "The Angel of the Crimea," whose death at the age of ninety occurred on Saturday at her London residence. At a time when our soldiers were left without proper care she, with a band of thirty-eight nurses, volunteered to go out to the Crimea, her devotion to the soldiers compelling universal admiration. Her work during the war actually brought the nursing profession into being. She followed it by establishing nursing-homes all over the world. Above Miss Nightingale is seen surrounded by a group of probationers at the Nightingale Home at St. Thomas' Hospital. Although the photograph was taken over twenty years ago, it is one of the last photographs in which she appeared.

1911

12 May The Festival of Empire opens at the Crystal Palace, south London

25 May Mexican rebels oust president Diaz, who has ruled as dictator for 45 years

23 June King George V is crowned

8 August The Army is called out to quell riots in London and Liverpool

10 August MPs will receive a salary of £400 for the first time

1912

'*Disaster of the Titanic*,' shrieked the front page headline of the *Mirror* on April 19, 1912, above a picture of the 46,300-ton ship steaming out of Southampton on her maiden voyage to New York six days earlier. Subdecks continued '*World's largest liner sinks after colliding with iceberg during her maiden voyage*' and '*all passengers safe*.' That last headline seems a monstrous error today but communications were slow in those days so the muddle over the fate of passengers and crew was understandable. As the day drew on, the awful scale of the disaster began to emerge and later editions grimly reported '*Many lives lost*' although it continued to carry the smug quote from the shipowners' organi- sation: 'The *Titanic* is unsinkable. We are not at all worried about the prospect of losing the ship. But we are extremely sorry for the annoyance and inconvenience to our passengers'. Details flooded into the paper as fast as the sea had rushed into the ill-fated liner. 'Immediately the wireless operator got going the alarm sounded within every wireless cabin within hundreds of miles. SOS SOS SOS flashed out the code signal that betokened to every operator who heard it the dark news of a ship in need.' Amid desperate scenes of heroism and cowardice as passengers struggled to board the pitifully few lifeboats 1,635 perished in the icy North Atlantic. Next day, the *Mirror* was sadly reporting: '*No Hope Left of Any Boatloads Being Picked Up*.' By April 18 the *Mirror* reported

REFLECTIONS

On June 28, 1912, the *Mirror* reported a huge protest meeting over the Liberal Government's decision to introduce what became national insurance: 'Over 15,000 people last night assembled at the Albert Hall to protest against the Servant Tax imposed by the Insurance Act. Ten thousand - mistresses and servants, governesses, clerks, farmers, nurses, labourers - crowded into the hall and cheered with the untmost enthusiasm the declarations of the speakers that "We will not pay." Outside over 5,000 were unable to obtain admittance. The great meeting was organised by the Servants' Tax Resistors' Defence Association. From the platform Mrs Morgan Dockerell said that the women of England had never brooked any political interference with their domestic life. This tax would interfere with the good relations between mistress and servant.'

harrowing scenes as relatives came to terms with the loss of loved ones. The wife of a crew member - 'poorly-dressed and middle-aged' – asked: 'Will they bother about the names of the crew as much as the others – the swells?' She was assured they would. But the *Mirror* wasn't just shocked at the tragedy. It was outraged at the complacency over safety. In a classic front page it demanded to know: '*Why were there only twenty lifeboats for 2,207 people on board the ill-fated Titanic?*' It ran a vociferous campaign on the issue which dominated the Board of Trade inquiry into the disaster. One downside of the *Mirror*'s *Titanic* reporting was that

The *Titanic* starts her fateful voyage

'Be British!' cried the noble captain through his megaphone

it had to apologise after reporting that the ship's skipper, Captain Smith, had shot himself. The next day the paper grovelled and praised his courage: 'Amid all the inhuman scenes stand out deeds of heroism that make one thrill with pride for England and the English tradition. "Be British!" cried the noble captain through his megaphone ere he went to a hero's grave – today proclaimed to the world an Englishman of Englishmen.'

1911

22 August A thief steals the Mona Lisa from the Louvre in Paris

20 October Italian troops seize Tripoli from the Turks

23 October Winston Churchill becomes First Lord of the Admiralty

12 December King George V is crowned Emperor of India, and founds the city of Delhi

14 December Norwegian explorer Roald Armundsen beats Captain Scott to the South Pole

The Daily Mirror

THE MORNING JOURNAL WITH THE SECOND LARGEST NET SALE.

No. 2,648.   Registered at the G.P.O. as a Newspaper.   FRIDAY, APRIL 19, 1912   One Halfpenny.

WHY WERE THERE ONLY TWENTY LIFEBOATS FOR 2,207 PEOPLE ON BOARD THE ILL-FATED TITANIC?

Something must be done by the Board of Trade to insist upon a larger number of lifeboats being provided for giant liners. Only twenty lifeboats were supplied by Messrs. Harland and Wolff for the Titanic, and even twenty, according to the Right Hon. A. M. Carlisle, the man who, as general manager to the company, was responsible for the building, was four in excess of the number required to comply with the Board of Trade regulations. "As ships grew bigger I was always in favour of increasing the lifeboat accommodation," said Mr. Carlisle, "yet it remains the same for a ship of 50,000 tons as for one of 10,000." The photograph shows the lifeboats on board the Titanic. It was taken while the giant liner was in Queenstown Harbour on Thursday of last week, in sight of land for the last time. Two boats, or even three if necessary, may be swung as easily as one on this type of davit. It will be seen that there is only one in the photograph.

6 January New Mexico becomes the 47th state of the American union

15 February A revolutionary republic is declared in China

7 March The first non-stop flight from Paris to London is made in three hours

23 March Militant suffragettes smash shop windows in the West End

27 March The introduction of the Coal Miners Bill establishes a minimum wage and ends a paralysing strike

1912

page 24 Thursday October 10 1912

Only nine years after first hitting the streets the *Daily Mirror* was already becoming an indelible part of British life, setting new standards for popular and informed journalism. Those were to be raised again with its coverage of the 1912 Balkan War, a conflict which was to lead directly to the outbreak of the First World War two years later. The paper proudly announced that to provide its readers throughout the British Isles with the 'most exclusive and very best service of photographs and news' it was despatching to the war zone a corps of seven photographic correspondents – three of them brothers – declaring: 'All are enterprising Britons – young men who are not afraid to brave great dangers to triumph in the end. All have had excitement and danger as their constant companions as they have

Young men who are not afraid to brave great dangers

secured exclusive photographs and newspaper stories from every nook and corner of the globe.' What more could readers ask? Head office chartered a special steamer from Italy to Tripoli and set up special lines of communication with depots in Malta, Naples, Rome, Milan, Marseilles and Paris to enable photographs to be rushed to London. As the paper remarked: 'Nothing will be left undone to secure the best and latest news and the finest and most exclusive pictures.' The conflict began when, to the astonishment of the world, tiny Montenegro declared war on Turkey. Its ruler, 71-year-old King Nicholas and his three sons led forces across the border into Albania and heavy fighting began. A midnight massacre of Turks by Bulgarians followed. The next day a four-hour artillery duel was followed by the Montenegrans attacking fortified Turkish positions. However, the *Daily Mirror*'s relish at covering the war did not extend to supporting it. An editorial said: 'The first fruits of the harvest of the war were not long in coming. Already we read of great battles in progress, of annihilated detachments and of what is yet more horrible, inter-racial massacres.' It called on the Christian Powers to intervene to halt the conflict and thundered: 'If they do not, they are conniving in murder and massacre.'

GENERAL

No. 37.

HOW TO AVOID ACCIDENT.

THE RIGHT WAY TO GET OFF A MOTOR-BUS.

Be sure to face towards the front of the bus.

1912

28 March The Oxford-Cambridge University boat race has to be re-run when both boats sink

9 May The House of Commons pass the third Irish Home Rule Bill

26 May Transport strikes across Britain bring the country to a standstill

31 May US Marines land in Cuba to protect American interests

6 July A foot and mouth epidemic breaks out in Ireland and England

The Daily Mirror

THE MORNING JOURNAL WITH THE SECOND LARGEST NET SALE

20 Pages

No. 2,797. — Registered at the G.P.O. as a Newspaper — THURSDAY, OCTOBER 10, 1912 — One Halfpenny

FIGHTING ON SERVIAN AND BULGARIAN FRONTIERS: SEVEN SPECIAL "DAILY MIRROR" PHOTOGRAPHIC CORRESPONDENTS GO TO THE FRONT.

Special *Daily Mirror* photographic correspondents will record every event of interest in the Balkan campaign for the readers of this journal, seven of them having been dispatched to various parts of the theatre of war. Portraits of four of them, showing them in different parts of the world, are seen above. The other three will be found on page 10. (1) Mr. A. Wyndham (on horseback) in Morocco with the French army. He is wearing native costume, which was essential for a correspondent. (2) Mr. Horace Grant being dressed in diver's uniform before descending to the Lutine, the British frigate which, laden with treasure, sank in the Zuyder Zee in 1799. (3) Mr. Ivor Castle (holding his camera) before making a sensational flight over the fleet at Weymouth. The pilot is Mr. Grahame White. (4) Mr. Frank Magee, whose fine work in Tripoli will be fresh in the memory of our readers. He is seen above behind the trenches mounted on a mule.—(*Daily Mirror* photographs.)

1913

REFLECTIONS

June 20, 1913: New York: The taking of action against women who appear in the streets in what is considered to be improper attire is spreading throughout the United States. At Rochester (New York) yesterday policemen obeying the instructions of the Morals Efficiency Committee of the city council stopped women walking in the streets and entering shops with the following formula: 'Sorry, madam, unless you agree to return home and change your mode of dress I must place you under arrest by orders of the Morals Efficiency Committee.' The surprised and indignant women demanding to know what was their offence were told: 'You are improperly dressed.' Slashed skirts, gauze hose and 'peekaboo' waists (blouses) are condemned by the council who later will issue a proclamation defining the length of skirts and the proper thickness of material. Hosiery, blouses and other articles of feminine apparel are to be classified by the august censors as 'permissible' or 'undesirable'.

Captain Scott

where Captain Amundsen had pitched his tent exactly five weeks earlier. Impelled by the pure spirit of adventure, the spirit that has made heroes since the world began, they plunged into the white unknown in quest of the unattained. There was a blizzard that kept them to their tent. At last, half starved, battered, but not yet beaten by the fury of the gale, they pressed on and one by one they dropped by the way. On, on, on, over the white infinity they struggled, to fall at last, 71 eternal days from the South Pole, eleven miles from food and life! (Photographs on pages 1, 3, 8, 9, 11 and 14).' The next day the paper published 'The last photographs of Captain Scott and his heroes: The photograph which will make the greatest and

They plunged into the white unknown in quest of the unattained

In yet another ground-breaking move, the *Daily Mirror* signed an exclusive deal with Captain Robert Falcon Scott before he set out on his attempt to become the first person to reach the South Pole. Early in April 1912 the paper ran a 'thrilling and remarkable narrative' describing the early part of Scott's epic endeavour. Unfortunately, the *Mirror* was unaware that just four days earlier Scott and his four companions had died on their return journey having discovered on reaching the Pole that Norwegian Roald Amundsen had reached there first. The Englishmen's fate was only discovered almost a year later, leading the *Mirror* to produce pages of reports and pictures and a special memorial edition showing the monument to the courageous captain in the Antarctic wastes. The national shock at the death of the explorers was evident from the tone of the initial report: 'Captain Scott has reached the South Pole with four companions and all have perished. In these few words is summed up one of the greatest tragedies in the world's history of high adventure. The gallant explorer died ere he could reach the outer world. The little band of five heroes had pushed forward to win the South Pole. Records found upon the body of the last to die, Captain Scott himself, show that on January 18 they reached that spot furthest south

most poignant appeal to English hearts is one showing the little tent of death in which the heroes lay down for the last time and calmly awaited the end with a stoicism which has been unsurpassed. It is just as it appeared after the search party had cleared the snow away from about its base. The little tomb of snow and ice is not visible at the present time. It is swallowed up in the Antarctic winter. It will remain invisible for five months in every year.' Within the tent were found the bodies of Captain R. F. Scott, Dr E. A. Wilson, chief of the scientific staff, and Lieutenant H. R. Bowers, of the Royal Indian Marine. The precious films of the last scenes at the Pole were found carefully packed away in their belongings. The following day the *Mirror* reported what it called 'Captain Scott's Dying Appeal To Manhood Of Britain'. Notes found by the explorer's body said: 'For my own sake I do not regret this journey which has shown that Englishmen can endure hardships, help one another and meet death with as great fortitude as ever in the past. (Signed) R Scott, March 25, 1912.'

1912

5 November Woodrow Wilson is elected President of the United States

11 November A Royal Commission on Divorce finds men and women should be treated equally

4 December Turkey agrees peace with Balkan allies except Greece. Fighting continues

1913

13 January The first sick and maternity benefits are paid under the Insurance Act

28 January The government withdraws the Franchise Bill, ending hopes for imminent female suffrage

CAPTAIN SCOTT'S TOMB NEAR THE SOUTH POLE.

The Daily Mirror

24 Pages

THE MORNING JOURNAL WITH THE SECOND LARGEST NET SALE.

No. 2,987. | Registered at the G.P.O. as a Newspaper. | WEDNESDAY, MAY 21, 1913 | One Halfpenny.

THE MOST WONDERFUL MONUMENT IN THE WORLD: CAPTAIN SCOTT'S SEPULCHRE ERECTED AMID ANTARCTIC WASTES.

 It was within a mere eleven miles of One Ton camp, which would have meant safety to the Antarctic explorers, that the search party found the tent containing the bodies of Captain Scott, Dr. E. A. Wilson and Lieutenant H. R. Bowers. This is, perhaps, the most tragic note of the whole Antarctic disaster. Above is the cairn, surmounted with a cross, erected over the tent where the bodies were found. At the side are Captain Scott's skis planted upright in a small pile of frozen snow.—(Copyright in England. Droits de reproduction en France réservées.)

18 March King George I of Greece is assassinated

3 April Emmeline Pankhurst is found guilty of inciting arson and sentenced to three years in prison

1 June French boxer Georges Carpentier beats Britain's bombardier Billy Wells to win the European Heavyweight title

31 July Chancellor Lloyd George declares that the House of Lords should be abolished

5 August The suffragettes bomb country homes belonging to government ministers

1914

REFLECTIONS

No single wartime act so outraged public opinion as the sinking of the luxury liner *Lusitania*. She was torpedoed by a German U-boat as she sailed for America. Of the 2,160 people on board, only 658 were saved. A surviving passenger, Mr D. A. Thomas, described the confusion: 'I found myself near a boat which was already three-parts filled with women and children and men. Quite near me two women and a child were standing helplessly. The one with the child overcame her hesitation and, taking a flying leap, landed safely in the boat. At this the other woman became hysterical. "Let me jump in," she shouted wildly, but she had not the courage to do so. It seemed an eternity before I induced her to jump.' The *Mirror* said: 'At first Germany was in ecstasies over the horrible crime she had committed. Later messages show that she is beginning to make excuses.'

In an effort to keep up morale among the wounded, the King and Queen made regular trips to hospital to visit them. The *Mirror* reported: 'Day after day their Majesties journey to some hospital and by their kindly, genuine and sincere words of sympathy help considerably to cheer the lot of the sufferers. At the Home for Wounded Officers, the King surprised patients by the way he knew the name of most of those in charge. Despite their agony, the officers cannot put behind them their sense of military duty when it comes to meeting the King. Directly the King and Queen enter the ward every man who can make an effort tries to straighten himself to attention, even though the attempt involves pain and the moving of a maimed limb. The men have an unbounded faith in the King doing what he can for them. He already has done something in the matter of railway passes for wives and children.'

The Lusitania heads for America

August 5, 1914, was a hot sunny day yet one of the bleakest in history. World War One began and millions of British lives were about to be lost in the mudbaths and trenches of Belgium and France, often for the sake of a few yards of land. The *Mirror* solemnly announced the start of hostilities with the words: 'Great Britain is in a state of war with Germany. War was Germany's reply to our request that she should respect the neutrality of Belgium, whose territories we were bound in honour and by treaty obligations to maintain inviolate. Germany tried to bribe us with peace to desert our friends and duty. But Great Britain has preferred the path of honour.' Not that it wasn't expected. Four days earlier, under a full-page photo of the Kaiser, the *Mirror* had warned: 'This is Armageddon. Germany has declared war on Russia, invaded France and seized the small independent state of Luxembourg.' But the mood of the country was upbeat. Admiral Sir John Jellicoe assumed the supreme command of the home fleets. The King sent him this message: 'At this grave moment in our national history I am

Europe is crossed and crushed by millions of armed men

confident the officers and men of the fleets will revive and renew the old glories of the Royal Navy, and prove once again the sure shield of Britain and of her Empire in the hour of trial.' The War Office appealed for doctors and motor-cyclists to join the army. They would be paid 35s (£1.75p) a week, with £10 when they signed on and another £5 when they left. The war was only a few days old when it was reported that the beautiful Belgian city of Louvain had been destroyed by the Germans. An editorial, headlined *'Only the Beginning'*, said: 'We are at the beginning of the 20th Century, which was to have been the century of the war against disease and poverty, against obsolete tyrannies and commercial ugliness, the century which at last (as dreamers said) was to bring in a civilisation worthy of the name, instead of the armed commercialisation that had too long strained and demoralised the world. That was a month ago, that other world now gone. Today Europe is crossed and crushed by millions of armed men. A famous and beautiful city is in ashes. Other towns are falling or in flames. Villages are destroyed. Crops are ravaged. Thousands and thousands of corpses scatter the fields and float down the rivers. Destructive insanity is everywhere. And we are only beginning!'

1913

10 August The Treaty of Bucharest brings an end to the second Balkan war

11 September A cholera epidemic breaks out in the Balkans

7 October Henry Ford unveils the first moving assembly line

25 November Riots erupt in Natal after Mohondas Gandhi is jailed

30 November Charlie Chaplin makes his screen debut in *Making a Living*

GREAT BRITAIN DECLARES WAR ON GERMANY.

The Daily Mirror

LATEST   CERTIFIED   CIRCULATION   MORE   THAN   **1,000,000**   COPIES   PER   DAY

No. 3,364.   Registered at the G.P.O. as a Newspaper.   WEDNESDAY, AUGUST 5, 1914   One Halfpenny.

DECLARATION OF WAR BY GREAT BRITAIN AFTER UNSATISFACTORY REPLY TO YESTERDAY'S ULTIMATUM.

Neptune's imps. They are torpedo-boats steaming in close order to enable them to send verbal messages one to another by means of a megaphone.

Field-Marshal Sir John French.

Rear-Admiral C. E. Madden.

Admiral Sir John Jellicoe.

Field-Marshal Earl Kitchener.

Remarkable picture of a submarine rising to the surface. Are we soon to know what these unknown quantities are capable of?

There are four men—two sailors and two soldiers—to whom the Empire will turn in her hour of need. The sailors are Admiral Sir John Jellicoe (known as "the future Nelson"), who has assumed supreme command of the Home Fleets with the acting rank of Admiral, and Rear-Admiral Charles E. Madden, who has been appointed to be his Chief of Staff. The soldiers are Lord Kitchener, whose achievements are known to everyone, and Sir John French, probably the finest cavalry leader in the world, who performed brilliant feats in South Africa, "the grave of reputations."—(Bassano, Symonds, Russell and Gale and Polden.)

18 February A British explorer discovers ancient Inca cities in the Peruvian jungles

25 February Ulster lies on the brink of civil war as the Ulster Volunteer Force prepares to fight

17 March Churchill presents the new Navy budget to the House of Commons, aiming to match the European arms build-up

4 April Hundreds rally in Hyde Park to protest at the potential use of British troops in Ulster

22 May The Suffragettes attempt to storm Buckingham Palace to present a petition to the King

1914

If ever there was a picture of how little men knew of the horrors that were about to greet them, one carried in the *Mirror* showing volunteers enthusiastically queuing to sign up to fight summed up the situation. Thousands responded to the call to arms. One report said: 'There are queues such as no first night has ever seen. The police are hard put to keep the men back.' Hundreds were pictured cramming the pavements outside Scotland Yard, the main recruitment office for London, 'every single one of them wanted to serve his King and country'. News of what was happening at the front, though, was hard to come by. But on August 24, 1915, came reports of the first skirmishes involving British soldiers – a cavalry outfit taking on a German equivalent. In the early weeks of war there were plenty of pictures of the preparations being made at home to repel an invasion. Flotillas of ships were seen establishing

REFLECTIONS

The outbreak of the first World War proved the making of the *Daily Mirror*. Within a year it boasted its July average daily circulation of 1,053,000. 'An average million a day is the almost impossible figure which newspapers in every land have been striving to attain. Some French newspapers claim they have passed this colossal figure – but their figures have never been checked. There is no doubt the *Daily Mirror* stands alone.' Six pictures of contemporary events surrounded the text in tribute to the newspaper's biggest selling point – its pioneering use of exclusive photographs 'which have made it famous the world over'. The paper said: 'Already we are leaving the mammoth figure behind. Already we are climbing steadily on the way upwards – shall we say another million?' Wrong. Ultimately, it was to be another four million!

Many an insult has been hurled at journalists through the ages. But it seemed the German army in World War One held them in lower esteem than most. A *Mirror* reporter was told in Brussels before an invasion party arrived: 'You had better get away at once. The Germans have orders to shoot all British newspaper correspondents because, they say, they are worse than spies.' He left just before the entry of the German advance guard. From Brussels he went to Ghent. Here he escaped on the last troop train when it was stated the Uhlans were on the outskirts of the old town.'

There were queues such as no first night has ever seen

defences off the south coast and sandbags and trees were used to build land defences. Fury against the Germans was stoked by a series of reports and pictures from Belgium, often contrasted with British humanity. One front page showed a destitute woman and her three young children weeping in the street under the headline: 'The Germans' Dastardly Work: Belgian Woman Whose Home Is Burnt Down Forced To Beg For Bread.' Later came dramatic photos

showing the result of bombs dropped from Zeppelins. Another front page was of 'An Englishman's Home' smashed by a raid. A mother and daughter had been thrown into the street and a boy had been trapped by the falling roof. A further picture showed children looking at the hole made in their bed by shrapnel. One had been sleeping in it but looked none the worse for his experience. Other youngsters were seen hunting for souvenirs in a huge crater left by a bomb. By the end of 1914, coverage from the front was improving. 'The world war is developing into a duel to the death between big guns,' the *Mirror* reported. 'Germany thought her great artillery would cow the world. Now the artillery of the Allies is mastering the heavy German batteries. Blow for blow and shot for shot, the guns of Great Britain and France are beating the guns of the Huns.' There was little indication behind this jingoism of the suffering in the trenches. But as Christmas approached the *Mirror* ran a remarkable front page showing an exhausted soldier asleep in the snow. It was an indication of how hard life was for the men at the front.

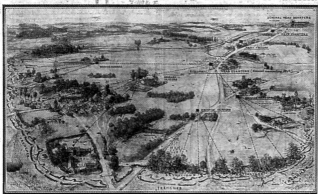

HOW A BATTLE IS CONDUCTED: THE IMPORTANT ROLE PLAYED BY WIRELESS.

A pioneering wartime graphic - nowadays all newspapers run them

28 June The Archduke Franz Ferdinand is assassinated in Sarajevo

23 July Austria issues an ultimatum to Serbia

4 August Germany invades Belgium

23 August British troops suffer heavy casualties at Mons and are forced to retreat

31 August St Petersburg is renamed Petrograd

OUR MONSTER CHRISTMAS NUMBER.

The Daily Mirror

CERTIFIED CIRCULATION LARGER THAN ANY OTHER DAILY NEWSPAPER IN THE WORLD

No. 3,470. Registered at the G.P.O. as a Newspaper. MONDAY, DECEMBER 7, 1914 **24 PAGES.** One Halfpenny.

A SOLDIER SLEEPS AMID THE SNOW: WHAT CHRISTMAS MEANS TO OUR BRAVE TROOPS AT THE FRONT.

Anyone who does not realise what a winter campaign means and what terrible hardships the men have to undergo has only to look at this remarkable study by a French photographer. While the civilian takes refuge from the cold in a soft blanket-covered bed, the soldier, who protects his home, must get his rest as best he can, often exposed to biting winds and driving snow. There are no eiderdowns or hot-water bottles at the front.

---

31 August Russia is heavily defeated on the Eastern Front in the Battle of Tannenberg

4 October The first German bomb falls on London

7 October The aeroplane transforms the face of war in Belgium and France

28 October The Eastman Kodak Company announces the invention of colour photographic processing

17 November British income tax is doubled to pay for the war

1915

By the spring of 1915, there was no disguising the horrors of the war, though the authorities did their best. But the *Mirror* did try to tell those back home how their loved ones were suffering. One headline said: 'Germans Gain Ground Near Ypres By Using Asphyxiating Gas.' Yet even in the darkest hours, tabloids feel a duty to cheer up their readers. And there was nothing like the latest clothing styles to bring a glimmer of light into people's gloomy lives. 'Youth and romance are personified in these summer fashions, which owe so much to days of long ago,' the *Mirror* simpered. The skirt, which was described as short because it showed a daring glimpse of ankle, was 'graceful, charming and demure'. And what could be more fascinating or feminine than the little loose coatee – 'braided, scalloped and ridiculously short'. As the weather warmed up, there were plenty of pictures of girls bathing in the sea. One tongue-in-cheek caption said: 'They reported sighting no U-craft during their swim.' However, the grim reality of war was all over the other pages. The *Mirror* printed pictures found at the front – family snaps of wives, girlfriends and children picked up near the trenches. The men who had taken them as a keepsake were dead. The official line, though, remained that set-backs were principally inflicted on our allies. The French were driven back at Ypres while British troops 'Hold Entire Crest of Hill 60' and 'Our front remains intact except on the extreme left'. It was claimed allied counter-attacks were a success. But the true toll was only learnt when the war was over. On the first anniversary of the start of hostilities, the *Mirror* gave a progress report. The Germans' initial advantage had been neutralised, it was claimed, though it admitted there was deadlock on the western front. A clue to the desperation of the real situation came when the King made a 'Stirring Appeal To My People'. He said: 'At this grave

THE MARTYRDOM OF A BRITISH NURSE

Edith Cavell is marked with a cross

REFLECTIONS

Edith Cavell was born in Norfolk and became a nurse when she was 20. In 1907 she moved to Brussels as matron of a large hospital. When the Germans invaded Belgium, she began to shelter British, French and Belgian soldiers, who were later able to escape to neutral Holland. The Germans discovered what she was doing and arrested her. She readily confessed. Her motives were entirely humanitarian, she said. But she was sentenced to be shot and, despite a huge international campaign to save her, the sentence was carried out. 'The Florence Nightingale of Brussels,' as she was known, became a symbol of courage. She is commemorated by a statue near Trafalgar Square.

When air warfare was in its infancy, raids by German Zeppelin airships posed an unnerving new dimension of terror. On May 11, 1915, the *Mirror* told in outraged terms how 100 bombs were dropped over Southend and surrounding seaside towns. 'Crowds Throng Streets to See the Air Huns at Work and Sleeping Woman Killed in her Bed', it reported, as it raged at German 'blood lust'. Five months later a fleet of the 'air butchers' killed 56 in London and East Anglia. 'Five aeroplanes of the Royal Flying Corps went up, but owing to the atmospheric conditions only one succeeded in locating an airship. The aeroplane, however, was unable to overhaul the airship before it was lost in the fog.'

Youth and romance are personified in these summer fashions

moment, more men and yet more men are asked to come forward so that Great Britain shall secure victory and enduring peace.' The King's plea, said the *Mirror*, 'is an intimate, personal letter to every man in the country, to men of all classes. His message is: "Take your share in the fight"!' The paper demanded: 'Are there any shirkers who will be able to stand out now?'

WILL BRITISH SOLDIERS HAVE TO FIGHT IN RESPIRATORS?

The War Office takes emergency measures

OUR NEW SHORT SERIAL, "A BARGAIN IN HEARTS," BEGINS TO-DAY

The Daily Mirror

CERTIFIED CIRCULATION LARGER THAN ANY OTHER PICTURE PAPER IN THE WORLD

No. 3,595. | Registered at the G.P.O. as a Newspaper. | MONDAY, MAY 3, 1915 | **24 PAGES.** | One Halfpenny.

SUMMER STYLES REPLETE WITH YOUTHFUL CHARM ARE PERHAPS DESIGNED TO MAKE US FORGET THE HORRORS OF THE WAR.

There is the charm of the old world in this summer evening gown by Reville and Rossiter, revealed in delicate sky-blue gros de Londres, trimmed with ruchings and garlands of shell-pink satin roses, with tulip-green foliage introduced at the hem of the skirt and on the corsage.

An original coat by Reville and Rossiter of royal purple woven with velvet stripes in black. This coat is worn with high Russian boots. A large cluster of lilies of the valley is worn at the waist.

Youth and romance are personified in these summer fashions, which owe so much to days of long ago. - The full short skirt is graceful, charming and demure in the softest of summer materials, and what more fascinating or feminine than the little loose coatee, braided, scalloped and ridiculously short.

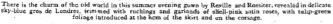

22 April The British launch a spring offensive at Ypres

3 May The government names the three main enemies as 'Germany, Austria and Drink'

8 May American liner the *Lusitania* is torpedoed off the Irish coast

13 May Street violence against 'aliens' erupts in London as anti-German feeling rises

25 May Herbert Asquith is forced to form a coalition government to avert a political crisis

1916

REFLECTIONS

Fat cats are nothing new – in 1916 the Bishop of London, Dr Winnington Ingram, revealed his income was £10,000 a year, £366,000 at today's prices. He nobly said he would be prepared to forego the bulk of the money and his Fulham Palace residence, but questioned whether 'having, say, a villa at Hampstead' would be the right place to entertain 'all the important men of England'. Also reported in the same issue was the case of a man of 41 who argued he should not be conscripted as his birth was not registered and therefore he had never been born. A tribunal sternly ruled: 'He is fit for the tanks.'

Gregory Rasputin was born in a small Siberian village in 1869 but rose to hold mystical power and unrivalled influence over the Russian royal family. Shortly before the revolution, he was brutally murdered by aristocrats jealous of the hold he had over the Tsar and his wife. The *Mirror* revealed that the man accused of killing him, Prince Felix Youssoupoff, had enticed Rasputin to his palace where he and other conspirators drugged, poisoned and then shot the shadowy, mysterious monk. Miraculously, he survived. But he drowned when he was thrown into the river. His body was found in an ice hole. The Prince's punishment was to be exiled from Russia – which saved his life when the Tsar and his family were butchered following the Revolution.

At Easter in 1916 the Government found itself having to fight on another front - only this one was nearer home. The IRA launched rebellion in Dublin and, with so many regular soldiers away in France, there were not enough troops to quell the uprising. There was a stunned tone to the initial account: 'Sinn Feiners, that is to say, Irish malcontents, mostly armed, occupied Stephen's Green, Dublin, at noon on Monday. They seized the Post Office and occupied nearby houses. Soldiers were brought from the Curragh and the situation is now well in hand.' It took a few days for the real scale of the bloody rebellion to come out, when the *Mirror* firmly nailed its colours to the Unionist mast: 'The rebellion is nearly over in Dublin. Leaders and bodies of the Sinn Feiners have either been killed or have surrendered and the insurrection as an organised conspiracy has ceased to exist. It received its death blow this afternoon when P.H.Pearse, the self-styled president of the Irish Republic and commander-in-chief of the rebel forces, was shot in the leg and captured. He is reported to have offered to parley terms of surrender with the commander of the King's troops. This we, of course, rejected and an unconditional surrender of a body of rebels is reported to have taken place in the central district of Dublin. The rebels' flag, which they had hoisted over their last main fortress, the Coliseum Music Hall, was hauled down. For some hours there has been a complete cessation of the rattle of machine gun and rifle fire which up to noon tortured the city, and very slowly, like men unexpectedly saved from the perils of imminent death, the people are beginning to come out of their houses again to look at the destruction and

'The insurrection as an organised conspiracy has ceased to exist'

count their dead. What they will see is that Dublin is a ruined city for months to come.' The tide turned against the Republicans when a troop of British forces arrived from the Curragh. A report stated: 'Lancers charged in a body down Sackville-street, clearing it of rioters. Side by side the cavalrymen galloped down, the hoofs of their horses ringing on the stones, and the rebels fled right and left. But in their charge the Lancers were enfiladed by rifle fire from the houses on each side of the street, and some horses, at any rate, were shot dead.' Pearse was executed within days of being captured and became a martyr of the Irish cause.

Count Rasputin

1 July 'Brides in the bath' killer George Joseph Smith is convicted and sentenced to death

11 November Winston Churchill resigns from the War Cabinet to go to France

20 December Allied Troops retreat from Gallipoli after a disastrous ten-month expedition

6 January The British Government introduces a Conscription Bill

21 February The Germans launch a devastating offensive on French positions in Verdun

THE DAILY MIRROR, Wednesday, May 3, 1916.

ARMY BILL TO-DAY FOR IMMEDIATE AND GENERAL COMPULSION

The Daily Mirror

CERTIFIED CIRCULATION LARGER THAN THAT OF ANY OTHER DAILY PICTURE PAPER

No. 3,908. Registered at the G.P.O. as a Newspaper. WEDNESDAY, MAY 3, 1916. One Halfpenny.

BRITISH SOLDIERS FIRING ON THE REBELS IN DUBLIN: MACHINE GUNS IN ACTION IN THE STREETS.

A machine gun section behind a street barricade in the South Dublin area. The photograph was taken during the actual fighting.

Mounted men in Sackville-street passing a horse lying dead in the road.

The balcony from which the first shot of the rebellion was fired.

The fighting in Dublin was enough to try the courage of seasoned troops, but the men engaged behaved with the utmost gallantry, although most of them had never been in action before. It was in the houses that the danger lay, as the snipers hid themselves within, and their chief efforts were directed against anyone in khaki. Soldiers could be seen lying behind barricades at every street corner, as in the top photograph, which was taken during the actual hostilities.—(*Daily Mirror* photographs.)

23 February Wealthy British families are asked to release their servants for war services

9 March Britain and France discuss the post-war division of the Ottoman Empire

4 May MPs approve plans to call up all men aged between 18 and 41

21 May British summer time is introduced in an attempt to save coal stocks

27 May President Wilson calls for a 'league of nations' to avoid future wars

1916

The bloody stalemate of the war was broken by the introduction of the tank. The first the British public saw of this revolutionary armoured vehicle was on the front page of the *Daily Mirror*. The paper had paid £1,000 to the Canadian Record Office for the photos – almost £70,000 in today's money. The cash went to war charities. There were vivid descriptions of tanks 'spitting forth fire and destruction' and 'taking ditches like kangaroos'. Only the men at the front knew how desperately the machines were needed to help stop the slaughter that was taking place. By this time the Battle of the Somme was at its height and the full horror was kept

Spitting forth fire and destruction and taking ditches like kangaroos

from readers. One front page showed Canadian soldiers climbing out of their trench and charging 'over the top' towards enemy lines. It was claimed the pictures proved the troops had mastered the foe. The report added: 'In this attack many of the men were laughing as they clambered out of the trench and made their way across the open to meet the Boche at close quarters.' The Battle of the Somme lasted for five months. At the end the allies had gained just 10 metres of ground and suffered 650,000 casualties. Today, we know much of what appeared in newspapers then was pure propaganda. The battle for Verdun was quaintly described as a struggle between the 80-year-old German Field Marshal Graf Von Haeseler, who was 'attempting to capture the place regardless of loss of life' and the French General Henri Petain 'who is 60, very modest and beloved by his men'. It's probably just as well the folks at home were ignorant of the grotesque level of casualties in the trenches, because the call for more men to sign up and fight got louder and louder. Lord Kitchener pleaded: 'We must have the married men (who were exempt from fighting). The position is an anxious one.' There was opposition, though. In a parliamentary by-election at Market Harborough, Mr Gibson Bowles, the Husbands' Candidate, pledged to keep married men out of the army, while at an election in Hyde, Mr W. P. Davies stood as an independent on a platform of 'fair play for attested married men and criticism of the Liquor Control Board'. The Board had been set up to answer worries about

excessive drinking by munitions workers. Its most significant a was to force pubs to close in the afternoon – a measure, as mar no doubt joyously remember, only repealed in 1988.

BRITONS
"WANTS"
YOU
JOIN YOUR COUNTRY'S ARMY!
GOD SAVE THE KING
Reproduced by permission of LONDON OPINION

31 May British and German dreadnoughts engage in an historic battle at Jutland

7 June Lord Kitchener, Commander of the British Expeditionary Forces, dies when his ship is hit by enemy fire

21 June Arab forces revolt against Turkey in a drive for independence

29 June Former diplomat Sir Roger Casement is found guilty of high treason and sentenced to death

1 July The Allies open an offensive on the Somme

1916

BRITAIN'S BIGGEST HOSPITAL SHIP SUNK—1,106 SAVED, 50 DEAD

The Daily Mirror

CERTIFIED CIRCULATION LARGER THAN THAT OF ANY OTHER DAILY PICTURE PAPER

No. 4,083. | Registered at the G.P.O. as a Newspaper. | THURSDAY, NOVEMBER 23, 1916 | One Halfpenny.

SOME MORE WONDERFUL PHOTOGRAPHS OF "TANKS" IN ACTION— EXCLUSIVE PICTURES FOR WHICH £1,000 WAS PAID.

Firing its guns during a battle. The Germans say that they are going to use tanks, and that theirs will be superior to the British.

Two "tanks" spitting forth fire and destruction from their guns.

Proceeding serenely on their way across a barren and trampled field.

"They take ditches like kangaroos, and simply love shell holes. Laugh at 'em."

To-day we publish four more wonderful photographs of the "tanks" in action. Those which appeared in our issue yesterday were the talk of the country, and there was a great rush to obtain copies of The Daily Mirror. The proprietors paid a record sum— £1,000—to the Canadian Record Office, and the money is to be given to war charities, while the whole of the proceeds of the world sales, which The Daily Mirror has undertaken, will be devoted to the Canadian War Memorials Fund.—(Exclusive.)

1917

By 1917, there was no disguising the terrible toll war was taking on men and morale. But, as far as possible, each military action was presented to the reading public as a positive advance rather than a hopeless and pointless slaughter. It was the year of Flanders, when hundreds of thousands of men struggled as much with the mud as they did with the enemy. Everybody was floundering in it, the *Mirror* said – horses, men and mules. There was no getting away from the horrible stuff –'its adhesive properties are superior to any glue on the market. It sticks to uniforms and the coats of horses. But', the paper added, 'our men don't despair.' On August 1 it was reported the British had advanced four miles in the first battle of Flanders. Fighting continued all day despite unfavourable weather. *Mirror* reporter W. Beach Thomas sent this dramatic eye-witness account from the War Correspondents' Headquarters: 'As I went forward in the morning, from the smoke of the heaviest

Men struggled as much with the mud as they did with the enemy

bombardment ever seen by soldiers came clear sign upon sign of a sterling victory during the first hours of the morning. News came back in many forms. Messengers arrived quickly and successively with the announcement of first and second lines captured. Our airmen, who were out at four o'clock flying very low, brought good, though sometimes vague, messages. One of them, wounded by a bullet, nevertheless dropped a series of welcome notes. Wounded men in the centre of the battle were a more slender stream than one had feared, and even the badly wounded beamed cheerfulness and victory. "We killed a lot", said one north country man with spartan brevity. Where we were held up, tanks, which proved most punctual all day, came up in a squad to clear out machine guns. North of them a body of cavalry were soon going into action, to the great delight of our infantry, who cheered them as the pioneers of victory. The wounded who first came back to our lines told a wonderful tale of creeping up in the dark to the shell-holes held by the enemy and, just before the time to charge, seeing the enemy fleeing. It was more than they could endure. They leaped forward in pursuit, rushed into our own barrage and

REFLECTIONS

With the war accelerating the development of the new-fangled aeroplane, an 'alluring' picture was presented to readers of 'commercial aerial services'. But many difficulties remained. How could a plane carry sufficient fuel for the journey? Carrying passengers would require 'delicate arranging'. Flying in fog was 'fraught with many perils'. The Mirror predicted: 'Those in a violent hurry for urgent reasons and thrill-mongers will travel by air. But they will not provide a sufficient stream, nor is flying likely to be popular with women.' On the same page a trenchant leader on Mesopotamia, now Iraq, declared: 'One impression emerges and remains with the mass of our people - a profound distrust and contempt for the bureaucratic mind and character, an utter contempt for the governing caste.'

Mata Hari was the stage name of the beautiful dancer Marguerite Gertrud Zelle. She created a sensation when she first appeared in Paris in the early years of the century and quickly became the toast of the French capital. When war broke out, the French asked her to spy for them, as she spent a lot of time with the Germans. But they became suspicious that she was really an agent for the enemy. When she crossed the border into France to visit one of her lovers, they arrested her. She confessed and the Mirror claimed that H21, as she was known to her handlers, was 'one of the Huns' most skilful women spies.' She was executed by a firing squad.

Mata Hari

followed the Germans beyond it.' How many British troops were killed or wounded by this early example of friendly fire is not recorded.

12 October The price of bread rockets to ten pence

21 November Franz Josef, leader of the Austro-Hungarian Empire since 1848, dies

28 November 650,000 Allies and 500,000 Germans have died on the Somme so far

7 December Liberal leader David Lloyd George becomes Prime Minister

25 December Christmas brings stalemate at the Front

The Daily Mirror

CERTIFIED CIRCULATION LARGER THAN THAT OF ANY OTHER DAILY PICTURE PAPER

No. 4,327. | Registered at the G.P.O. as a Newspaper. | THURSDAY, SEPTEMBER 6, 1917 | One Penny.

THAT ETERNAL MUD—FLANDERS ONE VAST QUAGMIRE

Bringing up bridging for the Yser.—(Official).

A party of stretcher-bearers from Boesinghe. Some of the men are knee-deep in mud. (Official photograph.)

Bringing up ammunition through such a quagmire is a difficult task.—(Official photograph.)

A horse gives up the struggle.—(Official photograph.)

Everybody's floundering in Flanders, and the man who whispers "mud" to the British soldier will soon endanger his popularity. There is no getting away from the horrible stuff. Horses, men and mules have to fight their way through it, and nowadays it is a greater enemy than Hindenburg. Its adhesive properties are superior to any glue on the market. It sticks to uniforms and the coats of horses, and produces wonderful eloquence on the part of the grooms. But our men don't despair. They are all Mark Tapleys.

1917

Getting the most sensational pictures ever seen was partly a matter of superb planning, a willingness to spend huge amounts of money and chunks of luck. One huge chunk of luck came the way of a *Daily Mirror* photographer who was on the French liner *Sontay* in May 1917 when it was hit by a torpedo. To many, that would sound like extremely bad luck. But for our intrepid snapper it presented a golden opportunity to record the drama of a sinking ship and the desperate efforts of its crew and passengers to flee it. After leaping into the icy water, he took 14 shots of the listing craft as he struggled to stay afloat. The quick-thinking photographer then wrapped his photographic plates in oilskin to keep them dry as he floundered in the sea for two hours before being rescued. His determination in recording the drama, despite his own predicament, resulted in some of the most fascinating pictures ever published in the *Mirror*. Two years earlier the paper had carried another incredible photograph of a sinking ship, the torpedoed liner *Falaba*. But that was taken by an ordinary passenger. He got £1,000 for

Advertisers took advantage of the servicemen's market

the shot – almost £70,000 in today's money. It was, the paper boasted, the greatest price ever paid for a photograph. The *Mirror* reported that the passenger was 'a cool, plucky Englishman who remained on board the doomed vessel, camera in hand, calmly snapping here and there, taking photographs oblivious of danger'.

REFLECTIONS

As the war neared its end, the *Mirror* posed the question – as the troops had, by necessity, learned the rudiments of domestic chores while under arms - 'will nearly every man be an expert in what was before regarded as woman's work in the house?' Certainly not, said one trooper. He announced: 'Don't let women think for a moment we shall want to do their work in the house. Not on your life. We're fed up with fatigues. I never want again to scrub, cook, brush, wash up, clean floors or even so much as look at a duster – I shall be quite content to come home and find my wife has been doing her bit.' Worse was to come: 'I warn you, and all women, there will be one great difference – men will come back to the home not merely experts, but expert critics.'

The aborted attack on Gallipoli – across the narrow strip of water that separates Europe from Asia Minor – was a particularly disgraceful episode. The commission which investigated the disaster was brutal in its criticism. The attack had been devised by Winston Churchill, the Navy minister, to defend Egypt. He stuck to his plan with typical determination but naval chiefs were accused of being 'half-hearted and hesitating' in planning and executing the operation. The report criticised the Sea Lord and War Council, and condemned Lord Kitchener for 'undertaking more work than one man could possibly do.' Seven hundred British lives were lost as well as three ships. But the greatest loss was the myth of the Royal Navy's invincibility.

He took fourteen shots of the listing craft as he struggled to stay afloat

It added: 'He helped to lower lifeboats and gave a man his lifebelt. He did his best to soothe frightened women and children and when there was a moment to spare he took photographs.' From its earliest days as a picture-driven newspaper, the *Mirror* had set huge store by getting photos first. As technology developed the paper was in the vanguard of developments. In June 1922 it filled its front page with a picture of the wedding in Belgrade of King Alexander of Serbia and Princess Maria, daughter of the King and Queen of Romania. It wasn't so much the obscure ceremony that fascinated the paper but the method used to rush the photographs back to London. Airman Mr A. J. Cobham was hired to fly the pictures across Europe and readers were treated to full details of his journey. It was, the paper proclaimed, the longest rapid commercial flight ever attempted. It included the 'daring enterprise' of flying over France and England in the dark.

27 March British troops defeat the Turkish army near Gaza

29 March Lloyd George announces plans to enfranchise married women over thirty

6 April The US enters the war, aiming to make the world 'safe for democracy'

16 April The Germans return Lenin to Russia in a sealed train.

2 May King George appeals to the country for restraint in its bread consumption

BRITISH ARTILLERY ON THE ITALIAN FRO.

The Daily Mirror

CERTIFIED CIRCULATION LARGER THAN THAT OF ANY OTHER DAILY PICTURE PAPER

No. 4,233.   Registered at the G.P.O. as a Newspaper.   SATURDAY, MAY 19, 1917.   One Penny.

"VIVE LA FRANCE!" SHOUTS A CAPTAIN AS HIS SHIP SINKS

Leaving the French liner Sontay a few seconds before she made her final plunge. The crew showed that France's sailors possess the same indomitable spirit as her soldiers, and the captain, seeing that all his men were not off the ship, refused to don a lifebelt and remained on the bridge until the water reached it. Then he ran to the stern, which was at pre water and when last seen was waving his cap and shouting "Vive La France!" For other photographs see pages 6 and 7 — (Exclusive to The Daily Mirror.)

1917

The start of the Russian Revolution was on the whole peaceful and bloodless. On March 16, 1917, the *Daily Mirror* reported that the Tsar had abdicated, handing over to his brother, Grand Duke Michael, but in reality giving power to a new government – the Provisional Committee of the Duma (Parliament). The soldiers, it was announced, had joined the people in the revolt and arrested members of the previous government. A communique from Petrograd, sounding like countless thousands which were to be delivered during the years of communist rule, said: 'The workmen

'We are all Russians and must avoid superfluous disorder and bloodshed'

express the determination to employ themselves on overtime in order to make up for all the work that has been lost.' The Imperial Palaces were taken over by troops and the Grand Duke Cyril lent his car to soldiers detailed to meet machine-gun regiments which joined in the revolution, addressing them in these words: 'We are all Russians and we must all try to avert superfluous disorder and bloodshed.' A *Mirror* correspondent wrote: 'I have been day and night in the streets for the last three days, and have seen long queues of hungry men, women and children at the bakers, wanton firing with rifles and machine guns, and civil war in the main thoroughfares, but I have not heard a single word against the war [with Germany]. Owing to the interruption of the tramway service and want of droshkies, it would have been difficult personally to watch the successive events.' Not getting a story due to shortage of droshkies is not an excuse many news editors accept. The comparative peace of the early days of the Revolution did not last, though. Lenin and others exiled from Russia were sent back by the Germans in the hope that they would demand an end to Russia's involvement with the war, which they did. Civil war broke out. On September 19, under the headline '*Crowd Mown Down by Machine Guns at Petrograd*' and a dramatic photo, it was reported: 'A terrible scene occurred in the Nevsky Prospect, Petrograd's famous thoroughfare. There were deadly encounters between the Leninites, the tools of German agents, and those who wished the war to be fought to a

Tsar Nicholas

finish. The photograph shows the panic which occurred when the Leninites opened fire with machine guns on the crowd. The peop are rushing wildly in all directions while in the centre of the roadway a mother can be seen trying to shield her children from the bullets.'

16 July Russia's provisional government crushes a Bolshevik coup

7 August Controversy grows over the sale of honours in return for party donations

8 October The British Labour Party plans a serious challenge for power in the post-war General Election

9 October The US government approves the creation of a black unit of the American army

9 November The Balfour Declaration recognises Palestine as a national Jewish homeland

The Daily Mirror

CERTIFIED CIRCULATION LARGER THAN THAT OF ANY OTHER DAILY PICTURE PAPER

No. 4,197. | Registered at the G.P.O as a Newspaper. | SATURDAY, APRIL 7, 1917 | One Penny.

THE RE-BIRTH OF RUSSIA: FIRST PHOTOGRAPHS TO REACH ENGLAND OF THE LIGHTNING REVOLUTION IN PETROGRAD.

Barricade erected in one of the principal streets. It is defended by field-pieces, from one of which the red flag is flying.

1918

9 December British forces take Jerusalem, ending the offensive against the Turks

22 December Peace talks between Russia and Germany open at Brest-Litovsk

19 January President Wilson proposes a 14-point plan for post-war peace

25 January Food shortages in Britain lead to a policy of two meat-free days a week

6 February The Representation of the People Act gives the vote to men over 21 and women over 30

1918

The *Mirror* wasn't totally supportive of the women's movement. A chauvinistic editorial said: 'The practical sex are to have the vote. Are they also to sit in the House of Commons? That will be the next question. But then, this sex only pretends to be logical – just as some animals (dogs, for instance) only pretend not to understand what men say to them – this insistent sex will logically demand seats, next, in the Cabinet. Once there, they will be everywhere. They will be judges, juries and policewomen. But let them try. Because one thing seems certain: They could not make a bigger muddle of things than made of so-called civilisation by men.'

The paper solemnly announced the death of Captain H. A. V. Harmsworth, killed in action. He was the second son of *Mirror* owner and Air Minister Lord Rothermere to lose his life in the war. Under a front-page picture of Harmsworth were the words: 'Captain the Hon H. A. V. Harmsworth, MC, Irish Guards, eldest son of Lord Rothermere, died yesterday of wounds received in the Battle of Cambrai. Lord Rothermere's second son Lieutenant Vere Harmsworth (R.N.D.) was killed in the Battle of the Ancre on November 13, 1916. He has one remaining son – a lieutenant in the R.M.A.'

Captain H A V Harmsworth

Bands paraded the streets followed by cheering crowds of soldiers and civilians

At the 11th hour on the 11th day of the 11th month, 1918, came the news to lift a weary nation – the war was over after four years, 14 weeks and two days. The Prime Minister, David Lloyd George, reported the formal conclusion to the House of Commons. There were scenes of unparalleled joy and relief throughout the land. The *Mirror* reported: 'London went wild with delight. Bells burst forth into joyful chimes, maroons were exploded, bands paraded the streets, followed by cheering crowds of soldiers and civilians, and London generally gave itself up wholeheartedly to rejoicing. There was a scene of

NOT A 'FLU MASK.

The latest fashion in veils

wonderful loyalty at Buckingham Palace, dense crowds gathering and shouting "We want the King."' He duly obliged and appeared on the balcony of Buckingham Palace with the Queen, Princess Mary and the Duke of Connaught. The report added: 'His Majesty spoke a few words. Indescribable scenes of enthusiasm followed. The Queen waved a Union Jack and the band played "God Save The King", "Tipperary" and the national anthems of the allies, and "Auld Lang Syne" was sung. Then the King, waving his hat to the crowd, left the balcony. Amazing scenes took place throughout London. Flags appeared on all sides with amazing rapidity. They floated proudly over public buildings, they appeared like magic from private houses, they were waved in the streets, they were worn in hats, pinned on coats, swirled frantically on bus tops, lorries, charabancs, taxicabs, costers' carts and on every description of vehicle that could pass through the surging, joyous multitude that thronged the main arteries of London's traffic. And the cheering! Never, not even on Mafeking night, has London resounded with such shouts of exultation. Right had triumphed over might, and the heart of the great City was filled to overflowing.' Londoners could now go about their business without the blackout which had been imposed for four years. One report said: 'London looked strange with its streets comparatively well lighted. Many shops and restaurants did not trouble to draw blinds and curtains, while in the West End the scene was quite a gay one.' There were similar scenes throughout the land. 'All the great cities and towns entered with joyous spirit into the peace celebrations, while villages and hamlets, too, had their rejoicing and peals of bells. Business was suspended generally, shops and houses were decorated with flags, and the people everywhere were delirious with delight.'

22 April The British government raises taxes and abolishes the penny post

23 April Irish workers strike in protest at conscription

13 March Plans to raise the school leaving age to 14 are outlined

1 July Dr Marie Stopes publishes the controversial *Married Love*

30 September Fears are raised of an influenza epidemic spreading across Britain

ALLIES' DRASTIC ARMISTICE TERMS TO HUNS

The Daily Mirror

CERTIFIED CIRCULATION LARGER THAN THAT OF ANY OTHER DAILY PICTURE PAPER

No. 4,696. | Registered at the G.P.O. as a Newspaper. | TUESDAY, NOVEMBER 12, 1918. | One Penny.

HOW LONDON HAILED THE END OF WAR

The King and Queen appeared on the balcony at Buckingham Palace to acknowledge the cheers of the crowd that gathered to congratulate their Majesties on the victory.

There never again will be such news for the Mercuries of the streets to cry.—(Daily Mirror.)

Nothing gave greater satisfaction to all of us than the news that the cessation of hostilities found the British armies once more in possession of Mons, where the immortal

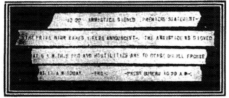

How news of the armistice signature came over the wire to the newspaper offices. A facsimile of it as automatically printed on the tape machine. The cheers which greeted it were the first to be raised.

A historic message as it came over the wire. It is dramatic that the last British war communiqué should proclaim our forces at Mons.

"Contemptibles" first taught the Huns what British valour and steadfastness could do. They left the town as defenders of a forlorn hope; they re-entered it conquerors indeed.

Goddesses in the car, accompanied by a man of war, celebrate the occasion.—(Daily Mirror.)

---

4 November English poet Wilfred Owen is killed in France

30 November Four new nations emerge from the ruins of the Habsburg Empire

28 December Women in Britain vote for the first time in a General Election

12 January A Communist revolt is quelled in Berlin

13 April Indian troops massacre protestors at the holy city of Amritsar

1919

The election of Nancy Astor as the first woman MP was the end of the beginning of women's suffrage. A lot had been achieved but there was still a long way to go. In February 1918, the struggle of the suffragettes finally got somewhere when the vote was given to women – as long as they were over 30 and married. Eight months later Parliament also voted to allow women to become MPs and some weeks on 17 of them stood in the general election. The only one to be elected was Countess Markievitz, who stood for Sinn Fein in Dublin. But as she would not take the oath of allegiance, she could not take her seat. A great effort was made to persuade first-time women voters to go to the poll. At a special rally the Prime Minister, Lloyd George, said he was told women were frightened to vote. They needn't be, he said.

'If they do not vote there is no stronger argument against having given the suffrage to them'

It was easy. 'If they do not vote there is no stronger argument against having given the suffrage to them. And it will not give them the influence which it is essential they should wield in order to ensure legislation on questions like housing, questions like temperance – (cheers) – questions affecting health, questions affecting equality of sexes, questions which affect war and peace.' The *Daily Mirror* had words of wisdom, too. It said: 'Go to the nearest polling station and ask for a ballot paper. Mark it with a cross, very distinctly, against the name of the candidate of whom you approve. It sounds, and is, simple.' It was almost a year before the first female MP took her seat in the Commons. And Nancy Astor was no commoner. She held a safe Plymouth seat for the Tories in a by-election caused by the elevation of her husband, the millionaire Waldorf Astor, to the peerage. The *Mirror* reported: 'Viscountess Astor began her campaign with a racy speech and yesterday, after being elected an MP, she made the raciest of them all. "The only man I am sorry for today is the poor old Viscount," she said. Billy, her son, also made a speech. Doffing his hat he said: "I saw you elect daddy to Parliament and now I see you have elected mother. Thank you very much for both".'

REFLECTIONS

Mary Pickford was America's Sweetheart and the first great female movie star. When she had flu the *Mirror* painted an adulatory picture of her career. 'Millions of people throughout the world were shocked' that she was ill. Although only 24, she was earning £300,000 a year. Born into a showbusiness family, she appeared on stage from the age of five and made her first film at 16. 'She has been up in an aeroplane, has jumped out of boats to rescue the hero, and has ridden like the wind to get help for the beleaguered garrison, and each part has been perfection,' the paper enthused. In a previous interview she had said: 'I believe in actuality. I believe in being practical.' Fortunately she recovered and lived for another sixty years.

A 1922 boxing match was the first sporting contest to be broadcast, being relayed from Marconi House in the Strand. A *Mirror* correspondent who 'listened in' on a home-made wireless set in Muswell Hill wrote: 'It was my first experience of this modern magic and nothing more thrilling can be imagined. The overture was alarming to the novice. "Hello, hello! Marconi House speaking. We shall describe this evening the progress of the Carpentier-Lewis fight at Olympia. We are in telephonic communication with the ringside and shall repeat to you the messages we receive. Stand by, please!" At 9.57 the eager "listeners in" were told that the seconds were out of the ring and the fight had started. A minute or so later came the announcement that Carpentier had won. Subsequent messages told the story of the brief encounter, concluding with a cheery "Good night! Good night!"'

Mary Pickford starring with Errol Flynn

1919

28 June The Versailles Peace Treaty is signed, despite German anger at the terms

1920

16 January Prohibition is introduced in the United States

16 November Russia's civil war ends in triumph for the Reds as the Whites are crushed

December The League of Nations is formed. Hopes that the United States will join are dashed

11 December Martial Law is declared in Ireland after increasing violence between the IRA, the British Army and 'black and tans'

"DAILY MIRROR'S" PLAN TO HELP EX-OFFICERS

The Daily Mirror

CERTIFIED CIRCULATION LARGER THAN THAT OF ANY OTHER DAILY PICTURE PAPER

No. 5,021. | Registered at the G.P.O. as a Newspaper | SATURDAY, NOVEMBER 29, 1919 | **[16 PAGES.]** | One Penny.

LADY ASTOR'S TRIUMPH: ENGLAND'S FIRST WOMAN M.P.

The scene at the declaration of the poll, showing Viscountess Astor, her husband, and Billy

Mr. W. T. Gay, the Labour candidate, speaking after the declaration.

---

17 March The first birth control clinic is opened in Holloway, London

30 June The Communist Party is formed in China at a meeting attended by primary teacher Mao Tse-tung

6 December The Irish Free State is created. Northern Ireland is partitioned

18 October The British Broadcasting Company is formed by radio set manufacturers

5 November Archaeologists discover the tomb of King Tutankhamun

1926

REFLECTIONS

Unbelievable as it may seem today, the *Mirror* felt the upper reaches of London society season were of such interest to its readers it devoted its entire front page to portraits of 11 aristocratic hostesses looking forward to what was expected to be a 'more than usually brilliant season'. In stark contrast, the paper also noted the discovery of a dying man in the first class compartment of the Dover-London train. 'A bloodstained razor lay beside him. He refused to give his name. All he said was "I am an outcast and in disgrace"'. The same page recorded that the wife of a guardsman in Aldershot gave birth to a record 24lb baby. It did not live. More than 53,000 spectators attended the FA Cup Final at Stamford Bridge. Huddersfield beat Preston North End 1–0.

He was the second son of the King. She was the youngest daughter of one of Britain's noblest families. Their wedding in April 1923 brightened the gloom of the post-war years but no one could foresee the roles they would play in the country's history. He would sit on the throne through the nation's darkest hours and she, as the Queen Mother, would live to see another century. This was the first royal wedding to be given the full tabloid treatment – page upon page of photographs, reports, comment and debate on every aspect of what it meant for the happy couple and the country. The *Mirror* said: 'For a few days we forget our private cares and joys and sorrows. And all because a gallant young gentleman is marrying a charming young lady.'

Royal Wedding Party

The General Strike of May 1926, when more than four million workers downed tools, was the closest Britain had come to revolution since the Civil War nearly 300 years earlier. Though print workers were among the first to be called out, the *Daily Mirror*, by dint of considerable subterfuge and the editor working almost single-handedly day and night, managed to publish throughout the nine-day dispute, appealing for volunteers to help secure supplies. The seeds of this cataclysmic event were sown when pit owners attempted to cut the wages and change the working conditions of miners. After a miners' lockout on April 30 the TUC called for a General Strike on May 4. Stanley Baldwin's Tory government declared a state of national emergency, King George V hurried to London and the British establishment geared itself to fight what it had always feared – open revolt by a deeply deprived working class. The middle class, who massed to oppose

Thousands of men besieged recruiting offices so they could help troops maintain services

the strike, came to its rescue. Thousands of men besieged national service recruiting offices so they could help troops maintain services. With newsprint in short supply, the *Mirror* produced skeleton issues which were mainly propaganda, containing claims that many strikers were returning to work and giving lists of strike-breaking activities. The paper loyally printed a list of places where those who wanted to blackleg could offer their help, and told readers: 'It is the duty of all citizens of whatever political opinion to rally round the Government and to support it in its effort to secure essential supplies.' There were photos of men and women joining those who volunteered to keep the nation moving and it was reported that 'the Government's appeal for volunteers to assist in the maintenance of supplies of food, fuel, light and power during the General Strike was widely responded to.' The strike collapsed on May 12 with the miners having achieved no significant concessions. They stayed out until November when they, too, were driven back to work. With the crisis over, the *Mirror* boasted it was the only 'picture newspaper' not to cease publication during the dispute. It said: 'During this emergency the paper was produced in no fewer than six places, one being a flat converted into an impromptu printing office. Emergency workers moved in the dead of night, papers were transported in suitcases and even Scotland Yard was informed of "mysterious goings on". The story is a newspaper romance.'

1922

30 December Russia is renamed the Union of Soviet Socialist Republics

1923

16 February Coco Chanel declares sweaters to be the height of fashion chic

28 April Wembley's Empire Stadium hosts its first football match, between Bolton Wanderers and West Ham United

8 June A new Bill allows women to divorce their husbands for adultery for the first time

12 November In Munich, Adolf Hitler is arrested after an attempt to seize power in the 'beer-hall putsch'

Daily Mirror

THE DAILY PICTURE NEWSPAPER WITH THE LARGEST NET SALE

No. 7,018   MONDAY, MAY 10, 1926   One Penny

London Strike Scenes : Top. Mounted Police in Action. Left. Sailors Travel by Lorry. Right. Wiring Motor-'bus Bonnets

1924

22 January Ramsay MacDonald forms the first Labour Government

6 April The Plague spreads in India. 25,000 have died so far.

1925

23 March American state Tennessee outlaws the teaching of evolution in schools

8 April The government announces assisted emigration to Australia

1 September The Charleston arrives in Britain with a flourish

1926

At 2.40am on April 21, 1926, at 17 Bruton Street, Piccadilly – the home of the Earl and Countess of Strathmore - a daughter was born to the Duchess of York. The *Mirror* reported: 'The baby is apparently a little below the average weight but very strong and healthy looking.' Just how healthy is evidenced by the fact that Queen Elizabeth II has now been on the throne for more than 50 years. At the time of her birth, Elizabeth was third in line to the throne and no one seriously thought she would ever become monarch. When her grandfather King George V died in 1936 her Uncle, Edward, Prince of Wales, succeeded to the throne. Baby Elizabeth – whose other names were Alexandra after the late Queen Mother and Mary after the then Queen – was the King and Queen's first granddaughter. After being woken with the news between 3 and 4am, the overjoyed royal couple motored from Windsor that afternoon to see the new arrival and to offer felicitations in person, while from Biarritz Edward telegraphed his

REFLECTIONS

As broadcasting grew in popularity, a commission was set up under Lord Crawford to decide how it should be run. It reported in March 1926, recommending that broadcasting should be conducted by a public corporation to be called the British Broadcasting Commission, which would consist of – 'men and women of judgment and independence, with business acumen and experienced in public affairs'. Everyone who had a wireless – except the blind – would have to pay a fee of 10 shillings (50p). Detection and prosecution of those who concealed their equipment would be vigorously pursued. The report added: 'Every effort should be made to raise the standard of style and performance in every phase of broadcasting and particularly music. A moderate amount of controversial matter should be broadcast provided the material is of high quality and distributed with scrupulous fairness.'

Vladimir Lenin

In January 1924, the death of Russian leader Vladimir Ilyich Lenin merited the headline 'Man of Terror'. Writing from Riga, the *Mirror*'s correspondent said: 'Lenin, Bolshevist Russia's dictator, was in his 54th year. Yet, what is strange, he belonged to a noble family. For the last two years he had been stricken with paralysis, unable to walk and capable of uttering only unintelligible sounds Like all tyrants, his life was always in jeopardy and several attempts were made to assassinate him. The Dictatorship of the Proletariat, he said a few years ago, was unthinkable without terror and violence against the deadliest enemies of the working class. It has been said that he had no feelings, no wishes, no instincts – nothing, in fact, but one invincible thought – the Red Terror.'

In accordance with ancient custom, the Home Secretary was present at the birth

congratulations. In accordance with an ancient custom designed to ensure that a royal baby was not another child brought in secretly as a substitute, the Home Secretary, Sir W. Joynson-Hicks, was present at Bruton Street at the time of the birth.

ROADSIDE MOTOR FUEL SUPPLY STATION

An up-to-date motor spirit bulk storage station installed on the Bath Road at Aldermaston by the A.A. and M.U. This station is the first of its kind in Great Britain and the first of a series being erected by the Automobile Association throughout the country with a view to popularising the bulk storage system.

Britain's first petrol station on the Bath Road at Aldermaston

The official proclamation announced that 'previous to the confinement a consultation took place at which Sir George Blacker was present and a certain line of treatment was successfully adopted' which must have left large sections of the public suitably baffled. The *Mirror* reported: 'All day long crowds, composed largely of women, waited outside the house, even during heavy rain. Callers were numerous and a line of motor cars stretched the whole length of the street. As their majesties left their car, the people cheered heartily and the womenfolk among the crowd waved handkerchiefs in salute. Her Majesty carried a bunch of carnations and spring flowers. Shortly before noon the Duke of York looked out of one of the windows of the house. He was smiling happily.' Poor George – his happiness was to be blighted on taking the throne, a role he never wanted. But his daughter never forgot his devotion to duty and, following his example, went on to become, like her father, a much-loved monarch.

---

27 January John Logie Baird gives the first public demonstration of television

18 February Five ancient Mayan cities are discovered in the Yucatan region of Mexico

23 August American fans are distraught at the death of Rudolf Valentino, at 31

31 October World famous escapologist Harry Houdini dies

20 November The British Empire is renamed the Commonwealth

£5,000 MUST-BE-WON RACING PRIZE: COUPON TO-DAY

Daily Mirror

THE DAILY PICTURE NEWSPAPER WITH THE LARGEST NET SALE

GREAT NEW SERIAL NEXT WEEK

No. 7,029 | Registered at the G.P.O. as a Newspaper | SATURDAY, MAY 22, 1926 | One Penny

FIRST PICTURE OF THE DUCHESS AND HER BABY

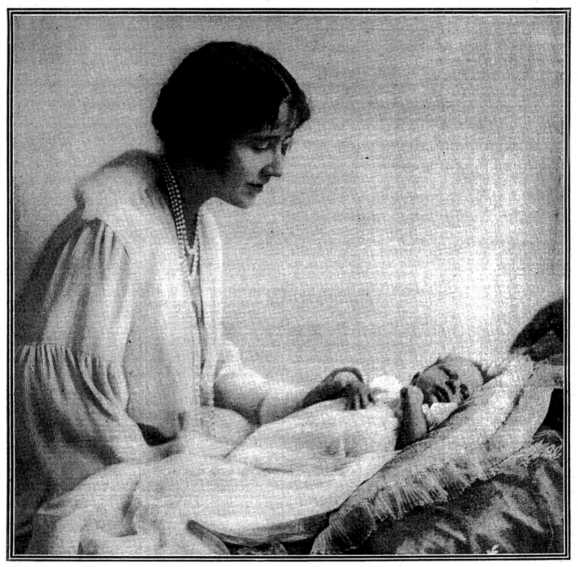

The first picture to be published of the Duchess of York and her baby daughter. The child is to be christened to-day week, in the private chapel at Buckingham Palace, and will receive the names Elizabeth, after the Duchess of York, Alexandra, after the late Queen-Mother, and Mary, after the Queen. Born at 17, Bruton-street, Mayfair, one month ago, the baby is the fourth lady in the land and a Royal Highness. She is in the direct line of succession to the Throne. The birth of the infant Princess was officially registered last Monday. A certificate will be lodged at Somerset House, but will not be available for public inspection. See also pages 8 and 9.

1927

31 January Britain sends troops to China to protect its nationals in Shanghai as fighting in the civil war worsens

6 February 10-year-old violinist Yehudi Menuhin performs before audiences in Paris

21 May Radio 2LO broadcasts on short wave to Australia, New Zealand, and South Africa, raising hopes for world radio

29 June The first total eclipse of the sun for 200 years occurs over Britain

6 October Warner Brothers release the first 'talkie', *The Jazz Singer*, starring Al Jolson

1927

page 52   Monday May 30 1927

Heroes exert an enduring fascination on the public mind and none was more intoxicating than 25-year-old Charles Lindbergh who in May, 1927, became the first man to fly solo non-stop across the Atlantic. Flying in the 1920s was still a dangerous adventure and the exploits of its pioneers were avidly followed. Lindbergh's precarious voyage into history captured the imagination of the world. For 1,000 miles of the 3,600-mile journey he battled in the open cockpit of his monoplane 'The Spirit of St Louis' with rain and snow; for hours he searched for good weather, sometimes skimming only 10ft above the ocean, at others soaring to 10,000ft where the cold ripped through his exhausted body; he could see ahead only by means of a periscope and he steered by one small compass. Extraordinary scenes of jubilation greeted the young

REFLECTIONS

Dancing aroused strong emotions among *Mirror* readers. L.V., of Ladbroke Road, West London, wrote: 'You cannot compel people to take an interest in politics. Dance maniacs are for the most part young and frivolous. You cannot persuade them that the Commons is more important than Ziggs World Famous Band'. On the same page A.W.K. of Lavender Hill, South West London, worried: 'English dancers have not the lithe gracefulness of the south Europeans nor the infectious vitality of the North Americans, but they have a distinctive nobility of movement. The Charleston is not suitable for English dancers because of its jerky precipitation.' Another correspondent asked: 'Who would wish pillion riding to be prohibited because a few careless motor-cyclists take unnecessary risks?'

'One of the brightest social events of the parliamentary season takes place at the Commons this evening when the bachelor MPs dine together. The party will include Sir James-Agg Gardner who at the age of 80 is still a bachelor. It was stated he has received a letter from a woman deploring the continued bachelordom of so many MPs.' Of course in those days the term 'bachelor' did not have the meaning later attributed to it.

In the Divorce Court a woman with nine christian names - Acie Bethel Kitzinger Firth Ishti Helena Goiga Pretoria Denver Hill - was granted a decree nisi. Judge: 'Is your first name Acie?' Mrs Hill: 'Yes.' Judge: 'That will do – it is not the woman's fault she has all these names.'

The excited mob broke down barriers and rushed to meet their idol

American's arrival in Paris after a gruelling 33hrs 49mins in the sky. More than 150,000 people broke down the barriers of the aerodrome where he landed, sweeping aside the guard which faced them with bayonets fixed and ripping pieces off the plane. Lindbergh's first words were: 'Hello boys, I'm here.' Then, almost in disbelief: 'I'm Lindbergh. Where am I?' He retired to the US embassy where, after a well deserved rest and still wearing a borrowed dressing gown, he told his remarkable story: 'It was very trying. I had no sleep. I used none of the stimulants I had with me as a precaution and drank only water. When I descended at Le Bourget I had some thirst, I can tell you.' A week later, Lindbergh flew to England where, to his astonishment, another 150,000-strong crowd was waiting for him at Croydon aerodrome. He made a circuit of the airfield, then swept down and landed. At this, the excited mob broke down barriers and rushed to meet their idol alarming him so much he promptly opened the throttle and shot into the air again. After making another circuit he landed for a second time. Hundreds of police held back the crowd though one man managed to climb on to the tail of the plane before being knocked off. Police had to lie at full length on the mudguards of the car taking Lindbergh to safety, blowing their whistles to clear a path. The next time the flying ace hit the headlines, it was to be in tragic circumstances.

Charles Lindbergh

1927

15 November Soviet leader Josef Stalin expels Leon Trotsky and Grigori Zinoviev from the Communist Party

1928

18 June 29-year-old Amelia Earhart is the first woman to fly the Atlantic

1 August The Morris Minor is launched

30 September Alexander Fleming discovers the penicillin mould staphylococcus bacteria

22 November The first £1 and 10s notes come into circulation

MORE PICTURES, MORE NEWS AND MORE SPORT

Daily Mirror | 28 PAGES

THE DAILY PICTURE NEWSPAPER WITH THE LARGEST NET SALE

No. 7,345 — Registered at the G.P.O. as a Newspaper. — MONDAY, MAY 30, 1927 — One Penny

CROYDON BATTLE TO WELCOME ATLANTIC HERO

The famous monoplane "Spirit of St. Louis," which brought her intrepid pilot, Captain Lindbergh, alone across the Atlantic, and yesterday from Brussels to Croydon, resting on the aerodrome there just after her arrival. Around her press closely some of the huge crowd of over 160,000 who flocked out of London for the occasion, and struggled wildly for a glimpse of the airman and his machine. The cars of the spectators were parked in a long line that reached for miles. Captain Lindbergh, escorted by six biplanes, flew over the metropolis before descending at Croydon. When he got out of his machine he said, "This is worse than it was at Le Bourget." See also pages 14, 15 and 28.

1932

REFLECTIONS

October 19, 1931: 'Thomas Alva Edison, the greatest inventor the world has ever known, died early yesterday at his home in West Orange, New Jersey, USA, aged 84. Up to a short time ago, he was working from 5am to midnight and rarely taking more than five minutes for a meal. He was a wizard who found the world dark and made it light. Our modern press-the-button existence is due in a large extent to his ingenuity in inventing the phonograph, the moving picture camera and electric power stations. No single genius has ever produced such a flood of revolutionary inventions as Edison. He more than any man changed the life of the world. More than 1,500 inventions stood to his credit but those relating to electric power were his greatest gifts to the human race. He made telephones and moving pictures practical realities in reach of all.'

In an early example of consumer rights it was announced that a law banning short weight or measure on foods would soon be on the statute books. Among articles 'to be retailed exclusively by net weight except when sold in quantities less than 2oz or in single pennyworths or less' were bacon, ham, butchers' meat (excluding heads, feet, hearts, lights and calves' sweetbreads), butter, lard and margarine, cereals, sugar, coffee, dried beans and peas, jam, marmalade and potatoes. 'All these articles should be delivered to the purchaser with a legible statement of the net weight. Powers are to be given to inspectors to weigh the contents of packages at wholesalers, packers and importers as well as retailers.'

Five years after Lindbergh's triumph the world was stunned by the audacious kidnapping of his 20-month-old son Charles from their home in New Jersey. The kidnappers, who used a ladder to pluck the child from his second-floor bedroom, left behind a ransom note demanding $50,000. As thousands of police joined the hunt and Lindbergh and other aviators scoured the countryside in planes, the family made it known they were prepared to pay up on the boy's safe return. But no clue was found. The *Mirror* reported: 'A small bed in the nursery of a New Jersey country house is empty and all America wants to know why. The kidnapping of the son of Colonel Lindbergh – America's idol – has aroused national excitement and anger. No crime committed by racketeers has aroused more widespread indignation and every device known to criminological experts is being employed. The child has been described as a chubby, golden-haired boy, with fair complexion, resembling his father, and just beginning to toddle and learn to talk. Footprints in the mud under the nursery window show that the kidnappers were apparently two men and one woman. Fears

No crime committed by racketeers has aroused more widespread indignation

The great inventor

that the kidnappers may not take proper care of her child were expressed by Mrs Lindbergh. She said "He had a severe cold and I am afraid that as the poor darling was clad only in his nightclothes he may suffer from exposure". Mrs Lindbergh released to the press details of her son's diet – a quart of milk, three tablespoons of cooked cereals morning and night, two tablespoons of cooked vegetables, one yolk of egg plus half a cup of orange juice on waking and half a cup of prune juice after his afternoon nap. This poignant list, with its pitiful assumption that the kidnappers would take any heed of a single part of it, was never needed. More than two months later, Charles's body was found near his parents' estate. An attempt had been made to bury it under a pile of leaves. It had probably been there since the day of the abduction. Almost three years later unemployed carpenter Bruno Hauptmann was found guilty of the murder and executed.

1930

30 July Uruguay wins the first football World Cup

1931

14 April King Alfonso of Spain is toppled. A Republic is declared

1 May The 1,245 ft Empire State Building opens in New York

24 August A Coalition government takes power as the Labour government falls

29 August The prospect of Indian Independence leads to violent rioting between Moslems and Hindus

BEGIN GREAT NEW SERIAL—P. 15

Daily Mirror

THE DAILY PICTURE • NEWSPAPER WITH THE LARGEST NET SALE

No. 8,830   Registered at the G.P.O. as a Newspaper.   **FRIDAY, MARCH 11, 1932**   One Penny

FOUR-PAGE LONDON FILM REVIEW

Wireless on Page 16

LINDBERGH KIDNAP—FIRST PICTURES

HOW THE BABY WAS STOLEN FROM BED

Police and photographers at Colonel Lindbergh's home.

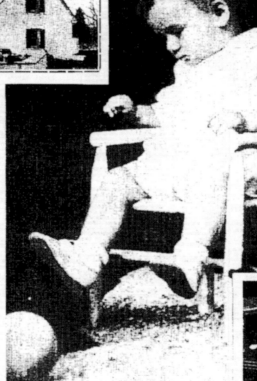

The pictures on this page are the first connected with the kidnapping of Colonel Lindbergh's nineteen-month-old son Charles at Hopewell, New Jersey, to reach London. Those above and on the right are photographs of the child taken shortly before his disappearance and that on the left illustrates the means adopted by the kidnappers to get through the 15ft. high window of the bedroom from which they removed him. Confusing messages from America yesterday deepened the mystery of the child's whereabouts. He was stated to be "alive and well."

A State trooper's questions near the Lindberghs' home. The child has been missing for ten days.

1931

18 September Japan attacks a Chinese garrison in Manchuria, sparking conflict over the region

20 September Britain is forced off the Gold Standard. Unemployment reaches a record level

22 October American gangster Al Capone is jailed for eleven years for tax avoidance

1932

29 March Republican leader and former IRA member Eamonn de Valera is elected to head the new Irish government

10 April Paul von Hindenberg beats Adolf Hitler to the German Presidency

1933

page 56 Tuesday January 31 1933

Few *Mirror* front pages can have been as prophetic as that of January 31, 1933, which announced the election of Nazi leader Adolf Hitler as Chancellor of Germany. The result of foreign elections rarely won much space in the paper. But however much it tried to close its eyes to the truth, all Europe knew this was an event with terrifying implications for the stabilty of the continent. Germany, its society fractured and economy wrecked, was in the hands of a right-wing demagogue who had created a party of political thugs intent on using the democratic process to destroy it. Tragically for Germany and the future of the world the German people were fatally seduced. Mockingly describing the new Chancellor as a 'one-time labourer, house-painter and army corporal', the *Mirror* reported: 'communists and Nazis (Hitler's followers) came to blows at Munich. A Communist was killed and combatants on both sides were wounded. The streets were filled with cheering and hissing crowds. The atmosphere in the capital is hourly growing more and more reminiscent of the heyday of

He abolished the title of president and decreed that he was to be known as Führer

Kaiserism, though without its glamour.' Two months earlier when Hitler had demanded the Chancellorship, President Paul von Hindenberg had replied that 'a presidential Cabinet led by you would necessarily develop into a party dictatorship with enormous aggravation of the antagonism in the German nation as its sequel'. Yet in 1933 the 86-year-old

Nazis demonstrate their physical prowess

statesman weakly agreed to the recommendation of former Chancellor Franz von Papen that Hitler should be given office in the hope that he could be controlled from inside the Cabinet. It took only weeks for that hope to be exposed as a terrible delusion. The following month Hitler used the burning of the Reichstag by a deranged Dutch Communist as the excuse for a general election in which the Nazis achieved a tiny majority though only 43 per cent of the popular vote. At first Hitler, backed by industrialists as well as his bullyboy SA brownshirts, relied on the support of coalition conservatives. But as soon as he was ready he flagrantly ignored constitutional safeguards, crushed dissent and effectively turned his country into a one-party state. When Hindenburg died in 1934, Hitler became head of state as well as Chancellor, decreeing that in future he should be known as Fuhrer. Over the next five years he consolidated his power, appointed himself Supreme Commander of the Armed Forces and launched a vigorous programme of rearmament and expansion which he knew would lead to war. The world is still living with the consequences of the demented megalomania and pitiless barbarity of the man Churchill called a 'bloodthirsty little guttersnipe'.

1932

17 April The Emperor of Ethiopia Haile Selassie abolishes slavery

25 April The government introduces new import tariffs on foreign trade

July Four-year-old Shirley Temple is a new star of the cinema

3 October The British mandate in Iraq ends

9 October Stalin purges his old allies Zinoviev and Kamenev to Siberia

THE DAILY MIRROR, Tuesday, January 31, 1933.

Daily Mirror

THE DAILY PICTURE NEWSPAPER WITH THE LARGEST NET SALE

No. 9,107   Registered at the G.P.O. as a Newspaper.   TUESDAY, JANUARY 31, 1933   One Penny

BEGIN OUR NEW SERIAL ON PAGE 15

WIRELESS PAGE 26   AMUSEMENTS PAGE 19

HITLER MAY RULE AS DICTATOR

Fighting in Germany Last Night

Herr Adolf Hitler, the new German Chancellor, receiving the salute from National-Socialist followers. Right: Herr von Papen, Vice-Chancellor.

A studio portrait of Hitler. Right, the new Chancellor surrounded by a surging, cheering crowd as he left his Berlin hotel to go to his official residence after his appointment yesterday.

TWO KILLED AND MANY INJURED AT MUNICH

NAZIS' MARCH

Germany was last night in the grip of wild excitement following the appointment of Adolf Hitler one-time labourer, house-painter and army corporal—as Chancellor.

Communists and Nazis (Hitler's followers) came to blows at Munich, when "Reds" evaded the police and attacked the guard at the Nazi headquarters.

A Communist was killed and several combatants on both sides were wounded.

Fighting also took place in the suburbs of Munich, where a Communist was stabbed to death. Fifty arrests were made.

The streets were filled with cheering and hissing crowds, says Reuter.

Serious trouble is also reported from several towns in Bavaria.

The atmosphere in the capital, says the Central News, is hourly growing more and more reminiscent of the heyday of Kaiserism, though without its splendour.

Great celebrations, including torchlight processions, are planned to mark the victory of the Nationalist movement.

From Doorn it is stated that the ex-Kaiser regards the change of Government as a step in the right direction, but the ex-Crown Prince is described as disappointed at Hitler's changed attitude towards the monarchy.

The entire storm troops of Berlin and the Brandenburg district, together with Steel Helmet detachments, last night marched down the Wilhelmstrasse. Some 15,000 men took part.

Earlier in the day it was stated that the procession was to be in honour of Hitler. But the new Chancellor made it known that he did not desire a personal demonstration. "Let it be in honour of President Hindenburg," he is reported to have said.

As, however, the President's Palace and the Chancellor's residence practically face one another in the Wilhelmstrasse, the demonstrators, as they filed past, gave rousing cheers for the new Chancellor as well as the President.

The principal men in the new German Cabinet are:—

Chancellor—HERR HITLER.
Vice-Chancellor—HERR VON PAPEN.
Foreign Minister—BARON VON NEURATH.
Minister of the Interior—DR. FRICK.
Minister for Defence—HERR VON BLOMBERG (formerly Commander of the First Division in Koenigsberg).

This is virtually a Coalition Cabinet, and seems to provide a check on Hitler, although his men hold important portfolios.

President's Future

"What is to be the future of President Hindenburg?" is the question being asked.

It is recalled that, when, only last November, Hitler demanded the Chancellorship President Hindenburg turned him down, and in the course of the letter sent to the Nazi leader on the President's behalf Dr. Meissner wrote: "The President fears that a Presidential Cabinet led by you would necessarily develop into a party dictatorship with enormous aggravation of the antagonism in the German nation as its sequel.

(Continued on back page)

1933

A terrible evil stalked the American Deep South in the early thirties. Racist white mobs were lynching black people. More often than not, those carrying out the vile attacks had the full support of their elected leaders. And most of the thugs caught escaped justice, being pardoned by the likes of Governor James Rolph of San Jose. Those who were arrested and locked up while awaiting trial were freed by gangs who smashed open jails to get them out. Further north, in Maryland, the State Militia had to be called out to one

They hurled tear gas bombs at the crowd who threw bricks back

Hunger march approaches London

such riotous act. They hurled tear gas bombs at the crowd, who threw bricks back. Shots were fired. The mob had been trying to free four lynchers arrested under the orders of Governor Albert C. Ritchie after the state attorney refused to act against them. Police, protected by troops armed with machine guns, had hauled the men from their beds and taken them to the state armoury at Salisbury. But word of their arrest spread like wildfire. A huge crowd soon gathered, infuriated by the governor's action, and a pitched battle ensued. Fire engines were summoned but their crews appeared sympathetic to the crowd for they sprayed water into the tear gas in an effort to deaden the effect of the fumes. The *Mirror* carried a front-page photograph of the man who had been lynched. The victim had been behind bars accused of attacking a 71-year-old white woman when a mob took the law into its own hands. Men, woman and children joined in the furore with thousands of onlookers cheering the spectacle. The *Mirror* report said: 'The negro for whose lynching the men were arrested was done to death by a mob at Princess Anne. Defying a barrage of tear gas bombs and the truncheons of 20 police, more than a thousand people burst into the county jail and carried off the negro. The victim was stripped and dragged through the town by a rope round his neck and hanged to a tree next to a judge's house. Later the body was cut down and burned in the public square.' On the same page was the story of how four mobsters were acquitted of kidnapping a young and wealthy brewer. In 1930s' lawless America, US juries were bribed or scared into passing not guilty verdicts.

REFLECTIONS

The dark days of the depression saw a series of huge hunger marches. On October 27, 1932, the *Mirror* reported how 2,000 marchers reached London headed by bands and men carrying banners. 'Comrade Wal Hannington, the Communist, paid flying visits to all the bands as they marched on London. He used a fast car and dashed from point to point in the London suburbs to talk with the leaders. The marchers were given accommodation in public baths, disused school rooms and church halls. Meals were provided by local people. At Edmonton they were also given cigarettes, free baths and free medical attention. Today the hunger marchers, who have gathered from all parts of Great Britain to put their case to the Government, will demonstrate in London and will be joined by many local unemployed.'

On November 8, 1933, an editorial asked: 'How Many More?' 'There were about 70,000 more motor-vehicles on the road each day during last September than during the same month in 1932. Good for the motor trade. Bad for human life. Confusing for the roads. Bad, also, for the beauty of the countryside. And in the future? If there were 50,000 more motor-vehicles in any month in every year, that gives us 500,000 more vehicles on the roads by 1943. And so on. Will it be possible to move in that year? What will the accident toll be? What will happen? Possibly relief (if you can call it that) will come from the air. We may "rise above" our earth-bound traffic problems!' Through the decade the *Mirror* continued to campaign for better road safety.

---

23 March The House of Commons endorses government plans for a federal constitution for India

7 May Fascists and Jews clash in the East End of London

16 June FDR signs 'New Deal' legislation for industrial recovery in America

22 February Government troops in Nicaragua assassinate Augusto Sandino, the main opponent of General Somoza

24 February English composer Sir Edward Elgar dies

Daily Mirror

Broadcasting - Page 24

THE DAILY PICTURE NEWSPAPER WITH THE LARGEST NET SALE

DRESS-SUIT ORDER FOR NEW POLICE —PAGE 2

No. 9,365 — Registered at the G.P.O. as a Newspaper. — WEDNESDAY, NOVEMBER 29, 1933 — One Penny

TRIAL BY FURY—U.S. LYNCH LAW

Frenzied Mob Storm Another Gaol

SOLDIERS' BOMBS DEFIED

Lynch law is spreading in the United States. Here are two contrasting pictures:—

IN MARYLAND
Something like civil war broke out yesterday when a mob attacked the State Armoury in an attempt to release four lynchers arrested by order of the Governor.

IN CALIFORNIA
The Governor publicly pardoned people involved in the storming of a prison and lynching two kidnappers, which was "a fine lesson to others."

The situation in Maryland grew so serious that the State Militia had to be mobilised. They hurled tear gas bombs at the mob, which replied with bricks. Shots followed, but it is not known whether they were fired by the crowd or the troops.

Martial law has been proclaimed.

SECRET SEARCH

Police Guarded by Troops Armed with Machine Guns

BALTIMORE, Tuesday.

A fierce clash between an infuriated mob and soldiers at Salisbury (Maryland) in which tear gas bombs and bricks were hurled and shots fired, came as a climax to the arrest of four lynchers by order of Governor Ritchie.

The men are alleged to have killed a negro who had attacked an aged white woman.

When the State Attorney refused to arrest the men a secret house-to-house search was ordered by Governor Ritchie.

Police, under the protection of troops armed with machine-guns, tear gas bombs and riot guns, hauled the wanted men from their beds last night. They were taken to the State armoury at Salisbury.

Yelling Crowd

The report of their arrest spread like wildfire, and crowds of townspeople soon gathered around the armoury.

Antagonism against the Governor's action flared up, and later a yelling crowd surged against the building.

The State Militia was called out, and a pitched battle took place.

Troops hurled tear-gas bombs into the advancing mob, but still they came on and drove the soldiers into the armoury.

A general fire alarm was sounded, and brought a fire brigade full speed to the assistance of the troops.

CAR OVERTURNED

A fusillade of bricks was launched against the armoury and shots followed.

The firemen appeared to be sympathetic towards the crowd, because they poured water into the tear gas, apparently in an effort to deaden the effect of the fumes.

After the riot had died down the troops departed in motor-cars, apparently heading towards Baltimore. It is not known if the arrested men were with them.

The crowd did not molest the troops, but they seized and overturned a motor-car which was said to belong to the State Attorney.

The negro, for whose lynching the men were arrested, was done to death by a mob at Princess Anne.

Defying a barrage of tear gas bombs and the truncheons of twenty police, more than a thousand people burst into the county gaol and carried off the negro.

The victim was stripped and dragged through the town by a rope round his neck and hinged to a tree next to a Judge's house. Later the body was cut down and burned in the public square.—Reuter.

According to Exchange, the Maryland authorities have proclaimed martial law.

Telegraphing and telephoning were banned during the arrests.

SHOTGUN GUARD

Four Gangsters Cleared of Kidnapping Charge

A jury at St. Paul, Minnesota, yesterday acquitted four gangsters, led by Roger Touhy, who were accused of kidnapping Mr. William Hamm, junr., a young and wealthy brewer, states Reuter.

The gang were also indicted by the grand jury in Chicago for the alleged kidnapping last July of Jacob Factor, the financier accused of share-pushing frauds.

Crowds jammed the corridors of the courthouse to learn the verdict. Guards around the court were reinforced and sheriffs stood on each stairway with shotguns ready.

Factor Case

After their acquittal the four men were served with "fugitive warrants" accusing them of participation in the kidnapping of Jacob Factor.

They will be taken to Chicago for trial in the Factor case, regardless of their acquittal yesterday.

Mr. William Hamm, junr., was kidnapped in June, but was released a few days later after a ransom had been paid. It was stated at the time that this ransom was much less than the $20,000 originally demanded.

Leaders of the mob battering in the doors of the county gaol at San Jose, California, prior to the lynching of Thurmond and Holmes, two alleged kidnappers.

Governor Ritchie, of Maryland, who has had four lynchers arrested.

Governor Rolph publicly pardoned people involved in the San Jose lynching.

The sentence of lynch law carried out at San Jose. Thousands of onlookers cheered the spectacle. (Pictures by radio.)

1936

REFLECTIONS

The triumph of Fred Perry in retaining the men's Wimbledon singles championship in 1935 was even greater than it seemed at the time. Sixty-seven years later, he remains the only Briton to have won the ultimate tennis contest. He beat Baron Gottfried von Cramm of Germany 6–2, 6–4, 6–4. *Mirror* sports writer H. E. Lainson Wood wrote: 'Some time after the match I found Perry sitting beneath a tree sipping a cooling drink with Miss Helen Vinson, the American film star. He could not remember a single detail of the match. "If you say I played well, I am satisfied," he told me. "But all I know is that I am out on my feet. I have just played the hardest match of my career."'

Perry with von Cramm

The Crystal Palace exhibition centre was the pride of Britain. Made entirely of glass and costing the enormous sum for those days of £2million, it was famed throughout the world. But on the night of November 30, 1936, the building burnt down. A team of *Mirror* reporters observing from various vantage points sent in sensational eye-witness reports: 'With flames rising to a height of 500 feet, streams of molten glass forcing back firemen and sparks being hurled three miles, the Crystal Palace was ablaze from end to end. Millions watched the greatest blaze London has seen for many years. It could be seen in Brighton, 50 miles away. An airliner pilot in mid-channel, 80 miles away, sighted the glare. By midnight two-thirds of the building was in ruins. Thousands raced from hundreds of surrounding towns and villages to see the spectacle. For three miles around roads were completely blocked by cars. Many fire engines found it impossible to get within half a mile. The Duke of Kent, accompanied by Lord Herbert, his equerry, motored down from the West End to see the fire. The entire London fire brigade was mobilised and 65 engines and 350 firemen were soon on the spot. The heat could be felt half a mile away. Firemen were unable to work near the flames for more than a minute. The noise as the roof crashed could be heard five miles away. Police cars raced through the thronged streets calling through their loudspeakers for Sir Henry Buckland, manager of the palace. At last he was

GO ON— KISS HER!

**Cary Grant and Jean Harlow –
stars of Hollywood's heyday**

Thousands raced from towns and villages to see the spectacle

traced – a pathetic figure standing in the road watching the fire with his daughter, Crystal, who had been named after the palace. Sir Henry said: "I am heartbroken. My Crystal Palace is finished. There will never be another one."

Mr D. H. Steel, the pilot of a *Daily Mirror* plane which flew over the blazing building, said: "It was like a scene in hell. I have never seen anything more beautiful nor more horrible. The whole of London was visible in the intense glare, except the north-east, which was wreathed in dense black smoke." Thousands of sightseers invaded Primrose Hill, ten miles away across the river. One onlooker remarked grimly: "This is the most spectacular firework display the Palace has ever staged." Planes were chartered to take sightseers over the blaze. Motor-coach tours were diverted to let passengers see the fire. One enterprising person hired out field-glasses at "twopence a look". Goldfish in the Crystal Palace ponds were boiled alive.'

1935

4 March Britain announces an increase in defence spending to counter German rearmament

17 April The League of Nations condemns Germany's unilateral rejection of arms limitations

6 May King George celebrates his Silver Jubilee

18 June Japan defeats the Nationalist Chinese government in Manchuria

19 September The Nuremberg decrees are announced, banning Jews from German public life

GODFREY WINN'S QUESTION—TO YOU! Page 11

Daily Mirror

THE DAILY PICTURE — NEWSPAPER WITH THE LARGEST NET SALE

TUESDAY
Dec. 1   No. 10297
ONE PENNY

Registered at the G.P.O. as a newspaper.

FIRE WRECKS CRYSTAL PALACE: ROYAL DUKE WATCHES

WHEN THE END DREW NEAR: The central portion of the palace, its acres of glass a molten mass in the inferno below, its steelwork twisting under the intense heat.

WITH FLAMES RISING TO A HEIGHT OF 500 FEET, STREAMS OF MOLTEN GLASS FORCING BACK FIREMEN AND SPARKS BEING HURLED THREE MILES, THE CRYSTAL PALACE, LONDON'S WORLD-FAMOUS £2,000,000 ALL-GLASS EXHIBITION BUILDING, WAS DESTROYED LAST NIGHT. ONLY ITS TWO 282-FOOT TOWERS WERE LEFT STANDING.

MILLIONS watched the fire. It could be seen in Brighton, fifty miles away. An air liner pilot in mid-Channel, eighty miles away, sighted the glare. At midnight two-thirds of the building was in ruins. The fire was then under control.

Thousands raced from scores of surrounding towns and villages to see the spectacle. For three miles around roads were completely blocked by cars. Many fire engines found it impossible to get within half a mile.

In their news bulletin the B.B.C. advised crowds not to go too near because of the difficulties that faced the police.

Ninety engines were on the spot with 400 firemen. The entire London Fire Brigade was mobilised and every machine stood by.

The tremendous heat could be felt half a mile away. Firemen were unable to work near the flames for more than a minute. Several were injured and taken away.

The noise as the roof crashed could be heard five miles away.

Police cars raced through the thronged streets calling through their loudspeakers for

(Continued on back page)

The Duke of Kent chatting with Mr. Morris, chief of London Fire Brigade.

DUKE OF KENT WEARS A FIREMAN'S HELMET

THE Duke of Kent, in evening dress, arrived by car shortly before midnight and chatted to fire fighters who took him up to the smouldering ruins.

At 2 a.m. he was still there—wearing gum boots and a fireman's helmet.

A cascade of water from a fire hose fell over the Duke. He retreated, still smiling, to have a cup of coffee at a brigade motor canteen which had just arrived.

He stood at the counter surrounded by firemen.

After his coffee, which the Duke said was "very good," he went with the chief of the London Fire Brigade in a staff car for a tour round the glowing wreckage to see for himself the extent of the havoc.

Then he visited the fire brigade intelligence headquarters, which had been established in a waiting room at Crystal Palace Station.

There he saw firemen and gas engineers busy with maps, working out the positions of the various mains, and directing parties of workmen who had been roused from bed to go and cut off the gas.

1936

Edward and Mrs Simpson

The 1936 Olympics in Berlin were supposed to be a triumph for Adolf Hitler and his theories of white supremacy. Instead they were dominated by the brilliant black American athlete Jesse Owens. The Black Flash, as he was known, smashed several Olympic records. On the same day that he took the 200 metres 'he returned to the track and now there'll be a new expression - 'Jumping Jesse'. For in the long jump he put up a new Olympic record of 8.06 metres, the third record he has beaten.' British athletes did not cover themselves in glory. The *Mirror's* legendary sports

Jesse Owens

writer Peter Wilson said: 'Great Britain might just as well not have entered for this Olympiad. Our athletes have been left as far behind as a donkey's tail.'

broke one of the most sensational stories of the century. The paper reported a grave issue affecting the King without mentioning Mrs Simpson. But it did say newspapers elsewhere in Europe were printing the story 'which involves an important constitutional issue affecting the King's relationship with his ministers'. That was enough to open the floodgates. The next day the *Mirror* revealed all, carrying a large exclusive picture of Mrs Simpson on the front page. In his autobiography *A King's Story*, Edward wrote how Wallis came into the drawing room that morning. 'In her hand

He was the People's Prince and now he was to be the People's King

When King George V died in January 1936 he was mourned as one of the greatest monarchs. But there was a consolation. His eldest son, Edward, was the most popular Prince of Wales imaginable. He had toured the country, visiting the poor during the depression, showing sympathy and understanding. He was the People's Prince and now he was to be the People's King. However, Edward was hiding a secret. He had fallen in love with a woman who was not only a divorcee, had not only remarried, but was still married to her second husband. His relationship with Mrs Wallis Simpson had been going on for months but was known only to a few Establishment insiders. Edward wanted to marry her when her second divorce came through but how was that possible for a King who was head of the Church of England, which did not accept divorce? Newspapers colluded with the cover-up, denying ordinary people knowledge of this crisis facing their popular royal, the monarchy and the country. Until, on December 3, the *Daily Mirror*

she had a London picture newspaper. "Have you seen this?" she asked. "Yes," I answered. "It's too bad." The world can hold few worse shocks for a sensitive woman than to come without warning upon her own grossly magnified countenance upon the front page of a sensational newspaper.' But the *Mirror* backed the King in his battle to remain on the throne. 'Tell Us The Facts, Mr Baldwin!' it screeched at the Prime Minister on the front page under the message 'God Save The King!'. It ran sympathetic features about the couple: 'They both love the sea. They both love gardening. They both love golf,' the paper revealed. And an editorial said: 'The nation loves this King. His good is the nation's good.'

7 March The Nazis enter the Rhineland, defying the Versailles Treaty

8 April Mustard gas is used in the Abyssinian war, creating widespread alarm

28 April 16-year-old Prince Farouk is crowned King of Egypt

19 July General Franco leads a rebellion of the Spanish army against the Republican government.

24 July The GPO begins a new speaking clock service

THE DAILY MIRROR, Saturday, December 5, 1936.

Daily Mirror

THE DAILY PICTURE NEWSPAPER WITH THE LARGEST NET SALE

SATURDAY
Dec. 5 No. 10301
ONE PENNY
Registered at the G.P.O. as a newspaper

GOD SAVE THE KING!

TELL US THE FACTS, MR. BALDWIN!

"Suggestions have appeared that if the King decided to marry, his wife need not become Queen. These ideas are without any constitutional foundation.

"There is no such thing as what is called a morganatic marriage known to our law. The Royal Marriages Act of 1772 has no application to the Sovereign himself . . . .

"This Act, therefore, has nothing to do with the present case. The King himself requires no consent from any other authority to make his marriage legal, but, as I have said, the lady whom he marries by the fact of her marriage to the King necessarily becomes Queen.

"She herself therefore enjoys all the, status, rights, and privileges which, both by positive law and by custom, attach to that position . . . . and her children would be in the direct line of succession to the throne.

"The only possible way in which this result could be avoided would be by legislation dealing with a particular case. His Majesty's Government are not prepared to introduce such legislation.

"Such a change could not be effective without the consent of all the Dominions. I am satisfied from inquiries i have made that this assent would not be forthcoming."
— MR. BALDWIN IN PARLIAMENT YESTERDAY.

THE NATION INSISTS ON KNOWING THE KING'S FULL DEMANDS AND CONDITIONS

The Country Will Give You the Verdict

30 July The board game 'Monopoly' is a hit in America

21 August The BBC broadcasts its first television pictures from Alexandra Palace

25 August A five day show trial in Moscow leads to the execution of 16 of Stalin's former allies

5 October 200 unemployed workers from Jarrow embark on a march to London

11 October Violent riots erupt when fascist followers of Oswald Mosley march through London's East End

1936

The *Mirror* fought hard to keep Edward VIII on the throne but, despite huge public support, it could not overcome the might of the Establishment. Pressure from the Government and Church was too great and on December 10 came the announcement that the King had decided to abdicate. His first act was to drive to Windsor from his home at Fort Belvedere and break the news to his doughty mother, Queen Mary, over a cup of tea. To avoid him being seen leaving the Fort, he drove down a rarely-used rough track. No one working in the grounds was allowed to see him leave – staff were told to hide in a garage. Later a Cabinet meeting was called and the Prime Minister, Stanley Baldwin, made a statement to the House of Commons while Lord Halifax did the same in the Lords.

REFLECTIONS

The Spanish Civil War was one of the most horrible and bloody conflicts of the past century. Many Britons who went out to fight fascism were among the thousands who died. But the *Daily Mirror* had a different worry: 'Your glass of sherry at Christmas may cost you more because the Spanish revolution is likely to raise the price and deprive Britain of nearly all supplies. Representations have been made to the Foreign Office to try to defeat difficulties looming ahead for the trade if the revolution continues. "Sherry has grown enormously in popularity during the last few years, particularly with women," one shipper said. "Mrs Smith and Mrs Jones will have their glass of sherry together at Christmas but after that the trade is in the lap of the gods."'

Shortly after the death of George V, the *Mirror* ran a remarkable article which had been sent in by a reader, Edven Crist, of Chelsea – 'a black man in a white man's country.' It began: 'I came to London as far back as 1887 and have made my home here ever since. Yet I am a stranger, cast out from amongst the people – uninvited, unwanted and unloved. My heart aches as I walk through the streets. Aches for one sign of sympathy, one hour's relief from the everlasting ostracism, one single genuine smile. Coloured folk like me are shut off, ignored, insulted, even though we live in the same land and breathe the same air. Yes, even though we are subjects of the same monarch. "Members of the one great family," as King George said. Please remember, your King is my King, too.

He broke the news to his doughty mother, Mary, over a cup of tea

Back at Fort Belvedere, Edward – still King – was visited by his brothers, the Dukes of York and Kent. The Duke of York did not leave until 9pm. He looked pale and worn, the *Mirror* reported, adding: 'In the event of abdication he will automatically succeed to the Crown.' Before he went to bed, Edward contacted the BBC to say he wished to broadcast to the nation the next day. He would be doing so as a private individual. The following day he performed his last act as monarch. He signed his abdication papers. A statement he had drafted was read to the House of Commons by the Speaker. It said: 'I would beg that it should be remembered that the burden which constantly rests on the shoulders of a Sovereign is so heavy that it can only be borne in circumstances different from those in which I now find myself.' As plain Edward Windsor, he was driven back to Fort Belvedere to prepare for his fateful broadcast – probably the most dramatic ever made in Britain. Millions huddled round their wirelesses to hear the man they believed would be their King for years to come explain why he was giving up the throne for the woman he loved. Vast crowds gathered in London to welcome Edward's brother Albert as their new monarch. They sang 'God Save The King' and 'For He's A Jolly Good Fellow.' They shouted 'We want King Albert!' and 'Long Live King Albert!' But Albert – his first name – had decided to take the title George VI. And that was how he and his Queen, Elizabeth, ascended the throne.

The exploits of Pip, Squeak and Wilfred delighted children and adults

1. "Who takes the pictures for *The Daily Mirror*, Uncle?" asked Squeak. "They are taken by expert photographers." I said. "Would you like to spend a day with one?" "Rather!" cried the pets. So I arranged things, and here you see them starting off.

1 November Italy and Germany form an anti-Communist axis

1 April The London County Council proposes a greenbelt around London to curb urban sprawl

6 May The giant Hindenberg airship explodes in the United States

28 May Neville Chamberlain takes over as Premier

7 July The British government unveils plan to partition Palestine to end violence between Jews and Arabs

THE DAILY MIRROR, Thursday, December 10, 1936.

Daily Mirror

No. 10305   Registered at the G.P.O. as a newspaper   ONE PENNY

THE KING DECIDES: ABDICATION PLANS

DRAMATIC VISIT TO QUEEN MARY

THE KING HAS DECIDED.

His abdication—unless he makes an eleventh hour change in his decision—is regarded by the Cabinet as imminent.

His Majesty's decision will be announced by Mr. Baldwin in the House of Commons this afternoon. Lord Halifax will make a similar statement in the House of Lords.

Last night the Labour and Liberal Opposition leaders were informed by the Government of the latest moves in the crisis, and advised that there is little hope of a happy solution.

YESTERDAY AFTERNOON THE KING SLIPPED SECRETLY OUT OF FORT BELVEDERE—THE FIRST TIME HE HAD LEFT THE FORT FOR SIX DAYS—AND HE DROVE TO WINDSOR GREAT PARK, WHERE, IN ROYAL LODGE, HE HAD TEA WITH HIS MOTHER, QUEEN MARY.

This meeting was of the most moving character and had been arranged with the utmost privacy.

Elaborate precautions were taken to enable King Edward to leave the Fort unobserved.

Over Rough-Track Roads

To avoid being seen, the King left by one of the rough track roads seldom used by anyone and was able to make the two-mile journey without being seen.

He therefore had only to traverse 200 yards of public roadway before it crossed from Ascot Road into the long private drive through Windsor Great Park to the Lodge.

No one working in the grounds was allowed to see the King leave the house. Workmen were told to remain hidden in a garage.

After spending half an hour with his mother the King returned as secretly to the Fort.

Queen Mary was accompanied by the Princess Royal and the Earl of Athlone. Later she dined with the Duke and Duchess of Kent.

In Mr. Baldwin's private room at the House of Commons last night a special Cabinet meeting was called and Ministers were frankly told of all developments.

The King had a further consultation with his brothers, the Duke of York and the Duke of Kent at Fort Belvedere during the day. The Duke of York did not return to London till 9 p.m. He looked pale and worn. In the event of abdication he would automatically succeed to the Crown.

Throughout the day dispatch riders with important messages from London had arrived at the Fort. The King's car drove out at 8.30 and shortly before eleven o'clock the royal shooting brake which has been used for the transportation of luggage left Fort Belvedere, and also a dispatch rider.

The Duke of Kent drove to Marlborough House shortly after 8 o'clock and at 9.15 a large car entered the gates with the Duke of York as its only passenger.

M.P.'s warned to be at the House to-day; Mrs. Simpson's drive.—Page 3.

KING EDWARD VIII

DIARY OF THE DAY'S EVENTS

Noon.—Mr. Walter Monckton, K.C., Attorney-General to the Duchy of Cornwall, and Sir E. Peacock back at No. 10.

1.15 p.m.—Cabinet meeting ended.

3.33 p.m.—Mr Baldwin made his statement in Commons.

4.5 p.m.—Duke of York arrived at Fort Belvedere.

5.0 p.m.—Queen Mary meets the King at Royal Lodge, Windsor Great Park.

9.0 p.m.—Duke of York arrives back at 145.

Piccadilly. The Prime Minister, Sir John Simon and Mr. Monckton at No. 10. Succession of messengers with brief cases.

9.15 p.m.—Mr. Malcolm MacDonald at No. 10.

10.0 p.m.—Sir John Simon and Mr. Monckton again at No. 10.

10.30 p.m.—Mr. Ramsay MacDonald at Colonial Office.

11.20 p.m.—Mr. Monckton left No. 10 in the King's car.

1938

29 August Japan bombs Shanghai in a new offensive against the Nationalist government

6 January Sigmund Freud arrives in London as a refugee from Vienna

14 January Walt Disney's *Snow White and the Seven Dwarfs* is released

14 March Germany invades Austria

11 May The price of refrigerators is cut to £22

1939

REFLECTIONS

War brings a few changes in people's everyday lives, to say the least. But fears that food prices would soar at the start of this conflict were allayed in a *Daily Mirror* article: 'Don't worry about your food supplies and prices. Prices will not alter. Milk will be delivered daily to people in London in daylight. There is no shortage of sugar and refineries are to increase output.' But there was bad news for those wishing to send telegrams to the Post Office to withdraw savings – the service was halted due to heavy telegraphic traffic. The limited BBC television service was also suspended until further notice.

Neville Chamberlain

Today's editorial writers are anonymous because their words are the Voice of the *Mirror*. But editorials used to be signed with initials. There was much pride about one leader writer in particular. On October 11, 1938, in a memorable piece of own-trumpet blowing, the paper crowed: 'Have you read what W.M. says about it in the *Mirror* this morning?' You've probably heard that remark made several times over the past few weeks of crisis. For that tribute to one man's far-sighted frankness has been paid by thousands of worried Britons during the fateful days that followed Hitler's speech at the Nuremberg Nazi Congress. One voice in this country has consistently, unswervingly "warned our people of what would happen next." One voice has consistently, unswervingly revealed the ultimate aims of the dictators. One voice has hammered home consistently, unswervingly the lesson that Britain must be strong. The voice of W.M. the *Daily Mirror*'s famous leader writer.' W.M. was Richard Jennings, the initials standing for William Morris, the nineteenth century radical.

D.S.

The first real signs of what sort of man Adolf Hitler was came almost a year after Prime Minister Neville Chamberlain returned from Munich in September 1938 waving a piece of paper declaring: 'I bring peace with honour from Germany. It is peace in our time. Go home and sleep quietly in your beds.' But the following September our quiet sleep was shattered when Germany's honour was thrown out of the window and Hitler embarked upon his quest for world domination by invading Poland. He had been planning the attack since March when his army marched into Czechoslovakia. After 21 years of peace, Britain was at war with its old enemy again. The UK's ultimatum to Hitler to withdraw his

WANTED!

FOR MURDER . . . FOR KIDNAPPING . . . FOR THEFT AND FOR ARSON

ADOLF HITLER
ALIAS
Adolf Schicklegruber,
Adolf Hittler or Hidler

Last heard of in Berlin, September 3, 1939. Aged fifty, height 5ft. 8½in., dark hair, frequently brushes one lock over left forehead. Blue eyes. Sallow complexion, stout build, weighs about 11st. 3lb. Suffering from acute monomania, with periodic fits of melancholia. Frequently bursts into tears when crossed. Harsh, guttural voice, and has a habit of raising right hand to shoulder

'It is peace in our time. Go home and sleep quietly in your beds'

invasion force was ignored. It was time for Chamberlain to cast another cloud of gloom over the nation with a broadcast from Number 10 on September 3, 1939. Gathered around their wireless up and down the land, the people heard these words: 'This morning the British Ambassador in Berlin handed the German government a final note stating that unless we heard from them by 11 o'clock that they were prepared at once to withdraw their troops from Poland a state of war would exist between us. I have to tell you that no such undertaking has been received and that consequently this country is at war with Germany.' A War Cabinet was set up with Winston Churchill as First Lord of the Admiralty. As he left Downing Street at the end of its first meeting, he was cheered. The people knew who they needed as wartime leader. The *Mirror* immediately set about raising the country's morale. It declared: 'Today and henceforward and until the end – endure! Rejoice that our choice is made. Rejoice that our choice is just. Know that we shall win through.' In a broadcast to the people, the King warned that this war would be different to the 1914–18 conflict and told them to prepare for death and destruction on these shores. He said: 'For the second time in the lives of most of us we are at war. Over and over again we have tried to find a peaceful way out of the difference between ourselves and those who are now our enemies. But it has been in vain. We have been forced into a conflict. The task will be hard. There may be dark days ahead and war can no longer be confined to the battlefield.'

---

21 June European governments approve a plan to enable foreign volunteers to withdraw from the Spanish Civil War

30 June A new 'Superman' comic strip begins

25 July 43 die when a bomb explodes in a busy market in Haifa, Palestine

21 October Japanese troops capture Canton, the largest city in South China

31 October A radio broadcast of H.G. Wells' *The War of the Worlds* starring Orson Welles causes a panic

DAILY MIRROR, Monday, September 4, 1939

Daily Mirror

No. 11,152 — ONE PENNY
Registered at the G.P.O. as a Newspaper.

BRITAIN'S FIRST DAY OF WAR: CHURCHILL IS NEW NAVY CHIEF

BRITAIN AND GERMANY HAVE BEEN AT WAR SINCE ELEVEN O'CLOCK YESTERDAY MORNING. FRANCE AND GERMANY HAVE BEEN AT WAR SINCE YESTERDAY AT 5 P.M.

A British War Cabinet of nine members was set up last night. Mr. Winston Churchill, who was First Lord of the Admiralty when Britain last went to war, returns to that post.

Full list of the War Cabinet is:—

PRIME MINISTER: Mr. Neville Chamberlain.
CHANCELLOR OF THE EXCHEQUER: Sir John Simon.
FOREIGN SECRETARY: Viscount Halifax.
DEFENCE MINISTER: Lord Chatfield.
FIRST LORD: Mr. Winston Churchill.

SECRETARY FOR WAR: Mr. Leslie Hore-Belisha.
SECRETARY FOR AIR: Sir Kingsley Wood.
LORD PRIVY SEAL: Sir Samuel Hoare.
MINISTER WITHOUT PORTFOLIO: Lord Hankey.

There are other Ministerial changes. Mr. Eden becomes Dominions Secretary, Sir Thomas Inskip goes to the House of Lords as Lord Chancellor, Lord Stanhope, ex-First Lord, becomes Lord President of the Council, Sir John Anderson is the Home Secretary and Minister of Home Security—a new title.

None of these is in the Cabinet, which is restricted to the Big Nine. These are the men who will be responsible for carrying on the war.

But Mr. Eden is to have special access to the Cabinet.

The Liberal Party explained last night that although Sir Archibald Sinclair had been offered a ministerial post, the Party had decided at this moment not to enter the Government

POLES ATTACK

POLISH troops are fighting on German territory, according to a Warsaw message.

A Polish counter-attack pushed back the Germans and penetrated East Prussia near Deutsch Eylau, it was claimed.

The Polish Embassy in London described a Nazi report that troops had cut the Corridor as " entirely false."

Later (according to the Havas Agency) the Polish Radio announced that Poland had retaken the frontier station of Zbarzn.

The German News Agency claimed that Nazi troops, operating on the Southern front had taken the town of Radomsko.

Radomsko, north of the industrial region round Kattowitz, is about forty miles from the Polish frontier.

1,500 Raid Casualties

The Poles' latest estimate of casualties in German air raids was issued last night in Warsaw.

It is alleged that 1,500 people were killed or injured in German air bombardment of open towns and villages during Friday and Saturday. A considerable proportion of the victims were women and children.

[The German Government had secured from

Contd. on Bk. Page, Col. 1

"BREMEN IS CAPTURED"

—French Report

The £4,000,000 German liner Bremen was reported to have been captured yesterday and taken to a British port.

A report from a high French source stated that the Bremen was captured at 4 p.m., but the area in which the liner was captured was not mentioned.

A French Government radio station broadcast the report which was picked up by the Mutual Broadcasting System of America.—Associated Press and British United Press.

Petrol Will Be Rationed

The first meeting of the new war Cabinet took place last night. Mr. Churchill was the first to leave and the crowd broke into a cheer as he walked out. Mr. Hore-Belisha was driven away by a woman chauffeur in uniform.

The Premier went from Downing-street to Buckingham Palace where he stayed with the King for three-quarters of an hour.

It was announced last night that as from September 16 all petrol will be rationed. In the meantime all car owners are asked not to use their cars more than is vitally necessary.

To-day all banks throughout Britain will be closed.

Australia yesterday declared war on Germany. " Where Britain stands, stand the people of the Empire and the British world," said Prime Minister Menzies in a broadcast message last night.

New Zealand has cabled her full support to Britain. There is a rush of recruits in Canada. At Toronto a queue of 2,000 men lined outside the Recruiting Office.

Japan has assured Britain of her neutrality in the present war.

Britain's last two-hour ultimatum to Germany was revealed to the people of Britain in a memorable broadcast from Downing-street by Mr. Chamberlain at 11.15 yesterday morning. By that time

cont'd in Col. 4, Back Page

The King to His People

" The task will be hard. There may be dark days ahead. . . . But we can only do the right as we see the right, and reverently commit our cause to God. If one and all we keep resolutely faithful to it, ready for whatever service or sacrifice it may demand, then, with God's help, we shall prevail."

These words were broadcast by the King last night. And to every household in the country a copy of his message, bearing his own signature facsimile, will be sent as a permanent record. The full speech is on page 3.

1940

you never know who's listening!

'careless talk costs lives'

'We shall fight on the beaches and landing grounds, in the fields and streets'

Things could not have got off to a worse start for the British in World War Two. In 1940, around 30,000 soldiers were killed and wounded as the British Expeditionary Force fled from Dunkirk. It was down to a superhuman effort by sailors in a flotilla of tiny boats from the coast of southern England that 350,000 British and French troops were evacuated from the port under German machine gun fire. The disaster was followed by what the *Mirror* described as the greatest speech ever made by a Prime Minister. Winston Churchill had taken over from the now broken Neville Chamberlain. As Nazi bombers targeted these shores, he defiantly declared: 'Even if large tracts of Europe fall into the grip of the Gestapo and all the odious apparatus of Nazi rule, we shall not flag or fail. We shall go on to the end, and shall fight in France, on the oceans and in the air. We shall defend our island, whatever the cost, and shall fight on the beaches and landing grounds, in the fields and streets. We shall never surrender.' A *Mirror* editorial said: 'The collapse of French resistance leaves us in our island alone as the last fortress and hope of civilisation in Europe. It is a grim position. It is not dishonourable. That is at least something.' The British people rallied to defend their country. More than 400,000 volunteered to serve in the Civil Defence and small bodies of highly mobile and strongly armed men, to be known as Ironsides, were organised in case we were invaded. The *Mirror* launched a crusade against what it called muddle and red tape which was holding back the war effort, asking readers to send in examples and promising to send them on to whichever government minister was responsible. In the summer of 1940, the blitz began, with hordes of German bombers coming over night after night. Thousands of homes were destroyed. The *Mirror* ran thrilling accounts of the blitz. One train passenger said: 'I threw myself flat on the floor as a bomber dived. The raider came down within a few feet and released a bomb. The back coaches of the train were riddled with shrapnel. The windows of my cabin fell in on me but I escaped without a scratch. It was a murderous thing.' Even royalty suffered. In September Buckingham Palace was bombed. Yet the following day the King and Queen went on another of their tours of bombed areas to sympathise with people who had lost their homes in the blitz.

1 May The Conscription Bill is passed

22 May Italy and Germany sign a 'pact of steel'

18 August *The Wizard of Oz*, starring Judy Garland, is released in Technicolor

23 August Hitler and Stalin sign a non-aggression pact

31 August The evacuation of British children from the cities begins

DAILY MIRROR, Wednesday, June 5, 1940.

Daily Mirror

(JUNE 5)

No. 11,385   ONE PENNY
Registered at the G.P.O. as a Newspaper.

LATE LONDON EDN.

WE NEVER SURRENDER

DUNKIRK —LAST MEN GO

UNDER the bullets of German machine-guns, the last of the Allied forces defending Dunkirk were embarked yesterday, it was officially announced last night.

Admiral Abrial, the French commander of the forces who have been defending Dunkirk while the embarkation operations were proceeding, was the last to leave the town, said the French radio commentator.

The evacuation ended at seven o'clock yesterday morning, it was stated.

And already some of the soldiers rescued from Flanders have taken their place in the defence line, stretching from the Somme to the Rhine, against which the next great German offensive is almost immediately expected.

The last two Britons to reach England from Dunkirk landed yesterday with a crowd of French troops—Corporal C. Huntington, of Shirebrook, Nottingham, and Private J. Cowlam, of Hull, both of the East Yorks regiment. They were picked up by a French fishing boat.

Last night's French official communique stated:—

"The embarkation from Dunkirk was completed today in conformity with the prearranged plan.

"Until the last moment, first in the suburbs and then in the town itself from house to house, the rearguard put up a heroic resistance.

Port Now Useless

"The enemy, constantly reinforced, ceaselessly continued his assaults and was ceaselessly counter-attacked. The last embarkation took place under the fire of German machine-guns.

"This implacable defence and the success of these difficult and vast operations under the orders of Admiral Abrial and General Falgade have had a definite influence on the development of the struggle.

"Admiral Abrial declares that the work accomplished by the British was magnificent."

An earlier French communique had stated that the port of Dunkirk had been made useless.

The French Navy, it was added, had lost in the Dunkirk operations seven destroyers—Jaguar, Chacal, Adroit, Bourrasque, Foudroyante, Ouragan and Sirocco—and the supply ship Niger.

"Most of the crews of our lost naval vessels were saved."

NEW CHARGE—SPREAD HAW-HAW RUMOUR

A charge of being responsible for a rumour that he had heard from a German broadcast by Lord Haw-Haw that the Nazis were going to attack a Mansfield school is being brought today against a man at Mansfield.

This was stated yesterday by Mr. J. L. Nicol, Regional Information Officer, at the inaugural meeting at Nottingham of the North Midland Regional Advisory Committee, which will function under the jurisdiction of the Ministry of Information.

This will be the first case of its kind under the new regulations.

"EVEN if large tracts of Europe fall into the grip of the Gestapo and all the odious apparatus of Nazi rule, we shall not flag or fail. We shall go on to the end, and shall fight in France, on the oceans and in the air. We shall defend our island, whatever the cost, and shall fight on the beaches and landing grounds, in the fields and streets. We shall never surrender.

"Even if—which I do not for a moment believe—this island or a large part of it were subjugated, our Empire abroad, armed and guarded by the British Fleet, would carry on the struggle until, in God's good time, the New World, with all its force and men, set forth to the liberation and rescue of the old world."

IRONSIDES FOR HOME DEFENCE

SMALL bodies of highly mobile and strongly-armed troops—to be called "Ironsides"—are being organised for home defence by General Sir Edmund Ironside, Commander-in-Chief, Home Forces. There will be many hundreds of these formed from the Regular Army.

The War Office, announcing this last night, sent to each "Ironside" a copy of the following saying by Oliver Cromwell:—

"Your danger is as you have seen: and truly I am sorry it is so great. But I wish it to cause no despondency, as truly I think it will not: for we are British . . . It's no longer despairing but out instantly all you can."

The name Ironside, first given to Cromwell himself by Prince Rupert after the battle of Marston Moor in 1644, was later given to the troopers of his cavalry — those "God-fearing men," raised and trained by him in an iron discipline.

It traditionally implies great bravery, strength or endurance.

400,000 Local

Defence Volunteers

Lord Croft, Under-Secretary for War, stated in the House of Lords last night that 400,000 had volunteered for the L.D.V.

"It is no mere outlet of patriotic emotion that we are endeavouring to recruit," he said, "but a fighting force which may be at grips with the enemy next week or even to-morrow.

"That is the attitude the War Office takes towards these forces. The response has been absolutely magnificent. I doubt whether it has been equalled in any part of the world."

Lord Strabolgi said that besides making open spaces unusable for the landing of invading planes we should do the same with large spaces of water.

Lord Breadalbane suggested that each local area should have a lorry armoured against splinters and bullets and armed with a couple of guns.

254 DEAD IN PARIS RAID

Death-roll in Monday's Paris air raid was 254, of whom 195 were civilians and fifty-nine soldiers, says the Paris War Ministry. It adds: 652 were wounded—545 civilians, 107 soldiers.

Twenty - five of the German bombers which took part in the raid were brought down.

MILITARY objectives in Munich, Frankfort-on-Main and the Ruhr were bombed by Allied warplanes as a reprisal for Monday's raid on Paris, the official Havas Agency announced last night.

A Berlin report yesterday stated that a "suburb of Munich" was bombed by an Allied plane, and eight people were killed. One bomb, it was stated hit a factory, causing much damage.

R.A.F. fighters maintained offensive patrols throughout Monday and early yesterday in the Dunkirk area.

In Germany refineries, oil tanks, supply depots and marshalling yards in the Ruhr, Rhenish Prussia and in the neighbourhood of Frankfort were among the important military objectives attacked.

Factories which were hit included one of the most important motor works in Germany. Many fires and explosions were caused.

At Monheim several attacks were made on a munitions works. Hundreds of incendiary bombs were released.

Paris Bombs Picture—page 3.

THAT proclamation of the unbreakable Allied will to fight on for freedom was made by Mr. Winston Churchill in his speech to the House of Commons yesterday — the greatest speech ever made by a Prime Minister of Britain.

Standing as the staunch embodiment of that will to fight, he declared

"I may myself full confidence that if all do their duty, and if nothing is neglected, and the best arrangements made—as they are being made—we shall prove ourselves once again able to defend our island home.

"We shall ride out the storms of war and outlive the menace of tyranny, if necessary for years."

A roar of cheers answered his superb, stark confidence

"The British Empire and the French Republic, linked together in their cause and in their need, will defend to the death their native soil, aiding each other like good comrades to the utmost of their strength," said Mr. Churchill.

+ + +

These were other vital points in the Prime Minister's speech (the full report of which starts on page 3):

WE MUST EXPECT ANOTHER BLOW ALMOST IMMEDIATELY—EITHER AT FRANCE OR OURSELVES.

We shall not be content with a defensive war. We shall build up the B.E.F. once again.

+ + +

Meantime we must bring Britain's defences to the height of efficiency

+ + +

From Flanders 335,000 British and French soldiers were evacuated. Our casualties were 30,000 dead, wounded and missing. The enemy's casualties were far heavier.

But thankfulness at the escape of the B.E.F. must not blind us to the fact that what happened in North France and Belgium was a colossal military disaster.

We lost 1,000 guns, and all the transport and armoured vehicles.

Yet in the record-breaking arms effort now on, that loss should be made up in a few months.

The Noble Story of Calais

Given an hour to surrender, 1,000 British and French troops, ordered to hold Calais to the end, spurned the demand to give in and kept the German hordes at bay for four days.

Then shells fell on the port. Thirty unwounded survivors were taken off by the Navy.

This noble story of the heroic defence of Calais is told on page 3.

Pictures of the Evacuation: Pages 8 & 9

1940

REFLECTIONS

One image of London during the war is of thousands sheltering from air raids in the London Underground. But in the first months of the war that was not allowed officially. So some people bought a ticket for the Tube and then spent the night on a platform. The Government wanted to avoid any interruption to train services, so refused to make the arrangement official. But the Ministry of Home Security was pressured into making the Tube night-time shelters after a campaign by MP James Hall. Objecting to other shelters, he said: 'If people have to turn out in the cold winter months and go to the present draughty and ill-ventilated shelters, there will be a high percentage of deaths from pneumonia.'

Women in wartime didn't only have to worry about being bombed. There was the problem of clothes rationing. But the *Mirror* was on hand to offer advice with 'Our New Clothes Service': 'Did you spend yesterday talking over the new clothes rationing; wondering this, asking that. We'll make it our job to end your worries. Send your queries to Clothes Rationing Service, Woman's Page, *Daily Mirror*, Fetter Lane, EC4, and each day we will answer a batch of them. The service will give advice on how best to distribute your 66 coupons. Tell us: 1. What clothes you have and mark them winter or summer; 2. What work you do; 3. Whether you sit down most of the day, stand or walk about a lot. We'll advise you then whether it would be better to spend more coupons on shoes, lingerie, dresses, coats, overalls

'It was nothing. Somebody had to look after the children.'

The battle for aerial supremacy produced an everlasting image of the dashing RAF pilot sweeping down from the sun in his Spitfire to repel wave after wave of Luftwaffe bombers intent on breaking the British spirit and paving the way for a Nazi conquest of these shores. While there was no questioning the heroics of these airborne gladiators during the Battle of Britain, the reality on the ground was one of extreme hardship. The German bombers did get through, in their hundreds, and wreaked untold damage on the towns and cities of England below them. But, as ever, the British spirit was proving harder to break than the houses they dwelt in. It was the spirit of the blitz. This *Mirror* front page captured it perfectly. It shows a young air-raid warden in a Kent village who ran to save three children standing paralysed in the street, terrified by the scream and thud of falling bombs. Gathering them in her arms, the *Mirror* said, she huddled over them, protecting them with her own body. Bombs were still crashing down only a short distance away. There she crouched to save the children from flying shrapnel and debris. Afterwards the *Mirror* photographer who took the picture said to her: 'You are a brave woman.' She replied: 'Oh, it was nothing. Somebody had to look after the children.' In the air, young men flew their fighters day after day, night after night in a courageous effort to stop the Nazi barrage. On one day alone, they shot down 175 planes. But not before some had dropped their deadly loads.

Once again a bomb fell on Buckingham Palace. The King and Queen were not there. Crowds would gather in the streets to cheer as bombers in flames fell from the sky. The *Mirror* proclaimed: 'This has been a week of suffering for many thousands in London. It has been a week during which the eyes of the world – particularly of America – have been turned towards London. This has been the week of our greatest hour. Our greatest week! Perhaps the greatest in the history of London. Never to be forgotten.' At the end of 1941, women were conscripted into the forces for the first time. The *Mirror* complained about 'the earlier failure to realise that modern warfare involves the complete participation of the whole able-bodied population for the forces or for the factories'. The impact of the Blitz and the spirit it evoked would ultimately be seared on to the collective memory of the British population.

Jane kept up the troops' spirits – mainly by taking off her clothes

9 April Hitler invades Denmark and Norway

28 May Belgium and Holland surrender to the Nazis

10 June Italy declares war on Britain and France

14 June The Germans take Paris. France sues for peace

21 August Leon Trotsky is assassinated by a Soviet agent in Mexico

DAILY MIRROR, Thursday, Oct. 17, 1940

Daily Mirror

OCT 17

No. 11,500
ONE PENNY
Registered at the G.P.O. as a Newspaper.

I WON'T LET THEM HURT YOU

The Story of a Great Picture

BY A SPECIAL CORRESPONDENT

MRS. MARY COUCHMAN, twenty-four-year-old warden in a small Kentish village, sat smoking a cigarette in the wardens' post. She was resting between warnings.

★

Suddenly the sirens sounded again.

She saw her little boy, with two friends, playing some distance away.

The cigarette still in her hand, Mrs. Couchman ran out of the post. Bombs began to fall as she ran.

The children, Johnnie Lusher, aged four, Gladys Ashsmith, aged seven, and her four-year-old son Brian, stood in the street, frightened by the scream and thud of the bombs.

Gathering them in her arms, she huddled over them, protecting them with her own body.

Bombs were still thudding down only a short distance away.

There she crouched, to save the children from flying shrapnel and debris.

★

A "Daily Mirror" photographer was on the spot when the incident occurred.

He took this picture.

Afterwards, when the planes had passed over, he told Mrs. Couchman, "You are a brave woman."

"Oh, it was nothing. Somebody had to look after the children," was her reply.

★

THE NAVY WIPES OUT A CONVOY, AND BLASTS DUNKIRK

—See Page Three

---

13 October 14 year old Princess Elizabeth makes her first radio broadcast to child evacuees

9 December The first major British offensive against North Africa begins

1941

8 January The anti-war British newspaper the Daily Worker is suppressed

17 March Ernest Bevin announces the mobilisation of women for war work

17 April Yugoslavia falls to the Germans

1941

"The price of petrol has been increased by one penny."—Official.

REFLECTIONS

One effect of wartime measures was a shortage in supplies of fresh milk, so people had to make do with the tinned variety. The *Mirror* explained, 'you may have wondered why tinned milk looks dark. Here is the reason: The milk is processed under pressure to preserve it hygienically. the heat causes the natural sugar which milk contains to turn slightly yellow. This tinned milk is creamy because it is "evaporated" which means the water has been reduced.' The paper also described how to open a can of tinned milk: 'Force two holes opposite each other into the lid. Tilt the tin over a jug and place it so that you can leave it for a while by itself to make sure all the milk runs out of the tin. Dilute the tinned milk every time you want to use it – one part milk, three parts water.'

As Britain's third Christmas at war approached, *Mirror* readers were warned that it would be very different from those they remembered in peacetime. 'It used to be like any Christmas card – snow, church bells, streaming lights, parcels, tinsel and holly. This year it will be a picture of tanks rolling off the lines; men on guard, men and women fire-watching, factories and training going full-blast. It will be a strange picture but one we want to put on record.' The paper asked readers to send in details of their Christmas plans, including 'you women who are spending a quiet Christmas Day at home because you're determined not to be a nuisance to anybody by travelling.' 10s 6d (52.5p) would be paid for every one published.

What began as a sleepy morning in Honolulu was to change the course of World War Two. The USA had steadfastly refused to enter the conflict raging in Europe – until its own shores were attacked on December 7, 1941. Japanese bombers pounded Pearl Harbour and America responded by declaring war on the Land of the Rising Sun. The *Mirror* reported how 'untold damage was done on the naval base and Honolulu'. Parliament immediately met to discuss how to support the US. It decided the two nations should unite against Japan, whose aggression threatened British colonies in the Far East. Churchill had foreseen this development. A month earlier he had declared: 'If the efforts of the United States to preserve peace in the Pacific fail, and should they become involved in war with Japan, the British declaration will follow within the hour.' As for newspapers, they were enjoying a less restricted role in reporting conflict than they had in the First World War. The *Mirror* was even allowed to question why the Germans were so far ahead of us in armaments after British troops had been badly beaten in the Libyan campaign – a far cry from the morale-boosting but propagandist articles during the 1914–18

Churchill did not like criticism aimed at his government

battles designed to mask the true horrors of the trenches. But by the beginning of 1942 the new-found press freedom had brought the *Mirror* and the Government into conflict. Churchill did not like some of the criticism aimed at his government, even though the paper could not have been more supportive of the war effort and the courage of the British people. The Cabinet had already discussed what should be done about the *Mirror* and when a Phillip Zec cartoon was published showing a torpedoed sailor adrift on a raft with the caption 'The price of petrol has been increased by one penny - Official', it was too much for the Prime Minister. He attempted to get the paper suppressed. The Home Secretary, Herbert Morrison, made a savage attack on the *Mirror* in the Commons but the crisis ended with only a threat to shut the paper. Had it been closed, it would not have been a popular move with the forces. The *Mirror*'s support for our soldiers in the field made it their most popular newspaper. Oh, and there was also the cartoon strip 'Jane', in which the attractive blonde constantly removed much of her clothing, which amused the troops and might even have helped to raise morale.

10 May Hitler's deputy, Rudolph Hess, parachutes into Scotland

11 May The Luftwaffe bomb the House of Commons

27 May Germany's fastest battleship, the *Bismarck*, is sunk

16 June The British government launches the V for Victory campaign

22 June Germany opens Operation Barbarossa against Russia, breaking the Nazi-Soviet Pact

DAILY MIRROR, Monday, Dec. 8, 1941.

Daily Mirror

DEC 8

No. 11,854   ONE PENNY
Registered at the G.P.O. as a Newspaper.

JAPAN DECLARES WAR ON BRITAIN AND U.S: 3 FLEETS IN BATTLE

2 tank fights open in Libya

BRITISH and enemy panzer forces last night began to fight it out in Libya. Two battles are now raging there.

General Rommel, who had the chance of escaping with his tanks to the west, is instead making strong attempts to smash our supremacy.

The tank battles were started with head-on attacks south of Tobruk. It was officially stated that forty-eight tanks, mostly Italian, were destroyed in the last three days.

As the new desert tank clash began German divebombers were sent to attack our forces. The R.A.F. smashed up this raid.

Troops danced like Dervishes around eleven blazing enemy planes on the ground.

The Fleet Air Arm followed this up by a night attack, on big enemy mechanical transport in the desert.

Battle in Moonlight

Last night's Cairo communique stated that in an action near Bir el Gobi, south of Tobruk, an enemy column of about 100 vehicles and two tanks was engaged by South African troops.

The transport was dispersed and the column forced to withdraw.

"Two other actions in this central area were still in progress when the latest reports reached Cairo. Fighting had continued in the moonlight.

"Further north again armoured forces of both sides were reported to have joined battle about midday on December 6

Reports of the progress of this engagement are not yet at hand.

Among losses inflicted by our mobile columns during December 6 are the destruction of twenty-three Italian tanks.

R.A.F. BOMB NAPLES.

R.A.F. planes attacked Naples in waves on Saturday night, yesterday's Rome communique admitted. Bombs fell on the Royal Arsenal at Naples and other war factories, stated a Cairo communique.

Jap navy is third largest

Japan's Navy is the third largest in the world. In the last eighteen months it has been strengthened by the addition of more than a dozen 2,000-ton destroyers alone.

It has at least nine capital ships, five aircraft carriers.

But information available suggests that Japan stands lowest in aviation development among the Great Powers. She is believed to have not more than 3,000 aeroplanes of all types.

America has aircraft carriers in the Pacific equipped with 100 planes, and her bombers could be brought within easy distance of their objectives.

AMERICAN RADIO CALL TO FORCES

AMERICA took prompt defence measures against Japan.

The Second Corps Army Area Headquarters in New York cancelled all leave, and ordered troops to report to their posts.

On the radio periodical announcements were made calling all naval personnel to report to their ships and stations.

All U.S. radio stations also broadcast an order to factories on war work to guard against sabotage.

All Japanese subjects in New York were ordered to remain in their homes until their status was determined.

Defences Manned

All aircraft and observation posts on the Pacific coast have been manned. Coast batteries were manned on a war basis.

The war between the U.S. and Japan has united the American people.

Even Senator Wheeler, America's leading isolationist, last night made the following comment: "The only thing now is to do our best to lick hell out of those Japs."

WAR WITH WHOLE AXIS?

Before dawn the United States may be in actual warfare with Japan, Germany, Italy and all satellites of the Axis Powers, said a Washington official last night.

Under the Tri-Power Pact Germany and Italy are expected to follow Japan in a war declaration.

JAPAN last night declared war on Britain and the United States some hours after seizing the Shanghai international settlement, sinking the British gunboat Peterel (310 tons) there and making big air and sea attacks on vital American army, navy and air bases in the Pacific.

Americans were asking: "What will Britain do?" when news was flashed from London that Britain and the U.S. are likely to declare war jointly on Japan today following a talk last night between Mr. Churchill and the U.S. Ambassador to Britain, Mr. J. G. Winant.

Both Houses of the British Parliament will meet in London at 3 p.m. today to hear Government statements.

Strong rumours were current at midnight that Japan had bombed British possessions.

One unconfirmed report from New York said that Singapore had been attacked by Japanese planes which "sank two cruisers."

British forces standing by in Malaya were said to have repulsed a surprise Japanese landing.

General Tojo, Japanese Premier, reported to the Emperor that a naval battle between Japanese, British and American naval units was going on off Honolulu.

Honolulu radio, broadcasting to the U.S., reported the destruction of six Japanese warplanes, four submarines, and the sinking of a Japanese aircraft-carrier. The carrier had been used for air raids on Honolulu, the Hawaii base at Pearl Harbour and on naval and military bases on the chief island at Oahu.

Continued on Back Page

350 killed by bomb on airfield

JAPAN'S bombers, bearing the insignia of the Rising Sun, caused severe damage in their attacks on the U.S. bases and towns.

At Hickam Airfield, on Oahu Island, 350 men were killed by a bomb which made a direct hit.

One hundred and four of the deaths occurred among Army men alone. In addition, 300 soldiers were wounded.

Admiral Block, U.S. naval chief at Hawaii, announced heavy damage and loss of life in raids there.

"Untold damage" was done to the Pearl Harbour naval base and the city of Honolulu, according to a radio message from Honolulu.

The Pearl Harbour raiders carried torpedoes and did considerable damage to shipping. Four vessels were left in flames and a fifth lay on its side.

Battleship on Fire

The U.S. battleship Oklahoma (29,000 tons), which was lying in Pearl Harbour, was bombed and set on fire.

Bombs fell on various parts of Honolulu itself and on Waikiki.

"A battle has been going on for nearly three hours," said a broadcaster. "It is no joke; it is real war. There has been severe fighting in the air and on the sea. Attacks have been very severe."

The attacks began at dawn when bombers, obviously from aircraft carriers, appeared over Honolulu and dropped bombs.

A broadcast message said

Continued on Back Page

Within one hour

Speaking at the Mansion House, London, on November 10, Mr. Churchill warned Japan:

"We do not know whether the efforts of the United States to preserve peace in the Pacific will be successful.

"BUT IF THEY FAIL, I TAKE THIS OCCASION TO SAY—AND IT IS MY DUTY TO SAY — THAT SHOULD THE UNITED STATES BECOME INVOLVED IN WAR WITH JAPAN, THE BRITISH DECLARATION WILL FOLLOW WITHIN THE HOUR."

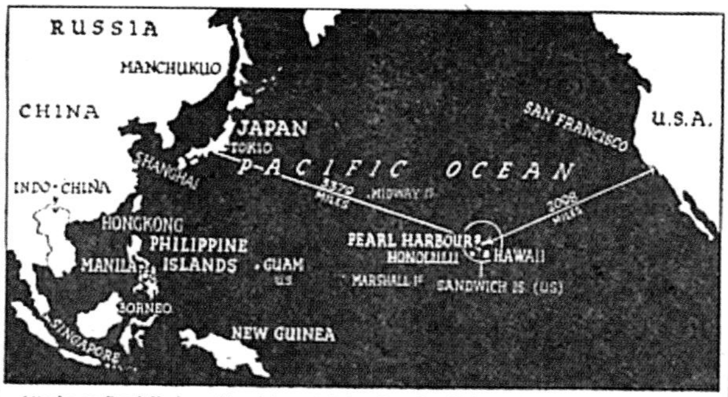

Attacks on Pearl Harbour, Honolulu and Oahu, Hawaii, which, as the map shows, are 3,379 miles from Japan, must have been made from aircraft carrier. Attacks on Manila may have been direct from Japan or Indo-China. Japanese warships are near Singapore and there are 125,000 Japs in Indo-China.

(Map showing Russia, Manchukuo, China, Japan, Pacific Ocean, Pearl Harbour, Hawaii, Philippine Islands, San Francisco, U.S.A., Midway Is., etc.)

27 July Japanese troops move into French Indo-China

14 August Churchill and Roosevelt sign the 'Atlantic Charter'

6 September German Jews are ordered to wear the Star of David

1942

22 March The BBC broadcasts its first Morse code bulletin to the French resistance

29 March Special envoy Sir Stafford Cripps offers Gandhi full post-war independence for India

1942

Many of the benefits we take for granted today – free health care and child allowances, for example – were alien concepts to pre-war Britons. But in November 1942 the foundations for change were laid by Sir William Beveridge, whose report into social division was to pave the way for the world's first welfare state. He proposed a system in which the Government provided maternity help, free medical, dental, eyesight and hospital treatment, increases in unemployment benefit, improvements in pensions and a funeral grant. And he recommended abolishing the hated means test. There was a charter for housewives which included a marriage grant, maternity payments, widow's benefit, separation and divorce provision and free help around the home in time of sickness. It would all be paid for by a new national insurance contribution which would replace the penny-a-week collected-at-the-door schemes of big insurance companies. Male employees would pay 4s 3d (21p) a week and women 3s 6d (17p), with their employers paying slightly less, between 2s and 3s 6d. Being a champion of the working classes, the *Mirror* welcomed the report with open arms. But it warned there would be those looking for an easy ride under the new system. It declared that when a worker lost his job he would not be allowed to continue in idleness indefinitely but would be required to undergo retraining. 'The generosity of the health service is designed to keep men and

REFLECTIONS

One wartime problem was the rapid spread of sexual diseases. The situation became so serious that it was debated in Parliament in December 1942. The Minister of Health, Mr Ernest Brown, said there were three main essentials in any attack on these diseases: public education; adequate free treatment; and indirect action to discourage promiscuity. To cheers from MPs Mr Brown told the Commons: 'The spread of these diseases hinders the war effort. We all agree there are moral, ethical and spiritual issues behind this evil. We know that self-control is the proper course. Personal purity is the only complete prophylactic.' Socialist MP Mrs Hardie said drink was the cause of the problem: 'We are now providing drink in women's canteens as well as men's. I don't know why women should want to copy men's vices.'

Things weren't going well on the nut front. The crop was not good and mass nut-picking parties had to be abandoned. But the *Mirror* had these words of advice: 'Pick nuts yourself. Not with the idea of eating them now, but storing them for the winter.' The paper then gave a list of nuts, when to get them and how to keep them. 'Hazel nuts grow wild in clusters, should be gathered on a fine day during a dry spell. Only ripe nuts should be chosen for storage. Pack in a box and cover with a layer of salt.' The advice was followed by hints on what to use the nuts for: flavouring, or in pastry to save fat.

'The decline in the birth rate must be reversed. Youth must provide for age.'

Sir William Beveridge

women fit for producing the wealth in which they will share,' the paper added. The *Mirror* also recognised that the Beveridge report was preparing the country for post-war reconstruction. It depended, said editorials, on future generations: 'With the present rate of reproduction the British race cannot continue. That is why children's allowances are to be introduced – to encourage people to breed.' In a *Mirror* article, Sir William wrote 'If the pensions plan is to work, the decline in the birth rate must be reversed. Youth must provide for age. The aim of the Plan for Social Security is to abolish want by ensuring every citizen willing to serve according to his powers has an income sufficient to meet his responsibilities. It is a plan for freedom from want.' The *Mirror* argued passionately for the Beveridge report to be adopted. How not to live, it said, was giving 'little bits of money to the sick, the old, the children. We are perfectly able to make sure that our standards of life make this sort of thing a forgotten nightmare'.

1942

25 June America appoints Major General Dwight Eisenhower to lead US forces in Europe

31 July Driving for pleasure is banned in the UK

31 July 'Bomber Harris' warns of devastating air raids on German cities

2 September 50,000 Jews die in the 'liquidation' of the Warsaw ghetto

1943

18 February Labour MPs lead a huge revolt over delays to the Beveridge Plan

DAILY MIRROR, Wed., December 2, 1942.

Daily Mirror

DEC 2

No. 12,159
Registered at the G.P.O. as a Newspaper.
ONE PENNY

Beveridge tells how to
BANISH WANT

Cradle to grave plan | All pay—all benefit

SIR WILLIAM BEVERIDGE'S Report, aimed at abolishing Want in Britain, is published today.

He calls his Plan for Social Security a revolution under which "every citizen willing to serve according to his powers has at all times an income sufficient to meet his responsibilities."

Here are his chief proposals:

All social insurance—unemployment, health, pensions—lumped into one weekly contribution for all citizens without income limit—from duke to dustman.

These payments, in the case of employees, would be:

Men 4s. 3d.   Employer 3s. 3d.
Women 3s. 6d.   Employer 2s. 6d.

Cradle to the grave benefits for all, including:

Free medical, dental, eyesight and hospital treatment;

Children's allowances of 8s. a week each, after the first child.

Increases in unemployment benefit (40s. for a couple) and abolition of the means test; industrial pension in place of workmen's compensation.

A charter for housewives, including marriage grant up to £10; maternity grant of £4 (and 36s. for 13 weeks for a paid worker); widow's benefit; separation and divorce provision; free domestic help in time of sickness.

Old age pensions rising to 40s. for a married couple on retirement.

Funeral grants up to £20.

To work the scheme a new Ministry of Social Security would open Security Offices within reach of every Citizen.

The 1d.-a-week-collected-at-the-door insurance schemes of the big companies would be taken over by the State.

Sir William says the Plan depends on a prosperous Britain, but claims that it can begin by July 1, 1944, if planning begins at once.

[See pages 4, 5 and 7]

Allies separate Axis armies in Africa

AMERICAN and French forces were reported last night to have driven a wedge between the two Axis armies in North Africa—between Nehring, fighting to hold Bizerta and Tunis, and Rommel, at bay at El Agheila.

Messages from North Africa and New York stated that the Allies have reached the Tunisian coast between Gabes and Sfax.

Nehring's land communications with Tripolitania—where the Afrika Korps is preparing for the next big attack by General Montgomery's Eighth Army—have thus been cut off.

The Americans and French are believed to have pushed to the coast through desert-like country from Gafsa, in Central Tunisia.

In the Bizerta-Tunis triangle, Morocco radio reported, the British First Army has crossed the Axis minefields to come to grips with the main defences.

The French are reported to have captured Pont du Fahs, a railway town 35 miles south of Tunis.

Quit Bizerta 'Drome'

The air battle over Tunisia is being fought with an intensity believed to be unequalled since the Battle of Britain.

As the struggle grows fiercer the Germans throw in planes rushed to North Africa from Western Europe and Russia.

One Nazi pilot shot down in Tunisia was flying over Stalingrad less than a fortnight ago.

Bizerta airfield has been so devastated that it was believed at Allied H.Q. last night that most of the Luftwaffe bombers and fighters have been driven back to Sicily.

Flying Fortresses have also pounded Tunis, Sfax and Gabes.

RAF Bombers rained explosives on Bizerta without a pause during Monday night, and daylight had scarcely appeared yesterday when other Allied aircraft took up the attack.

El Agheila spearhead

Patrol activity by the advanced spearhead of the Eighth Army on the El Agheila front yesterday means that the battle for this vital position may be looming.

Indications of our growing strength in this advanced area are our constant air attacks on enemy communications on the road between El Agheila and Tripoli, and on the two enemy bases of Misurata and Tripoli.

German radio last night admitted that the spearhead of the Eighth Army had pushed closer to Axis lines, and yesterday's Italian communique also reported activity between advanced units.

F D R AND DE GAULLE

President Roosevelt said yesterday that he would be glad to receive General de Gaulle, but he had not invited him to visit the United States.

Darlan is 'Chief of State'

ADMIRAL DARLAN has created an Imperial Council at Algiers and has assumed the powers of Chief of State in French Africa, Morocco radio announced last night.

The radio said Darlan has assumed the power of Chief of State "as representative of Marshal Petain, who is at present a prisoner."

"French Africa has resumed an official status which will enable it, pending the liberation of Metropolitan France, to defend the general interests of the Empire, to resume effectively the fight at the side of her Allies, and to represent France in the world."

The Imperial Council has already held its two first sittings.

Admiral Darlan presided over the sittings, which were attended by General Nogues, Governor - General Boisson, Governor - General Chatel, General Giraud, and General Bergeret.

STATEMENT ON DARLAN IN SECRET

The position of Admiral Darlan and the military developments in North Africa are to be subjects of a statement in secret session in the Commons.

When Mr. Eden announced this yesterday he added that an opportunity would be provided for a debate if desired.

NO COMMONS DEBATE BEFORE NEW YEAR

FIRST Commons comments on Sir William Beveridge's plan will be made at the next sitting, as the I.L.P. amendment to the Address is so broadly phrased that it will embrace any reconstruction proposals of this kind.

Mr. James Griffiths, from the Labour Front Bench, may indicate some of his party's reactions, but, as Sir William Jowitt indicated yesterday, the report will not be fully debated until the New Year.

The people of Occupied Europe are being told by radio of the report and its implications.

From dawn, in twenty-two languages, they will be shown how Britain, even in the midst of war, has grappled with social problems, just as in the past she took a lead on questions of social security.

Sir William will explain his report on the radio at 9.25 tonight.

Govt. give hint of post-war planning

CHOOSING the eve of the publication of Sir William Beveridge's long-awaited report on Social Security, the Government yesterday gave the country its first indication of their own plans for post-war Britain.

These include the continuance of rationing for some time and control of industry (some industries being taken over as public corporations); the development of agriculture, forestry and public utilities like electricity.

The Government also announced the immediate setting up of a new Ministry of Town and Country Planning, and the rejection of the Scott and Uthwatt Committees' proposals for placing main responsibility for planning in the hands of a permanent commission.

Victory First

Sir William Jowitt, Paymaster-General, answering a debate on reconstruction in the House of Commons, said:

"We must not allow ourselves to be distracted by talk of reconstruction from the stern task of securing victory.

"Talk of reconstruction is a mockery if the world is to remain hereafter under the constant fear of aggression."

Sir William referred to the Beveridge Report and said:

"The ideal of Social Security is one to which all thinking men and women can subscribe. We must survey his work as part of our reconstruction work as a whole.

"I hope that early in the New Year members will be in a position to discuss the main questions raised in the Report."

Sir William said it seemed obvious that the immediate

Continued on Back Page

Demobilisation fixed by age and length of service

Government plans for demobilisation after the war were outlined in the Commons yesterday by Sir William Jowitt, Paymaster - General. He said:—

No fighting man can expect to be demobilised at all if and so long as his services are required for some definite military purpose.

SUBJECT TO THAT THE BROAD PRINCIPLE ON WHICH WE HAVE DRAWN UP PLANS IS THIS: A DISCHARGE WILL BE BASED IN THE MAIN ON AGE PLUS LENGTH OF SERVICE.

I don't want to say any more about this at this time because it is probably undesirable to get into a demobilisation discussion at this stage of the war. To use a golfing metaphor, it would be a glaring case of taking our eyes off the ball.

In good time and in due course we may disclose to the House the plans that we suggest so that they may be debated.

In our plans we have not overlooked the question of education and training for the young whose educational careers were interrupted by the war.

Neither have we forgotten the disabled. We all owe it to them to see that special provisions are made for them.

We have passed all those matters under detailed review.

The Missing Link

OXO

LET OXO
MEAT YOUR VEGETABLES

1943

Field Marshal Montgomery

By 1943 the tide was beginning to turn against the Nazi war machine. Montgomery's Desert Rats had overcome the Germans in the African desert and Hitler's attack on Russia was doomed. His forces had been seriously beaten for the first time. A severe winter and a total underestimation of the opposition's will and determination ended with the destruction of the Wehrmacht in the Battle of Stalingrad. Fighting on two fronts would eventually herald the Führer's downfall. A telegram to Russian leader Josef Stalin from his generals, Voronov, Rokossovsky, Seledin and Malinin, reported: 'Completed the rout and annihilation of the enemy group. The total figure of German divisions wiped out and partly taken prisoner is 22, comprising 14 infantry divisions, four motorised divisions, three panzer divisions and one Romanian cavalry division.' It was one of the greatest massacres in history. Thousands of miles away at the sun-drenched port of Tripoli, Monty's conquest was hailed in a rather more upbeat fashion. A report said: 'Many hundreds of men in stained khaki lined up in the Piazza Castello overlooking the Mediterranean this morning and recited their thanks to God for the victory He gave the Eighth British Army. Towards the end a man stepped from the congregation and mounted the altar on the castle steps in the square. This man wore ordinary battledress. He was a man the soldiers knew well, for it was he – General Montgomery – who had sent them to battle at Alamein and brought them to the victory which this service commemorated.' Reporting battles was not the sole role of the *Mirror*. It also gave advice to troops and those at home. One such piece of advice had never before been dealt with by a newspaper. It concerned

A man stepped from the congregation and mounted the altar on the castle steps

venereal disease. A Dr Glenn wrote this radical article: 'It is my endeavour to give honest and simply understood facts about venereal disease. For too long there has been silence on this topic - mainly because it was considered shameful to discuss. The result has been ignorance and distorted knowledge which help to spread rather than check the disease. Very often the likely partner to be infected is the prostitute. It is usual to call prostitution a profession – I prefer to call it a commercial proposition, and to it applies the rule that applies to any business: No demand – no supply!' This discussion of taboo subjects did not appear again in newspapers until the sixties, when legendary agony aunt Marje Proops began writing about such things in the *Mirror*.

24 May The Allies gain the upper-hand in the U-boat war

8 July Jean Moulin, head of the French Resistance, is executed

13 July The greatest tank battle in history takes place between German and Russian troops near Kursk

25 July Mussolini falls from power

8 September Italy surrenders uncondi-tionally to the Allies

DAILY MIRROR, Wednesday, February 3, 1943.

Daily Mirror

FEB 3

No. 12,211 ONE PENNY

Registered at the G.P.O. as a Newspaper.

Montgomery and his conquering army give thanks for their victory

FROM T. E. A. HEALY

TRIPOLI, Tuesday.

MANY hundreds of men in stained khaki lined up in the sun-bathed Piazza Castello at Tripoli, overlooking the Mediterranean, this morning and recited their thanks to God for the victory He gave the Eighth British Army.

Towards the end of the service a man stepped from the congregation of soldiers, and mounted the altar on the castle steps in the square.

This man wore ordinary battle-dress. He was a man the soldiers knew well, for it was he—General Montgomery—who had sent them to battle at Alamein and brought them to the victory which this service commemorated.

Solemnly this great General, at whose bidding men had gone forth willingly to fight and die, recited the noble words of Laurence Binyon written in the last war in remembrance of the fallen:—

"They shall not grow old as we that are left grow old. Age shall not weary them, nor the years condemn. At the going down of the sun and in the morning, we will remember them."

And the soldiers in the square, recalling their fallen friends and comrades, as I, too, recall them in battle and in death, firmly and fervently answered: "We will remember them."

Service and Sacrifice

Then the General recited prayers for those who had given their lives in service and sacrifice.

This victory service was attended by men of many units who played an important part in our advance on Tripoli. There were kilted Highanders, tank crews and gunners from the North Country and Midlands, Home Counties, infantrymen and New Zealanders and South Africans.

There were two themes in this quiet and impressive service—thankfulness for victory, and remembrance of the sacrifice of those men who died for it.

The service was conducted by Lieutenant-Colonel the Rev. R. H. Royle, M.C., Vicar of St. Mark's, Swindon.

Two famous prayers were used—Lord Nelson's prayer written on the eve of the battle of Trafalgar, and Sir Francis Drake's prayer

Moment of Triumph

In Drake's prayer there is a line which gives the key to what we all feel here in this moment of triumph.

"Grant us so to know that it is not the beginning but the continuing of the same until it be thoroughly finished which yieldeth the true glory," the prayer says.

Apart from these famous supplications, the homely hymns and simple prayers used in the humblest village of their homelands were sung or recited by the soldiers.

From roof tops and balconies the local population looked on—Christians, Moslems and Jews.

After the service, Montgomery reviewed his men, who marched past to the music of bagpipes.

All the brushing and petrol-cleaning had not effaced from the uniforms the grease of tanks and guns or the dirt of the desert. But it was honourable dirt.

They would have looked out of place in The Mall on Sunday morning, but here in Tripoli, which they captured at the end of a 1,600-mile advance, they looked just what they are—the ~~bby, gallant fellows of ~~ain's finest fighting force.

In the adjoining column Healy tells how the men of the Eighth Army, led by General Montgomery, thanked God for victory with the prayers of Drake and of Nelson.

Here is Drake's prayer, composed before he sailed on Cadiz and destroyed thirty-three Spanish warships:

"O Lord God, when Thou givest to Thy servants to endeavour any great matter, grant us also to know that it is not the beginning but the continuing of the same, until it be thoroughly finished which yieldeth the true glory, through Him that for the finishing of Thy work laid down His life."

And here is Nelson's prayer on the eve of Trafalgar:

"MAY the great God, whom I worship, grant to my country, and for the benefit of Europe in general, a great and glorious victory; and may no misconduct in anyone tarnish it; and may humanity after victory be the predominant feature in the British Fleet. For myself, individually, I commit my life to Him who made me, and may His blessing light upon my endeavours for serving my country faithfully. To Him I resign myself and the just cause which is entrusted to me to defend. Amen. Amen. Amen."

NIGHT EFFORT TO AVERT STRIKE

EXECUTIVE of the Associated Society of Locomotive Engineers and Firemen sat in London till late last night without reaching a decision on their threat of a strike next week over the wages award.

Earlier, Mr. Bevin, Minister of Labour, had met the president and secretary of the Association, and it is understood that they brought back a reply from him, but its nature was not disclosed.

STALINGRAD FINAL FIGHT IS OVER

THE Battle of Stalingrad is over, after 142 days of some of the bloodiest fighting in history.

A Moscow special communique last night announced that the last Axis pocket, holding out in the ruined tractor factory in the north of the city, was forced to surrender during the day.

A brief telegram to Stalin told the first story. It read simply:

"All fighting in the Stalingrad area has come to an end." It was signed by four Russian generals—Voronov, Rokossovsky, Seledin and Malinin.

Later, Stalin received a fuller report from the four generals. This said:

"Carrying out your order, troops of the Don front at 4 p.m. on February 2, 1943, completed the rout and annihilation of the enemy group at Stalingrad.

"The total figure of German divisions wiped out and partly taken prisoner is twenty-two, comprising fourteen infantry divisions, four motorised divisions, three panzer divisions and one Rumanian cavalry division."

Stalin Expresses His Gratitude

Stalin, replying in an Order of the Day, congratulated Rokossovsky.

"I congratulate you and the troops of the Don front," he said. "I express my gratitude to all men, commanders and political instructors of the Don front for the successful battle operations."

"Today troops of the Don Front completely accomplished the liquidation of the German Fascist troops encircled in the area of Stalingrad.

"Our troops broke the resistance of the enemy encircled north of Stalingrad and compelled him to lay down his arms. The last nest of enemy resistance in the Stalingrad area was extinguished.

"General Streicher, com**mander of the troops left in the northern pocket, has been captured with his chief of staff and six more generals.**

"During the past two days the number of prisoners increased by 45,000. From January 10 to February 2, our troops captured in all 91,000 German officers and men.

"Altogether twenty-four generals and 2,500 officers have been captured."

The communique gave the names of twenty-two colonels of regiments who had also surrendered, and listed the booty captured since the final assault began on January 10.

It included 750 planes, 1,550 tanks, 6,700 guns, 8,135 machine guns, 90,000 rifles, 61,102 lorries, and 1,125 railway trucks.

"Other booty is being counted," said the communique, which ended simply, "This is the result of one of the greatest battles in the history of wars."

The German High Command admitted yesterday that the defensive ring of the last main Nazi position in Stalingrad had been broken at place after place during the night by an overwhelming Russian attack.

Their communique said the attack was carried out with far superior forces after the heaviest artillery preparation.

"During the night the enemy succeeded in breaking through at several points after our troops had used up almost all of their ammunition."

Berlin was last night making the most of an alleged Russian repulse south of Voronezh.

According to Moscow, however, at one point the Germans counter-attacked but achieved nothing, and were forced to fall back. The Russians followed up, broke into a fortified town and wiped out the German garrison there.

Rostov Trapdoor Is Closing

Meanwhile the tightening Red Army ring round Rostov, which the Germans called the gateway to the Caucasus, is making it a trapdoor which may at any hour be slammed in the faces of the enemy forces retreating from the south.

Russian troops driving towards the city along the railway from Salsk have advanced to within forty miles.

On the Donetz front General Vatutin has captured Svatova.

The Red Army columns pushing across the southern Kuban from Tikhoretsk and Kropotkin have already covered more than half of the eighty miles to Krasnodar.

BIG NAVAL BATTLE IN SOLOMONS

A GREAT NAVAL AND AIR BATTLE IS GOING ON BETWEEN UNITED STATES AND JAPANESE FORCES IN THE PACIFIC. THE JAPANESE HAVE LAUNCHED AN ATTACK WITH THE OBJECT OF REGAINING CONTROL OF THE SOLOMON ISLANDS.

This news was issued by the U.S. Navy Department early this morning.

A communique stated:

"Both American and Japanese forces have suffered some losses," the communique said, "but to reveal at this time details of the engagement would endanger the success of our future operations in this area.

"The increased activity on **the part of the Japanese indicates a major effort to regain control of the entire Solomons area."**

The communique follows Japanese claims a few days ago to have sunk two American battleships and three cruisers, and damaged another battleship and cruiser, for the loss of only ten planes off Rennell Island, in the Solomons.

The Japanese say the action occurred on Friday and Saturday, but the announcement by the U.S. Navy Department indicates that the struggle is continuing.

A Navy Department spokesman said last night: "Japanese claims to U.S. losses are grossly exaggerated, and their own losses under-stated."

Military observers in Washington pointed out that the Navy earlier reported a period of intensified air and sea activity covering a wide arc in the Pacific from the Aleutians to the Japanese stronghold of the Gilbert Islands and the air base of Munda in the South Pacific, which have been badly pounded.

Recent Navy communiques have reported constant bombing both by the U.S.A. and the Japanese of Solomons areas bases, shipping and installations.

If the Japanese suffer a major defeat in the all-out effort to regain the Solomons the military observers believe that their defensive position will be greatly weakened not only in the Solomons but also much further north.

A serious American set-back could badly disrupt American communications and shipping in the entire Solomons-Australian area

Round world for revenge story

A CHINESE whose father was robbed and murdered at Hong Kong four years ago was alleged to have taken an oath that he would get revenge on the slayer, and travelled round the world to England to achieve his purpose.

The man, Hung Leung, 24, a ship's steward, of Aigburth-road, Liverpool, is alleged to have been found struggling in the library of the Chinese Seamen's Welfare Centre and Club in Liverpool with Chank Lung Fok, warden of the club.

Leung had part of a knife in his hand, and Fok was fatally wounded in the throat, in which the pointed end of the broken knife was afterwards found embedded.

When arrested and charged with murder, Leung is alleged to have replied: "Fok killed my father in Hong Kong four years ago by poisoning. He stole my father's bank cheque for 50,000 dollars, a gold watch, gold ring and a diamond ring, and escaped to Portuguese territory."

This was the story told by the prosecution when Leung appeared in court in Liverpool yesterday.

Leung was remanded in custody.

MR. CHURCHILL PAYS VISIT TO CYPRUS

On his way back to Cairo after his visit to Turkey, Mr. Churchill called in at Cyprus where he was the guest of Governor and Lady Woolley at Government House, Nicosia.

In the course of a speech the Prime Minister described the United Nations as incomparably the strongest group of human beings that have ever been marshalled in arms in the whole history of the world.

MILK CAPS PLEASE

Aluminium milk bottle caps lost to salvage in eight months would provide the aluminium for ten Manchester or Halifax bombers, so housewives are urged to wash the caps in warm water, dry them and hand them to the milkman.

No-fight Huns—RAF browned off

MORE than 200 fighters escorted the RAF's new, fast twin-engined Venturas on two daylight bombing raids over occupied territory yesterday and carried out sweeps—without seeing a single German fighter in the sky or so much as the puff of an ack-ack shell.

Marshalling yards at Abbeville and railway targets at Bruges were bombed.

In the Abbeville attack a Spitfire wing circled the German airfield there, but though they saw F.W. 190s taxi-ing round the perimeter track, not a single Hun came up to try to "bounce" the Spitfires.

"They obviously did not want to fight and we came home because were so browned off," said the D.F.C. wing-commander.

"Although we were in the Abbeville - Boulogne area for about twenty-five minutes we were not even fired at by flak.

9 September Churchill envisages a future common citizenship between America and Britain

22 September The British government announces a new system of taxation, pay as you earn

24 October It is announced that the widespread use of penicillin on the Mediterranean Front is saving many lives

25 November The first meeting of the 'Big Three' – Churchill, FDR and Stalin takes place at Tehran

1944

19 January The Russian army defeats German forces at Leningrad, ending the two-year siege of the city

1944

page 78   Wednesday June 7   1944

The birth of modern war reporting came just as the end of this long conflict was finally in sight. On June 7, 1944, the D-Day landings began, and the *Mirror* was there to record the momentous event first hand. Under the dateline 'Aboard a British destroyer off North France, Tuesday' correspondent Desmond Tigbe sent this thrilling despatch: 'Guns are belching flames from more than 600 Allied warships. Thousands of bombers are roaring overhead and fighters are weaving in and out of the clouds. The invasion of Western Europe has begun. Rolling clouds of dense black and grey smoke cover the beaches south-west of Le Havre. We are standing some 8,000 yards off the beaches of Bernière-sur-Mer and from the bridge of this destroyer I can see vast numbers of naval craft. It is now exactly

The hour of destiny for Europe, and perhaps for the whole of mankind, has struck

7.25am and through my glasses I can see the first wave of assault troops crouching down on the water's edge and fanning up the beach.' Announcing D-Day, the *Mirror* said: 'The hour of destiny for Europe, and perhaps for the whole of mankind, has struck. A simple announcement, followed by the homely tones of General Eisenhower on the radio, proclaimed a world-shaking event, the like of which has no parallel in history. What began in Northern France yesterday morning marks the final phase of the greatest war of all time and is the largest, most elaborate, most intrepid operation of its kind ever undertaken.' A midnight communique from Supreme Allied HQ announced that 'our forces succeeded in their initial landings. Fighting continues. Our aircraft met with little enemy fighter opposition or AA gunfire. Naval casualties are regarded as very light.' Another *Mirror* report said powerful paratroop formations had dropped behind Boulogne and north of Rouen and were engaged in vicious fighting. A British-American group with light tanks was operating on dunes north-east of Bayeux trying to link up with the larger bridgehead. Fighting went on inside Caen, seven miles from the coast, and several bridges were captured. 'Battling still further inland, and well established, is the greatest airborne army ever flown into action. These troops were landed with great accuracy and very little loss. The airborne fleet consisted of 1,000 troop-carrying planes,

including gliders.' These dramatic and detailed reports, appearing in the paper only hours after the action, were very different from the late and distorted stories carried about the First World War .

20 January The RAF drops 2,300 tons of bombs on Berlin in one night

22 January The Allies advance on Rome, meeting little German opposition

1 February Clothing restrictions end in Britain

17 February R. A. Butler outlines the Education Bill, introducing a new system of secondary education

19 March Allied forces advance on Japanese troops in Burma

1944

Page 6

Daily Mirror

JUNE 7

No. 12,627
ONE PENNY
Registered
at the G.P.O.
as
a Newspaper.

4,000 ships and 11,000 planes take part in attack

5,000 tons of bombs on 10 batteries

WE HOLD BEACHHEAD

Bristol
0   50 Miles
Chatham
Dover
Calais
Dunkirk
Southampton
Portsmouth
Newhaven
Boulogne
Weymouth
Cherbourg
Dieppe
Abbeville
Amiens
R. Somme
Barfleur
Guernsey
Havre
Rouen
Jersey
Trouville
R. Seine
Caen
Versailles   PARIS
Chartres

WITHIN a few hours of the mightiest assault in history Allied troops established a beachhead on the Normandy coast yesterday.

Airborne troops are fighting some miles inland. More than 640 naval guns—from 4 to 16 inches—had practically silenced the German coastal batteries, on which 5,000 tons of bombs were dropped on Monday night.

All through the day, from the 7 a.m. landings until dusk, Allied fighter-bombers were dive-bombing, glide-bombing and strafing German defences and communications. Their war paint was blue and white stripes, and they carried coloured lights.

ALLIED PLANES WERE TO FLY 20,000 SORTIES IN THE DAY. BUT HOUR AFTER HOUR THE EXPERTS WERE ASKING: WHERE IS THE LUFTWAFFE?

Scaled the Cliffs

Berlin provided the only place-names in the news. They said they were fighting Allied troops on an eighty-mile front between Trouville and Barfleur, on the Cherbourg peninsula.

They spoke of hard fighting around Caen, and of "strong landings" at St. Vaast, below Barfleur.

Tanks, they said, were landed at Aromanches, fifteen miles from Caen, nine hours after the main landings.

In this landing there were 200 boats, and Berlin spoke of :—

"THE ENEMY TRYING TO SCALE THE STEEP COAST WITH THE AID OF SPECIAL LADDERS."

Other landings were being made under strong air protection at Ouistreham and Marcoeul, and Berlin added: "The landing parties were at once engaged in extremely costly battles."

Several Miles In

There is no word at all from the Allied side to support the German statement that we have landed paratroops on Guernsey and Jersey, which lie off the coast.

Hitler's biggest admission was that between Caen and Isigny the Allied tanks had penetrated several miles to the south.

Mr. Churchill gave the House the facts at noon. "This is the first of a series of landings," he emphasised.

BEFORE SUNRISE YESTERDAY AN ARMADA OF 4,000 SHIPS, WITH SEVERAL THOUSAND SMALLER CRAFT, HAD CROSSED THE CHANNEL—WHICH WAS NOT TOO KIND

Mass airborne landings had been successfully effected. The fire of the shore batteries had been

(Continued on Back Page)

20,000 SORTIES

CHANNEL ISLAND ATTACK

—German Report

What the Huns said

THE German radio made the first announcement to the world yesterday morning and throughout the day their military commentators and experts never stopped talking.

"They are coming, they are coming," shouted Captain Sertorius, and Lieutenant-Colonel von Olberg more dignified, said: "D-Day has dawned—the invasion has begun. There is every indication that the present Allied intention is a triphibious offensive which MUST BE TAKEN VERY SERIOUSLY INDEED."

The enemy radio said the invasion began with the landing of airborne troops near the mouth of the Seine and asserted that the operations extended from Le Havre to Caen to Cherbourg.

Their early reports said that

"First British prisoner"

Private James Griffith, of Newcastle, was one of the first prisoners to be captured by the Germans, said German radio. He had been fighting in the Caen and Cherbourg region. "The fighting was tough," he said.

German naval forces were in action off the coast and later claimed that a large Allied warship had been set on fire off the Seine where many Allied ships were gathered.

Le Havre harbour was being bombarded, the Germans announced, and Anglo-American paratroops "baled out on the northern tip of Normandy to capture several airfields."

Airborne landings were made "in great depth"—and shortly after this was altered to "greater depth."

Allied troops, they said, were fighting ten miles inland from the coast.

The German Official News Agency said that the British 1st, 2nd and 6th Airborne Divisions took part in the Seine estuary landings.

The U.S. 28th and 101st Airborne Divisions attacked the Cherbourg peninsula area, the radio claimed.

German air defence forces attacked, it was claimed, and a further statement insisted that "many sections of parachute units have been wiped out." Another report, not quite so certain, said that they were only "badly mauled."

The Germans admitted that the Anglo-American troops fighting at the mouth of the Seine had been reinforced but added hopefully:—

"Strong winds and rain showers are harassing the enemy units laden with tanks and troops, in particular the smaller ones. They are trying to evade the withering fire of

Caen was William the Conqueror's (1066) home. Cherbourg and Havre are the great liner ports. Trouville is a summer resort. Dieppe is a cliff town, with radiating railways. The Isle of Wight is about seventy miles from the peninsula.

"FIGHTING ALONG 80 MILES"

•

Sky troops sweep in

•

MINEFIELD HAZARDS OVERCOME

Continued on Back Page

1945

May 2, 1945

Daily Mirror

Page 7

"GERMANY WILL BATTLE ON"

HITLER DEAD

Killed in Berlin, says new Fuehrer, Admiral Doenitz

HITLER was killed in action yesterday afternoon, according to a broadcast from Hamburg at 10.30 last night.

His successor is Rear-Admiral Doenitz, the C.-in-C. of the German Navy, who made the announcement himself.

Doenitz said: "The Fuehrer has fallen at his command post in Berlin. He fell for Germany."

"MY FIRST TASK," SAID DOENITZ, "IS TO SAVE THE GERMAN PEOPLE FROM DESTRUCTION BY BOLSHEVISM. IF ONLY FOR THIS TASK THE STRUGGLE WILL CONTINUE.

"Give me your confidence. Do your duty."

'Lay down your arms' —Graziani to his Army

MARSHAL GRAZIANI

Adolf Hitler, leader of the Nazi Reich since January 30, 1933, the world's chief criminal, now dead at the

---

REFLECTIONS

Although broadcasting was restricted to a few hours a day, *Mirror* editorial writer B.B.B. was worried about its impact on the British people: 'Broadcasting is a permanent part of the machinery of modern life. It has come to stay and universal television will soon be a practical proposition. There is too great a tendency to regard everything which is new as of obvious benefit to mankind. But in our opinion the BBC has not only done harm to children but to everyone else as well who listens in. The effect of broadcasting as a whole is bad because there is too much of it. The inveterate listener is in danger of losing the capacity for personal effort. He is liable to acquire a habit for mental laziness. In the long run he may even cease to think for himself. A spoon-fed generation goes from bad to worse.'

War was over. The light at the end of the long tunnel had finally been reached. And Patience Strong, as ever, had the words that captured the spirit of the nation: 'Sunshine is a tonic. It uplifts, it thrills and cheers. Thoughts take on a brighter hue and all our doubts and fears fade away like mists that vanish when the light breaks through. From the windows of the mind we see a fairer view. Sunshine has a magic touch, transforming everything. Ugly streets are paved with gold. Its glory seems to bring life and strength. Beneath it buds swell and burst apart. Hope returns and joy breaks in upon the weary heart.'

On April 30, 1945, as Russian troops closed in, Hitler – the man the *Mirror* called the 'world's chief criminal' – killed himself in his Berlin bunker. His mad dream of a 1,000-year Reich was over at a cost of an estimated 30 million dead, including six million Jews murdered in death and labour camps. The defeated German nation, which had long lost faith in their deranged Führer, was told he was killed fighting and 'fell for Germany'. As leading Nazis made an undignified scramble to save their own skins Hitler's successor, Grand-Admiral Doenitz, ordered the military struggle to continue, but surrender was imminent. On May 7 it was all over. A million Germans in Holland, Denmark and north-west Germany laid down their arms to Field Marshal Montgomery. Their capitulation followed the surrender of 900,000 Germans in Italy three days earlier. The *Mirror* trumpeted: 'It is triumph day for Field Marshal Montgomery and his men. They have beaten the Hun to his knees along the whole of their front, and have written "finis" to the German Reich. Today they bring salvation to the starving millions of Holland, and freedom to the people of Denmark, crushed for five long years under the Nazi

Gangs of girls and soldiers are waving rattles and shouting and climbing lamp-posts

jackboot.' In the first known piece of its kind, the *Mirror* ran an article by former German supreme commander Field Marshal von Rundstedt on 'Why we lost'. Von Rundstedt hailed Monty as Britain's greatest general, citing his triumphs in Libya, Tunisia, Sicily, Italy and his advance to Germany after D-Day. He added that much as Germany had wanted to invade Britain it had never seriously made the attempt, recognising that the superior British fleet would have destroyed its hopes. VE (Victory in Europe) Day was greeted with incredible scenes of jubilation. It was, said the *Mirror*, 'the day for which the British people have fought and endured five years, eight months and four days of war.' A reporter in Piccadilly Circus enthused: 'We are all going nuts! We are dancing the conga and the jig and "Knees up, Mother Brown". We are singing and whistling and blowing paper trumpets. The idea is to make a noise. We are. We are dancing around Eros in the blackout but there is a glow from a bonfire in Shaftesbury Avenue. Gangs of girls and soldiers of all the Allied nations are waving rattles and shouting and climbing lamp-posts and swarming over cars that have become bogged down in this struggling, swirling mass of celebrating Londoners. A paper-hatted throng is trying to pull me out of this telephone box now. I hold the door tight but the din is drowning my voice.'

---

25 August The Allies enter Paris

27 August The first Nazi death camps are uncovered in Poland

9 September Britain, China, America and Russia announce plans for a post-war United Nations

17 September Blackouts end after five years

14 October British troops take control of Greece

Daily Mirror

MAY 8

Tuesday, May 8, 1945
No. 12,911   ONE PENNY
Registered at G.P.O. as a Newspaper.

VE-DAY !

IT'S OVER IN THE WEST

TODAY is VE-Day— the day for which the British people have fought and endured five years, eight months and four days of war.

With unconditional surrender accepted by Germany's last remaining leaders, the war in Europe is over except for the actions of fanatical Nazis in isolated pockets, such as Prague.

The Prime Minister will make an official announcement—in accordance with arrangements between Britain, Russia and the U.S.— at 3 o'clock this afternoon. ALL TODAY AND TO-MORROW ARE PUBLIC HOLIDAYS IN BRITAIN, IN CELEBRATION OF OUR VICTORY.

We also remember and salute with gratitude and pride the men and women who suffered and died to make triumph possible—and the men still battling in the East against another cruel enemy who is still in the field.

War winners broadcast today

You will hear the voices of the King, Field-Marshals Montgomery and Alexander, and General Eisenhower when they broadcast over the B.B.C. Home Service to-night.

After the King's speech, at 9 p.m., and separated from it by the news bulletin, comes "Victory Report," a special programme which will contain the recorded voices of Ike and Monty, and other famous personalities of the war.

Additional features of the B.B.C. Home programme, which will end at 2 a.m. to-morrow, include, at 8 p.m., an address by the Archbishop of Canterbury at a Thanksgiving Service for Victory, and at 8.30 a tribute to the King.

VE-SCENE

TRAFALGAR SQUARE

It was a high old time in Trafalgar-square last night. Everybody wanted to climb something. This party of Wrens and Allied soldiers celebrated by clambering on to the lions. Army policemen present—like Nelson on his column—turned a blind eye.

London had joy night

"Daily Mirror" Reporter

PICCADILLY CIRCUS, VE-EVE. THIS is IT—and we are all going nuts! There are thousands of us in Piccadilly-circus. The police say more than 10,000—and that's a conservative estimate.

We are dancing the Conga and the Jig and "Knees up, Mother Brown," and we are singing and whistling, and blowing paper trumpets.

The idea is to make a noise. We are. Even above the roar of the motors of low-flying bombers "shooting up" the city.

We are dancing around Eros in the black-out, but there is a glow from a bonfire up Shaftesbury-avenue and a news reel cinema has lit its canopy lights for the first time in getting on for six years.

A huge V sign glares down over Leicester Square. And gangs of girls and soldiers of all the Allied nations are waving rattles and shouting and climbing lamp-posts and swarming over cars that have become bogged down in this struggling, swirling mass of celebrating Londoners.

We have been waiting from two o'clock to celebrate. We went home at six when it seemed that the news of VE-Day would never come, but we are back now.

And on a glorious night we are making the most of it. A paper-hatted throng is trying to pull me out of this telephone box now. I hold the door tight, but the din from Piccadilly Circus is drowning my voice.

It is past midnight. We are still singing. A group of men liberated from German prison camps are yelling—"Roll out the Barrel."

"We sang it when we went to France in 1939 and we sang it as we tried to get out in 1940," they told me. "Now we sing it for victory."

Amid terrific cheers a New Zealand sailor climbed on the bonnet of a bus and from there to the roof.

He stood there swaying above the crowds as the American army swarmed up.

Continued on Back Page

1945

REFLECTIONS

On May 11 the *Mirror*'s front page carried the first ever 'Forward With The People' logo on its masthead. The British people were beginning to have their first taste of freedom since the war began. Restrictions were slowly being lifted. The public was promised a basic petrol ration. Other embargoes began to disappear. Those listed in the *Mirror* included: 'Restrictions limiting dog racing to one meeting a week have gone. Police no longer have the power to limit the size of crowds at sports meetings. You can change your name by advertising the fact in the London Gazette. Death penalty for looting is abolished. Sentries no longer have the right to shoot to kill on the public highway.'

It probably doesn't sound too far-fetched in these hi-tech days but, according to US intelligence chiefs, Adolf Hitler had planned to use giant mirrors in space to reflect the sun's ray on to London and scorch the city out of existence. An American army colonel said: 'If the sun's rays had been so focussed on a small patch of earth they would destroy any living thing. Water would turn to steam, forests set alight and cities wiped out.' Fortunately, Hitler's scientists could not work out how to get the mirrors into space. Other secret German plans uncovered included a rifle that shoots round corners and rockets that could be fired from U-boats underwater.

President Harry S Truman

A great pall of smoke hid from Allied airmen the destruction the bomb had wrought

The Nazi threat was over but already a new cloud hung over the world, the fear of which is still with us today – the awesome peril of nuclear weapons. The first atomic bomb was dropped on Hiroshima on August 6, 1945, killing and wounding an estimated 150,000 people. It was the moment, said the *Mirror*, when 'the basic power of the universe was brought under human control in the greatest scientific revolution of all time'. Three days later a second A-bomb devastated Nagasaki. This time the toll of dead and injured was 75,000. The two strikes forced Japan to surrender on August 14 drawing to a close the Second World War. But this was a terrible new dawn. The *Mirror* said: 'Last night a great pall of smoke hid from Allied airmen the destruction the bomb had wrought on Hiroshima and its population of 300,000. Though its explosive charge is exceedingly small, an atomic bomb contains more power than 20,000 tons of high explosive and is more than 2,000 times as effective as the biggest bombs ever before used in war. It is so powerful that with it one plane can cause as much damage as five 1,000-plane RAF raids.' The paper reported that the first A-bomb to be exploded as a test turned a steel tower from which it was suspended into vapour. 'There was a blinding flash as the explosion occurred and the whole area was brighter than the brightest daylight. Two men 17,000ft away were knocked down and windows were shaken 180 miles away.' Announcing the strike on Japan, President Truman said: 'The force from which the sun draws its power has been loosed against those who brought war to the Far East.' He went on to disclose that the Allies had spent £500 million on the 'greatest scientific gamble in history' and that 65,000 people had worked on the project. The *Mirror* said: 'To save the rest of the world from the danger of sudden devastation, the secrets of how the bomb is made will for the time being be kept.' But that secret was already out. Two years earlier, the *Mirror* revealed, a British-Norwegian paratroop raid on a factory at Telemark, in Norway, succeeded in stopping work on Hitler's plans to produce his own A bomb. German output of heavy water used in making the bomb had reached a critical level. But the raid, led by 26-year-old Sverre Gaugen destroyed six months supply, a blow from which the German scientists never recovered. Soon Russia, aided by spies in the West, would also be in possession of the gravest threat ever to the future of mankind. The Cold War had been declared.

---

12 February The Big Three outline the post-war map of Europe

14 February Dresden is devastated by Allied bombing, killing 50,000

12 April President Roosevelt dies of a cerebral haemorrhage

28 May Mussolini is executed by Italian Partisans

26 June The United Nations is formed, embracing fifty states

Daily Mirror

TUES AUG 7 1945

FORWARD WITH THE PEOPLE

No. 12,988 — ONE PENNY
Registered at G.P.O. as a Newspaper.

British and U.S. scientists harness basic power of the universe

ATOMIC BOMB IN USE AGAINST JAPS — TOTAL RUIN SOON

Holiday folk soaked by freak storm

"*Daily Mirror*" Reporters

THE Big Storm—thunder and torrential rain — which travelled the holiday spots on Sunday, hit London at lunchtime yesterday.

As it broke, holidaymakers in Brighton, only fifty miles away, lazed on the beach in blazing sunshine.

In London the millions who couldn't get off for the weekend were caught napping. Girls in gay summer dresses and men in sports shirts ran for shelter as the rain cascaded down.

Thunderstorms swept towns along the Straits of Dover during the afternoon and crowds ran from beaches for shelter.

Several storms were raging in adjoining areas at one time, and forked lightning was almost continuous, while thunder boomed like a cross-Channel gun bombardment. Within an hour, however, the sun was out again.

At Folkestone the rain fell in torrents, while the sun was shining brilliantly for a part of the time and a storm was at its height a few miles out in the Channel.

Thousands of young Londoners defied the threat of showers and went camping and hiking.

"We haven't one vacant bed in any hostel in the South of England," an official of the Youth Hostels' Association reported.

Blast moved the clouds

This is what happened when the atomic bomb was first tested, according to a U.S. War Department expert last night:

The bomb vaporised the steel tower from which it was fired and sent a massive cloud billowing into the stratosphere. There was a blinding flash of lightning and the whole area was brighter than daylight.

Then came a tremendous sustained roar and heavy pressure which knocked down two men outside ten thousand feet from the explosion.

Immediately afterwards a huge, multi-coloured, surging cloud boiled up to over 40,000 feet. Clouds in the path of it disappeared.

One as destructive as five thousand-plane raids

THE basic power of the universe—atomic energy—has been brought under human control in the greatest scientific revolution of all time and turned against the Japanese.

British and American scientists have produced an atomic bomb which contains more power than 20,000 tons of high explosive and is more than 2,000 times as effective as the biggest bomb ever before used in war.

Last night a great pall of smoke hid from Allied airmen the destruction the bomb has wrought on one of Japan's cities. And the enemy have been warned that it will be used to destroy their land entirely unless they capitulate.

First news of this tremendous advance, with its incalculable possibilities for the future of civilisation, were given by President Truman in a statement released from the White House last night.

"The force from which the sun draws its power has been loosed against those who brought war to the Far East," he declared.

The atomic bomb is so powerful that with it, one plane can be expected to do as much damage as five 1,000-plane RAF raids did to Berlin.

It is more destructive than three mass raids by Super-Forts.

"With it," said President Truman, "the United States is now prepared to obliterate more rapidly and completely every productive enterprise the Japanese have above ground in any city.

"We will destroy their docks, factories and communications. Let there be no mistake. We shall completely destroy Japan's power to make war.

"If they do not now accept our terms, they may expect a rain of ruin from the air the like of which has never been seen on this earth."

Target No. 1 for the atomic bomb was Hiroshima, fortified port with a population of 300,000, on Tokio's island, Honshu. The Japanese said merely that the fort was raided.

SPLITTING THE ATOM

An atom is made up of minute electric particles—one or more making up a core, and others strung around the core like moons round a sun. Splitting the atom means knocking off some of the particles—and thereby releasing the terrific force locked up in the atom. Other atomic particles are used as "bullets", shot by powerful electric currents.

AND NOW WHAT OF FUTURE?

FURTHER research into the new wonder bomb promises to lead to even greater developments in its use.

"It is now for Japan to realise what the consequences will be of an indefinite continuance of this terrible means of maintaining a rule of law in the world," Mr. Churchill's statement warned.

"This revelation of the secrets of Nature, long mercifully withheld from man, should arouse the most solemn reflections in the minds and conscience of every human being capable of comprehension."

May Serve Industry

"We must indeed pray that these awful agencies will be made to conduce to peace among the nations, and that instead of wreaking measureless havoc upon the entire globe they may become a perennial fountain of world prosperity."

Dr. E. Slade, research controller, Imperial Chemical Industries, said last night: "We know now how to bottle it and release it. The next thing is to discover how to harness it so that it will serve industry."

Scientists are confident. Mr. Henry Stimson, U.S. War Secretary, said, that over a period of years the atom bomb would be developed into a still more powerful weapon.

Mr. Stimson, however, warned that much further research into the conversion of atomic energy into useful power. "How long this will take, no one can predict, but it will certainly be a period of many years," he said.

They said 'it can't be done in time'

PERFECTION of the atomic bomb meant so great a mastery of the unknown that when the war began no British scientist was prepared to predict that it would be ready for use by 1945.

But, said a statement by Mr. Churchill prepared before the election and issued by Mr. Attlee last night, its potentialities were so great that Britain decided that research should be carried on.

Responsibility for co-ordinating the work was placed in the hands of a committee of leading scientists presided over by Sir George Thomson.

There was a full interchange of ideas with America and such progress was made that by the summer of 1941 Sir George reported that there was a reasonable chance of success before the war ended.

The Chiefs of Staff recommended immediate action with the maximum priority.

Mr. W. A. Akers was released from Imperial Chemical Industries to take charge of a special division to direct the work.

And it was called, for purposes of secrecy, "The Directorate of Tube Alloys."

Under the chairmanship of Sir John Anderson a council composed of the president of the Royal Society, the chairman of the Scientific Advisory Committee of the Cabinet, the secretary of the Department of Scientific and Industrial Research and Lord Cherwell.

The Minister of Aircraft Production at that time, Lord Brabazon, also served on the committee.

Under Mr. Akers there was also a technical committee on which sat the scientists who were directing the different sections of the work, and some others.

This committee was originally composed of Sir James Chadwick, Professor Peierls, Doctors Halban, Simon and Slade.

Later it was joined by Sir Charles Darwin and Professors Cockcroft, Oliphant and Feather.

Continued on Back Page

PARATROOPERS SAVED US FROM ATOM BOMB

BRITAIN was saved from the atomic bomb by a British and Norwegian paratroop raid on a Norway factory in February, 1943.

For the atomic bomb was to have been Hitler's V3. The Germans had been working on it for a year before the Reich collapsed and their experts believe that, given a few months more, they would have brought it into operation.

The paratroop raid was made on Rjukan, when German output of "heavy water," used in making the bomb, had reached 11lb. a day.

Success of the raid was due to the co-operation of a workman at the laboratories, who instead of raising an alarm allowed the raid to proceed.

The paratroopers, led by a 26-year-old Norwegian, Sverre Gaugen, eluded the sentries at the heavily guarded Vemork plant at Rjukan, slipped into a basement room and blew up 286 cells in which the "heavy water" was concentrated, thus destroying a six months' supply.

This raid followed another British-Norwegian paratroop attack earlier that winter.

Saboteurs and planes also took a hand. In March, 1943, Norwegian-speaking saboteurs wearing British uniforms were reported to have been landed from a British plane and to have blown up part of the plant.

In November, 1943, Fortresses and Liberators blasted it in a pinpoint attack again. Huge explosions were reported.

Later the Nazis had another plant in Norway but the RAF ended this venture and destroyed.

Continued on Back Page

Out of all proportion

A little OXO enriches food out of all proportion to its size.

1945

Winston Churchill had led Britain to victory in war, but the *Daily Mirror* believed a new Prime Minister was needed to win the peace. A Labour Prime Minister. In the summer of 1945 it ran one of the greatest newspaper political campaigns ever seen, under the slogan 'Vote For Them' – a reference to all those who had fought and died for their homeland. The day before the election, the *Mirror* filled its front page with 'A message to the voters of Britain'. Aimed particularly at the women waiting at home for their men to return, it said: 'Tomorrow the future of Britain and of yourselves is at stake. Your hearths and homes, your families,

For five long years the lusty youth of this great land has bled and died...fighting for YOU

your jobs, your dreams. Vote for Them! For five long years the lusty youth of this great land has bled and died. From Berlin to Burma, through desert and jungle, on the seas and in the air, they have fought and are fighting still for *you*. Vote for Them! You women must think of your men. For five years you have depended on them. Tomorrow they depend on you. The choice is plain: to march forward to a better and happier Britain or turn back to the dangers that led us to the brink of disaster. You know which way your men would march. Vote for Them!' On election day the paper reprinted a cartoon by Phillip Zec depicting a weary, wounded soldier holding out the laurel of peace and uttering the plea 'Here you are – don't lose it again!' The paper again urged voters: 'As you, with whom the destiny of the nation rests, go to the poll, there will be a gap in your ranks. The men who fought and died that their homeland and yours might live will not be there. You must vote for *them*. Remember the issues. They are national not personal. Your own interest, the future of your children, the welfare of the whole country demand that today you do your duty and *vote*.' The election result was a triumph for the *Mirror*, Labour and its leader, Clem Attlee. For the first time the people chose a Labour Government with a clear majority. On July 27, the paper reported: 'Last night

REFLECTIONS

The *Mirror* was in real trouble with doctors. At a British Medical Association meeting, chairman Dr Guy Dain drew applause and cheers when he declared: 'The press on the whole has treated us fairly. Unfortunately there is one striking exception. This paper (the *Mirror*) insinuates we are concerned with midwifery simply because it gives us large financial rewards.' The *Mirror* had voiced concerns over doctors carrying out obstetric procedures without proper qualifications in maternity care. But, at its meeting, the BMA proposed a motion that they block efforts to take the role away from them. It was passed without one vote against it.

After the gloom of war lifted, the *Mirror* tried to brighten things up even more by declaring production of the atom bomb could bring all-year good weather to these shores: 'When science has harnessed the new discovery to the needs of peace, there are several things that could happen: our weather could be made warm and sunny. Clouds over experimental stations in America where the first atom bomb exploded vanished in the heat of the explosion. The dull, grey clouds over England could be dispersed in a similar controlled emission.' Thankfully for our fragile environment, the idea came to nothing.

Prime Minister Clement Attlee

Mrs Attlee, wearing a bright red hat, drove her husband in a small car to Buckingham Palace. There the King invited Mr Clement Attlee to become Prime Minister. He accepted. Half an hour earlier a red-eyed Mr Churchill, smoking a cigar and giving the V-sign, had driven to the Palace and tendered his resignation.'

---

22 January The first 'GI brides' leave Britain to join their husbands in America

5 March Churchill warns of an 'Iron Curtain' descending across Europe

6 March Communist Ho Chi Minh establishes the Democratic Republic of Vietnam

18 April America recognises General Tito's People's Republic of Yugoslavia

1 May Britain and America unveil a plan to partition Palestine

Daily Mirror

Thur. JULY 5 1945

FORWARD WITH THE PEOPLE

No. 12,960   ONE PENNY
Registered at G.P.O. as a Newspaper.

DON'T LOSE IT AGAIN

Vote for them

WE reproduce on this page Zec's famous VE-Day cartoon. We do so because it expresses more poignantly than words could do the issues which face the people of this country today.

As you, the electors, with whom the destiny of the nation rests, go to the poll, there will be a gap in your ranks. The men who fought and died that their homeland and yours might live will not be there. You must vote for THEM. Others, happily spared, are unable for various reasons to have their rightful say in this election. You must represent them.

Vote on behalf of the men who won the victory for you. You failed to do so in 1918. The result is known to all. The land "fit for heroes" did not come into existence. The dole did. Short-lived prosperity gave way to long, tragic years of poverty and unemployment. Make sure that history does not repeat itself. Your vote gives you the power. Use it. Let no one turn your gaze to the past. March forward to new and happier times. The call of the men who have gone comes to you. Pay heed to it. Vote for THEM.

Remember the issues. They are national not personal. Your own interest, the future of your children, the welfare of the whole country demand that today you do your duty and

VOTE

"Here you are—don't lose it again!"

(Reproduced from our VE-Day issue without apology.)

---

16 May Clement Attlee announces plans for the creation of a united and independent India

29 June Indonesian President Sukarno launches a fight for full independence from the Dutch

22 July Zionist terrorists blow up the King David Hotel in Jerusalem

19 August Civil war breaks out in China

1 September The first English League football matches since 1939 are held

1946

The post-war years were hard for the British people. Exhausted by war they struggled to return to a normal way of life against a grim backdrop of rationing and a desperate housing shortage. In an attempt to cheer its women readers the *Mirror* announced the dawning of a new age of fashion. After the long, grey years of austerity back came the pleats, tucks, embroideries and other gay fripperies of pre-war days. Non-austerity blouses and skirts went on parade in London showrooms at prices from three to five guineas. Designers had let themselves go, the *Mirror* trilled. Evening blouses were in delicate coloured chiffons, sporting silver or gold sequin epaulettes. Others were embroidered with heavy crustings of coloured beads. Among other goods reappearing in shops were famous-name lipsticks, face creams, lotions and nail varnishes which had been practically unobtainable since war began. The Board of Trade diverted six million yards of Government service cloth in various

Goods reappearing were face creams, famous-name lipsticks, lotions and nail varnishes

shades of pink to corset manufacturers. 'This will save the corset situation,' a Board official told the *Daily Mirror*. But prospects looked bleak almost everywhere else. Britain was short of manpower. Industry had lost many of the two million women who had gone to work during the war and hundreds of thousands of older people were ready for retirement. Meanwhile the production and distribution of food was a huge problem. You cannot have six years of fighting and colossal destruction without suffering for it, said the *Mirror*. 'Neither nature nor man can recover by magic.' Trying to encourage its readers not to moan, it told them: 'Since the war the grousers have had a non-stop gala. The bread is too dark; there's not enough beer; cigarettes are short; there's nothing in the shops. It's bellyache after bellyache. But why don't the grumblers take a reasonable view? The nation smokes twice as much as it did. It drinks more beer. Demand is outrunning supply. We fought a great war and we won it. Surely that is something to be going on with.' One threat, however, could not be shrugged off - the development of the atomic bomb. A feature shortly before another test was headlined 'The Last Chance' and read: 'In just two days' time the most important dress rehearsal in recorded history will be staged on a tiny atoll in the sun-drenched Pacific. It will be a dress rehearsal for the end of the world. If atomic bombs are dropped in another international war, the curtain will rise only once more – on the final act in the human tragedy: the annihilation of mankind.'

REFLECTIONS

'How do I get rid of legs that feel like a pair of shapeless sausages at the end of a hot day?' Miss H. L., of Truro, asked. The *Mirror* Beauty Parlour page had the answer: 'There are a lot of legs like this. But there would be far fewer if their owners slept with the foot-end of their beds slightly raised off the floor. Eight hours spent with the legs just that bit higher than the rest of the body lets the blood drain back to the heart and relieves a lot of the work of the veins. All you need is a couple of wooden cubes about four inches each way and you'll soon find your legs improving because they'll start off each day as nature made them.'

In 1947, six weeks after Britain's partition of the Indian sub-continent into predominantly Muslim Pakistan and Hindu India, Cassandra reported on the bloody religious war that erupted as millions of people were uprooted from their homes. 'The victims die of stabbing, shooting and burning. For the most part they are hacked to death with swords. Children are torn in two and women subjected to unspeakable atrocities. There is no mercy – only the limitless fury of mobs gone berserk in the name of religious zeal.' Cassandra estimated the death toll at twice the then official figure of 50,000. Tragically that figure would reach a million before the violence burned itself out. The tensions of partition are reflected in today's bitter enmity between India and Pakistan.

QUALITY CARRIES ON...

DRINK Coca-Cola

When restrictions are removed there will be increased opportunities of enjoying the refreshing goodness of Coca-Cola — more people will be getting it, more often. Coca-Cola will have the same high quality that has prevailed for the past fifty years.

THE COCA-COLA COMPANY LTD., SOUTHFIELD ROAD, LONDON, W.4

1946

16 October Ten leading Nazis are executed for war crimes at Nuremberg

22 November The Biro, invented by a Hungarian journalist, goes on sale for the first time

1947

12 March The United States declares a crusade against Communism

5 June American Secretary of State George Marshall announces a plan for financial aid to Europe

10 August Clement Attlee appeals for a wartime effort to tackle the national economic crisis

Daily Mirror

FORWARD WITH THE PEOPLE

No. 13,231   GNE PENNY

Registered at G.P.O. as a Newspaper

TUES MAY 21 1946

GLAMOUR IS BACK FOR WOMEN AT LAST

MORE COSMETICS MORE CORSETS AND NICER CLOTHES

HONEY BLONDE MANICURIST FOUND STRANGLED AS RUSH-HOUR CROWDS FILL STREET

A TALL oney-blonde manicurist was found stabbed and strangled to death in her saloon in Liverpool during the evening rush-hour yesterday.

She was Ella Staunton (or French), aged about 30. She had been stabbed about the head and face and strangled with the flex cable of an electric table lamp.

The police are seeking to interview a young man in connection with the murder.

It is stated that there were signs of a desperate struggle in the saloon and that screams were heard.

MacDonald wooed her in 5 weeks

MR Malcolm MacDonald, former High Commissioner for Canada and Governor-Designate of Malaya, is to marry a 30-year-old widow whom he met in Ottawa.

The bride-to-be is Mrs. Audrey Fellowes Rowley, widow of Lieutenant-Colonel Rowley, who was killed in action.

Mr MacDonald, who is 45, courted and proposed to her in the five weeks before he left Canada. Date and place of the wedding have not yet been fixed.

Engagement Surprise

Mrs. Rowley, who is tall and blonde, and was considered one of Ottawa's most beautiful debutantes, has two children, a boy aged three and a girl of two.

Although she and Mr. MacDonald have been seen together frequently at functions this year, the engagement came as a surprise.

She refused to comment on her betrothal yesterday. But her family said Mr. MacDonald would return to Ottawa soon and the wedding would take place there.

After the wedding, they will go to the Malay States.

SOCIALITE DOGS COST MORE AT THIS HOTEL

A DOG'S life at the Torbay Rise Hotel, Chelston, Torquay, involves some tricky etiquette.

For, says a tailpiece to the hotel's elegant brochure, "Guests' dogs are charged for at the rate of either 1s. or 1s. 6d. each day, according to the size and social standing of the dog."

"It is difficult to say exactly how we arrive at the distinction between the 1s. a day dog and the 1s. 6d. a day dog," admitted Mrs. Reid, the hotel manageress, yesterday.

"Size, of course, is quite a factor. But many smaller dogs of the more pampered sort would equally qualify.

"There is something about dogs—as about people—you can more or less tell by looking at them."

Despite the fact that the city was virtually isolated by patrol cars almost immediately after the discovery, the man the police wish to interview had left the city.

Special radio messages were flashed to North Wales and a town in the south of England asking police to make inquiries at addresses there.

Police stations and ports throughout the country were warned.

An inspector of the C.I.D. told the Daily Mirror last night: "We have a perfect description of the wanted man, and I think it is only a matter of time before he is found."

Discovery of the crime is said to have been made by police passing the building.

The saloon, known as "Bobby's," is in a basement in Tempest Hey, in the heart of the city's commercial centre.

Crowds of homeward-bound typists and business people gathered outside the saloon when police cars raced up.

The dead woman was known to hundreds of people. She had been married.

Dr. W. H. Grace, the pathologist, and Dr. J. B. Firth, Home Office, have been called in.

U.S. Consul tells Americans to get out of Azerbaijan

BECAUSE, he says, "the security situation has deteriorated," the U.S. Consul in Tabriz, Persia, last night advised the six American citizens in the city to leave Azerbaijan.

This follows unconfirmed reports of clashes between Azerbaijan and Persian forces, says British United Press.

CRUISES AGAIN

Royal Eagle, pre-war pleasure steamer now released from war service, goes back to her old run — London, Southend, Margate and Ramsgate — on Saturday, June 8.

Here's the "free-style" fashion for the mother-to-be—a special skirt with graduated pleats falling from the left hipline.

"Danger in quest for security"

MR JAMES BYRNES, U.S. Secretary of State, stated over the American radio early today (British time) that if the peace conference were not called this summer, the U.S. would ask the UNO General Assembly to take up the matter of the peace settlements.

He said that last December Marshal Stalin personally gave him wholehearted support for

—SAYS MR. BYRNES

his proposal for a twenty-five-year Four Power treaty for Germany, to which Mr. Molotov, Soviet Foreign Minister, at the Paris meeting raised serious objections.

Mr. Byrnes's broadcast, says Reuter, was on the results of the latest Foreign Ministers' Conference.

He continued: "Progress towards peace at Paris was infinitely greater than I expected.

"We differed considerably on a number of fundamental points, but we did come to know what those fundamental points were.

"Security is the concern of every nation, but the quest for security may lead to less, rather than more, security, in the world."

AFTER the long grey years of austerity, glamour is coming back for Britain's women.

More and better cosmetics, with the reappearance of famous brands, more corsets, and nicer clothes with all the pleats, tucks, embroideries and other gay fripperies of pre-war days are on the way.

Here are the details of today's happy news for the womenfolk:—

COSMETICS: Manufacturers have done so well with their exports—they produced £700,000 worth in the first quarter of the year as against a target of £300,000—that the Board of Trade is allowing them to put more goods into Britain's shops as a kind of "bonus."

Some of the "bonus" goods in the shops in the next three months will include famous name lipsticks, face creams, lotions and nail varnishes which have been practically unobtainable since the war.

And there may be a few good perfumes as well.

CORSETS: Six million yards of Government service cloth in various shades of pink have been diverted to the corset manufacturers by the Board of Trade.

Still on Coupons

"This will save the corset situation," a Board official told the "Daily Mirror" last night. "Many firms have already started production."

But corsets will remain on coupons, and no appreciable drop in price can be expected.

CLOTHES: First non-austerity blouses and skirts for the home market went on parade in London showrooms yesterday.

They are autumn models which will reach the shops in August at prices from three to five guineas.

Fashion details are given below.

Through the years of drabness women have waited for the silver lining on the cloud of austerity. It's here at last.

Above is one of the non-austerity blouses and skirts —the first for the home market — featured in a Bruton - street (London) fashion parade yesterday.

The skirt is sky blue barathea embroidered with plastic beading. Blouse features tucking and pin-pleating details

DRESSY SKIRTS AND BLOUSES—THE PLEATS AND FRILLS ARE GAY

TUCKS and frilling are the main features for daywear of non-austerity blouses in London yesterday.

But designers have let themselves go on the evening blouses.

Some, in delicate coloured chiffons, sport silver or gold sequin epaulets. Others are embroidered with heavy crustings of coloured beads.

Prettiest blouse in the collection was in white moss crepe, embroidered on the breast

and wrists with little green and gold sequined hearts.

Day skirts have plenty of swinging pleats. The more dressy cocktail type gauge at the back to fall into tiny bustles.

Most novel idea was a scarlet skirt with collapsible concertina pleats which fold for travelling.

Special skirt for the young mother-to-be will be just as useful after baby arrives. It is a wrap-around model with five graduated pleats

BONFIRE NIGHT— FIREMEN KNEW IT

It was bonfire night in Edinburgh last night—celebrating Victoria Day—and the fire brigade was out seven times.

One blaze was in a tenement basement—among waste paper boys had collected for a fire—and two people, overcome by fumes, were rescued.

1948

Muffin the Mule

July 1948 saw two revolutions which were to change the British way of life – the launch of television and the National Health Service. On July 30, the *Mirror* reported: 'At half-past eight tonight in more than 70,000 homes in and around London, people will switch on their 'radio set with a window' and watch the window light up. They are the television audience watching the modern miracle, pictures plucked from the air, and the diagram is a reception test. When they have twiddled the

People will switch on their 'radio set with a window' and watch the window light up

controls and got it clear the pictures that follow will be distinct and bright. In about five years eight out of 10 of Britain's homes will be able to *see* as well as hear the sort of show hitherto reserved for those able to visit London's West End.' Viewers paid £2 a year for a combined TV-sound licence with reliable sets costing £50–£60, a considerable sum at the time. But the *Mirror* – which called the new medium 'the eighth wonder of the world' – pointed out: 'For your money you can get two to three full-length plays each week, many of them acted by famous stars of stage and screen. Then there are variety shows, a television newsreel changed twice weekly, documentary and foreign films and outside broadcasts of great public events.' The paper went on to paint a rosy picture of a more innocent age: 'Every Sunday afternoon thousands of children sit entranced at the adventures of Muffin the Mule and his puppet friends. They see lessons by experts in tennis, cricket, football, riding, swimming and running, not to mention Percy Edwards and his imitations of bird songs. Make no mistake about it: television is no toy. It is as up to date as the jet engine and the atom bomb.' Although the fanfare that greeted the National Health Service was less jubilant, the

Women of Oldbury (Worcs) don't like using analgesia - painfree birth, the paper reported. Out of 236 births in the last six months, only 20 mothers had used the free analgesia equipment. Others had been invited to take experimental whiffs at demonstrations but few were interested. Nurse M. Bishop, midwife, said: 'I think the mask scares the mothers. They think they might become unconscious and miss the greatest joy of a woman's life – the first glimpse of her child.' A public health official said: 'It must be that the women are too tough or too scared for some reason we can't understand. We thought the publicity given to the Princess' – Elizabeth had pioneered painfree birth when she had Charles – 'would change their minds. It hasn't.'

On the night of November 14, 1948, the future Queen Elizabeth gave birth to her first child. 'The Duke of Edinburgh stood outside the Buhl Room at Buckingham Palace at 9.14 with the King and Queen. Inside were Princess Elizabeth, her doctors and nurses. The door of the room opened. Sister Rowe came out, went over to the Duke and said with a smile "It's a boy and they're both well." "Thank God," said the Duke. He turned to the King and Queen. The Queen embraced him, the King shook him warmly by the hand. The Empire had a new prince. Outside, women in the waiting crowd joined in circles and sang "Isn't it marvellous!" Others shouted "We want Philip!" though he did not oblige.' The *Mirror* approvingly noted the 'highly modern character' of the happy event. 'This was shown in the ease and normality of the birth and in the pre-natal behaviour of the mother'.

breakthrough of free treatment for all was widely welcomed. Even the head of the British Medical Association had complained that under the previous system many people could not afford to be ill. The *Mirror* crowed: 'Nobody in the world has such a powerful force ranged on his side as *you* have now: nearly 19,000 family doctors plus thousands of specialists.'

27 February Communists seize power in Czechoslovakia

1 April The Russians begin a blockade of traffic between Berlin and the West

13 May A baby boom is announced, as the highest number of births is recorded for 25 years

14 May The State of Israel is founded after weeks of escalating violence

1 July The first Oxfam shop opens in Oxford

Daily Mirror
Geraldine House,
Fetter-lane, E.C.4.
Holborn 4321.
And at
42-48, Hardman-st.,
Manchester, 3.
Blackfriars 2313.

FORWARD WITH THE PEOPLE

IT'S A SHOCK!

YOUR electricity may cost you more! It is a melancholy thought that the Government, instead of going all out to reduce the cost of living, are prepared, apparently, to sanction expedients which will make domestic expenses higher. The Minister of Fuel has for some time played about with the idea of checking consumption of current in the winter by making it dearer. He now has the backing of an official committee, despite the obvious unfairness of the scheme.

No one denies that some means must be found to limit the electric load during the cold weather, for it will be two or, perhaps, three years before supply catches up with demand. But why choose the method of rationing by price? This means that if you have plenty of money you can snap your fingers at economy, and that if you have not you must turn off the heat and put out some of the lights.

Had such a thing been proposed in years gone by, think how the Labour Party would have denounced it. Imagine the caustic epithets that would have gone hurtling across the House. **"The rich can welter in warmth while the poor shiver."** It would have been a sheer gift to the most "corny" tub-thumper. No, no, Mr. Gaitskell. Use your brains. Think out something else—and something **better.**

SEEING DAYLIGHT

DENTISTS in Salford have reversed a decision refusing to enter the National Health Service. They were threatened with ruin because people flocked to those who have joined the scheme. This indicates (1) that the public want the Service, and (2) that Salford dentists are beginning to acquire a little common sense.   **B. B. B.**

Out of Doors

IT was a heavy day in the field, combing woods for shade-loving plants. Last locally on the list had yet to be found; a small wood known to a few naturalists as the haunt of the great brown-winged or lady orchid, sometimes prettily styled the "Maid, of Kent."

Knew I was weeks too late for this tall and handsome rarity, but a glimpse of the basal leaves was all I wanted. Turned down a lane, dived into a wood, and hunted through every part of it—without success. The map was consulted; and found to my dismay that I had gone down the wrong lane!   JOHN ARMITAGE

KENTISH ORCHID

TELEVISION: *Britain's Baby Starts to Walk*

AT half-past eight tonight in more than 70,000 homes in and around London people will switch on their "radio set with a window" and watch the window light up with this diagram:—

BBC TELEVISION SERVICE

TUNING SIGNAL

They are the television audience watching the modern miracle—pictures plucked from the air—and the diagram is a reception test. When they have twiddled the controls and got it clear, the pictures that follow will be distinct and bright.

Regular viewers in the present television area of forty miles around London number about 300,000. On big occasions more than half a million look in. The number rises daily

NEXT year television is due to stride out from Alexandra Palace to the middle of England. Work has begun on the second transmitter at Sutton Coldfield, near Birmingham.

It will serve about six million people in a circle 100 miles across: from South Yorkshire to Oxford and Gloucester and from the Welsh border country to Peterborough.

Relay stations will pick up London programmes and beam them on to Birmingham.

In about five years most of the big centres of population are likely to be covered by the television network. Eight out of ten of Britain's homes will then be able to SEE as well as hear the sort of show

hitherto reserved for those able to visit London's West End.

Viewers pay £2 a year for a combined television-sound licence. Reliable sets cost £50 to £60. But prices are coming down as demand develops.

☆

FOR your money you can get two to three full-length plays each week, many of them acted by famous stars of stage and screen. Then there are variety shows with acts from British and Continental theatres, a television news reel changed twice weekly, documentary and foreign films—and outside broadcasts of great public and sporting events.

Mobile cameras bring close-ups of Bradman batting in a Test, of tennis stars battling at Wimbledon, international Rugby at Twickenham, the F.A. Cup Final at Wembley, the Boat Race, swimming, speedway, boxing, rowing, racing and a dozen other sports. This month viewers will see the major Olympic Games events.

In the past year we have seen Princess Elizabeth drive to her wedding, the King at the Cenotaph, the Royal Family leaving for and returning from South Africa, Mrs. Roosevelt unveiling her husband's memorial—and happy children tobogganing in the snow

☆

EVERY Sunday afternoon thousands of children sit entranced at the adventures of Muffin the Mule and his puppet friends of the television children's hour. And they see lessons by experts in tennis, cricket, football, riding, swimming and running. Not to mention Percy Edwards and his imitations of bird songs.

Television means more than entertainment. It means big overseas markets for British factories as the world follows our lead and starts to look as well as listen.

Make no mistake about it; television is no toy. It is as up to date as the jet engine and the atom bomb. By the time our children reach adolescence television will be the big brother of radio; today's sound broadcasting will be its auxiliary.

Britain still leads in presentation. But America, France, Holland and Russia are chasing us. America has

gone television crazy, with stations springing up everywhere

THIS is what Alistair Cooke, famous broadcaster, says of the televising of the two great U.S. party conventions three weeks ago:

"Six million people saw more than any newspaper reporter or radio commentator — one minute watching and hearing confidential whispers on the rostrum, the next soaring out, unseen and unsuspected, to the delegation from Maine or California and looking in on a quarrel or a deal.

"When the roll-call of the States was started they moved from delegation to delegation and saw the sincerity or the bitterness of the man who got up to speak ... the man who watched by television conducted a personal probe into one of his democratic processes more withering than any expert Congressional Committee.

TELEVISION fulfilled the hungriest, most irresistible of simple human wishes—to be a fly on the wall when mighty or scandalous deeds are brewing.

"America will pay dearly for this constant privilege, but it certainly will pay, and the price will be undreamed of changes in the public behaviour of our leaders, perhaps in our institutions themselves."

British viewers have already seen similar intimate scenes—the impulsive clutch of a bridal Princess at her husband's sleeve, the Queen waving to friends from the Royal dais, a worried Edrich at the wicket, a solemn statesman holding forth but glancing at his watch.

THESE ARE THE THINGS WHICH MAKE TELEVISION THE EIGHTH WONDER OF THE WORLD.

By
ROBERT CANNELL

NORMAN COLLINS
Television's chief sees to it that you see clearly.

Sun Gives Film Men £50,000

A FULL day's sunshine is worth £10,000 to a unit on location with a colour camera. So "Trottie True," Jean Kent's latest film, which has a lot of outside-London scenes, is at least £50,000 to the good as a result of the heat-wave.

On the other hand, the cinemas have caught it in the neck. Hot weather makes audiences melt away. But they come back with the clouds and the cool winds. This is what they will come back to.

"NIGHTMARE ALLEY"
(Plaza, West, now)

This drama, adapted from an American best-seller, concerns the rise and fall of Tyrone Power as a phoney from the fairground who achieves fame as a mind-reader. Joan Blondell figures prominently.

Gripping moments.

YOU WERE MEANT FOR ME"
(New Gallery, West, now)

This is an American austerity musical, but I quite enjoyed it.

It tells of very attractive Jeanne Crain and a small town-girl, who marries a famous band-leader—and finds out the snags.

Popular melodies of the 1930's make pleasant hearing.

"TO THE ENDS OF THE EARTH'
(London Pavilion, now)

Dick Powell and Signe Hasso are the stars in this somewhat long-winded yarn about the rounding-up of an opium gang

Plenty of changes of setting, but a famine in thrills.

"DAISY KENYON"
(Leicester-square, West, now)

Joan Crawford is the pivot of this so-so melodrama about a dress designer who falls for one character (Dana Andrews) and marries another (Henry Fonda).

But what a story! I'm surprised at you, Joan!

'THE PIRATE (Empire, West, now)

An opulent Hollywood musical, with Caribbean backgrounds, in which Judy Garland sings and Cole Porter supplies the melodies.

Good entertainment.

REG. WHITLEY
Talking Pictures

VIEW POINT

Mother Love

Readers comment on the letter of an unmarried mother who had been advised to have her baby adopted.

I WAS left a war widow four years ago, when I was nineteen, with a son a year old. I let my mother-in-law adopt him, as I was told "he would have a better chance."

How I wish I had kept him. I have married again, and we have a seven-roomed house. I pine for my son, especially as I found out I may not have any more children. — (Mrs.) P., Whitley Bay, Northumberland.

I TOO had a baby without being married. I carried on alone until my little girl was four. Then I found a husband—none better. He was killed in 1944, and I was left with my little girl and another baby on the way. It was a boy, and it

was hard bringing him up. But I met Mr. Right, and he loves my children as I do. We were married a month ago.—(Mrs.) G. F., Norfolk.

MY girl is now seventeen. God has been good to me in helping me to bring her up. It has not been easy, but to see her radiant happy face, to hear her laughter, makes everything worth while. — (Miss) T., Staffs.

I FOOLISHLY let my baby be adopted. Now look at me—a sour, embittered, nervous wreck at twenty-three. My baby girl would now be two years old. I still cry myself to sleep thinking of her.—Another Unmarried Mother, Wilts.

1949

Haigh as a choir boy

Editor Bolam

Being editor of the *Daily Mirror* is often hard but no one had it tougher than Silvester Bolam. He was the only editor of the paper – or of any British newspaper in the 20th century – to be sent to jail. On March 2, 1949, the *Mirror* reported that a man had been arrested for killing Mrs Olive Durand-Deacon, 69. The killer had tried to dispose of her body in a bath of acid. He was named as John George Haigh. But the *Mirror* did not stop there. It asked 'How many rich widows died?' and went on to speculate that

The editor pleaded guilty to contempt and was sent to Brixton prison for three months

several other elderly women could also have been murdered. The next day it went further. 'Vampire horror in Notting Hill' shrieked the front page, and it was claimed that police were investigating cases in which it was believed a murderer drank his victims' blood. There could be no doubt that the paper was saying this was Haigh, as it later reported: 'Vampire – man held' going on to name five other alleged victims. The next step was: 'The Vampire Confesses - The Vampire Killer will never strike again. He is safely behind bars, powerless ever again to lure his victims to a hideous death.' It was too much for the lawyers. The editor was charged with contempt of court. Three weeks after Haigh's arrest, Mr Bolam pleaded guilty and was sent to Brixton prison for three months. The Lord Chief Justice, Lord Goddard, told him: 'Anyone who has had the misfortune as this court has had to read these articles must be left wondering how it can be possible for that man to obtain a fair trial. Not only does it describe him as a vampire but. . . it says he has committed other murders and gives the names of persons who they say he has murdered. In the long history of this class of case there has in the opinion of this court never been a case approaching such gravity as this or one of such a scandalous and wicked character. This has been done not as an error of judgment but as a matter of policy, pandering to sensationalism for the purpose of increasing the circulation of this paper.' After serving his three months, Silvester Bolam returned for a short while to the editor's chair. Since then, the *Daily Mirror* has never been convicted of a contempt of court and those newspapers which have been are punished with a fine rather then imprisoning the editor.

12 May The Soviet blockade of Berlin ends

10 June George Orwell publishes *1984*

14 August Dr Konrad Adenauer becomes the first leader of the German Federal Republic

18 September The pound is devalued as the British economic crisis continues

1 October Mao Tse-Tung's Chinese Communist Republic is recognised by the USSR

Daily Mirror

FRI MAR. 4 1949

ONE PENNY

FORWARD WITH THE PEOPLE

No. 14,095

Registered at G.P.O. as a Newspaper.

THE VAMPIRE CONFESSES

★ No. 79—room of horror

In tins, bags and little parcels, detectives bring specimens from the back-basement of 79, Gloucester-road, London, S.W., in which the McSwans are believed to have been slain. Police digging, found false teeth in the floor.

THE Vampire Killer will never strike again. He is safely behind bars, powerless ever again to lure his victims to a hideous death.

This is the assurance which the *Daily Mirror* can give today. It is the considered conclusion of the finest detective brains in the country.

The full tally of the Vampire's crimes is still not known.

It will take squads of police many weeks to test the ghastly tale which has come tumbling from his own lips as he sat, wild-eyed and drawn, under a powerful guard.

But as the police have listened appalled, to his sadistic story of mass murder, mutilation and the drinking of his victims' blood, confirmation has been flashed back of his earlier boasts.

During the interrogation the monster explained that he was not happy about the first murders.

"It was a messy business," he said. "I found that my technique improved later."

It was as if a great artist were looking back on his handiwork.

He told his questioners that he cut the throats of the people he had killed, and sucked their blood through a lemonade straw.

And so far he has named on his catalogue of murder five people only. They are:

Dr. Archibald Henderson;
Mrs. Rosalie Mercy Henderson, his wife;
Mr. Donald McSwan;
Mrs. Amy McSwan, his wife; and
Mrs. Donald John McSwan, their son.

Dr. and Mrs. Henderson disappeared in February of last year.

Mr. Donald McSwan, property owner, and his family, of Kenilworth-avenue, Wimbledon, S.W., vanished three years or more ago

Genteel

Hour after hour, to relays of detectives and shorthand writers crowded into the buff-painted interrogation room of a London police station, the Vampire has recalled his orgies.

Drinking mug after mug of strong police tea—but never forgetting to crook his little finger genteelly away from the coarse china—the maniac has shown himself a man of easy manners.

He wears a quiet suit, of immaculate cut, with a discreet tie. His hair is sleekly brushed, his nails well-kept.

From the interrogation room he has now gone back to his cell. Here he is already awaiting trial for other offences.

The Director of Public Prosecutions now awaits police and medical reports before deciding on what action the Crown shall take.

Scotland Yard men working on the dossier of the McSwan family had by last night put together the final pieces of a strange jigsaw.

Mr. and Mrs. Donald Mc-

Continued on Back Page

IT WAS A WOMAN'S HUNCH THAT TRAPPED HIM

A WOMAN'S intuition first put the police on the trail of the Vampire.

It was that intuition that made Woman Police-Sergeant Maud Lambourne study the "missing persons" file at her police station recently.

And the same sixth sense made her decide to investigate a report personally, although there seemed nothing unusual. Similar reports are filed three times a week at her station.

She put routine questions. She put them to a man. Her intuition told her she was no longer investigating a disappearance. It was murder.

Maud Lambourne went back to her station, where the C.I.D. had come to respect her intuition.

They knew she already held four commendations from the Chief Commissioner of Scotland Yard for her detective work.

They listened—and took over the investigation.

From that moment the story of the greatest series of murders since Palmer the Poisoner, nearly a hundred years ago, began to crystallise in the test tubes of the Scotland Yard scientists.

Police-Sergeant Lambourne, eight years in the Force, has played her part.

DEFENCE: PREMIER TO SEE CHURCHILL

MR. ATTLEE revealed last night that he is ready to give Mr. Churchill details of our defences—"but Mr. Churchill has not so far informed me of the time when he would see me."

The Government, he added, are advised that in present conditions a great deal of information should not be released.

War of science will not find us unready.—Page 7.

Kept alive a month to sign killer's notes?

Mrs. Rosalie Henderson, 41, victim of the Vampire-murderer. Last night her brother said: "I am convinced she was kept under duress and forced to sign letters for a month before she was shot." Story on Back Page.

Advertiser's Announcement

Reduced Prices of FRY'S Chocolates

As from February 27th all Fry's chocolates are reduced in price or increased in weight. Better value. Quality unchanged.

FRY'S NEW PRICES

Sandwich Assortment	1/- ¼lb. ctn.
Silver Lining Assortment	1/2 ¼lb. ctn.
Crunchie	4d. each
Chocolate Cream	2d. & 3½d. each
Sandwich Block	5d. each
Quality ¼lb. Block	11d. each

FRY'S MAKERS OF GOOD CHOCOLATE

3 thirsty Russians rush the barricade

THREE of the eight Russian officials besieged in a Frankfurt building by American troops broke from the building last night.

Ignoring calls to halt and the glare of searchlights, they dashed to a garage behind the building and tried to start up a car. American military police sent them back into the building.

The officials have been ordered by the Russian authorities to return to the Soviet Zone, Berlin radio said last night.

Gas, light and water services to the building have been cut off. The phones have been disconnected, and no food is being allowed in.

One of the Russians yesterday asked the American guards for newspapers. "We are cut off from the world," he said.

He was given a copy of *Stars and Stripes*, the U.S. Army newspaper.

The Russians' job had been to advise Russians how to get back to the Soviet. Americans found few wanted to go and told the Russians to quit by March 1 but they refused to leave.

His booby trap tripped the wrong man

The wrong man — a motorist—fell into the trap which Alfred Hatcher, 26, admitted he had set one night for his rival in love, Rex Moore.

Hatcher had tied a piece of twine across the road. It was said at Ashford when he was fined £2.

Edith Scott, 16, said last night she thought Hatcher imagined Moore was meeting her.

16-STONE WIFE SAT ON HIM

WHEN the husband of a 16st. woman took refuge with a neighbour after a quarrel, she sought him out and mastered him by pinning him down and putting her knee on his chest, said Judge L. C. Thomas at Cardiff Divorce Court yesterday.

The wife, Olive Pretoria Evans, of Bryn Hirgoed, Pencoed, Glam, was described by the judge as being "quite capable of looking after herself" in a physical contest with her husband, a small man.

She wept when her husband, Ernest Rees Evans, a chemist, was awarded a decree on the ground of cruelty.

1951

The original Dome

REFLECTIONS

Shortages caused by the war persisted, leading the *Mirror* to address the burning issue of a lack of wool: 'Mending socks is about the dullest job in the world, yet if we cannot get new socks we must continue to wear that substitute which consists of a collection of holes neatly joined together. Let us hope, therefore, for the sake of masculine comfort and domestic peace, adequate supplies of wool will soon be forthcoming. By the way, when the Brains Trust reassembles it might like to answer the question: What becomes of the wool when it goes out of the hole?' Nobody could accuse the *Mirror* of not involving itself in its readers' concerns, however trivial they may seem at this distance.

In 1949, a year after the launch of the National Health Service, Clement Attlee's Labour government continued its vigorous policy of reform by announcing the nationalisation of Britain's 107 biggest steel firms. The giants, which produced 90 per cent of the nation's output, would still compete with each other. But the paper said: 'Their policy will have to be different. They must put the national interest before profits although they will be expected to pay their way.' A more intimate scheme was dreamed up to bring much needed dollars into the country. Britons could buy from 60 mail order firms top quality export-only nylons, underwear, shirts and other clothes – as long as they were paid for by a friend or relative living in the US or Canada.

of British products and the value of the British way of life. That diffidence must be shed.' From the start the festival showed that Britain, still labouring under drab austerity, was desperate to party. In cities, towns, villages and hamlets, millions joined the celebrations that marked its launch. But the centre of the festivities was the then startlingly modern new Royal Festival Hall in London. A breathless *Mirror* report on the South Bank exhibition gasped: 'Britain has done it. The Festival of Britain is colourful and exciting – a gay adventure as thrilling as the story of Britain that it unfolds. All the nations in the world will look and judge it. But we need not fear. Every man, woman and child in the country should feel proud of this great achievement, a first-class advertisement for the nation's "we fought back" effort.' The exhibition was dominated by the Dome of Discovery, the biggest dome

Every man, woman and child in the country should feel proud of this great achievement

Even postwar Britain could come up with a winner that puts present-day efforts to shame. The 1951 Festival of Britain succeeded in everything the London Millennium Dome failed at 49 years later – it was thrilling, enormously popular, great fun and a massive success. On its opening night, 2,000 bonfires blazed around the kingdom to welcome an extravaganza which not only marked the centenary of the great 19th-century exhibition which led to the construction of Crystal Palace but was supposed to herald the dawn of a new, more exciting, era. The *Mirror* explained that 100 years before 'we in this country held an enormous position by virtue of the fact that we had a monopoly of many new industrial processes. Today, our task is to hold our place among many able competitors and to restore our industrial greatness by the quality of our output. We have been bad publicists, both as to the virtues

in the world. Under its 350ft aluminium roof were stories weaving the fabric of Britain's history from early explorers to atom scientists. Three giant figures represented the fisherman of England, his wife and child. Thirteen pavilions housed exhibits including ones on transport, power and production, and the countryside. A particular favourite was a huge model of a human head cut away to show how the brain works. The *Mirror*'s Noel Whitcomb enthused: 'The place is so young, alive and new that it surprises you at first by making you feel rather proud – proud to think that this is Britain.'

---

30 May The rationing of petrol ends in the UK

17 June The first kidney transplant takes place in the US

25 June Communist North Korea invades the South. America offers aid to the South

11 July Frank Sinatra makes his British debut

26 July British troops are sent to Korea

1950

Daily Mirror.

FRI MAY 4 1951

ONE PENNY

No. 14,766

FORWARD WITH THE PEOPLE

Registered at G.P.O. as a Newspaper.

MILLIONS ENJOY FIRST NIGHT OF FESTIVAL

—and here are two of them

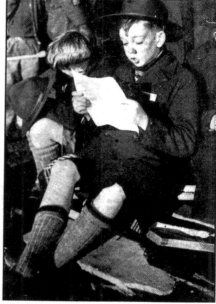

Great crowds jam roads at South Bank

"DAILY MIRROR" REPORTER

MILLIONS throughout Britain last night began the nation's great Festival celebrations. Everywhere people set out to make Festival Night the opening of their own Festival of Joy.

Two thousand bonfires blazed across the land from Northern Ireland through Scotland down to the Channel Isles telling the news in joyous leaping flames.

Streets in cities were packed with happy family crowds. In villages and hamlets the people danced on the greens. Bells pealed out and buildings famous in national and local history were everywhere ablaze from roof to ground in floodlight.

Hundreds Press Forward

But the centre of the celebrations was London and its great new Royal Festival Hall, where the King and Queen, cheered by thousands, arrived to hear the first Festival Concert.

As the packed audience in the £2,000,000 hall listened to the conducting of Sir Adrian Boult and Sir Malcolm Sargent, the crowds outside grew and swelled to VE Day size.

Police were there, heavily reinforced, to hold the way open for the Royal Family to leave. But everyone in the crowd was striving to get to the main entrance.

Just before the Royal Family left, hundreds of people were still pressing through from Charing Cross and the Embankment across Hungerford footbridge to get to the pavement lined with policemen.

The policemen leaned back against the ever-growing wall of people. They tried to persuade screaming women and children to move away towards Waterloo Bridge. But the pressure from the crowds moving in the opposite direction was too great and the dam of blue-uniformed men broke.

2,000 at the Palace

Mounted policemen took control and forced the crowds back, pleading with them to turn and go.

Finally the crowd obeyed—but not before many dozens of elderly women and girls had fainted.

Then the police outriders swept from the Festival grounds followed rapidly by the Royal car with the King and Queen and Princess Margaret.

At Buckingham Palace, 2,000 people waited to greet the Royal Family's return from the Festival Hall.

The King's car was slowed to walking pace by the cheering crowds. They were happy people, and the Queen had a smile for them.

In the shadow of St. Paul's Cathedral, meanwhile, the youth of London—over 10,000 of them—lit their Festival bonfire on a site that was fired by Hitler's bombers.

Then a 1,000-strong choir of teen-agers sang "The Song of the Festival" around the blaze. Then they burst into the traditional songs of the English, Welsh, Scots and Irish.

As the fire blazed into the sky, Londoner's swarmed towards it all round the

Continued on Back Page

For a Princess and for a Boy Scout—and for millions of other happy young folk —it was Britain's Festival night.

Princess Elizabeth, in her sparkling crinoline gown of cyclamen silk, was at the Royal Festival Hall's opening concert. Diamonds sparkle in her tiara and necklace.

The Scout, Trevor Sharp, 12, of the 7th City of London troop, was joining in the community singing around the Festival bonfire at St. Paul's Cathedral.

More Festival pictures in the Centre Pages.

And they never even kissed

A MAN was ordered to pay £150 breach of promise damages in Sydney, yesterday, to a girl he had never been out with alone, cables a *Daily Mirror* correspondent.

After the verdict Mark Salakas, a twenty-one-year-old Greek, commented: "It seems a lot to pay to a girl I have never even kissed."

So ends one of the most sensational and strange love stories ever to have been made public in an Australian court.

At one stage the father of the girl collapsed and died in the courtroom.

Then the jury was discharged, and the case was heard by the judge alone.

This love story began when the family Salakas and the family Ramales met and arranged the marriage of the girl, twenty-two-year-old Arero, and the boy, Mark.

The matchmakers, according to Greek custom, decided that a dowry of £500 was to go with the bride, and a golden sovereign was handed over by the future in-laws as the traditional token of engagement.

Then the families threw a party. Two hundred and fifty guests were invited, and a priest announced the betrothal of the boy and girl who had never even kissed.

But the boy Mark shattered this Greek love story when he decided he was "through" with old customs.

He did a very natural thing. He met another girl. He kissed her one day, and fell in love. And then he married her.

And so this story of love, according to an older Greece, ended in modern Sydney yesterday.

The girl now says: "I will never get a good offer of marriage again..."

1951

REFLECTIONS

The Korean War, which broke out when the Soviet-backed North invaded the US-supported South in 1950, raged for three years. It was the first war of the nuclear age and the only one fought by UN forces, to which Britain contributed. A typical *Mirror* report said: 'Eighth Army troops yesterday advanced between one and two miles in their drive on the central Korean front. Infantry had to slog their way through artillery and mortar fire. On the eastern front a Communist battalion was routed and Allied troops killed 115 men.' The war ended after the UN retook all land seized south of the 38th parallel along which the peninsula was partitioned. Half a century later, the armistice signed on July 27, 1953, has yet to be turned into a lasting peace agreement.

The early years of the 1950s witnessed some of the worst smogs ever to strike Britain. A great dense blanket fell on cities and towns, caused mainly by pollution from fires. After one of them the *Mirror* reported: 'Road transport came to a near standstill. Nearly all bus services stopped. Motorists abandoned their cars by the roadside. Torch-bearers walked ahead of ambulances on emergency trips. Train services were disrupted and airliners grounded. Fires blazed unchecked while fire brigades groped through the thick murk. Crime had a holiday – cosh thugs and break-in thieves struck silently out of the smog, made their coups – and vanished without risk of pursuit. BBC programmes were upset because broadcasters could not get to the studios.' It would be more than a decade before non-smokefree fuel was banned and the pall of smog lifted.

Another successful sortie over Korea

Despite carrying out a spectacular programme of reform, Labour found its huge majority at the 1945 General Election cut so drastically that in 1951 Winston Churchill returned to 10 Downing Street at the head of the Conservative Party. The *Mirror* made no secret of its support for Labour and ran a brutal and dynamic campaign against the old warrior under the slogan 'Whose Finger on the Trigger?' The *Mirror* feared that Churchill could drag Britain into another war in the atomic age and in a passionate call to arms urged its readers to vote Labour to preserve the peace and maintain the development of the welfare state and health service. Condemning Churchill's close association with America, the paper declared: 'In spite of our esteem for Mr Churchill we must point out that there are forces at work in the world which he dangerously misunderstands.' It added in a passage that was to be echoed in events 52 years later: 'He suggests that we must sit passively attendant upon a grave decision that might be taken in Washington and perhaps by a US administration more bogey-ridden than that of President Truman. Are we to wait for our foreign policy to come to us from across the Atlantic? Whose finger do we

Must our foreign policy come to us from across the Atlantic?

want guarding our trigger? At least let it be Britain's own finger.' A front page featured comments by readers proclaiming the benefits of a Labour government. Shop assistant Mrs Pauline Boddy, 29, said: 'In deciding how to vote I put a sane foreign policy at the top. So I shall vote Labour.' The Revd Leonard H. Sugden, 35, said: 'I believe Labour gives us the best chance. God has given us the resources of the world to share and Labour has shared them as fairly as possible.' Cotton worker Fred Fish, 36, said: 'Before the war I was earning 32s a week at the mill. After the war I went back to cotton. Now I get 10 guineas for a five-day week.' Welsh miner Percy Dober, 52, added: 'While I was on the dole in the bad days all I was allowed to keep my seven small daughters was 14s a week. Now I have seen contentment come to the Welsh valleys.' Housewife Mrs Olive Mahoney, 29, said: 'Labour has saved our child's life, housed us and made a country that's good to look forward in.' Family doctor Charles W. Brook weighed in: 'Before the war I used to see on the doorsteps maybe a half-pint bottle of milk. Now I see perhaps six pints. I would see a sick child and realise the small fee I had to charge might mean the family would have to go without their dinner next day. I had to wage a constant battle against malnutrition and the effects of semi-starvation. Today, thank God, that battle is over. My greatest joy is the health of the children.' But the *Mirror*'s efforts came to nothing. Churchill and the Tories won the election comfortably.

22 April Minister of Labour Aneurin Bevan resigns over plans to charge for teeth and glasses

12 May The first hydrogen bomb is tested in the Pacific

14 May The South African Government ends the vote for all mixed race citizens

14 August US newspaper tycoon William Randolph Hearst dies aged 88

23 September George VI has a major operation to remove part of his left lung

Daily Mirror

THURS
OCT. 25
1951

1½d

No. 14,915

FORWARD
WITH THE
PEOPLE

Registered at G.P.O. as a Newspaper.

WHOSE FINGER ?

BIG ISSUES OF 1951

Today YOUR finger is on the trigger

Dunkley

SEE YOU DEFEND

PEACE with SECURITY and PROGRESS with FAIR SHARES

VOTE FOR THE PARTY YOU CAN REALLY TRUST

The 'Daily Mirror' believes that Party is Labour

27 September The dispute over Iranian oil worsens when national troops seize control of a British-owned refinery

17 October The German Porsche is unveiled at the British Motor Show

19 October British troops seize control of the Suez Canal, leading to anti-British riots

24 November Austin and Morris announce a merger, creating the largest British motor firm

29 December The Italian colony of Libya becomes independent

1952

The last picture of the King

This is the front page Britain remembered ever afterwards as 'The Three Queens'. It shows King George VI's mother, Mary, his widow Elizabeth and daughter Elizabeth in deepest mourning as the monarch's coffin is carried to the lying-in-state. George – his health broken by years of duty – was found dead in bed at Sandringham royal estate, in Norfolk, on February 7, 1952, by his valet Jimmy Macdonald. He was only 56. Alerted by staff, the Queen went to George's room where she was joined by her younger daughter, Princess Margaret. The Queen, a devoted wife who had given immeasurable support to her husband, was in tears. Two thousand miles away her elder daughter Elizabeth was relaxing with her husband Philip, the Duke of Edinburgh, at the Royal Lodge, in Nyeri, Kenya, not knowing that she had become Queen. The couple were enjoying a private joke when the Princess's private secretary, Lieutenant Colonel Martin Charteris, entered. At

REFLECTIONS

When the Queen Mother died, a BBC newsreader was accused of being disrespectful for not wearing a black tie. A completely opposite complaint was made about the Corporation when her husband, George VI, died 50 years earlier and broadcasting was stopped: 'Have the BBC failed Britain? This is the great argument that has sprung up in millions of homes in the midst of our sorrow. For many who looked to the Corporation for information and, indeed, comfort on the day of the King's death remain critical at finding so little of either. To them, silence-bound speakers and blank TV screens came as poor companions for their grief. The BBC was not operating to a plan. There was not only sorrow but consternation at Broadcasting House. Nothing was ready for such an emergency. Nothing had been prepared. No radio or TV programmes were standing by. No one knew what to do. The truth is, the BBC were forced to close down. They couldn't help themselves. Once off the air, no one had any clear idea how to start up again. A national crisis can happen any time. It is to be hoped Broadcasting House have learned the lesson.'

The crowning of the young Queen Elizabeth was eagerly anticipated by millions who would be able to see a coronation for the first time thanks to the marvel of television. But their hopes were dashed. Buckingham Palace decreed that TV cameras would not be allowed to show the ceremony in Westminster Abbey. A top BBC executive told the *Mirror*: 'We are flabbergasted. We are being allowed to put cameras inside the Abbey – but they cannot be focussed on the altar to show the one thing Britain wants to see – the Coronation. There is not a man in the BBC who is not hoping that the Queen herself will intervene on behalf of both ourselves and the public.' Perhaps she did. Six weeks later the Palace changed its mind and her subjects were able to witness their monarch being crowned.

At the sight of his sombre expression the laughter died on the couple's lips

the sight of his sombre expression the laughter died on the couple's lips. Philip swiftly moved to Charteris who whispered the news of George's death. The Duke turned to Elizabeth, whose face had drained of colour. Tenderly, he told her: 'The King has passed away peacefully in his sleep.' For an instant the Princess stood quite still. Then, hands to her face, she burst into tears. Gently, Philip led her to a private room. A few minutes later, pale and composed, 26-year-old Elizabeth began planning her return to her country and the duties of monarchy that lay ahead. Nine days later the King was buried at Windsor in the first televised royal funeral. A million people lined the route of the procession. As the bier moved along The Mall and drew level with Marlborough House

there came the most moving incident of all. The blind of one window was raised and aging Queen Mary was seen standing there motionless, saying a final farewell. On June 2 the following year, Queen Elizabeth II was crowned at Westminster Abbey under the all-seeing eye of television. The *Mirror* gleefully reported that when she entered the State Coach viewers could glimpse 'something no woman, not even a queen, likes to be without – her handbag'. *Mirror* columnist Cassandra wrote prophetically of that day: 'For me, there were moments of deep sadness. The young and tender and lovely Queen I think felt it, too. Stretching down the highway of the years that lie before her is the unending duty and the burden of the Throne.' The Coronation Special Edition brought joy to the *Mirror*, too – it sold seven million copies, the highest circulation ever reached by a daily newspaper.

1952

26 February Churchill announces that Britain has developed its own atomic bomb

21 March Dr Kuame Nkrumah becomes the first African Premier

26 April The French launch a push to defeat Viet Minh forces in South Vietnam

2 May The Comet Jet airliner makes its maiden flight

16 May The House of Commons votes for equal pay for women

DAILY Mirror

TUES FEB. 12 1952

FORWARD WITH THE PEOPLE

1½d

No. 15,007
Registered at G.P.O.
as a Newspaper.

A sorrowing family group of three Queens——Elizabeth the Second, Queen Mary and the Queen Mother——stand at the entrance to Westminster Hall as the King's coffin is carried past them to the Lying-in-State. On the right is Princess Margaret.

1 June The Soviets establish a three-mile security belt between East and West Berlin

15 June The diary of 13 year-old Jewish refugee Anne Frank is published

26 June A non-violent protest against South Africa's apartheid laws begins

26 July The charismatic leader Eva Peron dies in Argentina

6 September Twenty-six die when an aircraft crashes into the crowd at the Farnborough Air Show

1953

Guilty: Christie

Innocent: Evans

REFLECTIONS

The dramatic trial of 55-year-old clerk John Christie for the murders of his wife and three other women held the nation in thrall. It was, said the *Mirror*, 'the story of a house of death.' Christie killed his victims over 11 weeks at his home in 10, Rillington Place, Notting Hill, admitting 'I must have gone haywire'. On the first day of the trial the paper dutifully reported that the madman had a 3s 8d' lunch of roast beef and two vegetables, jam roll and custard and a bottle of lemonade. Christie, who was hanged, eventually confessed to strangling seven women and may well have killed the infant daughter of Timothy Evans for which Evans was wrongly executed. He was posthumously pardoned in 1966.

Something is wrong with the railways. You read that often enough nowadays. But the *Mirror* was saying it 50 years ago. On January 13, 1953, it devoted a full page to troubles with the trains. Railway workers had sent in dozens of examples of neglect, indifference and incompetence. One claimed that inexperienced men were allowed to make repairs so didn't do a proper job. Another revealed he had seen engines being sent out with brake blocks so thin they would not hold the train. An express driver with 36 years of footplate experience wrote: 'Drivers are made to take engines unsafe for work. One driver who refused to take out an engine with a loose tyre was given a day's suspension.' For balance, the *Mirror* carried a statement from Railway Executive chairman Mr John Elliot, who dismissed all the accusations as 'unfounded statements'.

'Cheerio Dad, cheerio Mum, cheerio Iris. I'll see you tomorrow.'

At 9am on January 28, 1953, petty crook Derek Bentley – a boy of 19 with the mental age of a 10-year-old – was hanged by the neck until he was dead for a murder he did not commit. Bentley had taken part in a break-in at Croydon with his 16-year-old friend Christopher Craig, not knowing Craig had a gun. Approached by police, Craig shot dead PC Sidney Miles, a crime for which he was too young to go the gallows. When he appeared in court, Craig was detained indefinitely. But Bentley was convicted of murder and sentenced to death. In a chorus of public outrage thousands of people backed by 200 MPs wrote to Home Secretary Sir David Maxwell-Fyfe, and even the Queen, begging for clemency. But their appeals were in vain and after a last-ditch request for a reprieve was rejected. The day before his execution he was visited in jail by his mother, father and sister Iris who brought him a photo of his dogs, letters from neighbours and a rosary. Mr Bentley said: 'Derek was cheerful, even under the shadow of the gallows. His last words were "Cheerio Dad, cheerio Mum, cheerio Iris. I'll see you tomorrow".' He never saw them again. Bentley's execution, however, was not in vain. People were shocked that a simple-minded youth whose only involvement in a killing had been that he was present had now been killed himself in the name of justice. As a result, the campaign to abolish capital punishment was given new urgency. Another aspect of the murder raised an issue which resurfaced half a century later: the easy availability of guns to young men. During Bentley's trial the public was horrified by revelations of the trafficking in weapons by teenagers. The *Mirror*, under a photo of the pistol which killed PC Miles, asked 'How many more are there in boys' hands?' and launched a campaign to outlaw ownership of small arms. The Home Office weighed in by considering a nationwide 'Give up your guns' appeal. The Home Secretary told the paper: 'I am tremendously alive to the danger of any section of the community getting into the habit of carrying offensive weapons, which, of course, include firearms.' He announced that he was considering taking 'severe steps' against people carrying guns. But private possession of guns was not banned for another 45 years, after the Dunblane tragedy in which crazed gunman Thomas Hamilton killed 15 school-children. Tougher action on carrying illegal firearms is still awaited. Craig was released in 1963. In 1998, Bentley's murder conviction was overturned.

DAILY Mirror

WED JAN. 28 1953

1½d

No. 15,305

Registered at G.P.O. as a Newspaper.

FORWARD WITH THE PEOPLE

Bentley dies today
NO LAST-MINUTE REPRIEVE

Their grief became nation's problem

200 M.P.s SIGN PLEA —'DON'T HANG HIM'

Police are called to Home Office crowd

'Daily Mirror' Reporters

THERE is to be no last-minute reprieve for Derek Bentley. The execution, fixed for 9 a.m. today at Wandsworth, will be carried out.

The final decision was sent over to the Commons from the Home Office late last night, in a letter which the man with the power of life or death, Home Secretary Sir David Maxwell Fyfe, wrote in his own hand.

IT WAS THE REPLY TO A DRAMATIC LAST-DITCH PETITION BY MORE THAN 200 M.P.s FOR AN ELEVENTH-HOUR ACT OF CLEMENCY.

The letter said that Sir David had given careful consideration to the arguments of the six M.P.s who had presented the petition two hours earlier, but that he could find no reason to revise his decision.

Mr. Tom Driberg, M.P., broke the news to Bentley's father, who was waiting in the part-darkened lobby of an almost deserted House with his wife and daughter.

Then the party which included the mother of gunman Christopher Craig, walked slowly out to cars.

Mrs. Bentley and her daughter Iris were both sobbing when the family reached their Norbury home.

A friend said: "The Bentleys are completely worn out. But, as a final gesture, they are going to send a telegram to the Queen."

A crowd of about 500

2,800 'protest' wires

mostly young people, staged a "reprieve Bentley" demonstration.

They marched to the Home Office, but found a line of police barring the doors.

They were told Sir David was not in his office—then they marched to a block of flats in Great Peter-street.

Four policemen were at the door. As the crowd raced forward one constable said : "Sir David does not live here any more. He has moved."

Off went the demonstra-

tors—to seek Sir David at his Temple Gardens flat.

The gates were closed, but the crowd chanted slogans. Bentley's father joined them at 12.50 a.m. and the demonstrators, with Mr. Bentley, then moved towards Mr. Anthony Eden's house in Carlton House-terrace.

In their last-minute appeal to Sir David the deputation of M.P.s urged that since he decided not to reprieve Bentley a new factor had entered the situation—public reaction. If Bentley was hanged,

they said, his execution would, in the opinion of the great majority of his countrymen, be contrary to fair play. They said they were sure that the Home Secretary would not ignore this.

They had in their minds, the fact that nearly 2,800 telegrams have been received by M.P.s nearly all opposing execution.

It is believed that other

Continued on Back Page

'Cheerio,' he told them

A MOTHER weeps for her son . . . a sister for her brother. Mrs. Bentley and Iris Bentley, 21, leave Wandsworth Prison yesterday afternoon after a last family visit to see condemned nineteen-year-old Derek Bentley.

But it had not all been tears. Mr. Bentley, who was also there, said: "Derek was cheerful, even under the shadow of the gallows.

"He fired questions at us and asked: 'How are we getting on outside ?'

"I told him we were putting up a fight to save him.

"We gave him a photograph of his dogs, a letter from some neighbours and a rosary which someone had sent for him.

"His last words were 'Cheerio Dad, cheerio Mum, cheerio Iris, I will see you tomorrow.'"

But shortly after the family got back

to their Norbury (London) home a Home Office messenger called. He bore a letter saying that Sir David Maxwell Fyfe, Home Secretary, had considered "representations" made by Mr. Bentley that morning, but that he was unable to find grounds for changing the "No reprieve' decision.

The "representations" concerned points arising from conversations between Mrs. Craig and her son Christopher, 16, Bentley's accomplice. It was Craig who shot Police-Constable Miles on a Croydon rooftop, and who was sentenced to be detained until the Queen's pleasure is known. He is too young for the death sentence.

Mr. Bentley also urged that evidence on his son's mental condition should have been given at the trial—he is said to have had head injuries during the bombing and to have had black-outs.

GOVT. SAY 'NO' TO £200 HOME GIFTS

THE Government have turned down Kidderminster Rural Council's plan to give couples £200 to help them build their homes and save council-house subsidies.

The Housing Minister yesterday told M.P.s he saw no prospect of the legislation needed for such grants.

See "The House that Pat builds"—Page Two.

---

26 March A vaccine against polio is successfully tested

17 April Charlie Chaplin is accused of Communism and banned from America

25 April James Watson and Francis Crick unveil the DNA structure of genes

31 May The American government warns of a 'domino effect' in the Far East

1 June Edmund Hillary and Sherpa Tensing conquer Everest

1954

REFLECTIONS

On March 6, 1953, the Soviet despot Stalin died and *Mirror* columnist Cassandra wrote his obituary: 'He died in his bed. That was the last, triumphant, exultant trick of Josef Vissarionovich Djugashvili – otherwise Joseph Stalin, the most powerful man in the world . . . His seventy-three hideous years have been enough. In his time he did titanic things and the whole world was his chess board. No tyrant ever planned on such a scale, and continents rather than countries were his prey. Probably he was brave. Certainly he was shifty and cruel. His skill in power politics was unsurpassed. But his purpose was evil and his methods unspeakable. Few men by their death can have given such deep satisfaction to so many.'

The pride which drab, post-war Britain felt in Roger Bannister's achievement in becoming the first person to run a sub four-minute mile leapt from the jubilant headline '4-minute mile – it's OURS'. Bannister, a 25-year-old medical student, clocked 3mins 59.4secs at an athletics meeting at Iffley Road, Oxford despite running against a strong cross wind which could have added almost two seconds to his time. The *Mirror* gushed: 'It was the greatest achievement in athletics history.' But Bannister's first love was medicine - 'it must come first,' he said. Unfortunately the *Mirror* did not have a reporter at the run. The sports editor refused to send one because he insisted it was impossible to run a mile in under four minutes.

Roger Bannister

Such awesome power left people horrified, shocked and genuinely concerned

Josef Stalin

Fears of a dangerous and uncertain future did not stop the *Mirror* celebrating the explosion of Britain's first atom bomb. Seeing the nation's membership of the nuclear club as a source of national pride, it trumpeted: 'This Bang Has Changed The World. Today Britain is Great Britain again.' But by 1954, when initial hydrogen bomb tests were held, the *Mirror*'s attitude had changed. No wonder. Britain's first H-bomb – which the paper branded 'The Monster' – was six times more powerful than the device dropped with such devastating effect

on Hiroshima. Exploded on the Pacific island of Elugelab it punch into the water to a depth of 175ft, creating a hole large enough to take the bodies of everyone on earth. Such awesome power, far removed from the bombs of conventional warfare, left peopl horrified, shocked and genuinely concerned for the future of mankind. The *Mirror* had originally supported the decision to make the H-bomb, declaring: 'If Britain is to enjoy the protectio of Western defence, we must share the burden. We are not a nation of cowardly men and wome But the paper wanted to end or limit tests. Now it led the opposition to the terrifying weapons. In a poll of readers 92 per cer backed the *Mirror*'s proposals that testing be halted and a conference called between the three nuclear powers, America Russia and Britain. Only two per cent of readers wanted tests to continue Four years later came th first of the Aldermaston Ban the Bomb marches that led to the formation of the Campaign for Nuclear Disarmament. T *Mirror* did not agree with what the protesters said

but valiantly defended their right to say it: 'The *Mirror* salutes the Aldermaston marchers. Blistered feet and all. There have been many sneers at this Ban the Bomb demonstration. At the rank-and-file marchers. At leaders who sometimes marched and sometimes stayed at home. The *Mirror* is not among the sneere Everybody wants to get rid of the bomb. The argument is about the best way to do it. We think the Aldermaston marchers are o the wrong tack. But at least they upped and did something. The gesture will set people everywhere thinking and arguing.' At about the same time Russia announced it was stopping all nuclear tests. The *Mirror* had no doubt what the reaction of the new Conservative Prime Minister, Harold Macmillan, should be suspend Britain's H-tests, ground the H-bombers and delay buildir missile sites.

26 July Cuban President Batista crushes a rebel uprising led by Fidel Castro

14 August Russia announces that it has developed nuclear weapons

22 August The Shah of Iran is restored to power following a coup

13 November The British government announces plans for a commercial television service

3 February The Quee makes the first visit to Australia by a reigning monarch

Daily Mirror

FRI APR. 2 1954

1½d FORWARD WITH THE PEOPLE

No. 15,670

THE MONSTER

Shoe-life stories... *continued*

YOU WERE THE SMARTEST WOMAN AT THE PARTY, DARLING. AND I DO LIKE THOSE NEW SHOES!

FLATTERER! THOSE ARE THE SHOES I WORE AT JOAN'S PARTY.

BUT THAT WAS AGES AGO!

EXACTLY! SHOES FITTED WITH *PHILLIPS* STAY NEW SO MUCH LONGER.

Take it from me— *PHILLIPS* double the life of your shoes

Phillips 'STICK-A-SOLES' AND HEELS

● This is the first picture, just released, of an H-bomb explosion. It was taken from a plane fifty miles away.

● The monstrous mushroom cloud reached nearly eight miles high within two minutes of the detonation — at the Pacific Marshall Islands in 1952.

[*Other pictures are in the Centre and Back Pages.*]

● Please send your views about the H-bomb tests by filling up the voting form on the right.

'Daily Mirror' H-BOMB inquiry

1. Should Churchill at once OPENLY INVITE Eisenhower and Malenkov to a conference on the H-Bomb? YES ☐ NO ☐

2. Should Churchill ask Eisenhower and Malenkov to STOP further H-Bomb tests in the meantime? YES ☐ NO ☐

Mark with a tick like this ✓ *the answer you wish to give.*

NAME ....

ADDRESS ....

....

Please post your form IMMEDIATELY, in an unsealed envelope (1½d. stamp), to: H-Bomb, "Daily Mirror," 127, Stamford-street, London, S.E.1.

✂ CUT ROUND THE DOTTED LINES ✂

---

24 February American Evangelist Billy Graham arrives in England

21 March There are rumours of a 'third man' involved in the diplomatic spying scandal

9 April The British government grounds all Comet Jet airliners after a second fatal crash

18 April Colonel Nasser becomes Prime Minister of Egypt after a power struggle

8 May The French fortress of Dien Bien Phu falls to the Viet Minh

1955

REFLECTIONS

Grumpy Gilbert Harding was an early TV star who behaved strangely during one 'What's My Line' programme. When the *Mirror* rang him the next morning he said: 'I am lying in bed.' The intrepid reporter asked: Could drink have played a part in his erratic performance? 'Asthma aided by fog,' Harding said. 'I may have over-fortified myself against it. If I appeared a bit tiddly then viewers were not wrong in thinking I was a bit tiddly.' Such refreshing honesty.

The fuss about adapting TV sets for digital or satellite was nothing compared with the time when ITV began. Six months before the eagerly-awaited second channel was launched TV editor Clifford Davis revealed how much viewers would have to pay to get the service. 'To adapt existing TV sets will cost between £7 and £12 while new aerials will cost anything from 7s 6d to £10. The Independent Television Authority, which will be responsible for the commercial stations, said that nearly a million sets will be unable to pick up the new programmes.' But there was a further problem. There would be much more electrical interference from cars, hair driers and vacuum cleaners, 'as existing suppressors will be unable to prevent interference on the wave band used by the commercial programmes.'

By the mid 50s the car, arguably the most significant product of the 20th century with its capacity to transform ordinary people's lives at the same time as wreaking dramatic change on the environment, had celebrated its half-century. It was no longer simply a possession of the wealthy. Mass production had taken off and families relished the freedom afforded them by their not-always-reliable Ford Prefects, Austin A30s and Morris Minors. But as ownership grew, so the old roads became less able to cope and drivers were increasingly frustrated by the long time journeys took. In February 1955 the Government came up with a plan to ease the traffic chaos – a motor-traffic-only road from which pedestrians, horses and cyclists would be banned. Thus was born

the M1, the country's first motorway. Announcing the plan in the Commons, Transport minister John Boyd-Carpenter hinted that tolls might be charged to help pay for the vast cost of what was planned to be a network of super-highways. (The *Mirror* pointed out that most of Britain's toll roads were abolished at the end of the previous century). Mr Boyd-Carpenter said: 'There have been few improvements in our road system since 1939. The problem

A motor-traffic-only road from which pedestrians, horses and cyclists would be banned

facing us is immense. Our plans are intended to provide an up-to-date road system adequate for the traffic it has to bear.' The first motorway – originally 150 miles long and costing £45 million – would run from the St Albans bypass north of London and end near Rugby. Later it would be extended to Doncaster with spur roads linking to Birmingham and Sheffield. The *Mirror* breathlessly explained: 'The road will be of the dual-carriageway type throughout. The motorist will drive *Under* or soar *Over* all existing roads. Speed cops will patrol the roads – *to warn drivers who go too slowly*'. Building began in the late 1950s and by 1960, 200 kilometres (125 miles) were open. Within 20 years the figure had leapt to 2,600 kilometres (1,625 miles) and by the year 2000 it was up to 3,500 kilometres (2,200 miles). Everyday life, and the face of Britain, was transformed. But the problems the motorways were designed to solve never went away. There were little more than two million cars on the roads when the M1 was designed but more than 10 times that number by the end of the century. Fifty years after their launch, the

highways planned to make motoring easier and faster were as congested and jammed as the smaller roads they replaced. Another sensational project was announced on the same day as the motorway: 'A road running through the sea in a gigantic concrete tube.' It would span the Firth of Forth 'and allow people using it to ignore the weather.' The Firth Subway has never been built, although more than 30 years later the Channel Tunnel opened - though motorists cannot drive through it.

17 May The American Supreme Court outlaws racial segregation in schools

24 May IBM announces the development of the first computers for public use

3 July All rationing ends in Britain after 14 years

19 July Elvis Presley releases his first single, 'That's All Right Mama'

21 July Fighting in Vietnam ends with the division of the country into two regions

Daily Mirror

THURS FEB. 3 1955 | THE BIGGEST DAILY SALE ON EARTH

Britain's Four Year Plan to end traffic chaos

A ROAD THROUGH THE SEA

—And a road where drivers MUST hurry

WILL AMERICA DEFEND THOSE OFFSHORE ISLANDS?

Ike sends secret Note to Chiang

● The American Ambassador in Formosa, Mr. Karl L. Rankin, last night gave Chiang Kai-shek, anti-Communist Chinese leader, a vital secret message from President Eisenhower.

● The message, says Reuter, was believed to clarify whether or not America would defend Matsu and Quemoy islands, just off the mainland, if Chiang pulled his 20,000 troops out of the Tachen Islands.

● Chiang is reported to have told Eisenhower that if the Tachens are evacuated this must be the last step backwards, says B.U.P. (American).

SEVENTH FLEET SAVES EVACUEES

A DESTROYER of the United States Seventh Fleet yesterday escorted a shipload of civilian refugees from the Tachen Islands after they had escaped from four Communist gunboats.

The Reds were said to have fired on the refugee ship, a 1,000-ton landing craft. No casualties were reported.

HE TELLS WORLD: 'MY POLICY IS CRYSTAL CLEAR'

PRESIDENT Eisenhower claimed last night that he has made his China policy "crystal clear."

He said America was determined to defend "the great island barrier" of Formosa, stronghold of anti-Red Chiang Kai-shek.

America tried to avoid being truculent, he told a Washington Press conference.

His aim was to make sure that no conflict occurred through a miscalculation by "the other side" of America's concern over Formosa.

'Technical'

But the President still would not say if America would take in defence of the offshore islands of Matsu and Quemoy.

Those were technical details about which he felt he could not be specific now, he said.

There were constant conversations between America and Chiang, but their views did not always coincide.

In general, Eisenhower stated, America would not let international Communism expand in the Pacific. Her only aim was to prevent war.

Britain makes arms offer

Britain yesterday refused to join any "above governments" European arms production pool, as proposed by France.

But, at a Paris conference, she offered her co-operation in efforts to standardise weapons among future members of the Western European Union, to which Germany will belong.

55 SURRENDER

Fifty-five terrorists have surrendered in response to the Kenya Government's amnesty offer made on January 18. It was stated in the Lords yesterday.

DAILY MIRROR REPORTER

TWO sensational projects were announced last night as part of the Government's plans to revolutionise Britain's antiquated road communications—

● A road running through the sea in a gigantic concrete tube—the first of its kind in the world; and

● Britain's first motor-traffic-only highway, from which pedestrians and all other vehicles will be banned.

These are the two most imaginative schemes in a £147,000,000 Four Year Plan for the Roads—the first instalment of a big new drive to catch up with the fifteen-year stagnation in the nation's transport network.

Details were announced by the Minister of Transport, Mr. John Boyd-Carpenter, in the House of Commons.

He hinted that TOLLS may be charged to help pay for the vast cost of some of the fast motorways to be constructed.

[Most of Britain's toll roads were abolished at the end of last century.] Mr. Boyd-Carpenter said: "There have been few improvements in our road system since 1939. The problem facing us is immense.

"Our plans will take a good many years to complete. They are intended to provide an up-to-date road system adequate for the traffic it has to bear."

Road Through the Sea

These are some of the features in the Four Year Plan:

THE plan is to build an amazing UNDER-WATER HIGHWAY to span the Firth of Forth almost alongside the existing Forth Bridge in Scotland.

A massive concrete pipe, two-thirds of a mile long, would be laid on the sea bed, instead of under it like every other underwater tunnel ever made.

Through this pipe would run two 22ft. roads, wide enough to carry two streams of traffic in each direction.

A bridge would cost £15,000,000 and take eight years to build.

The subway could be built for £5,500,000 in three years.

It is up to the local authorities to decide between this proposed subway and a new bridge.

But the Minister quoted some comparisons which left little doubt about the Government's preference:

Traffic on the bridge would be hampered by gales which sometimes reach 125 m.p.h.

People using the subway could ignore the weather.

The painting of the existing Forth Bridge is a non-stop job.

The road through the sea would need hardly any maintenance.

Finally, the Government points out—

The construction of the Forth Subway would be of outstanding interest in all countries of the world.

As the first of its kind it would have a high prestige value for Britain.

It would lead to an increasing demand for British engineers and their products overseas.

A Road for Motors Only

THE Government has approved Britain's first-ever fast motor road from which all horses, cyclists and pedestrians will be banned.

It is to be the first stage of a new road from London to Yorkshire, starting on the St. Albans by-pass and ending near Rugby.

Later, it will be extended to Doncaster, with "spurs" linking up to Birmingham and Sheffield.

Total length: 150 miles. Cost: £45,000,000.

The road will be of the dual-carriageway type throughout. The motorist will drive UNDER or soar OVER all existing roads.

Fly-overs, under-passes and clover-leaf junctions will keep traffic flowing smoothly.

Speed cops will patrol the road—

To warn drivers who go too slowly.

A second motor-traffic-only road is planned to link Preston, Lancs. with Birmingham — about eighty miles.

The Four Year Plan takes in many schemes to widen existing roads, build new bridges and by-passes, and ease the traffic pile-up in the big cities.

These are a few of the projects in a list of scores:

● The Dartford-Purfleet tunnel under the Thames is to be started.

● A "fly-over" is to be built over the busy Western-avenue in Middlesex.

In LONDON:

● The Strand will be widened, the Albert Bridge rebuilt, roundabouts laid down at the Elephant and Castle, and the Holborn-Kingsway junction.

A daughter for Elspet

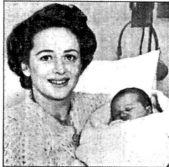

ELSPET GRAY, 25, the TV, stage and screen actress, nurses her daughter Louise who was born yesterday at the Princess Beatrice Hospital, Chelsea, London. Elspet is the wife of Hull-born Brian Rix, 31, the actor-manager now appearing in the London comedy "Dry Rot."

THE QUEEN GIVES A PARTY

THE Queen entertained Commonwealth Premiers to dinner in the State dining room at Buckingham Palace last night.

With her were the Duke of Edinburgh, the Queen Mother, the Duke and Duchess of Gloucester and the Princess Royal.

The Queen sat between Mr. St. Laurent (Canada) and Mr. Menzies (Australia). The Duke sat between Mrs. Swart, wife of the South African Minister of Justice, and Mrs. Mathieu Samson, Mr St. Laurent's daughter.

The Queen wore a crinoline-type dress of white lace with the skirt lifted on either side to show an underskirt of white tulle.

The company numbered more than sixty. There were no formal speeches.

At yesterday's Commonwealth conference, India's Premier, Mr Nehru said that all production of hydrogen bombs should be stopped.

There should, he added, be no more H-bomb experiments.

Sir Winston Churchill, who spoke on atomic defence for forty minutes, said he expected that America and Russia would have equal strength in A-weapons in a very few years.

Today, it is expected, Mr. Butler, Chancellor of the Exchequer, will warn the Premiers that the Commonwealth is being hit by prosperity.

WEATHER Bright periods and showers, with chance of hail in the evening. OUTLOOK: Changeable.

1955

REFLECTIONS

Early television sets were bulky and extremely heavy. Then in 1955 came a sensational innovation. 'It's arrived at last,' the *Mirror* announced breathlessly. 'The Carry It Around television set. It can be watched in moving buses, cars and trains.' Developed by the Southend firm E.K.Cole, the set weighed about 30lb, worked up to 30 miles from a TV transmitter and cost around £60. 'The Carry It Around set does not need a rooftop aerial. It has a special collapsible aerial of its own. A 12-volt car battery or mains electricity can supply the power.' Although the size of the screen was limited to 9 inches 'the arrival of the portable set will bring television to millions of people in caravans and cottages where there is no electricity supply. And families will be able to take them on picnics.'

Senator Joseph McCarthy provided a spectacle unmatched in American political history. He insulted Presidents, humiliated generals and flouted the authority of the United States Senate with his investigations into 'unAmerican activities' – in reality a witch hunt against anyone with Communist, or any left-leaning, sympathies. His hold on American public opinion was so great that he overrode the US constitution. Yet he did serious damage to his country's reputation abroad. On April 22, 1954, the *Mirror* reported that another set of hearings was about to start, this time against the army, which McCarthy accused of harbouring Communist influences. But it was during these hearings that the evil Senator finally went too far and his swift downfall followed.

McCarthy

denied murdering David Blakely, 25, outside a Hampstead pub but admitted manslaughter. Dressed in black, the 28-year-old nightclub hoste cut a dramatic figure as she sat in the dock with nurse holding a first-aid box at her side. It was clear she was not in her right mind. Ellis claimed she was provoked by Blakely who had threatened to jilt her an evidence was given abou the 'primitive reactions women in the grip of jealousy'. But the most compelling evidence wa

'He ran a few steps and I thought I'd missed so I fired again'

Platinum blonde Ruth Ellis shot dead her racing-driver lover in passion, freely confessed her guilt and blithely accepted her fate of death by hanging. She was the last woman in Britain to be executed. The *Mirror* reflected an increasing national distaste at the death sentence though many remained to be persuaded that it should be abolished. On the day of Ellis's death, July 13, 1955, columnist Cassandra wrote with fierce compassion: 'It's a fine day for hay-making. A fine day for fishing. A fine day for lolling in the sunshine. And if you feel that way – and I mourn to say that millions of you do – it's a fine day for a hanging. If you read this before nine o'clock this morning, the last obscene preparations for hanging Ruth Ellis will be moving to their sickening climax. If you read this at nine o'clock then, short of a miracle, you and I and every man and woman in the land with head to think and heart to feel will, in full responsibility, blot this woman out.' At the Old Bailey Ellis

Ellis's statement to police. She said that after Blakely failed to c her 'I took a gun and put it in my bag. I got a taxi to Tanza Road then walked to the nearest pub where I noticed David's car. I waited till he came out. David went to his car door, turned and saw me, then turned away. I took the gun and shot him. He ran few steps and I thought I'd missed so I fired again. He was still runing and I fired a third shot. I don't remember firing more but must have done.' Outcry greeted her conviction and sentence fo murder. Yet Ellis refused to appeal, declaring 'Why the fuss? I killed David and that's that.' But there was a huge fuss and it w led by the *Mirror*. The day after she died, the paper launched a campaign to abolish hanging. It was another decade before it succeeded.

19 January The Kenyan government offers Mau Mau terrorists an amnesty

8 February Plans are announced for a new London tube line between Victoria and Walthamstow

10 February The South African Government begins a policy of clearing black townships

28 February Israeli troops launch a reprisal raid on Egyptian forces in the Gaza strip

26 March An electricians' strike halts the production of all national newspapers for a month

Daily Mirror

WED JULY 13 1955

1½d

FORWARD WITH THE PEOPLE

No. 16,045

THE WOMAN WHO HANGS THIS MORNING

EXECUTION EVE

Crowd break police cordon round gaol

DAILY MIRROR REPORTER

MORE than 400 people staged amazing scenes outside Holloway gaol last night—the eve of Ruth Ellis's execution.

There were even attempts to storm the prison gates.

Police were drawn up outside, but time after time sections of the crowd broke through the cordon and hammered on the massive oak doors.

They demanded to see Mrs. Ellis, crying: "We want her to kneel in prayer with us."

But they were told: "Mrs. Ellis does not wish to see anyone else tonight."

Then anti-capital pun-

ishment leaflets were thrown in the air. They fluttered down in the light shining from the prison windows.

People began shouting: "Give her a reprieve."

And a woman clutching a bunch of flowers kept repeating: "There, but for the grace of God, go I."

Despite official statements that "there would be nothing to see," the crowd refused to disperse.

One section chanted "Evans —Bentley—Ellis" and the chorus was taken up by the rest of the crowd.

Police on foot and in patrol cars tried to move

Continued on Back Page

By CASSANDRA

IT'S a fine day for hay-making. A fine day for fishing. A fine day for lolling in the sunshine. And if you feel that way—and I mourn to say that millions of you do—it's a fine day for a hanging.

If you read this before nine o'clock this morning, the last dreadful and obscene preparations for hanging Ruth Ellis will be moving up to their fierce and sickening climax. The public hangman and his assistant will have been slipped into the prison at about four o'clock yesterday afternoon.

There, from what is grotesquely called "some vantage point" and unobserved by Ruth Ellis, they will have spied upon her when she was at exercise "to form an impression of the physique of the prisoner."

A bag of sand will have been filled to the same weight as the condemned woman and it will have been left hanging overnight to stretch the rope.

Our Guilt . . .

If you read this at nine o'clock then—short of a miracle—you and I and every man and woman in the land with head to think and heart to feel will, in full responsibility, blot this woman out.

The hands that place the white hood over her head will not be our hands. But the guilt—

and guilt there is in all this abominable business —will belong to us as much as to the wretched executioner paid and trained to do the job in accordance with the savage public will.

If you read this after nine o'clock, the murderess, Ruth Ellis, will have gone.

The one thing that brings stature and dignity to mankind and raises us above the beasts of the field will have been denied her—pity and the hope of ultimate redemption.

The medical officer will go to the pit under the trap door to see that life is extinct. Then in the barbarous wickedness of this ceremony, rejected by nearly all civilised peoples, the body will be left to hang for one hour.

Dregs of Shame

If you read these words of mine at mid-day the grave will have been dug while there are no prisoners around and the Chaplain will have read the burial service after he and all of us have come so freshly from disobeying the Sixth Commandment which says thou shalt not kill.

The secrecy of it all shows that if compassion is not in us, then at least we still retain the dregs of shame. The medieval notice of execution will have been posted on the prison gates and the usual squalid handful of louts and rubbernecks who attend these legalised killings will have had their own private obscene delights.

Two Royal Commissions have protested against these horrible events. Every Home Secretary in recent years has testified to the agonies of his task, and the revulsion he has

felt towards his duty. None has ever claimed that executions prevent murder.

Yet they go on and still Parliament has neither the resolve nor the conviction, nor the wit, nor the decency, to put an end to these atrocious affairs.

When I write about capital punishment, as I have often done, I get some praise and usually more abuse. In this case I have been reviled as being "a sucker for a pretty face."

Well, I am a sucker for a pretty face. And I am a sucker for all human faces

RUTH ELLIS: *CASSANDRA SAYS: "In this case I have been reviled as being 'a sucker for a pretty face.' Well, I am a sucker for all human faces, good or bad. But I prefer them not to be lolling because of a judicially broken neck."*

because I hope I am a sucker for all humanity, good or bad. But I prefer the face not to be lolling because of a judicially broken neck.

Yes, it is a fine day.

Oscar Wilde, when he was in Reading Gaol, spoke with melancholy of "that little tent of blue which prisoners call the sky."

THE TENT OF BLUE SHOULD BE DARK AND SAD AT THE THING WE HAVE DONE THIS DAY.

1955

Two hundred years after the birth of the first industrial revolution, a new upheaval beckoned – the age of high technology. The *Mirror* called it Automation and painted an arresting picture in which industry and business would be staffed by robots. The paper breezily warned readers: 'It will change your life. It is already at work in America and Russia. We dare not lag behind. Developed without planning, it will cause unemployment. Harnessed intelligently it will bring more leisure, happiness and a higher standard of living.' Every day for a week, the *Mirror* explained the robot revolution which, it said, promised less drudgery for all. 'They can bake pies. They can make motors. They can answer the telephone. They can fashion jig-bores. They can add up, subtract, divide. They can write. They can speak. They can pen love-letters. They can do all

Even the lowly office boy is being replaced by a dark-green robot

these things without any help from you. Whatever your job is, the chances are that one of these machines can do it faster and better than you can.' Eagerly explaining the benefits, the *Mirror* predicted that automation could lead to a four-day week and bigger pay packets. Less encouragingly, you could be out of a job. 'Within 10 years eight out of 10 of all the typists, filing clerks, secretaries and adding-machine operators in London's big offices will not be needed. There are few pursuits of the office girl that machines cannot do. Even the lowly office boy is being replaced by a dark-green robot that transmits messages from one office to another.' The paper interviewed one Gilbert Soto, a New York factory worker whose job making vacuum-cleaner wheels had been taken over by a robot. At first he was worried but now he was delighted, as he looked after the machine which stole his job. 'It's a cinch,' said Gilbert. 'Now I ain't tired no more. I'm ready to take in a movie or play a little baseball.' Inspired by automation's awesome possibilities, the paper challenged its readers to multiply 2368.912941062 by 867124.0510296. How many took on this mind-boggling task is not known, but it took an experienced accountant fifteen minutes to reach the correct 26-figure answer – 2054141385.99012550. A robot, the paper announced triumphantly, reached it in 31-millionths of a second. The *Mirror* believed the Robot Revolution – no mention of

computer or calculator in those days – could 'bring about somethin[g] which Socialists fundamentally believe in – a shorter working wee[k] for all, less drudgery for all and therefore more leisure for all.'

Fashion spotlight on PARIS

DIOR's

NARROW SHOULDER INSET SLEEVE

EASY WAIST

WIDTH AT HIP

Classic Fifties fashion

31 May Kruschev and Tito normalise relations between their countries, conceding different roads to Socialism

31 May The government declares a national emergency to deal with the national dock strike

June Marilyn Monroe appears in *The Seven Year Itch*

11 June Eighty people are killed in a three-car crash at Le Mans race track in France

18 July Disneyland opens in Los Angeles

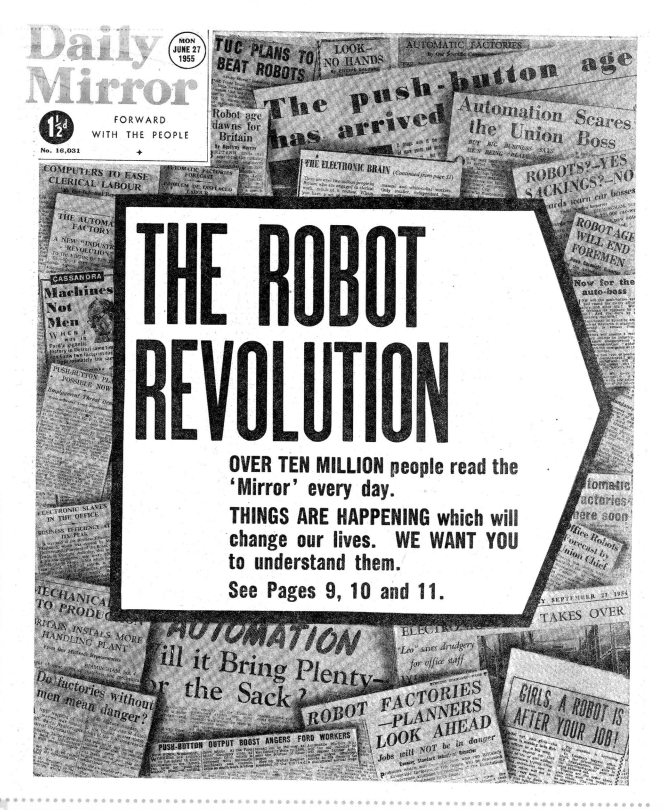

1955

Even by the standards of sensational journalism, the front page of the *Daily Mirror* on August 19, 1955, was a shocker. 'Come on Margaret!' it shrieked. 'Make up your mind.' No one had ever talked to royalty like that before. But the Queen's 25-year-old sister was not the real target of the *Mirror*'s venom – it was the Establishment. Margaret was in love with dashing Group Captain Peter Townsend. But Townsend had been married before and Government and Church were not prepared to see a royal wed a divorcee, even though Margaret would never become Queen. Other papers savaged the *Mirror* for its bold stance. It was accused of 'plumbing hitherto unreached depths of self-importance, impertinence and plain bad manners'. In true style, the *Mirror* proudly reprinted all the criticisms on its front page adding that the chairman of the Press Council, Sir Linton Andrews, 'nearly fell off his chair in pious horror' when he saw the paper. Though

Daily Mirror

MARGARET DECIDES :

DUTY BEFORE LOVE

PRINCESS MARGARET, in this dramatic announcement from Clarence House last night, told the world that she had renounced the love of Peter Townsend:

"I would like it to be known that I have decided not to marry Group Captain Peter Townsend. I have been aware that, subject to my renouncing my rights of succession, it might have been possible for me to contract a civil marriage. But, mindful of the Church's teaching that Christian marriage is indissoluble, and conscious of my duty to the Commonwealth, I have resolved to put these considerations before any others. I have reached this decision entirely alone, and in doing so I have been strengthened by the unfailing support and devotion of Group Captain Townsend. I am deeply grateful for the concern of all those who have constantly prayed for my happiness.
(Signed) Margaret."

Peter Townsend leaves—alone SEE BACK PAGE

'Plumbing hitherto unreached depths of self-importance, impertinence and plain bad manners'

readers were divided between those who thought Margaret should do what her heart told her and those who believed duty came first, the *Mirror* pursued its campaign relentlessly. The only reasons that prevented Margaret from marrying Townsend, it said, were because 'the young man concerned was born a member of

Captain Peter Townsend

the middle-class and divorced a wife who had deserted him'. By October, the paper was saying 'the time has come for plain speaking' – as if it had not been speaking bluntly all along. It said Throne, Church and Nation had been forced into an increasingly humiliating position by Margaret's continued silence. It attacked the Church for falling into 'a more foolish position with every sermon' and boldly proclaimed that advice

offered to the Queen was the most appalling ever given. Then what the *Mirror* called 'the first sinister move in a cruel plan' was hatched. It was suggested to Margaret that she must give up Townsend or be banished forever from the royal circle - 'to spend the rest of her life like the luckless Windsors, without roots, without purpose and without hope'. On November 1 the *Mirror* sadly reported 'Margaret decides: Duty before love'. In an announcement from Clarence House the Princess said she had renounced Townsend, declaring: 'Mindful of the Church's teaching that Christian marriage is indissoluble, and conscious of my duty to the Commonwealth, I have resolved to put these considerations before any others.' She then fibbed: 'I have reached this decision entirely alone.' Margaret never fully recovered from this cruel treatment though she went on to marry photographer Anthony Armstrong-Jones in 1960. The marriage was dissolved in 1978.

---

22 September A new era in commercial television begins with the launch of ITV

20 October The BBC demonstrates colour television at Alexandra Palace

26 October South Vietnam is declared a republic under Ngo Dinh Diem

28 November A state of emergency is declared in Cyprus following a revolt against British rule

4 December Rosa Parks sparks a boycott of segregated buses in Alabama, USA

Daily Mirror

FRI AUG. 19 1955

1½d FORWARD WITH THE PEOPLE

No. 16,077

- *The Princess is 25 on Sunday.*
- *Will she wed? When will she announce her decision?*

COME ON MARGARET!

FOR two years the world has buzzed with this question:

Will Princess Margaret marry 40-year-old Group Captain Peter Townsend?—OR Won't she?

Five months ago, Group Captain Townsend told the Daily Mirror: '. . . the word cannot come from me. You will appreciate it must come from other people . . .'

On Sunday the Princess will be 25. She could then, if she wished, notify Parliament direct of her desire to marry without first seeking the consent of her sister the Queen.

She could end the hubbub.

Will she please make up her mind?

Please make up your mind!

---

12 January British troops are sent to Cyprus to control nationalist rebels

26 January Briton bans the import and export of heroin

6 February The French Premier is attacked by mobs of French settlers in Algeria

16 February British MPs vote against the death penalty

29 February American Civil Rights activists clash with whites over segregation

1955

The disappearance in 1951 of two British 'diplomats' in the early years of the Cold War was the tip of a traitorous iceberg. For years Eton-educated Guy Burgess and fellow public schoolboy Donald Maclean – both graduates of Trinity, Cambridge – spied for the Soviet Union. Burgess, an alcoholic homosexual, worked for the BBC and MI5 and in 1950 was secretary of the Washington Embassy. Maclean, a shifty introvert, was head of the American Department at the Foreign Office. Both defected to Russia shortly before the security services nailed them, having been tipped off by another mole, MI6 officer Kim Philby. The press could not quite understand the story when it broke and the hunt for the two agents was made harder by the refusal to release photos of them, 'a decision taken at the highest level'. French police, supplied with the pictures, obligingly passed them to the press. Four years later,

The hunt for the two agents was made harder by the refusal to release photos of them

when the official report on Burgess and Maclean exploded on a shocked public, it became clear why the authorities had been so keen to remain silent. It was revealed that Burgess, prone to drink-fuelled indiscretions, was a known security risk while Maclean was allowed to continue working even after he was suspected of spying. The *Mirror* complained: 'Now we know the behaviour of the Foreign Office over the traitors Burgess and Maclean is an example of monstrous stupidity.' The paper blamed those who worked at the FO – 'intellectuals, the Old School Tie brigade, long-haired experts and the people-who-know-the-best-people.' Keith Waterhouse, then a *Mirror* reporter, wrote a devastating expose headlined 'Buckets and

Guy Burgess

buckets and buckets of whitewash'. The report, he said, was an indictment of the 'slap-happiest bunch of incompetents who ever graced a government department.' It contained no criticism of the hare-brained way in which the affair had been handled and no assurance it could not happen again. Waterhouse wrote: 'The hawk-eyed investigators for our security services learned some years earlier certain information had leaked out to the Soviets. Nothing happened. But eventually they narrowed the suspects down to "two or three" - and this takes two years! Meanwhile the two actual villains are packing their toothbrushes and preparing to depart.' He concluded: 'It is obvious somebody in the British Foreign Office gave Burgess and Maclean the tip-off. Who was it?' It was another eight years before Philby was exposed as the third man. He, too, defected after being tipped off by a *fourth* member of the spy ring, the respected art historian and Surveyor of the Queen's Pictures, Sir Anthony Blunt. Blunt was exposed in 1979.

1956

6 March The head of British Transport announces the introduction of electrified train services

9 March Britain deports Archbishop Makarios, the leader of the Greek-Cypriot community from Cyprus

18 March Soviet leader Kruschev denounces Stalin as brutal and despotic

22 March Martin Luther King declares a policy of 'passive resistance' to fight for black civil rights

17 April The government launches a premium bond scheme to encourage saving

Daily Mirror

SAT SEPT 24 1955

2D · FORWARD WITH THE PEOPLE

No. 16,108

THE FOREIGN OFFICE SCANDAL

Buckets and buckets and buckets of whitewash

WHODUNIT?

Don't ask the chaps at the Foreign Office—THEY DON'T KNOW!

By KEITH WATERHOUSE

THE Report on the Burgess-Maclean fiasco published last night is not a White Paper, it is a pallid paper—written with a brush dipped in buckets and buckets and buckets of whitewash. Some people call it a thriller. BUT IT IS THE DULLEST WHODUNIT OF ALL TIME.

MR. MACMILLAN says with great gallantry, "I take the blame." But his gallantry is ridiculous. No one man can possibly take the blame for all the follies committed in The Case of Burgess and Maclean.

THE report is an indictment of the slap-happiest bunch of incompetents who ever graced a Government department.

But the White Paper contains no criticism of the hare-brained way in which this affair was handled, and no assurance that it could not happen again.

Leak to the Soviet

Consider the plot of this burning, mystery yarn.

In Chapter One the hawk-eyed investigators of our security force learn that SOME YEARS EARLIER certain information has leaked out to the Soviet.

Nothing happens for several chapters. The armchair detectives are at work.

But eventually, by diligent research, they narrow the suspects down to "two or three." AND THIS TAKES TWO YEARS.

Meanwhile, the two actual villains are calmly packing their toothbrushes and preparing to depart. In the last chapter they leave the country. And that is the end of the book.

See how this investigation was handled.

> Maclean was watched only while he was in London. It was considered "a risk" to follow him into the country in case he smelled a rat.

As things turned out it WAS a risk—for Britain.

What kind of a trail is it that finishes at London's boundaries?

A decision to search his house was put off for A MONTH, "when Mrs. Maclean, who was then pregnant, was expected to be away from home."

They Sat Back —and Waited

Security was threatened—but the Sexton Blakes of the security force sat back drumming their fingers, waiting for a woman to have a baby.

The idea of questioning Maclean was put off because he might leave the country and "the authorities would have had no legal power to stop him."

Couldn't they have FOUND some power?

Mrs. Maclean was allowed to fly off to Geneva on her way to join her husband—"it was only natural that she should wish to bring up her children in new surroundings." says the White Paper.

Didn't they think to keep an eye on these "new surroundings"?

The simplest reader of a single Agatha Christie novel could have handled this affair more completely than the snail's-pace investigators who took two years to close in with a net that turned out to have great yawning holes in it.

Sleuths with Butter-fingers

Why, for instance, instead of cutting Maclean off from secrets and thus arousing his suspicions, couldn't he have been fed with false secret papers?

It is no use Harold Macmillan magnanimously taking the blame.

What about the sleuths with the butter - fingers who let these two traitors give them the slip?

It is obvious from the White Paper that somebody employed in the British Foreign Office gave Burgess and Maclean the tip-off that they were being watched.

WHO WAS IT? IS HE STILL AT THE FOREIGN OFFICE? AND CAN IT HAPPEN AGAIN?

The answers to these questions are not forthcoming. *NOBODY KNOWS.*

The White Paper says that searching inquiries were made and that "insufficient evidence was obtainable to form a definite conclusion or to warrant prosecution."

Are these searching inquiries still going on?

And if they are, are they going on in the same half-baked manner in which the inquiries about Burgess and Maclean were made?

IF SO, WE MIGHT AS WELL RUN OUR SECRETS OFF ON A DUPLICATOR FOR GENERAL DISTRIBUTION AND HAND THE SECURITY FORCE OVER TO THE CRAZY GANG.

WHAT THE WHITE PAPER ADMITTED

See Page 2

1956

REFLECTIONS

'Two towns yesterday banned the riot-rousing rock 'n' roll film *Rock Around the Clock*.' Such was the outrage that greeted the arrival in Britain of the then sensational movie featuring kiss-curled Bill Haley and the Comets. Teenagers literally danced in the aisles and jived down the streets as rock captured the rebellion and turbulence of youth. The authorities moved to crush these worrying signs of young people enjoying themselves, declaring that the 'jazz film' contained 'matter likely to lead to public disorder' and barring it from screens. Psychologists were called in to explain the links between rock 'n' roll and rioting youth. One sensibly told the *Mirror*: 'This type would tear the cinema down with Mickey Mouse on the screen if they felt that way.'

action. This is Eden's War.' It was also his downfall. US President Dwight Eisenhower was furious at the invasion. In a speech that would have George W. Bush choking on a pretzel, the great World War Two soldier said: 'We do not accept the use of force as a wise or proper instrument for the settlement of international disputes.' Britain's actions were condemned by Canada, India and Pakistan. Not one European nation other than France supported what we had done. The *Mirror* said: 'Eden still wields the truncheon but the world has stripped him of his phoney uniform.' Within 48 hours of the marines going in, the UN had passed a resolution demanding withdrawal. Eden to his lasting shame had to pull out our troops. Two months later he resigned, a broken man.

There is no treaty, no international authority, no moral sanction

The Suez adventure was the most humiliating international episode for Britain in the 20th century. Only France and Israel supported the military action launched by Anthony Eden, Churchill's successor as Prime Minister, after Egypt's leader Colonel Nasser moved to take control of the Suez canal. Just about every other country opposed it. So did the majority of the British people, steadfastly led by the *Daily Mirror*. As it would argue in 2003 over an invasion of Iraq, the paper argued there must not be war without the backing of the United Nations. It urged the Government to negotiate before sending in troops. Opinion polls showed that four out of five voters felt the same way. The paper's message to the Prime Minister was: *Si sit prudentia* – three Latin words which were the Eden Family Motto and which mean 'If there be but prudence ...'. But Eden was deaf to the plea and blind to the public mood. On November 1 came the first reports of the attack on Egypt, spearheaded by the RAF and British Navy. The *Mirror* lamented: 'Time and again we have warned of the dangers of gunboat diplomacy. Today those warnings stand fully justified. British bombs fall on Egypt. British and French troops are poised to seize Egyptian territory. Tory spokesmen claim Eden's action is a triumph for diplomacy. That is claptrap. The truth is this: There is *no* treaty, *no* international authority, *no* moral sanction for this desperate

29 June Marilyn Monroe marries playwright Arthur Miller

10 July The House of Lords votes against the abolition of the death penalty

30 August Britain will introduce traffic wardens when parking meters are installed

17 October The Queen opens Britain's first full-scale nuclear power station

29 October Israel crosses the Egyptian border into the Gaza strip

1956

Daily Mirror

THURS NOV 1 1956

2ᴰ FORWARD WITH THE PEOPLE
No. 16,451

RAF BOMB EGYPT

'Airfield was all lit up'

CAIRO says: 5 CITIES RAIDED, 7 DEAD

EDEN'S WAR

FOR three months the Mirror has warned the nation that Sir Anthony Eden's handling of the Middle East crisis might lead us into war.

Time and again the Mirror has attacked gunboat diplomacy.

Today those warnings stand fully justified.

British bombs fall on Egypt.

British and French troops are poised to seize Egyptian territory.

Tory spokesmen in the Commons and some Tory newspapers claim that Eden's action against Egypt is a triumph for the rule of law. That is claptrap.

The truth is this:

There is NO treaty, NO international authority, NO moral sanction for this desperate action.

This is Eden's War.

Unlike some newspapers which are whooping with joy at this grave news, the Mirror has no shameful record of appeasement to live down.

Orders

Clearly everyone's thoughts at this moment must first be with the British soldiers whose job it is to carry out the Government's orders.

This newspaper has taken no part and will take no part in inciting discontent among the troops.

But in a democracy that must not mean that all criticism of the Government has to be stifled once shooting starts.

The Mirror declares that the attack on Egypt is the culminating blunder in Eden's disastrous Middle East record.

Where has Eden's policy left Britain today?

● The **country** is deeply divided. The Labour Opposition has challenged the Government. Labour is right to move a vote of censure and to rouse the nation.

● The **Commonwealth** is split. India is appalled by the Anglo-French ultimatum. Canada regrets that it was

Continued on Page Two

BRITISH and French forces began an air and naval bombardment of military targets in Egypt at 4.30 p.m. yesterday, it was officially announced last night.

A twenty-word communique issued by Allied Forces H.Q. at a packed Press conference in Nicosia, Cyprus, said: "An air offensive by bomber aircraft under Allied Command is at this moment being launched against military targets in Egypt."

RAF Canberra jet bombers attacked Egyptian airfields exactly twelve hours after the expiry of the Anglo-French "Stop fighting" ultimatum.

The ultimatum—accepted by Israel and rejected by the Egyptian President Nasser—said that with or without Nasser's permission Britain and France intended to occupy key points to protect the Suez Canal.

One RAF crew, returning to their base in Cyprus, said that they had bombed an airfield which was "beautifully lit up."

Cairo radio said that the RAF dropped incendiaries and high explosive bombs on five cities—Cairo, the capital, Alexandria, Port Said, Suez and Ismailia.

Light damage was caused, and there

Continued on Back Page

WORLD FLASHPOINT—Egypt and the Suez Canal Zone where British and French forces have attacked.

CRISIS DEBATE
—see Page 4

1956

5 November The United Nations votes to create a peace force for the Middle East

13 November The American Supreme Court declares Alabama's bus segregation rules illegal

19 November Anthony Eden flies to Jamaica to recuperate from strain following the Suez crisis

13 November British Communists resign from the Party in protest at Russia's action in Hungary

10 December The IMF issues a $1,300 million loan to bolster the British economy

1956

He was outrageous, he was dangerous, he was, said the *Mirror*, 'sex, love, hate, sorrow, joy – everything that was ever pent up in a young breast.' He was Elvis Presley. In an age of ballad crooners Mississippi-born Elvis, who combined white country and western music with black rhythm and blues, was a sensation. Quite simply, he changed the world of popular music forever. By 1956, the 21-year-old was selling more records in a month than 50

British artistes together. The *Mirror* deftly managed to reflect both the sneers and fears of an older generation and the enthusiasm of the younger. Referring to Elvis as an 'alleged' singer, it declared: 'He tries to sound like a guitar when he loosens his larynx. In the ensuing chaos, words get mangled to death. Elvis has something else. Not for nothing is he known as the Pelvis. When he sings he vibrates. He shimmers from the shoulders right down to his little toes. A gurgling, choking jelly, he stands with legs astride. After every few bars or so his quivering left leg seems to snap at the knee and cave in. His hips swivel and perform contortions that have resulted in him being called "a male Marilyn Monroe" and "obscene". Parents attack Elvis. He leads youth astray with that rebel, strangled voice, they say. Churches attack Elvis. There have even been prayer services that Elvis may be granted salvation.' Then the adulation. 'Yet he is the biggest driving force ever in show business. He is fantastic.

REFLECTIONS

Liberace was a camp American pianist who dressed in sequins and put candelabra on his piano. Cassandra was the *Mirror*'s brilliant but irreverent columnist who found Liberace too tempting a target. He called him 'this deadly, winking, sniggering, snuggling, chromium-plated, scent-impregnated, luminous, quivering, giggling, fruit-flavoured, mincing, ice-covered heap of mother love'. Liberace claimed the article suggested he was gay. He sued and won, receiving £8,000 in damages. But the *Mirror* recouped far more in publicity.

Almost 40 years after the first female MP was elected, women were still not allowed to sit in the House of Lords. The Government proposed changing that when Life Peers were created but not all their Lordships agreed. The 83-year-old Earl of Glasgow protested: 'Many of us do not want to sit beside them. Nor do we want to meet them in the library.' Jutting out his beard he went on: 'This is a House of men – a House of Lords. We do not want it to become a House of Lords and Ladies.' He said women did excellent work, especially in welfare, but they were not suited to politics. There was laughter when Lord Glasgow said: 'The emotional urge which exists in a woman's make-up does not help towards good judgment.'

When he sings he vibrates. He shimmers from the shoulders right down to his little toes.

He is, without hesitation, the Rage of the Year.' In 1950s Britain, the other most significant development in popular culture was the launch of ITV in opposition to Aunty BBC. The *Mirror*'s TV Editor Clifford Davis was critical of the opening programme. It was, he said, a yawn – not surprising as it was composed of 45 minutes of pompous speeches from London's Guildhall. Why, asked Davis, did ITV have to go all high-hat instead of setting the screen sizzling from the start? Like the rest of Britain, he was fascinated by the £1,000-a-minute commercials – never seen before on British TV. The first started with snow falling, then the camera panning down to a block of ice with a toothbrush inside. 'It's tingling fresh…it does your gums good…it keeps your teeth as white as snow,' boomed the gooey, off-screen voice of some unknown man, wrote Davis. Then came the pay-off – a picture of a tube of Gibbs SR toothpaste. It was the start of what the owner of one ITV station, Roy Thomson, would later call 'a licence to print money.'

1956

11 December The government allows the BBC and ITV to broadcast between 6pm and 7pm

1957

16 January British troops invade Aden in the Yemen

25 March The Rome Treaty comes into force

24 April Mao tse-Tung promises reform and greater openness in China

16 May The GPO announces plans for direct dialling within two years

THE RAGE OF THE YEAR

THIS time last year you had never heard of Mississippi's rockin' 'n' rollin' Elvis Presley, who is close on twenty-two, wears sideburns and used to drive a lorry for a living.

This time this year, as a singer ("alleged," some people preface it) he is a world personality, commands a far bigger TV audience than Eisenhower, sells more records in a month than about fifty British disc artists lumped together for a year, has become a Hollywood film star and as near as dammit is a millionaire.

● **WHY?**

Elvis has a voice enough to make Caruso spin in his grave.

Says Presley, very honestly, of himself: "I've got nothing in common with Johnnie Ray, except that we both sing—**if you want to call it singing. . . ."**

He tries to sound like a guitar when he loosens his larynx. In the ensuing chaos, words get mangled to death.

Elvis has something else. Not for nothing is he known as the Pelvis. **When he sings he vibrates.**

He shimmies from the shoulders right down to his little toes. A gurgling, choking jelly, he stands with legs astride. After every few bars or so his quivering left leg seems to snap at the knee and cave in.

His hips swivel and perform contortions that have resulted in him being called "A male burlesque dancer," "A male Marilyn Monroe," "obscene."

But for countless teenagers the world over, he is sex, love, hate, sorrow, joy. **Everything that was ever pent up in a young breast.**

Parents attack Elvis. He leads youth astray with that rebel, strangled voice, they say.

Churches attack Elvis. There have even been prayer services that Elvis may be granted salvation.

What does he say ? "If I thought that my rock 'n' roll singing was causing juvenile delinquency, I would go back to driving a truck. I don't love money that much."

For one TV show in New York Elvis is paid £17,000. . . .

He is the biggest driving force ever in show business. He is fantastic. **He is, without any hesitation, the Rage of the Year.**

IN a year, Elvis has stormed the world. Even The Times, which is about as hep on disc singers as a Tibetan monk, takes notice.

When Elvis bought his parents a house (and a few odd Cadillacs) they ran a story headed: "Singer's father retires at age of 39." That's fame. . . .

Pat Doncaster

---

3 July An attempted coup against Kruschev fails

20 July Harold MacMillan tells the British they have 'never had it so good'

8 August Myxomatosis spreads across the English counties

30 August The last major British colony, Malaya, gains independence

25 September President Eisenhower sends Federal troops to quell riots over school segregation in Little Rock, Arkansas

1957

In September 1957, a great sexual revolution was unveiled. No, not the appearance on these shores of actress Jayne Mansfield and her 41-inch bust. It was the publication of the Wolfenden report on homosexuality and prostitution which led to the law being dragged – at least part of the way – out of Victorian prejudice. The *Daily Mirror* welcomed it as being 'no whitewash, no prudery and no hypocrisy'. It urged readers: 'Don't be shocked by this report. It's the truth. It's the answer. It's life.' Until then, prostitution and homosexuality had been illegal. But Wolfenden said criminal law should not play a part in private morals. Its enlightened findings were: 'Prostitutes exist ... Prostitution cannot be eradicated by the criminal law. Most prostitutes choose their life because it gives them an easier, freer and more profitable style of living than any other occupation. And there are enough men to keep the trade alive. The law should not try to abolish prostitution. But it should

REFLECTIONS

Man's dream of exploring the heavens grew ever closer when the Soviets put the first living creature in space, a dog called Laika. As the animal, who the *Mirror* at first called Curly, orbited 1,000 miles above the earth, she was fed through a nozzle shaped around her mouth and drank from a sponge filled with water under pressure.The *Mirror* enthused: 'Some scientists believe the Russians may have a live microphone inside the satellite which can be switched on and off by radio. If this is done, the world will soon hear barking from space - to prove that it is possible to live out there.' Sadly for Laika the Soviets had not mastered re-entry and she was condemned to die in space. Animal-lovers throughout the world protested. In a lame defence, Moscow Radio said: 'We in Russia love dogs, too, but the dog in space is a real hero, a dedicated hero.'

The fight against racism by American blacks was a long and bitter road. A defining moment in the march to freedom was the Battle of Little Rock when eight black children were slipped into an Arkansas high school in defiance of a colour bar. The *Mirror* reported: 'Inside the school, the children were chased and attacked by their white classmates. Outside, an angry mob of 250 beat up one of four Negroes who had acted as decoys.' The brave flame of revolt was swiftly extinguished with President Eisenhower saying he would use 'whatever force may be necessary to prevent any obstruction of the law by extremists.' That the law was savagely unjust and the 'extremists' ordinary families seeking basic human rights did not, sadly, seem to matter.

Don't be shocked by this report. It's the truth. It's life

clear prostitutes off the streets.' Wolfenden was even more revolutionary on gay relationships. He said: 'It should no longer be an offence for homosexual acts to take place in private between consenting adults of 21 or over.' The *Mirror*'s uncompromising reaction to the 'sensible and responsible' report was: 'It is the answer to the nauseating parade of vice in the streets which has led tourists to call London "The Shocking City". If the Government

accepts the report and acts on it quickly, the streets will be cleaned up. The youth of this country will not be exposed to the temptations of blatant and corrupting vice. Tarts will no longer cling to every lamp-post asking passers-by whether they are "lonely".' As the sexual barriers were pushed back, so the *Daily Mirror* joined in, often in a tongue-in-cheek way. The arrival of Jayne Mansfield was not by traditional standards a big story but the paper saw fit to blast her and her bosom all over the front page with the ironic question 'Has the bust had it?' The *Mirror* clearly thought not. In fact, it was having a field day when it came to women's boobs. It trumpeted 'the Celebrity Bosom'. It gave her statistics (41-18-35) as well as its own (24 pages – 13million readers – price 2d). It asked the crucial question: 'Can you still win friends and influence people with a tape measure? Has inflation gone too far? London airport had become the bustling, bust-y capital of the world. Those who had passed through it recently included 38 inches of Sophia Loren (the well-known bosom from Rome); 42 inches of Sabrina (the notable bosom from Blackpool); 38 inches of Marilyn Monroe (the distinguished bosom from Beverley Hills); and 37 inches of Diana Dors (the celebrated bosom from Bray).'

The first Anti-nuclear protests to Aldermaston

17 October A fire at the Windscale atomic works in Cumberland is blamed on mismanagement

30 October The House of Lords admits women and life peers

20 January Sir Edmund Hillary reaches the South Pole, beating Dr Vivian Fuchs

17 February The Campaign for Nuclear Disarmament is formed

18 March Buckingham Palace announces its final season for debutantes

Daily Mirror

THURS SEPT 26 1957

2⅟₂ FORWARD WITH THE PEOPLE

No. 16,730

PAGE ONE QUESTION

HAS THE BUST HAD IT?

★ **H**ERE it is again—the Celebrity Bosom. Yesterday Miss Jayne Mansfield, that bronzed and strapping Hollywood film star, bobbed across the tarmac at London Airport and coyly announced:

"I am 41 . . . 18 . . . and 35½. I'm tanned all over—every little inch of me."

Then she said how happy she was to be in Britain.

The Bust came first.

PAUSE NOW — for a question from the Daily Mirror (Vital statistics : 24 pages . . . read by 13,000,000 every day . . . price at present, 2d.)

HAS THE BUST HAD IT? CAN YOU STILL WIN FRIENDS AND INFLUENCE PEOPLE WITH A TAPE MEASURE? HAS INFLATION GONE TOO FA—

We don't, of course, mean FINALLY. We do not advocate a bust-less world. But we're just wondering.

London Airport has become the bustling, bust-y rendezvous of the world. Famous beauties, with their even more famous busts fly in (or out) almost every day.

38 inches of SOPHIA LOREN (the well-known bosom from Rome).

40 inches of SABRINA (the notable bosom from Birmingham).

38 inches of MARILYN MONROE (the distinguished bosom from Beverly Hills).

And 36½ inches of DIANA DORS (the celebrated bosom from Bray).

Ladies and gentlemen — HAVE WE HAD IT ?

What do you think ? Anyway, you had better turn to Donald Zec (AND JAYNE MANSFIELD) on the Centre Pages today.

For lovely hair!

Silvikrin
Liquid Shampoo

7d

in the green sachet

Only Silvikrin Shampoo contains Pure Silvikrin, the hair's natural food—essential for your hair's health and beauty.

---

24 March Elvis Presley joins the American army

13 May Violence is revived between nationalists and French settlers in Algeria

16 June The former Premier of Hungary, Imre Nagy, is hanged

14 July The monarchy in Iraq is overthrown in a bloody coup

9 September Race riots erupt in Notting Hill, London

1958

1958

GHANA A wind of change was blowing through Africa, Prime Minister Harold Macmillan said, and the first country to reap its benefits was Ghana. On March 6, 1957, it became the first British colony there to gain independence. At midnight a colour sergeant lowered the Union Jack from the parliament building. In its place was raised the flag of a new country – the red, gold and green of Ghana. Keith Waterhouse wrote in the *Mirror*: 'It flutters from the forts that were once slave depots. It is clutched in every hand from here to the Ivory Coast and it sparkles in fireworks across the sky of Africa. The drums beat, the bells ring and there is singing in the streets. For Ghana has become the first all-African member of the Commonwealth. Red, gold and green. The green is for the cocoa forests, the gold for the gold mines and the red for blood. But there has been little blood spilt to give this rich land its freedom. The Prime Minister is Kwame Nkrumah, who worked as a liftboy and a washer-up to educate himself in America and London. He sees Ghana as a centre to which all the peoples of Africa may come and where all the cultures of Africa may meet.'

The drums beat, the bells ring and there is singing in the streets

MUNICH On February 6, 1958, football suffered one of its bleakest days. A young Manchester United squad, nicknamed the Busby Babes after their manager Matt Busby, had just reached the European Cup semi-final following a 2–2 draw with Red Star Belgrade. On their way home from Yugoslavia the plane stopped off in Munich. Later, it took off in a snowstorm and crashed, killing 23 of the 43 on board. Eight players from the team that had been English champions for the previous two years died in the disaster. Among them were captain Roger Byrne, England centre forward Tommy Taylor and Irish international Billy Whelan. Two weeks later, Duncan Edwards died in hospital. He was the David Beckham of his day, only 21 yet already capped 18 times by England and considered to be the complete player. Matt Busby was badly injured but survived. Archie Ledbrooke, the *Mirror*'s famous northern sportswriter, was also killed. The paper solemnly ran his last column, a report of the match in Belgrade. The crash was the greatest disaster to players in English sporting history. With the exception of the young Bobby Charlton, it almost wiped out the greatest club side not just in the country but in the world. Matt Busby had been critically injured. 'The great manager who brought Manchester United world fame is 'doing badly' in hospital. A doctor said he had little chance of survival.' Yet Busby recovered and went on to manage United for many more years. Bobby Charlton, who was more famed in those days for being the nephew of former Newcastle star Jackie Milburn than for his own footballing prowess, escaped with minor head injuries. 'He is doing his army call-up,' the *Mirror* said. The only other player to escape from the crash so lightly was Harry Gregg – 'the world's most expensive goalkeeper, recently bought from Doncaster Rovers for £23,0000 – and the crowds think him worth it.'

26 October The Boeing 707 begins regular flights across the Atlantic

5 December Britain's first motorway is opened

21 December General De Gaulle is elected President of the 5th Republic in France

31 December The anti-sickness drug Thalidomide is linked to birth defects

1 January Fidel Castro's rebels take power in Cuba

Daily Mirror

FRI
FEB 7
1958

2½ FORWARD WITH THE PEOPLE
No. 16,843

SOCCER AIR TRAGEDY

Manchester United plane crashes

22 dead

THE END The chartered Elizabethan airliner in which the Manchester United team was travelling home lies shattered in a snowfield near Munich. The pilot, Captain James Thain, escaped alive from the crashed machine on the left of the picture.

AN Elizabethan airliner, on charter to the fabulous Manchester United football team, crashed in flames at Munich Airport, Germany, yesterday, and plunged the world of Soccer into mourning.

Last night twenty-two men—among them some of the brightest stars in British football—were feared to have died in the crash.

Seven of them were members of the champion Manchester United football team—such international stars as Roger Byrne, the team captain, and centre forward Tommy Taylor.

Twenty-two of the forty-four people aboard the plane survived, including Matt Busby, the team's famous manager, two air hostesses and a baby.

Among those who died was Archie Ledbrooke, the Mirror's famous Northern sports writer.

● THE CRASH—Story and pictures: Back Page.
● THE TEAM in the Tragedy—See Centre Pages.

—Blackest Day of—
All—By Peter Wilson
—See Page 23—

THE BEGINNING This picture was taken when the team, accompanied by sports writers, boarded the plane at Manchester on Monday. Left to right, with known survivors marked with asterisk*: Jackie Blanchflower*; Billy Foulkes*; Walter Crickmer, secretary; Don Davies, Manchester Guardian; Roger Byrne, captain; Duncan Edwards*; Albert Scanlon*—just visible behind Scanlon is Frank Swift, News of the World; Ray Wood*; Denis Violet*; Archie Ledbrooke, Daily Mirror; Geoff Bent; Mark Jones and Alf Clarke, Kemsley Newspapers.

22 January The number of people owning television sets in Britain has grown to 24.5 million

2 February Indira Gandhi is elected President of the ruling Congress Party in India

3 February American singer Buddy Holly is killed in a plane crash

27 February The government of Rhodesia announces a state of emergency to suppress African nationalist rebels

31 March China suppresses nationalists in Tibet. The Dalai Lama flees to India

1960

At the height of the Cold War, the world's leaders agreed to meet in Paris for a summit aimed at easing international tension over potential nuclear war. The *Mirror* considered the 1960 event so important, editor Jack Nener decided to run the paper from the French capital. In a personally signed article he wrote: 'The *Daily Mirror* believes in the Summit. That is why I have come to Paris to edit the paper from the city that is today the world's capital. With me are a top team of *Mirror* writers and photographers. They will report, interpret and portray the big news and the big personalities of this historic week. And the gay news, too.' He concluded: 'The statesmen must not let the people of the world down. Mankind has lived too long under the shadow of war.' But the Summit hardly got started, thanks to Russian leader Nikita Kruschev. Before the first session he launched a vicious attack on American president Dwight Eisenhower over US admissions that it spied on the Soviets with U-2 planes. The *Mirror* called his outburst 'a slap in the face to millions of people all over the world who had pinned their hopes of peace on the Summit'. It also branded it 'abominable, full of hypocrisy, violence and rash folly'. Kruschev, a master actor, played the innocent. Raising his hands above his head he exclaimed: 'As God is my witness, my hands are clean and my soul is pure.' The *Mirror* wasn't fooled. Nor was it statesmanlike. It could be as crude and blunt as the Soviet leader and on its front page demanded: 'Mr K! (If you will pardon an olde English phrase) *Don't be so bloody rude!*' Even though the language of the world leaders was more dignified, they let Kruschev know they felt the same. The Summit collapsed

REFLECTIONS

Opponents of Britain joining the euro make much of wanting the Queen's head on our notes. But it wasn't until 1960 that she made her first appearance on the currency. On March 16 of that year, the *Mirror* reported: 'The new £1 notes bearing a portrait of the Queen will be out tomorrow. The notes – the *first* Bank of England notes to carry a picture of a reigning monarch – are mainly green, but other colours have been added to defeat forgers. Your old £1 notes will not be affected.' This was also the first time the Bank of England allowed newspapers to picture a banknote. It laid down strict conditions: the picture must not be more than 4.5 inches long, copies of the Bank's pictures and the printing blocks must be destroyed and the picture can only be printed once.

One of the most important discoveries of the past century was the Pill, which has freed women from the fear of unwanted pregnancies. Yet its invention was only reported in the *Mirror* in a short story on Page 20 on March 3, 1960: 'British scientists have discovered a new substance for making birth-control pills. Reports have suggested that British Drug Houses are making a break-through in the family planning field and are developing a pill to limit the size of families. A BDH spokesman said: "We think the discovery of this new substance is comparable to the discovery of insulin or penicillin. It is 200 times more active than any previously known similar substance. It has been tested on animals as an oral contraceptive and has been immensely effective and efficient. A month's supply of fifteen will cost only 1s 6d – roughly a penny each".'

Queen's head appears on bank notes for the first time

'As God is my witness, my hands are clean and my soul is pure'

the next day and the *Mirror* mourned. It labelled Kruschev 'the loneliest man in the world today' and announced: 'Wickedly – wantonly – tragically, Kruschev has killed the Summit. He could have saved it by behaving like a sensible man. Instead, he has acted like a spoilt child. He spurned the mediation attempt by Harold Macmillan and Charles de Gaulle. He ignored an invitation to return to the conference table and get on with the real work of the Summit – which is world peace. He is playing a perilous game

of Russian roulette with urgent world problems. The unlucky one blows his own brains out. Kruschev has only himself to blame if the West now believes that his talk of peace was never sincere. That he came to Paris only to wreck the Summit. This he has done The world will never forgive him.'

6 May The Cod Wars escalate between Britain and Iceland

18 May The Mini is launched

18 June South Africa's slum clearance scheme fuels rioting

31 August President Eisenhower and Harold MacMillan hold an armchair conversation on British television

17 November Duty Free shopping is introduced

Daily Mirror

2½d.   Tuesday, May 17, 1960   No. 17,547

MR. K!

(If you will pardon an olde English phrase)

DON'T BE SO BLOODY RUDE!

PS

Who do you think you are?
STALIN ?

1960

SHARPEVILLE Seven weeks after Harold Macmillan made his famous 'winds of change' speech about Africa, it became apparent that not all of this continent was being blessed by the gentle breeze of change that Ghana had enjoyed. Until now the world had turned a blind eye to the South African government's policy of apartheid which segregated the black majority from the white minority. But it couldn't ignore it after Sharpeville. When thousands of blacks peacefully demonstrated against the Pass Laws, the police opened fire with rifles and machine guns. Fifty-six people, including women and children, were killed and 162 wounded. A *Mirror* reporter wrote: 'The dusty town square looked like a battlefield. It all started when hordes of natives surrounded the police station. My car was struck by a stone. If they do these things they must learn their lesson the hard way. Demonstrators dropped like ninepins. The air was filled with the cries of the injured and wails of women who found their menfolk dead. A dog howled beside the body of its murdered master.' An editorial written after Sharpeville said: 'These deaths lie grimly at the door of the people who wilfully deny the wind of change. Those people are the government of South Africa who still believe that in this day and age they can keep the country's nine million Africans in servitude. Yesterday's tragedy could be the beginning of the revolt in South Africa.' But it would be more than 30 years before apartheid was defeated.

Daily Mirror 2d No. 17,500 TUE. MAR. 22 1960

FURY IN SOUTH AFRICA

LIKE a battlefield. . . . Some of the 56 Africans killed and 162 wounded sprawled in a street after police had opened fire with rifles and sten guns at Sharpeville, near Johannesburg, South Africa, yesterday.
Women and children were among the victims.
Now turn to Back Page.

56 SHOT DEAD 162 WOUNDED

The average jail term for those convicted of child cruelty was four months

CHILD ABUSE The *Mirror* produced a shock issue to tackle head-on the horrendous, and largely unspoken of, subject of child abuse. Long before Esther Rantzen founded ChildLine, the paper told of another Esther. She was two years old and had made her father angry by soiling the carpet. So he rubbed the poor girl's nose in it for 10 minutes, banged her head on the floor and thrust her under a tap which poured water into her screaming mouth. Her skull had been fractured and her little body covered with bruises. The *Mirror* said: 'If your heart goes out to this pitiful mite, spare some of your sympathy for the other tear-stained kids who are beaten, kicked, punched and flogged in British homes every year – *More than ten thousand of them*. And this is only part of the hidden horror in British homes.' This issue was produced with the National Society for the Prevention of Cruelty to Children, which revealed the shockingly inadequate punishments meted out to the adults who abused children. The average jail term for those convicted of child cruelty was four months and the fine was £12. But nearly half those convicted weren't even fined. This was the first campaign that exposed the horror of what was happening to so many children.

Daily Mirror

MON MAR. 14 1960

2½ · No. 17,493

THE HIDDEN HORROR

SHOCK ISSUE

to fight cruelty in BRITISH homes

SHOCK ISSUE

to expose the appalling neglect of children

HELL'S KITCHEN

Their home had ONE chair, ONE cup.

They took turns to drink from a jam jar.

You could have slid on the mud on the kitchen floor.

Their parents were gaoled for six months for NEGLECT.

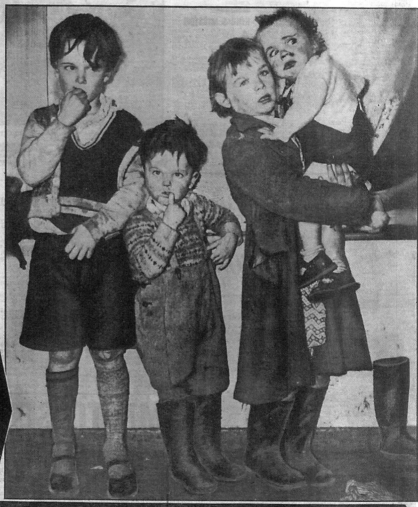

YES, BUT WHAT CAN I DO ABOUT IT? SEE PAGE 15

1960

1961

REFLECTIONS

Adolf Eichmann was the 'banality of evil' – a timid, desk-bound Nazi who organised the wartime slaughter of six million Jews with clinical efficiency and a heart of granite. After fleeing to Argentina he was kidnapped by Israeli agents in 1960 and brought to Jerusalem for trial. The *Mirror's* Cassandra reported: 'Compared with him Genghis Khan was a welfare worker. It is odd that all the maniacal madness of mankind gone berserk should be symbolised in one who would go unnoticed at a church service in Balham.' Eichmann, who said he could not stand the sight of blood, showed no emotion as the prosecution detailed the gas oven genocide and bestial atrocities for which he was responsible. He said: 'I don't deserve mercy. I'm prepared to hang myself in public.' The monster was executed in 1962 aged 56.

Eichmann

Daily Mirror

THURS APR. 13 1961

3°   No. 17,828

Salute to the pioneers

● LITTLE LEMON
Russian Space Pioneer

● HAM
Russian Space Pioneer

● GARTH
Mirror Space Pioneer

MAN IN SPACE

HE went into Space just after 7 yest[er] fresh-faced 27-year-old Russian Gagarin. Gagarin means Wild Duck. he went. Flashing over ocean Reporting simply: "The flight is norr[mal] The Wild Duck landed somewhere i[n] 9 o'clock. Rush-hour time for Earthboun[d] words…"I feel well. I have no i[?] Who cannot fail to be stirred by this n[?] Today the Mirror salutes the Russians—

MAN IN SPACE

Printed and Published by THE DAILY MIRROR NEWSPAPERS, Ltd., at Holborn Circus, London, E.C.1. Tel. Fleet Street 0246, and at Mark-lane, Manchester, 4.—Thursday, April 13, 1961.

The voice said: 'The sky is very, very dark and the Earth is a light blue. Everything can be seen very clearly.' For the first time in the history of the universe, a man was speaking from Space. The voice belonged to Yuri Gagarin, a young Russian who had been hurled into the sky in what the *Mirror* described as 'the greatest adventure ever undertaken by man.' Under the byline: 'By *Mirror* Space Age Reporters', the paper said: 'At a height of 125 miles, whirling round the world at five miles a second, Gagarin talked by radio to his base

in Russia about what he saw on a television screen in his spaceship And from him, for the first time, the world learned what it feels like to be a man out in soundless space, alone in a great emptiness where no man had been before.' Gagarin's spaceship blasted off at 7.07am British Summer Time and landed back in Russia at 8.55am. A journey of only one hour, 48 minutes, but one which changed the world. The first spaceman reported how he found himself hovering over his chair and objects swam about in the cabin. He said he was

1960

3 October The Labour Party Conference votes for unilateral nuclear disarmament

2 November A jury rules that D.H. Lawrence's *Lady Chatterley's Lover* is not obscene

9 November John F. Kennedy is elected President of the United States

31 December National Service ends in the UK

1961

8 January The French vote in a referendum in favour of Algerian home rule

Daily Mirror

Thursday, April 13, 1961 ✦ ✦ No. 17,828

Today the Mirror celebrates
the greatest story of our lifetime..
the greatest story of the century

MAN IN SPACE

morning. A
man. Yuri
the world
continents.
feel well."
just before
s. His first
or bruises."
chievement?
Wild Duck.

MAJOR YURI GAGARIN—his name means "Wild Duck."

MAN IN SPACE

He walks on Earth as the greatest, bravest pioneer in history

full of joy and sang a stirring Russian song, 'The Homeland Hears, The Homeland Knows' as he was coming down. Gagarin's ambitions now, he added, were to visit Venus and see if there were any canals on Mars. After all, when you've just become the first man in space, anything must seem possible. He was given the ultimate hero's welcome by the Soviet Union. The *Mirror* was bursting with praise. A profile by Tony Miles, later the paper's editor, enthused: 'The name is Yuri Alexeyevitch Gagarin. Son of a carpenter. Today, with the world at his feet, he walks on Earth as the greatest, bravest pioneer in history. Yuri Gagarin is the kind of hero that science fiction is made of. Young. Handsome. Even his name has the apt meaning of Wild Duck.' But America's new President, Jack Kennedy, declared: 'The exploration of our solar system is an ambition which all mankind shares. I am tired of being second in the space race.' It was the moment the United States committed itself to being first to land a man on the Moon.

8 February The BBC announces the end of Children's Hour

15 March South Africa states its intention to leave the Commonwealth

21 March The United States grants military aid to Laos to defeat insurgent Communist rebels

19 April American-backed Cuban exiles invade the Bay of Pigs hoping to overthrow the Marxist Government

8 May Former diplomat George Blake is jailed for 42 years for spying

1961

It wasn't until the start of the 1960s that humans woke up to the threat to hundreds of species of animals and birds. That was when the idea for the World Wildlife Fund began, with its symbol of a giant panda designed by Sir Peter Scott. The organisation was launched in a shock issue of the *Daily Mirror* on October 9, 1961,

REFLECTIONS

On March 8 1961, the *Mirror*'s move to its £9 million 15-storey new home at Holborn Circus in London was hailed with the boast 'This dominant, dynamic building is the most efficient newspaper headquarters ever known'. At the time, the 5,000 sq ft editorial floor was the biggest in the world. *Mirror* chairman Cecil King said: 'There is no reason why the most successful newspaper in the country should not conduct its affairs in the finest building.' Three years later the paper hit new heights with an average daily sale of 5,018,000 – 700,000 more than nearest rival the Daily Express – saying: 'The *Mirror* salutes its vast family of readers, acknowledges splendid service given by the newsagents and congratulates the entire staff on a magnificent achievement.' In 1995, the paper moved to Canary Wharf in London' Docklands.

The foolishness, greed and neglect of the most superior animal on earth – Man

with eight pages – a large proportion in those days – devoted to this one issue. The *Mirror*, as ever, pulled no punches. It placed the blame for the threat to animals like the rhino pictured on the front page squarely on 'the thoughtless foolishness, greed and neglect of the most superior animal on earth – Man himself.' It explained that the lovable giant panda was the symbol of the new organisation because '*He* was saved from extinction because Man acted in time' and that the WWF was a crusade 'to beat the 20th-century death flood.' Inside pages revealed the varied reasons why entire species were threatened, including failure to manage land properly and poaching as well as the obscene slaughter of thousands of animals. One article said: 'Look at this picture. It shows elephant feet being turned into wastepaper baskets as trophies for tourists. There is a big market in trophies. Zebra tails, elephant and rhino tusks, skins and paws of lions, are sold so that so-called sportsmen can boast to their friends about the animals they have shot. If something is not done quickly to stop man's mad misuse of the world's living treasure . . .we may be too late.' Another page listed some of the creatures that 'may become as dead as a dodo . . .The short-sighted and likeable ugly rhino has been butchered and robbed of his natural surroundings. His numbers have dwindled to a dangerously low level. There are only two varieties of elephant left in the world. Humans have been the gorilla's worst enemy, killing off adults to capture the young ones alive for zoos. Gorillas are rare today. The plump little pigmy hippopotamus of Africa does not wish to be a bother to anyone. Yet this little hippo is in serious danger as man invades his home.' The article concluded: 'state of emergency is facing the world's wildlife.' An editorial attacked the Queen for encouraging the killing of animals: 'Bang, bang, bang, bang! Four stags killed with four shots, one after the other. This, we are told, is the Queen's latest "bag" while hunting on her holidays at Balmoral. Splendid marksmanship. But is Her Majesty shooting at the right target?' The paper called on the Queen 'to enjoy her richly-deserved holidays without indulging in a massacre of animals' and pointed out that Prince Philip had agreed to be a patron of the World Wildlife Fund.

16 June Russian ballet star Rudolf Nureyev defects to the West

31 July Great Britain applies to join the Common Market

12 September Dozens of anti-nuclear demonstrators in Trafalgar Square are arrested

28 September 20 year-old folk singer Bob Dylan makes his debut in New York

16 October South Vietnam declares war against Vietcong guerrillas

Daily Mirror

3d. Monday, October 9, 1961 · · · No. 17,981

SHOCK ISSUE · · SHOCK ISSUE

DOOMED

—to disappear from the face of the earth

due to Man's FOLLY, GREED, NEGLECT

UNLESS

. . . unless something is done swiftly animals like this rhinoceros and its baby will soon be as dead as the dodo, a duck-like bird last seen nearly 300 years ago. All because of the thoughtless foolishness of the most superior animal on earth —Man himself. Greedily he slaughters indiscriminately for the cash a tusk or a tail will bring. Neglectfully, as civilisation marches on, he bulldozes wildlife out of its natural haunts and deprives it of water, food, shelter and space to live and breed. From jungle to hedgerow, tragedy is stalking the living wonders of the world. The giant tortoise of the Galapagos Islands, the Asian bactrian camel, the Ceylon elephant, the North American whooping crane, and even the songbirds and butterflies of Britain are among the startling number of creatures on the danger list. There is only one hope for them—symbolised by the lovable giant panda. IT was saved from extinction because Man acted in time. Now the panda is the emblem of a world crusade for a new "Noah's Ark" to beat the 20th century death flood—the WORLD WILDLIFE FUND. This crusade needs YOUR support. If you don't want the phrase "dead as the dodo" to be replaced by "dead as the rhino," read on . . . .

PLEASE TURN TO PAGE THREE

SHOCK ISSUE · · SHOCK ISSUE · · SHOCK ISSUE

1962

1 November The British Government announces tighter immigration controls

7 December The construction of high-rise tower blocks in London is approved

4 January President Kennedy steps up US aid to South Vietnam

February British recording company Decca reject the Beatles

17 February After the longest murder trial in British history, James Hanratty is sentenced to death for the A6 murder

1962

For one nerve-shredding week in October, 1962, the world held its breath as it teetered on the brink of nuclear war. The crisis blew up after the Soviet Union built a number of missile sites on the island of its ally Cuba, within rocket-shooting range of the US coast. When Russia despatched the freighter *Polotavia* to Cuba with a cargo of rockets, youthful US President John Kennedy knew he had to act to stop the build-up. He ordered the American fleet to blockade Cuba – though he used the more diplomatic word 'quarantine' – and intercept the *Polotavia* before she could reach her destination. Russian President Nikita Khruschev was faced with two alternatives: either recall the ship or raise the stakes to a deadly new level by providing her with a naval escort. The latter move would inevitably lead to a sea battle which could only escalate into all-out war and the unthinkable use of nuclear weapons. As the two superpowers

The future of mankind depended on which President blinked first

faced each other down, the Americans assembled a massive strike force of jet fighters in Florida while the army built a huge tent city for thousands of troops who would be needed in any invasion of Cuba. At a dramatic meeting of the UN Security Council, US Secretary of State Adlai Stevenson produced spy-plane photographs proving the build-up of Russian missiles and planes on Cuba and warned Khruschev to halt his 'ominous adventure'. He told the Soviet President he must not think America lacked the will or nerve to use her weapons of mass destruction. The world has never been closer to nuclear war, with the future of mankind depending on which President blinked first. Thankfully, it was Khruschev. After a six-day stand-off, on October 28 the Soviet leader ordered that the Cuban rocket bases be dismantled and shipped back to Russia under UN supervision. In return, the US agreed to withdraw missiles from Turkey. Kennedy immediately issued a statement welcoming Khruschev's 'statesmanlike decision' as an important and constructive contribution to peace. Clearly showing his relief that the crisis was over, he admitted the situation had been approaching a point where events could have become unmanageable. It was later discovered that Khruschev's peace move was made only hours before the US planned to launch a devastating air strike against the rocket bases.

The Street's Ena Sharples

26 March The French Army launches a final offensive to end the Algerian civil war

1 April Hundreds die in Iraq after fighting erupts between the army and Kurdish rebels

10 May American Marines are sent to crush communists in Laos

2 June Britain's first legal casino opens in Brighton

1 July The Commonwealth Immigration Act becomes law

Daily Mirror

3d. Wednesday, October 24, 1962   No. 18,304

Ships, planes move in for Cuba blockade

U.S. HUNTS TARGET NO. 1—THE RED ROCKET RUNNER

12   SOVIET MISSILES ?

5 MISSILE DOLLIES ?

MISSILE TRANSPORTERS ?

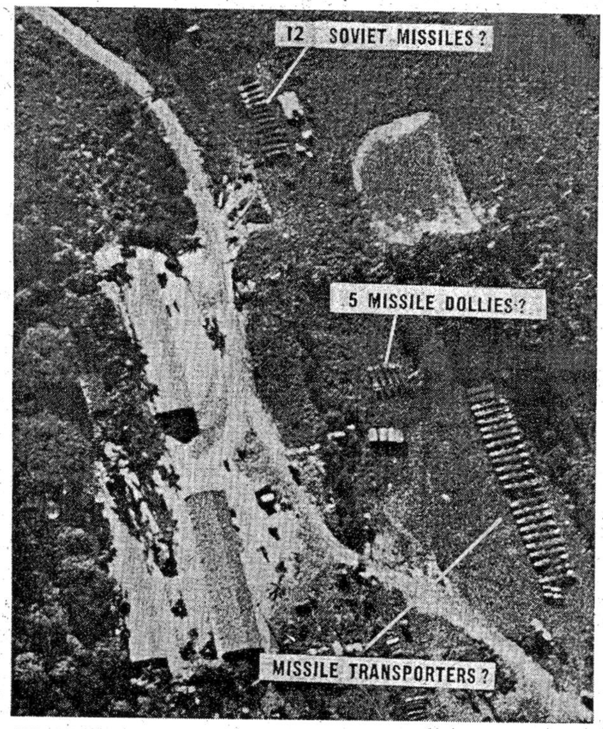

THIS IS AMERICA'S EVIDENCE

THIS is one of nine aerial pictures taken by US Spy planes of the Russian missile build-up in Cuba. The pictures were released by the American Embassy in London last night.

The Americans say that the picture above, taken well inside Cuba, shows a surface-to-air missile base.

On the base, it is claimed, are Soviet missiles, missile dollies and transporters.

It was after seeing this and the other photographs, said to show Russian MIG fighters, IL28 bombers and missile-launching PT boats, that President Kennedy ordered the blockade of Cuba.

From RALPH CHAMPION, New York, Tuesday

AMERICAN warships now fanning into the Atlantic to enforce President Kennedy's blockade of Cuba are lying in wait for the Soviet rocket-carrying freighter Polotavia.

This Red rocket-runner is their Target No. 1. She was specially designed to carry the 67ft. long missiles which the Russians have been setting up in Cuba within range of Washington and US bases.

Tonight there were reports that US warships—at least forty are on blockade duty in undisclosed areas, with jet fighter support—had made radio contact with a Soviet ship bound for Cuba.

Details of the exchange of messages—and the name of the Soviet ship—were not known.

Convoy

The Polotavia has been running a regular service from Russian ports to Havana, Dictator Castro's capital. If she maintains her usual time-table, she should be making a Westerly voyage across the Atlantic again within a few days.

The American ships have been ordered to intercept her at all costs.

President Kennedy's official proclamation of the blockade—or "quarantine" as he prefers to call it—was made tonight. The proclamation comes into effect at 3 p.m. (British time) tomorrow.

Moscow can recall the Polotavia to Russian waters—or throw down the gauntlet by providing her with a naval convoy.

Washington does not expect much trouble with chartered ships.

Those carrying contraband are most likely to turn back. Others with legitimate cargoes will probably submit to search.

★ AT KEY WEST, Florida, a massive strike force of American jet fighters is being assembled for patrol missions over Cuban waters.

And a children's playing field has been taken over by the Army to build a tent city for thousands of troops.

Strike

The troops would be used if Mr. Kennedy felt a strike against Cuba was necessary.

★ IN HAVANA, the Cuban militia are now "on a war footing," said Castro's government.

Two Russian freighters sailed into port today. They

Continued on Back Page

K warned: End this ominous adventure ..

MR. KRUSHCHEV was called upon by America last night to halt his "ominous adventure" in Cuba.

And he was warned against thinking that America lacked the will or nerve to use her weapons.

The speaker was Mr. Adlai Stevenson at a tense emergency meeting of the United Nations Security Council in New York.

He was speaking on a US resolution demanding that the Council order Russia to remove all the offensive weapons she has sent to Cuba. Mr. Valerian Zorin, Soviet

Deputy Foreign Minister, presided over the 11-Nation Council.

He said that America's move in asking for a UN meeting was a "clumsy attempt to cover up her unprecedented aggressive actions against Cuba."

The Cuban delegate said President Kennedy's case was "dishonest."

Veto

The debate was continuing early today. Russia tabled a resolution condemning "US aggression," and is almost certain to veto the American resolution.

America will then take her case to the 110-nation General Assembly.

BRITISH SHIPS FACING A SEARCH

THREE British ships are likely to be among the first affected by the "stop and be searched" order.

Steaming towards the blockade zone are the 5,929-ton Linkmoor, the 7,150-ton Beech Hill and the 6,523-ton Eastern Star.

Two other British ships, the tankers Athelcrown (11,149 tons) and Athelknight (9,087 tons), were last night in port in Cuba.

In London, shipowners' representatives met Ministry of Transport officials to discuss shipping problems in the Caribbean.

It is understood that the shipowners have been asked to be as

co-operative as possible with the American authorities.

British shipbroking firms were yesterday approached by Russians who wanted to buy six war-built Liberty ships to operate on the Cuban route.

The brokers believe the Russians need them to replace chartered ships now being withdrawn by the owners because of the blockade.

Under a clause in the charter agreement, a shipowner can refuse to allow his ship to be sailed in an area where there is a threat of war.

1963

Soviet embassy, Commander Yevgeny Ivanov. What indiscreet pillow-talk by the War Minister could Keeler have passed to her Russian lover? Such lurid speculation was boosted by the *Mirror* getting hold of a sensational letter which showed that the Soviet did, indeed, want Keeler to extract atomic secrets from Profumo. The can of worms was not yet empty. It emerged that Profumo met Keeler at the home of society osteopath Stephen Ward, who

REFLECTIONS

The Congo – now Zaire – had been riven by violence ever since it won independence from Belgium in 1960. The UN moved in but before long its peace-keeping troops were fighting for their lives as warring factions brought terror and violence to the country. The *Mirror* published a dramatic front-page picture showing a Belgian cowering by his shot-up car as he appealed to advancing UN troops 'Don't kill me!' The nervy soldiers had fired at the car, killing the man's wife and another woman, during the capture of the Katangan town of Jadotville. The tragedy summed up the complex strands running through post-colonial Africa – the victims were white, once dominant, settlers, the town they were fleeing was being fought over by blacks, and the UN troops were Indian.

As millions struggled in the grip of an unofficial power strike, the *Mirror* exposed 'The Most Hated Man in Britain'. This was Charles Doyle, founder member of the rogue National Committee of Power Station Shop Stewards and leader of the dispute. The paper revealed that Doyle was thrown out of the US for his Communist activities, returning to the land of his birth where he became a shop steward in the Electrical Trades Union. 'He is the man behind the completely *Unofficial* power station go-slow which is inflicting untold misery, hardship and suffering throughout arctic Britain,' the *Mirror* thundered. 'This is how one man thanks the people for his freedom.' Just in case readers should miss him, the *Mirror* published a huge picture of Doyle and printed his home address in the opening paragraph of its front-page story.

Christine Keeler

was having an affair with the model's friend Mandy Rice Davies. Ward claimed to have warned the security services about Profumo's fling. But instead of being discreetly thanked he was accused of living off immoral earnings and committed suicide. Still there was more. The shocked public now learned that Keeler and Profumo attended torrid parties at Cliveden, the country home of Lord Astor, where the rich and famous mingled with the low and louche – the lurid scenes could only be imagined. A public inquiry was held under leading

What indiscreet pillow talk could Keeler have passed to her Russian lover ?

He was the War Minister in a Tory Cabinet. She was a 21-year-old model with a shadowy circle of friends. Together they caused Britain's greatest political scandal of the 20th century – the Profumo Affair. Rumours that Christine Keeler was linked with 48-year-old John Profumo emerged after Keeler failed to attend court as a witness in a trial involving her former boyfriend. Harrow and Oxford-educated Profumo told the House of Commons the rumours were unfounded. But he was lying. The married MP was intimately involved with Keeler and, as more evidence surfaced, was forced to confess his deceit and resigned in disgrace. But worse was to come. At the same time that Keeler was sleeping with Profumo she was having an affair with an attaché at the

judge Lord Denning who, among other things, had to consider a photograph of a masked man, said to be a well connected member of the Establishment, committing an indecent act. His identity was never revealed. The *Mirror*'s conclusion to this astonishing episode in British public life: 'Nobody expects all people in high places to be plaster saints. What we can expect, and what we must expect, is that they keep out of shady company and behave with some degree of decorum.' Profumo paid personal penance for his folly by withdrawing from public life and devoting himself to charity. He was awarded the CBE in 1975.

3 September 20,000 are feared dead after an earthquake devastates Iran	**30 September** Rioting breaks out when a black student attends the University of Mississippi	**15 October** Amnesty International is created	**22 October** British civil servant William Vassall is jailed for spying for the USSR	**26 October** Heavy fighting erupts on the Indo-Chinese border

Daily Mirror

d. Thursday, June 6, 1963   No. 18,494

WAR MINISTER SCANDAL

'I have come to realise that, by this deception, I have been guilty of a grave misdemeanour'

PROFUMO QUITS

e lied to MPs over Christine to save his family

BEFORE THE STORM

Smiling happily, before the storm broke . . . Mr. John Profumo pictured with his beautiful wife, former actress Valerie Hobson. Now he is a Minister no longer   And his political career is in ruins.

Mirror Comment

THE BIG LIE

THE Daily Mirror does not kick a man when he is down.

Mr. Profumo, who married a beautiful and pleasant woman, is now down and out.

There can be nothing but pity for a suave but tarnished politician who has to admit—in a letter to his Prime Minister—that he is guilty of lying, of misleading, of deception, and of a grave misdemeanour. The words of the confession were chosen by Profumo himself.

God knows, he was never a good Minister: it seems now that he is not a very important man. But there is guilt in many a human heart, and skeletons in many cupboards.

The question is:

What the hell is going on in this country ?

Morals

All power corrupts—and the Tories have been in power for nearly twelve years. They are certainly enduring their full quota of fallen idols, whited sepulchres, and off-white morals.

In the Commons, Mr. Profumo made a personal statement in March,

---

By VICTOR KNIGHT

WAR MINISTER JOHN PROFUMO caused a political sensation last night by resigning from the Government.

In a dramatic letter to the Prime Minister Mr Profumo admitted that he lied to the Commons about his association with red-haired model Christine Keeler "to protect my wife and family."

This admission finally clears away the cloud of rumour and suspicion which has hung over the political scene for more than three months.

The first public hint of a scandal building up around 48-year-old Mr. Profumo came during a Commons debate in the early hours of March 22.

Three Labour M Ps referred to rumours surrounding 22-year-old Miss Keeler, who was then a missing witness in an Old Bailey shooting case.

A few hours later Mr. Profumo made a personal

Christine Keeler

was anything improper in his association with Miss Keeler.

And he threatened to take legal action against anyone spreading these rumours.

Prime Minister Harold Macmillan and other senior Ministers were in ...

Continued on Back Page

1963

Slick, professional and marred only by a single act of violence the 1963 Great Train Robbery was the most audacious of its age, netting the villains who carried it out the then fantastic sum of £2.5 million in cash. On the night of August 8 the mail train from London to Glasgow was halted by red lights at Sears Crossing in Buckinghamshire. Driver Jack Mills was clubbed with an iron bar – an attack from which he never recovered – and was forced to drive the diesel train and two uncoupled coaches carrying more than

Ronnie Biggs is arrested

100 mail bags packed with old bank notes to a bridge where the robbers' getaway truck was waiting. Mills later told the *Mirror*: 'I think they might have killed me, but I was too important to their plans. It was a fantastic operation, timed with military precision. There were between 20 and 30 men but it was all done in almost complete silence. Everyone seemed to know what he had to do, and did it.' As the gang fled, they told him: 'Keep your trap shut. There are right bastards in this crowd.' Britain was enthralled by what seemed the perfect crime, revelling in its obvious daring and skill and choosing not to dwell on poor Mills's injuries. But a £260,000 reward for information soon tempted squealers from the underworld. An informer revealed that the

Most Britons still holidayed in their own country in the early sixties with seven out of 10 visiting a seaside resort, 13 per cent caravanning and five per cent staying in one of 97 – by today's standards, exceedingly grim – holiday camps. Blackpool attracted eight million visitors and Butlins one million campers. For adventurous souls travelling abroad there were some bargain breaks – 10 days in Nice for £27 5s, eight days in Copenhagen for £44 14s and 15 days in Ibiza for £46 18s. The *Mirror* advised first-time travellers: '*Do* take the sun, as well as food and drink, in small quantities to begin with. *Don't* take Great Britain with you. Live the life of the country you visit. *Don't* forget to take soap - many Continental hotels do not supply it.'

It spelt dramatic new freedom for women, yet millions worried about the long-term effects of the Pill. Despite the doubts, by 1962 150,000 women were taking the revolutionary oral contraceptive. Asking 'Is there peril in the Pill?' *Mirror* writer Audrey Whiting revealed that though the Health Ministry had given doctors the go-ahead to prescribe, it was not up to the Ministry to assess the drug's safety. She quoted one doctor expressing concern at the way the Pill interfered with the balance of hormones and another who was so confident of the Pill's safety he said he would prescribe it for his daughter. Rather unhelpfully, Audrey told readers: 'This is a subject second only in importance to the nuclear bomb. My job is to provide you with facts about the Pill. What you decide must be for your own judgment.'

gang had hired a farmhouse not far from the scene of the robbery where they could divide up their money. The police swiftly identified Leatherslade Farm, an isolated building at the end of a country lane. A search uncovered empty mailbags scattered around a half-dug pit in which the gang planned to bury the evidence before ditching the idea and fleeing in panic. But, crucially, the robbers had broken their own rigid security, removed their gloves and left vital fingerprints by which they were traced.

'It was a fanastic operation and was timed with military precision'

Only £250,000 of the haul was ever recovered and the gang's leading members were jailed for a draconian 30 years, the longest jail sentences ever handed down for the crime of robbery. But the saga was not over. Two of the guilty, South London petty crook Ronnie Biggs and mastermind Bruce Reynolds escaped from jail. Reynolds was recaptured in Canada and brought back to jail. Biggs fled to Australia and then Brazil where he evaded extradition by making his girlfriend pregnant. In pitifully poor health and seeking medical treatment he voluntarily returned to Britain in 2001 to serve the rest of his sentence.

15 January The BBC will no longer ban the mention of politics, royalty, religion or sex in its comedy programmes

4 February Two journalists are jailed for refusing to name their sources in the Vassall spy trial

18 May President Kennedy sends in troops to control race riots in Alabama

27 May Jomo Kenyatta is elected premier in Kenya's first General Election

1 April The underground magazine 'Oz' is launched in Australia

Daily Mirror

3d. Monday, August 12, 1963 • No. 18,551

Hundreds go after £260,000 reward

SEARCH FOR TRAIN GANG'S LOOT NARROWS

By TOM TULLETT and ALAN GORDON

THE £2,525,000 treasure-train haul may be hidden within twenty miles of the ambush spot. The robber-gang may be hiding there, too.

Those were the theories being followed yesterday by Scotland Yard men leading the hunt for the gang.

The ambush was staged at 3.15 a.m. last Thursday. The GPO Travelling Post Office train from Glasgow to London, carrying £2,525,000 in banknotes, was stopped and looted at Sears Crossing, in Buckinghamshire.

Wires

The gang would have taken ninety minutes to reach London down the M1 motorway. Though they had cut phone wires, they could only reckon on fifty minutes start before the alarm was raised.

In fact, roadblocks were set up within sixty minutes of the ambush. And the four police car crews patrolling the M1 saw none of the vehicles thought to have been used in the hold-up—two lorries and a jeep.

Hundreds of phone calls have been received by police and insurance investigators following the offer of a £260,000 reward for information leading to the gang's arrest.

A police spokesman at Aylesbury said last night: "We have had a little over 400 phone messages at this station alone."

Check

Meanwhile detectives seeking the gang's hideout have started checking on all house agents around Sears Crossing.

They are listing everybody who has bought or rented a house within getaway distance of the ambush spot during the last few months.

Yesterday, seventy policemen with dogs swept across the countryside near Sears Crossing. They went to farms, barns and cottages.

And police in Buckinghamshire's neighbouring counties — Bedfordshire, Hertfordshire and Oxfordshire—were warned that the gang might be hiding in their areas.

Bandaged driver Mills yesterday.

❝ I think they might have killed me .. but I was too important to their plans ❞

By MIRROR REPORTER

JACK MILLS, the diesel driver who was beaten up in his cab during the Great Train Robbery, said last night: "I think they might have killed me, but I was too important to their plans."

Mr. Mills, 57, his head swathed in bandages after being discharged from hospital, spoke about the robbery at his home in town.

He said: "It was a complete surprise, timed with military precision.

Expert

"There were between twenty and thirty men and it was all done in almost complete silence. Everyone seemed to know what he had to do, and did it.

"There must have been railwaymen on the job because of the expert way they managed the coaches with the money in.

"But I'm certain that they didn't know how to drive the diesel and that's what saved me."

Mr. Mills, whose train was stopped by a faked red signal at Sears Crossing, was attacked with an iron bar wrapped in cloth when he tried to stop a masked man entering his cab.

The man said: "I wouldn't have hurt you, but you retaliated."

Mr. Mills was then forced to drive the diesel and the two uncoupled coaches to the bridge where the robbers' getaway truck was waiting.

Warning

Later he was told: Keep your trap shut. There are right bastards in this crowd."

Mr. Mills is going to a British Railways convalescent home in Devon.

And he said: "I don't know whether I'll ever be fit enough to drive again."

DRIVER TELLS HIS STORY

BRAVE DOG SAVES A FAMILY

THIS is Schutzen the dog who spotted a fire and raised the alarm . . . and saved the lives of a family.

With him are Leslie Chandler 8 and sister Christine 7 two of the people he saved.

Schutzen, an Alsatian, is three years old and weighs seven stone. When he spotted the fire at home in historic Lauderdale House in Highgate early yesterday Leslie and Christine were asleep.

So were their parents, park keeper John Chandler 71 and his wife Doreen, 30.

Schutzen leaped swiftly to John's bed and began to tap him heavily with his paw. He kept on tapping and whining too, until John woke.

By now flames were roaring through Lauderdale House, a 17th century building once occupied by Nell Gwynne, mistress of King Charles II.

John leapt out of bed and roused the rest of the family.

He said last night: "I tried to get the family down the stairs but flames blocked the way. Then I dashed back and looked out of the bedroom window and saw three policemen.

"I lowered the two children and my wife to them.

Then John added someone got a ladder and I slid down to carry the Schutzen.

His name is German for protect, you know."

1963

US President John F. Kennedy – glamorous, dynamic and married to the beautiful Jacqueline Lee Bouvier – was the symbol of an impossible dream and the king of America's own Camelot. A scion of the nation's leading family he was the youngest person to be elected president when he took office in 1960 at the age of 43 and won his spurs by facing down Russian president Nikita Khruschev in the Cuban missile crisis. He seemed to the West a beacon of hope amid the Cold War chill and at the start of 1963 the *Mirror* made him its Man of the Year – a 'Year of Hope that took a darned long time a-coming'. But before the year was out Kennedy was dead, cut down by an assassin's bullet as he was driven in an open-top car with his wife through Dallas, Texas, on

He fell forward and his wife cradled his head in her arms

November 22. The *Mirror* reported the assassination in graphic detail: 'A bullet ripped through his head. He fell forward and his 34-year-old wife cradled his head in her arms. As the car raced to a nearby hospital, Jackie kept crying "Oh, no!" Her clothes were spattered with blood. Mr Kennedy lived only 25 minutes after he was hit.' The world was transfixed in shock. British Prime Minister Sir Alec Douglas-Home spoke for the nation when he said: 'There are times in life when the mind and heart stand still. One such is now.' West Berlin's leader Willy Brandt said: 'A light has gone out for all who hoped for peace, freedom and a better life.' Even Russian radio paid unprecedented tribute. The *Mirror* said: 'The man who stood for all the precious values of the West is dead. He defended all the freedoms which we hold dear. But he was gentle and magnanimous. It is a cruel blow he should be struck down in the heat of mankind's great battle.' Within hours of the shooting, police arrested 24-year-old Lee Harvey Oswald, a Marxist and former US Marine. But two days later, as Oswald was transferred between jails, he was shot dead before millions of TV viewers by Jack Ruby, a Dallas nightclub owner. Ruby said he did it to spare Mrs Kennedy the ordeal of Oswald's trial. At first it was claimed Oswald acted alone. But evidence soon suggested a far wider and more sinister conspiracy. To this day it remains a source of constant debate who was responsible for the assassination of the young President, with the US Secret Service, big business and the Mafia all fingered as likely parties in an unholy alliance of murder.

1963 was the year of the Profumo scandal but Britain was almost equally riveted by the then outrageous revelation that 14-year-old Prince Charles had paid 2S 6D (about 12p) for a glass of cherry brandy in a bar on the Isle of Lewis. The Palace originally said there was 'not one vestige of truth' in the claim but then admitted the story was accurate. 'Charles will have to face the music when he returns to school,' warned the *Mirror*. On the same day it was reported that the independent Jet Petroleum company had knocked a penny off its premium grade in a price war, bringing the cost of a gallon down to 4S 6D (23p). Shell-Mex-BP said it was unlikely to cut prices further in response as 'profit margins are slender'. Sounds a familiar gripe.

Inflation was scandalously high an the *Mirror* wasted no time in attacking the Tory government for it. In May 1964 the cost-of-living index zoomed up for the eighth month in a row. And there was a beef crisis which could turn into a milk shortage, the paper warned. What was this sky-high inflation rate? It was 3.2 per cent – certainly high by the standards of those days but nothing compared with what was coming. Little more than a decade later, inflation reached 27 p cent during the oil crisis of 1975 an it remained in double figures for most of the following 20 years. In fact it took almost 40 years for inflation to fall below its 1964 level

Prince Charles on the Isle of Lewis

8 August Britain, America and the Soviet Union sign the Nuclear Test Ban Treaty

28 August Martin Luther King makes his 'I have a dream' speech in Washington

30 August A 'hotline' is installed between Moscow and the 'White House'

10 September The first British credit card is launched by American Express

1 October Labour leader Harold Wilson claims Britain faces the 'white heat of [a] scientific revolution'

Daily Mirror

3d. Saturday, November 23, 1963 ✦ ✦ No. 18,640

KENNEDY ASSASSINATED

Jackie spattered with blood

Mrs. Kennedy, her clothes spattered with blood, bends over her dying husband as their car rushes to hospital.

THE world was horror-struck last night with the news that President John F. Kennedy was dead — shot down by a hidden assassin.

Mr. Kennedy, only forty-six and the leader of the West, was riding in an open car with his wife Jackie in Dallas, Texas.

A bullet ripped through his right temple. He fell forward, and his 34-year-old wife cradled his head in her arms.

As the car raced to a nearby hospital, Jackie kept crying: "Oh, no!" Her clothes were covered in blood.

Mr. Kennedy lived only twenty-five minutes after he was hit. In hospital, surgeons opened his throat to relieve breathing and to give him blood.

But he died—at about 1 p.m., local time, 7 p.m. British time. And shocked millions throughout the world heard the announcement soon afterwards.

Texan Governor John Connally, who was in the Presidential car, was also hit by one of the assassin's three shots. After an operation his condition was satisfactory.

Waiting

Police were questioning a man last night. They had found a rifle with a telescopic sight. And they said that the assassin had been eating fried chicken at a fifth-floor window while waiting for the President.

Automatically, Vice-President Lyndon B. Johnson, 55, takes over at the White House.

Last night, as Mr. Kennedy's body was being flown to Washington, world leaders spoke with deep emotion of the youngest man ever to become President of the United States.

Full dramatic story by RALPH CHAMPION, Chief of the Mirror's American Bureau

1964

REFLECTIONS

With the death of Winston Churchill at 90 the nation lost its greatest Englishman. In a turbulent political career running from 1900 to 1955 this restless genius held a range of offices of State culminating in his inspirational wartime Premiership. The Queen said his death caused her 'inexpressible grief'. In a tribute headed 'The Saviour of the Nation', *Mirror* Political Editor John Beavan wrote: 'He was overweight and took a drop to drink. He wore old-fashioned clothes and used elaborate oratory that went out with Queen Victoria. Yet this plump Victorian gentleman became our greatest public hero.' Born the son of a duke, Churchill - present at the Battle of Omdurman in 1898 - first achieved notoriety by escaping from imprisonment during the Boer War. He entered Parliament as a Tory but six years later joined the Liberals. Recovering from the fiasco of the First World War Dardanelles expedition, for which as First Lord of the Admiralty he bore heavy blame, Churchill remained almost continually in office until 1929 before falling out of favour. A voice in the wilderness, he repeatedly warned of the Nazi threat and re-emerged in 1940 as Tory Prime Minister in the wartime coalition. His brilliant oratory strengthened the nation in its darkest hour and by drawing America into the war he dealt a death blow to Hitler. Churchill, who won the Nobel Prize for Literature, was voted out in 1945 but returned as Premier in 1951. His coffin lay in state for three days and tens of thousands lined his funeral route.

girls left their seats and rushed to the stage. Two fans fell into the orchestra pit. Programmes were thrown onstage with phone numbers written on them in lipstick. 'Beatles leader John Lennon bawled for quiet. It just brought more squeals.' The report was accompanied by pictures of hysterical girls gripping their heads and screaming. When the group visited the US for the first time, pandemonium broke out among the thousands of waiting fans. A bemused cop who worked at New York's JFK airport said: 'I think the world's gone mad.' Hundreds of reporters and photographers attended a press conference at the airport but they did not discover much. Q: 'Will you sing something?' John: 'No.' Q: 'Can you sing?' John: 'Not without money.' Q: 'How much money do you expect to make in the USA?' George: 'About half-a-crown.' Q: 'Are you going to get haircuts?' John: 'We had one yesterday.' The *Mirror* devoted an entire editorial to explaining the phenomenon: 'You have to be a real sour square not to love the nutty, noisy, happy,

It seemed as if the whole world was in the grip of hysteria

Fans had screamed for other idols but never like they did for the Beatles in 1964. The scenes of adulation which greeted tousle-headed Liverpudlians John Lennon, Paul McCartney, George Harrison and Ringo Starr had never been witnessed before and their intensity has never been repeated since. It seemed as if the whole world was in the grip of hysteria. Wherever they went the Fab Four were mobbed. Their concerts could have been sold out 100 times over yet no one could hear a word they sang over the screams of the baying girl fans. Their records held the top five places in the US charts. The *Mirror* gushed: 'Everyone, everywhere is catching it. It is called Beatlemania. Last week it swept Sweden. Last night it hit sedate Cheltenham – traditional home of retired brigadiers, colonels and the Ladies College. And Cheltenham loved them.' A report of the group's gig there said that as the Beatles tried to make themselves heard above the weeping and screaming, handsome Beatles. If they don't sweep your blues away – brother you're a lost cause. If they don't put a beat in your feet – sister, you're not living. Fact is that Beatle People are everywhere. From Wapping to Windsor. Aged seven to seventy. And it's plain to see why. They're young, new. They're high spirited, cheerful. What a change from the self-pitying moaners crooning their love-lorn tunes from the tortured shallows of lukewarm hearts. The Beatles are whacky. They wear their hair like a mop, but it's *Washed*, it's super clean. So is their fresh young act. Youngsters like the Beatles are doing a good turn for show business – and the rest of us – with their new sounds, new looks. *Good luck Beatles!*'

15 March Elizabeth Taylor and Richard Burton are married

19 March The UN attempts to maintain peace between warring Greek and Turkish communities in Cyprus

28 May Jawaharlal Nehru, Prime Minister of India since 1947, dies

2 June The Palestine Liberation Organisation is created in Jerusalem

14 June Nelson Mandela is sentenced to life imprisonment in South Africa

Goodbye, Britain—then the Big Hello

Fans on a roof at London Airport wave goodbye to the Beatles yesterday.

YEAH! YEAH! U.S.A!

That old Beatlemania hits New York as a screaming girl tries to reach the Beatles.

Paul, Ringo, George and John answer questions at the Press conference.

IRENE GOES HOME TODAY

PRINCESS Irene of Holland, whose romance has started a constitutional crisis, is going home today.

This was announced in The Hague last night by the Dutch Government.

Retreat

The announcement added that Irene—who recently became a Roman Catholic—had been spending several days in a "house of retreat" in Spain.

A second Government statement denied rumours that Queen Juliana might abdicate because of differences with the Cabinet over the romance.

Meanwhile Holland's Crown Princess Beatrix and her sister Margriet returned home yesterday from Austria, where they have been watching the winter Olympics.

Their father, Prince Bernhard, flew his own plane to Austria to collect them.

Meanwhile, in Madrid, Irene's secretary said that she "will soon be able to announce some good news in respect of her private life."

'Some good news soon'

Overcome

It went on: "The princess has overcome the difficulties she had encountered in her spirit."

The statement denied that 24-year-old Irene's suitor was Prince Alfonso de Bourbon, grandson of the last King of Spain.

From BARRIE HARDING
New York, Friday

FIVE thousand screaming, chanting teenagers—most of them playing truant from school—gave the Beatles a fantastic welcome here today.

More than 100 extra police were on duty to control the crowd as the group's jet landed at the John F. Kennedy Airport.

'Mad'

Pandemonium broke out among the stamping, banner-waving fans as the Beatles—John Lennon, Paul McCartney, George Harrison and Ringo Starr—stepped from the plane.

One policeman who has worked at the airport for ten years said: "I think the world has gone mad."

5,000 scream 'welcome' to the Beatles

And a veteran airport employee said: "I see it—but I don't believe it."

Then, when the group had left the plane, thousands of their screaming fans rushed to the balcony above the Customs Hall to watch them pass through.

There were screams and shouts as their guitars appeared, surrounded by a luggage trolley.

There were fresh squeals as the Beatles finally appeared, surrounded by a "bodyguard" of New York policemen.

Fans waved huge posters. There was a huge banner which proclaimed "Welcome to Beatlesville, U.S.A."

One of the fans had travelled 1,500 miles from Arkansas to see the group arrive—and many more had travelled up to 300 miles.

Airport officials said the crowd rivalled anything since General MacArthur returned from Korea.

The airport Press conference which followed the Beatles' arrival was chaos.

Hundreds of reporters and photographers, plus seven TV cameras, had the room bursting at its seams.

Part of the question-and-answer session between reporters and Beatles went like this:

"Will you sing something?"
John Lennon: "No!"
"Can you sing?"
"Not without money."
"How much money do you expect to make in the USA?"
George Harrison: "About half a crown."
"Are you going to get haircuts?"
Lennon: "We had one yesterday."

Hits

They were also asked what they thought of an anti-Beatle campaign in the mid-West, where some motorists were exhibiting stickers saying: "Stamp Out The Beatles."

Lennon replied: "We have a campaign to stamp out Detroit."

● The Beatles were told just before leaving London that their records "I Wanna Hold Your Hand" and "She Loves You" were joint No. 1 in the US Hit Parade.

1964

They waged a series of bloody pitched battles at seaside resorts

REFLECTIONS

In the half-darkness, the guitars and the drums started to twang and bang – a pulsating rhythm and blues, wrote Patrick Doncaster, described as 'the *Mirror*'s DJ'. He was reporting from the Station Hotel in Richmond, Surrey, where a new band called the Rolling Stones were performing. Its members were student Mick Jagger, 19, former lorry driver Brian Jones, 19, ex-Post Office worker Keith Richard, 19, Bill Wyman, 21, who likes poetry and Charlie Watts, 21, who collects pocket handkerchiefs of which he has 100. They had just released their first record – 'Come On' (Decca), which Doncaster said was quite exciting. Though he didn't suspect they would still be rocking and rolling in 40 years time.

Radio was not tailored for young people in the early 1960s. They had to be content with a few hours of pop a week. So offshore pirate radio stations began pumping it out 24 hours a day. They were such a huge success that the Government worried it would lose control of the airways. So it came up with a plan for an official pop network financed by advertisements. This outraged the Musicians Union which saw any greater use of records as a threat to its members. It threatened to refuse to make records or tape radio and TV shows. Assistant General Secretary Ted Anstey announced: 'We believe services at present available from the BBC are fully adequate.' The union's Canute-like attempt to stem the tide of progress was short-lived. Before long the venerable Light Programme became poptastic Radio I – with DJs mainly hired from pirate radio.

The Rolling Stones

Before flower power bloomed and hippies sang the mantra of peace and love, 1960s youth moved to darker urges. Seeking release from grey conformity in the comfort of the tribe, thousands of youngsters split into the rival bands of scooter-riding Mods and leather-clad motorcycling Rockers. Their mutual loathing exploded in the summer of 1964 as they waged a series of bloody pitched battles at seaside resorts up and down the country. The *Mirror* reported how in Brighton the Mods blew a whistle then chased a gang of Rockers. One fell sprawling on the beach and was savagely kicked in the face. The *Mirror* said: 'There are no rules in the war between Mods and Rockers. And no mercy.' In Margate, too, there

Pirate radio ship 'Radio Caroline'

was blood on the sands as rival teenagers spent the day fighting and smashing their way around the town. As night fell, 800 Mods were still at large strutting cockily through the streets while 200 Rockers tried to keep their heads down. More than 80 youths were arrested. Magistrate Dr George Simpson said: 'It is not likely that the air of this town has ever been polluted by hordes of hooligans male and female, such as we have seen this weekend. These long haired, unkempt, mentally unstable, petty little hoodlums – these are the sawdust Caesars who act like rats and hunt in packs.' The *Mirror* applauded Dr Simpson but did not like it when the Mayor of Margate blamed the press for fuelling the riots by publicising them. The *Mirror* retorted: 'If the Blinkers Brigade imagine that this newspaper is going to suppress the ugly activities of the lunatic fringe, they had better think again. There are matters more important, Mr Mayor, than a slump in the day's takings of a whelk stall at Margate. And the future of the youth of Britain is one of them.' The paper explained the teen gang phenomenon: 'Teenagers with an urge for group identification are likely to join the Mods or Rockers. They are the two "in" cults and there is no compromise between them. This *West Side Story*-style rivalry has created in every city and town in Britain two distinct teenage camps. It's the black leather jacket versus the blue nylon mac. The motorbike versus the motor scooter. The crash helmet versus the French beret. Make-up versus no make-up. If you don't understand the difference, you're a dead duck.'

Daily Mirror

Tuesday, May 19, 1964 • No. 18,789

In two dramatic pictures — all the fury and the hate of the scrap-happy Whitsun Wild Ones

LIVING FOR KICKS

Portrait of a Mod in action at Brighton yesterday

THEY met on the beach at Brighton yesterday—the Mod and the Rocker. And the boot went in.

In the picture on the left, the Rocker is lying full-length on the beach.

He was one of a gang of Rockers who fled from a gang of Mods. He tripped and fell. He lay face downwards. Helpless.

There are no rules in the war between Mods and Rockers. And no mercy.

The Mod kicked the Rocker in the face. And when the Rocker (below) was able to lift his head, it was smeared with blood.

This was just one moment of violence out of the many which flared in Brighton and Margate over the Whitsun holiday.

Fines

There was fresh trouble at both resorts yesterday while Sunday's Wild Ones—as reported in Page Four—troops into court to face the music.

The chairman of Margate magistrates, Dr. George Simpson, made no distinction between Mods and Rockers.

Sawdust Caesars. That was how he described all the young hooligans who turned a holiday into a time of fear and violence.

Fines totalling £1,918 were imposed on forty-five youths at Margate. Thirty-five more were dealt with at Brighton. More will appear in court at both towns today.

The victim, a long-haired Rocker, raises his head after the attack. His face is smeared with blood.

THE BOOT GOES IN Moment of violence as Mod meets Rocker. The Rocker, lying defenceless, takes a savage kick in the face after falling down on the beach at Brighton.

MORE BATTLES ON THE BEACHES—BACK PAGE

---

30 April American troops back a military coup in the Dominican Republic

15 June The Beatles are awarded MBEs

29 June US ground troops are deployed in Vietnam

15 August America's worst race riots for twenty years erupt in Watts, Los Angeles

6 September India launches a full-scale attack on Pakistan over Kashmir

1966

It was mid-morning on October 21, 1966, when the giant slag heap that brooded above the small Welsh town of Aberfan began to move, slowly at first then gaining speed as it slid down the mountainside destroying everything in its path. At the bottom lay the town school. Minutes later 116 children and 28 adults lay dead, suffocated under the choking black avalanche. An army of rescuers – many of them panic-stricken parents – tore at the slurry, too exhausted for tears, searching for survivors. Deputy headmaster David Benyon was found dead with the bodies of five children in his arms. Ten-year-old survivor Dilys Pope told of the appalling moment her school was engulfed: 'We heard a noise and saw stuff all flying about. The room seemed to be flying around. The desks were falling over and the children were shouting and screaming. We couldn't see anything. But then the dust began to go away. My leg was caught in a desk and could not move and my arm was hurting. Children were lying all over the place.' The school caretaker recalled: 'I heard a noise from the mountain. It sounded like the rush of giant waves on the seashore. I rushed out and the mountain was moving down towards the school. Teachers were

Desks were falling and children were shouting and screaming

breaking windows and screaming for help. I helped to get twenty children out. The black mud just kept moving. It was hopeless trying to reach the others.' The Queen visited the scene of the tragedy and was moved to tears. But besides the national grief there was a consuming rage. The tip was made up of waste from coal pits – as one miner put it 'the scar men left so everyone could see what coal mining meant' – and there had been constant warnings about the danger of these ever-growing heaps. There had been slips before, shockingly twice at Aberfan. But as the *Mirror* said: 'The information was buried away in files. Or never got taken seriously. Or never got pressed hard enough. Or was never fully understood.' A devastating report on the disaster said it 'could and should have been prevented'. Investigators blamed the Coal Board for a catalogue of ignorance, ineptitude and failure. But no one was sacked and no one resigned. The lasting legacy of Aberfan was the removal of slag mountains throughout South Wales – and a grief that would never die.

REFLECTIONS

1966: England's World Cup victory was the nation's greatest sporting triumph but it only rated a single inside page in the *Daily Mirror*. Under the headline 'Salute them one, salute them all!', chief sports writer Peter Wilson said the match 'beggars description and stifles all criticism'. His poetic report even managed to describe the rain which fell during the match as 'the heavens joined in like some celestial orchestra playing "The Ride of the Valkyries" – only these were *English* Valkyries – with the thunder heads massing lividly, thunder shaking the giant stadium, lightning stitching the empurpled skies and finally the sun peeping out.' But what of the football? There was a short interview with hat-trick hero Geoff Hurst, who said: 'I wasn't sure until we got to the dressing room that my last goal counted. I thought the game might have ended before I put the ball in the net.' The report added: 'The lanky inside forward started the World Cup as reserve and didn't expect to play. He said: "I certainly didn't expect things to work out as they did."'

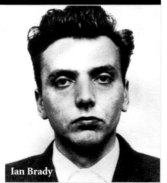

Ian Brady

Few crimes have fed such revulsion as those of Ian Brady and Myra Hindley who abused, tortured and finally killed five youngsters then buried their bodies on the lonely moors. Horrific evidence of their pitiless cruelty, including a tape of one of their victims being tortured, was produced at their trial at Chester Assizes. Yet the prosecution asked the jury: 'Did you see the slightest flicker of emotion when the most poignant and harrowing details were being discussed with them?' Brady, 28, and girlfriend Hindley, 23, were each jailed for life. Successive Home Secretaries have decreed that life must mean life for them, so heinous were their crimes. Brady remains behind bars saying that he never wants to be freed. Hindley died of cancer in 2002.

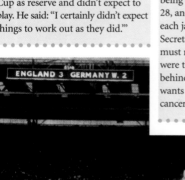

ENGLAND 3 GERMANY W. 2

11 November White Rhodesia issues a Unilateral Declaration of Independence

29 November Mrs Mary Whitehouse launches the 'Clean Up TV' campaign

21 December The government plans to introduce legal alcohol limits and random breath tests

8 January America launches the largest offensive of the Vietnam war

8 February Freddie Laker sets up the first low-cost package holiday airline

1965 1966

Daily Mirror DISASTER

4d. Saturday, October 22, 1966   No. 19,543

HOUSES SWEPT AWAY

swept mercilessly down on the village   *Picture by Mirror Cameraman FREDDIE REED*

In the words of a little girl of 10

❝ We heard a noise, and we saw all stuff flying about. The room seemed to be flying around. The desks were falling over and the children were shouting and screaming. We couldn't see anything.

But then the dust began to go away. My leg was caught in a desk and could not move, and my arm was hurting. The children were lying all over the place. ❞

IN these words little Dilys Pope last night told the story of the disaster that stunned the nation.

Scores of people died when the gigantic slag heap that brooded over Aberfan, Glamorganshire, swept down into the village to flatten a school and fourteen houses.

Dilys lived to tell the tragic story. But she was one of the lucky ones.

Early today, 85 bodies had been taken out of the wrecked school. One hundred and twenty-four people, mostly children, had been rescued alive — many of them seriously injured. And about 45 were still buried under the creeping wall of death.

Toiled

Hours after the disaster, as more than 2,000 rescuers toiled, and clergymen toured the homes of stricken relatives, the wall of death was still moving forward, inch by inch

And South Wales miners' president Glyn Williams said: "The valleys of Wales have seen their tragedies but never one like this . . "

Full Story of the Horror—See Pages 2 and 3

More Pictures—See Pages 9 and 11

---

12 March General Suharto takes power in Indonesia after a bloodless coup

27 March The missing World Cup trophy is found in a garden by a dog called Pickles

8 April Leonid Brezhnev emerges as leader of the Soviet Communist Party

23 May A seamen's strike paralyses Britain, leading to a state of emergency

2 June Eamonn de Valera becomes President of Ireland once more, aged 83

1967

Moshe Dayan

Ever since the state of Israel was founded in 1948, its Arab neighbours had refused to accept its existence. There had been war between them the following year and again in 1956, both won by the Israelis. But the Arabs, with overwhelming superiority of numbers, would not accept defeat. In 1967 they began to prepare for an invasion. There were a series of clashes with Syria before Egypt launched a massive troop build-up along its Sinai border, at the same time blockading the Gulf of Aqaba, Israel's only southern sea link. On June 3 Israel appointed General Moshe Dayan, the one-eyed hero of the 1956 campaign, as its Defence Minister. Two days later, before the Arabian invasion could be launched, Israel struck in a brilliant and devastating pre-emptive action. Legendary *Mirror* foreign correspondent Donald Wise, in the heart of the action, wrote from Jerusalem: 'The crump of shellfire and the rattle of machine-guns sound over the Holy city tonight. Jordanian shells and mortars rain down in one part while Israeli planes dive down to attack in the other. I moved up to the relief of the beleagured city with an Israeli armoured column, driving up through the Judaea hills overlooked by Jordanian positions. Children from farm settlements

The crump of shells and the rattle of machine-guns sound over the Holy City

came out of the villages to throw oranges to the troops.' An earlier report from Wise, from Tel Aviv, said: 'Radio broadcasts told the nation that fierce air and tank battles were being fought in the Sinai Desert. Men, vehicles and equipment were called up by announcers who read out code words like "Peace and blessings," "Love of Zion" and "The uncle is shaving." The good-looking women in the traffic-police stayed at their posts to direct lorries and cars. I saw surfers run from the sea with their boards when the first air-raid sirens sounded. When they heard the all-clears they ran back to the water.' *Mirror* reporter Ron Ricketts cabled from Cairo: 'War was served up with bacon and eggs. It came with a loud crash –like a heavy bomb exploding – and the hotel shook. It continued with the crunch, crunch, crunch of heavy gunfire. It was 9am. All traffic halted. Crowds gathered on pavements to listen to Cairo Radio on transistors. The mood here is one of excitement, almost exhilaration. There is no panic although anti-aircraft shells explode in the sky every few minutes. War has arrived and the Egyptians appear to welcome it.' It was all over in six days. Not only had Egypt, Syria, Jordan and Iraq been beaten, but Israel had pushed back its borders to claim large swathes of new territory, including Jerusalem, which it still holds today.

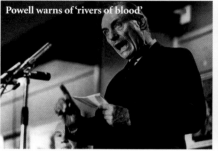
Powell warns of 'rivers of blood'

King

13 August Mao Tse-Tung proclaims a cultural revolution in China

4 October The government attempts to halt the economic slide with the introduction of a Prices and Incomes Act

18 October Timothy Evans is pardoned for the Christie murders

22 October The Soviets help double agent George Blake to break out of his London jail

22 December Rhodesia leaves the Commonwealth

Daily Mirror

4d. Tuesday, June 6, 1967 • No. 19,734

Both sides claim victory in Gaza Strip battle

THE TANKS ROLL AGAIN OVER THE DESERT

The Suez illusion— and the principle

THE Daily Express is a dubious and wayward guide on international affairs.

It said there would be no war in 1939—an error of judgment.

It seeks to withdraw our troops from Germany at the very moment when Britain is trying to join the European Common Market and say goodbye to "East of Suez."

It said that Sir Anthony Eden's Suez campaign in 1956 was right. Wrong again.

That robust but erratic newspaper is now peddling views on the new Suez Crisis which are so woolly that you can count the sheep before you fall asleep. The Great Illusion lingers on.

MIRROR PAGE ONE COMMENT

The Daily Express has publicly "re-affirmed our support for Lord Avon." Lord Avon was, of course, Sir Anthony Eden, the statesman who served his country splendidly until he was plagued by illness.

Says the Daily Express:

"In truth, recent spectacular events have converted all sensible people in the free world to his opinion."

Lord Avon, speaking last week in the House of Lords, was quick to expose this unctuous bosh.

"I do not feel myself back ten years ago," he said. "I feel myself very much in the 1930's at the present time."

The Middle East crisis of 1967 has

Continued on Page Two

In action, somewhere in the Negev Desert . . . an Israeli tank rumbles into war.

By MIRROR REPORTERS

EGYPT and Israel were last night locked in bitter conflict along their 117-mile Sinai border.

Tanks of both nations were once more rolling over the desert battlefield as they did eleven years ago during the Suez campaign.

And both countries were last night claiming major victories.

Israel reported that her forces were smashing their way into Egyptian territory and had cut off all President Nasser's troops in the Gaza Strip.

'Invading'

Shortly afterwards, Egypt said she was invading Israel after repelling Israeli attacks.

Iraqi troops were also advancing into Israel, according to Baghdad Radio.

Another large-scale battle appeared to be raging in the divided holy city of Jerusalem between Israeli and Jordanian forces.

Three Indian soldiers of the U.N force were killed in

Big peace bid begins

the fighting. As the land forces swung into action, Arab and Israeli jets battled in the air and swooped on airfields, villages and cities.

Almost as soon as the outbreak of war was announced, the rest of the world began efforts to stop the fighting.

Premier Harold Wilson started contacts with Premier Alexei Kosygin of Russia, President Lyndon B. Johnson of America, President de Gaulle of France, and U N Secretary U Thant.

President Johnson declared his neutrality in the conflict in "thought, word

and deed", and offered to talk to anyone who might end the war.

President de Gaulle announced he was stopping arms supplies to both Arabs and Israelis.

Capture

And in New York, a meeting of the U N Security Council was adjourned so that private peace talks could be held.

Meanwhile, in the Middle East land war, Israeli forces claimed they were advancing into Sinai in all sectors.

They reported capturing the key town of Khan

Continued on Back Page

see the Holy City ravaged by war

From DONALD WISE, Jerusalem, Monday

In a joint Press despatch

THE crump of shellfire and the rattle of machine-guns sound over the Holy City tonight.

Jordanian shells and mortars rain down in one part—and Israeli planes dive down to attack in the other.

Burnt-out trucks litter the streets, and shop fronts are caved in.

Government House was taken by the Jordanians—and then recaptured by Israeli tanks.

The shellfire started early this morning, catching children already at school and housewives at the supermarket.

We moved up to the relief of the beleaguered city with an Israeli armoured column driving up through the Judea hills overlooked by Jordanian positions.

Children from farm settlements came out of the villages to throw oranges to the troops. We were all wearing red roses in our shirts, given to us by the children.

Earlier we had driven down from Tel Aviv to the Gaza Strip, where Egyptian field guns had been shelling the border settlements.

It is reported tonight that Israeli forces have completely cut off the Strip.

Continued on Back Page

1968

REFLECTIONS

On August 12 1968 Czech leader Alexander Dubček was arrested in Prague by Soviet troops after the Russians invaded his country. By the end of the day, the whole reformist leadership had been rounded up with the exception of President Ludvic Svoboda. He managed to make a defiant radio broadcast to the nation calling the Russian occupation illegal. The *Mirror* reported: 'As he spoke Russian troops opened fire in Wenceslas Square. The Czechs put up strong resistance. The people tried to stop the tanks with their bodies.' A week later it was clear the Russian tanks had won. An editorial declared: 'A dream died in Prague. The Kremlin has slammed the door on the Czech bid to interpret Communism its own way. Soviet might has triumphed. But the Kremlin cannot forever resist the wind of change.'

Five years earlier he had told the American people: 'I still have a dream. I have a dream that one day this nation will rise up and live out the true meaning of its creed: "We hold these truths to be self-evident, that all men are created equal". Now, on a hotel balcony in Memphis Tennessee, Martin Luther King's dream that he would see an end to discrimination against America's black population died as he was gunned down. He had been the most inspirational leader of the US civil rights movement as it fought to change an attitude that dated back to the time of slavery. He wanted black and white to live in harmony, telling his followers: 'Let us not seek to satisfy our thirst for freedom by drinking from the cup of hatred and bitterness.' But the path to integration continued to be a tortuous one.

Martin Luther King

Mother seals nose around the shapeless carcases looking for their young

This 1968 picture by *Mirror* photographer Kent Gavin of a seal hunter clubbing a baby pup to death was possibly the most shocking, and certainly the most sickening, ever to appear on the paper's front page. Gavin travelled to icy Canada in March, when seals which had swum down from Greenland gave birth to their young in the Gulf of St Lawrence. Waiting to welcome the babies into the world were hunters whose only aim was to kill them for their valuable pelts. In one week 42,000 pups were clubbed to death. The Canadian government called it the seal harvest. *Mirror* readers called it mass murder. Reporter Alan Gordon wrote of one hunter: 'He has his one-dollar licence to kill from the Government. He has in his bloodied hands the standard baseball bat. He has the skinning knife clipped to his belt and a hooked rope for dragging the pelts away.' Another picture showed a line of dead baby seals awaiting the skinning knife, their blood draining away and staining the ice red. Gordon also noted the tragic aftermath: 'Mother seals slither acro the silent floes, nosing around the shapeless carcases looking for their young. But their babies all look the same now that the hunters have taken their soft, white furry coats. They have gone to make jackets and furs for women in Europe.' He quoted one observer, saying: ' saw a mother seal weeping over her butchered pup. She was covered in blood as if she had tried to nurse it. I saw tea in her eyes and she was wailing.' A hunter told the *Mirror*: 'I just do it for the money. Killing them is a messy job but how else can I live?' *Mirror* womens' editor Felicity Green wrote a message to any woman who owned a baby seal coat: 'It is doubtful if, when she chose it, she had the slightest idea of the way in which a pansy eyed seal pup sitting a few flippers' lengths away from its mother was battered to death with all the finesse of a mass murderer on th rampage. But it's important that she does know, even if it makes painful reading. Even if the seal pups look alarmingly like her ador pet dog.' Gavin's picture was syndicated around the world and made the brutal slaughter of animals for their pelts an international issue The *Mirror* campaign was instantly successful. Before the followi year's massacre, the Canadian government called off the 'harvest

Daily Mirror

5d.   Tuesday, March 26, 1968   →   No. 19,984

THE PRICE OF A SEALSKIN COAT

See Pages 3, 15, 16, 17

9 April Riots spread across America after the death of Martin Luther King

14 May Rioting students and striking workers bring France to a standstill

6 June Senator Bobby Kennedy is shot dead in America

31 October The first abortion clinic will open in London

6 November Richard Nixon becomes President of the United States

1969

Our early ancestors worshipped it. Lovers gazed longingly at it. Scientists theorised over it. And then came the day when Man walked on it. The space race had become a sprint since President Kennedy ordered that America should overtake the Russians. Gradually, the Apollo series of space shots had got closer and closer to the Moon. On July 16, 1969, the eleventh in the series, with three astronauts on board, was launched from Cape Kennedy. Its mission: To land on the Moon's surface. Of all the great explorations humans had undertaken, this was the greatest. Five days later, while the spacecraft orbited around the Moon, Neil Armstrong and Buzz Aldrin fired off in the lunar module Eagle. At 3.56am British Summer Time, it landed on the

'The surface is like a fine powder. It has a soft beauty all its own.'

Sea of Tranquillity and, as Armstrong stepped on to the Moon's surface, he uttered the immortal words: 'One small step for man, one giant leap for mankind.' He reported: 'The surface is like a fine powder. It has a soft beauty all its own, like some desert of the United States.' After less than a day the two astronauts returned to Apollo and the third crew member, Michael Collins, before heading back to Earth. The *Mirror* saluted them: 'This has been the most audacious and heroic achievement in the history of human endeavor.' When Armstrong and Aldrin set foot on the Sea of Tranquillity, they diminished the dimensions of the Universe and expanded the compass of the human mind. It seems almost unbelievable that the Space Age began only twelve years before with Russia's Sputnik One. Like all the great discoveries and explorations of the past, this is an accomplishment for all mankind. The astronauts brought back a large collection of rocks which, like the men, were put in quarantine. There were fears that organisms from the Moon could infect life on earth – someone at NASA had been reading too many scary science fiction stories. They worried that if life did exist on the Moon, it might run riot in the more favourable conditions on Earth. In the next three years there were five more successful moon landings. Astronauts even went for a drive in a moon buggy. But despite the astonishing achievement and incredible excitement of the first landing, man has not now set foot on the Moon for more than 30 years.

REFLECTIONS

The brutal Kray gang, known as 'The Firm', ruled London's East End in the 1960s with an iron grip. Led by twins Ronnie, a homosexual psychopath, and Reggie it seemed they were untouchable as their empire of protection rackets and illegal clubs blossomed. Showbiz stars and Establishment figures who should have known better flirted with their company, boosting their aura of invincibility. The end beckoned after Ronnie shot dead hoodlum George Cornell and both twins butchered to death Jack 'The Hat' McVitie. Fearful witnesses finally came forward and, in 1969, the 35-year-old thugs were each jailed for 30 years. The *Mirror* reported: 'To stay on top in the Terror Trade, the Krays had to be the most terrifying of all.' Ronnie died in jail in 1995 and Reggie from cancer while on parole in 2000.

The birth of a legend was announced on June 2, 1969: 'BBC's New Space Thriller Zooms in for the Viewers' – *Star Trek* was on its way. Describing what was destined to become cult viewing, a BBC spokesman said: 'Despite a staggering collection of computer weapons, communication systems and navigating devices the creators claim there is nothing in the series which is technically impossible.' The *Mirror* reported that *Star Trek*, which would replace *Dr Who* as the Saturday teatime space thriller, would run to the end of the year. In fact, *Star Trek* films are still being made for the massive following of 'Trekkies' who to this day mourn the passing of the original team of Captain Kirk, Dr Spock, Scotty and fellow crew members of the legendary spacecraft Starship Enterprise which was forever going 'where no man has gone before'.

Star Trek's Spock and Captain Kirk

17 December Mary Bell, 11, is jailed for life for the murder of two boys

10 January The government considers changing the law on 'soft' drugs

March John Lennon and Yoko Ono stage a 'love-in' for peace in an Amsterdam hotel

30 June 4 million people face starvation in Biafra after the Nigerian Government bans Red Cross aid

15 August British troops are deployed in Northern Ireland after weeks of escalating violence

Daily Mirror

The time: 3.56 am, July 21, AD 1969

5d.   Monday, July 21, 1969   09   No. 20,393

MAN WALKS ON THE MOON

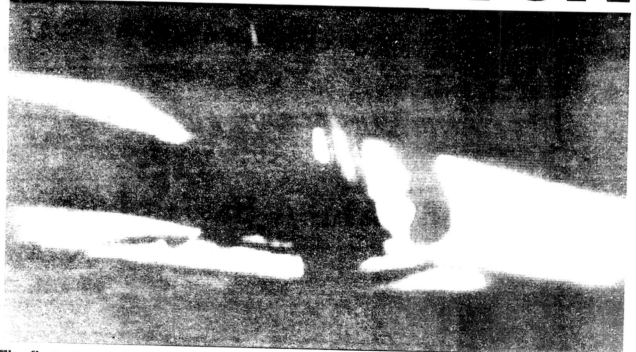

The first step . . Astronaut Armstrong feels gingerly with his foot for the Moon surface

---

1 September Mu'ammer Gaddafi overthrows the monarchy in Libya

15 October The largest ever anti-war demonstration takes place in America

17 October The Divorce Reform Bill is passed

1970

1 March American planes bomb the Ho Chi Minh trail in Vietnam

23 March Damages are paid to 18 victims of Thalidomide

1971

Concorde takes off

REFLECTIONS

Under the headline 'Up, Up And Away', the *Mirror* told of the Concorde's maiden flight. Reporter Peter Harris wrote from Toulouse, where the test pilot André Turcat took the airliner on a 28-minute trip: 'The Concorde flew yesterday, not with a bang, but a whisper. The drawing board dream had become a reality. Turcat's aim was to prove Concorde was more than big and beautiful. He had to show the world it worked. And he did. He came back to earth and announced: "finally, the bird flies." On April 9, British test pilot Brian Trubshaw, 44, flew the jet for 22 minutes from Filton air base. Later he declared: 'It was wizard.' The *Mirror* carried a picture of the world's most exclusive flying club. The Concorde club. And these two are its only members.

Of all space exploits, none has been more incredible than Apollo 13. What began on April 11, 1970, as the third manned landing on the Moon quickly became a rescue mission when shortly after take-off the craft was disabled by an explosion in one of the oxygen tanks. But the astronauts and engineers at Mission Control combined to steer the spaceship round the Moon and head it back towards Earth. Six days after it had first blasted off, Apollo 13 splashed down safely in the Pacific. The world had watched enthralled throughout this extraordinary, nail-biting endeavour.

The nation viewed the change with a mixture of bafflement and trepidation

The *Mirror* had three words of wisdom for the British people on February 15, 1971: 'Keep your cool. Take your time. And don't let them rush you. That is our advice on this Happy (we hope) D-Day.' The momentous event was the greatest social change of the century – the switch to decimalisation. Until then, there had been twelve old pence in a shilling and twenty shillings to a pound. In future there would be a hundred new pence in a pound. It sounds simple today but the nation viewed the change with a mixture of bafflement and trepidation. Hence the *Mirror*'s page one advice – though some of it must have added to the confusion. For instance: 'Take plenty of small change out with you this morning. Soon you'll be paying with decimal bronze coins. But as you haven't got any yet, when you go into decimal shops you will have to pay in £sd amounts made up to the nearest sixpence above the price. That's because sixpence is the lowest £sd sum with exact decimal value – 2.5p. If you don't pay in 6d units you'll be diddling yourself because the shopkeeper won't be able to give you the correct change'. Even shoppers who understood the new currency might have been muddled by that. The paper appointed reporter Sally Moore as its Decimal Watchdog Girl, produced a Shoppers' Guide and set up Decimal Watchdog Helplines, which readers could ring in an emergency. To add to the confusion, there were £sd shops and decimal shops. Buses had not been converted to the new currency so fares had to be paid in the old money. Full-page adverts from the Decimal Currency Board gave more advice: 'Some shopping examples: In a decimal shop, you want to buy a small tin of soup marked 4p. You can pay exactly with decimal coins – for example, with two 2p coins. Or you can hand the shopkeeper a 5p coin (or an old shilling) and get 1p change. Or you can pay with £sd coins by giving, say, two 3d bits and a sixpence. That equals 1/-, of course, and is the same as 5p, so you'll get 1p change. In a £sd shop you want to buy a packet of sweets marked 1s 2d. You can pay exactly with an old shilling (or a 5p coin) and two old pennies. Or you can hand the shopkeeper a 5p coin, a 2p coin and 1/2p coin. That equals 7.5p and since 7.5p is 1s 6d in the old money, you'll get 4d change.' In his *Mirror* column, Keith Waterhouse put it in perspective: 'Shut up and pay attention. Now this is what we call a new penny. OK? OK. Now then. These three old pennies and this threepenny bit are equal to two and a half new pence. Am I getting through to you? Of course I'm not guessing, you stupid twit! It's all here in this conversion table. Don't use that tone of voice to me – I didn't write the damned booklet!'

1970

9 April The Beatles announce they will split up

30 April President Nixon sends American troops into neutral Cambodia

4 May The US National Guard shoot dead four Kent State University student anti-war protestors

15 December The Industrial Relations Bill is passed in a bid to avoid further strikes

1971

2 January 66 football fans die when safety barriers collapse at Glasgow's Ibrox Park Stadium

DAILY Mirror

2½p (6d.) Monday, February 15, 1971   No. 20,876

ALL CHANGE!

Good Morning! It's D-Day

WATERHOUSE

has already been driven dotty..
See Page 6

KEITH WAITE

has seen it all before
See Page 5

YOUR MIRROR

● The Daily Mirror is today priced at 2½ new pence, which is the exact equivalent of the 6d. you have been paying.

But you can still buy your Mirror—Britain's biggest-selling newspaper—with a sixpenny piece which is remaining in circulation.

IT'S GOING TO BE A GREAT WEEK IN THE MIRROR —YOUR BEST BUY IN ANY CURRENCY

BRITISH RAIL went decimal yesterday. One of the first customers at Brighton, Sussex, was Jenny Farley, 16. She's still at school, and knows all about the new money. There are obviously no problems for Jenny.

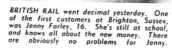

NEW PENNY JENNY

KEEP your cool. Take your time. And don't let them rush you. That is our advice on this Happy (we hope) D-Day.

Three thousand readers have already had their decimal problems solved by the Mirror Decimal Watchdogs—the best and most active service of its kind in Britain.

Now D-Day has arrived. So here is how to get through this historic Monday as painlessly as possible!

To start with, it's all much easier than most people imagine.

1—TAKE plenty of small change out with you this morning.

Soon you'll be paying with decimal bronze coins—½p, 1p, 2p. But as you haven't got any yet, when you go into decimal shops you will have to pay in £sd amounts made up to the nearest sixpence above the price.

That's because sixpence is the lowest £sd sum with **EXACT** decimal value—2½p. If you don't pay in 6d units, you'll be diddling yourself because the shopkeeper won't be able to give you the correct change.

2—TAKE your Mirror Shoppers' guide, which is printed today on Page 5, if you want to compare the old £sd prices with the new decimal ones.

But remember that you cannot use this table to choose whether you pay in £sd or the £p prices. Think — and pay—**DECIMAL.**

Remember also that in decimal shops where you buy

> **By SALLY MOORE** the Mirror's Decimal Watchdog girl

several items, like the local newsagents for instance, the shopkeeper must total up each of the items separately in decimals—then charge you the decimal total.

He can't just convert the £sd total to decimals.

3—TAKE your time. If you think a mistake has been made, don't worry about holding up the queue. Ask the cashier immediately. But try not to lose your patience.

Fair

Most shopkeepers, who have spent a lot of time and money going decimal, intend to play fair—but it's likely to be a rather fraught start to the week for them too.

4—IF you get really confused and decide it's all too much for you, pick up the nearest telephone and ring the Mirror's Decimal Watchdogs.

We're here to help you.

DIAL (01) 822 3962 if you live in these areas: London, Birmingham, Bristol, Cambridge, Cardiff, Leicester, Nottingham, Oxford, Plymouth, Southampton, Wolverhampton.

DIAL (061) 829 2225 if you live in these areas: Manchester, Belfast, Carlisle, Chester, Hull, Leeds, Liverpool, Middlesbrough, Newcastle, North Wales, Preston, Sheffield.

DIAL (041) 248 7000 if you live in these areas: Glasgow, Aberdeen, Dundee, Edinburgh.

And good luck!

1972

First edition of a revolutionary magazine

REFLECTIONS

Headlined 'Heath's Darkest Hour', the *Mirror* carried a front-page editorial on Britain's gravest industrial crisis since the General Strike of 1926. The country was in the grip of a miners' strike and the Tory Government's response was to cut power to factories to three days a week. The *Mirror* said: 'The Government has picked the right enemy – inflation. It has picked the wrong battlefront – the pits. They picked on the relatively poor-paid and long-patient miners, who do the lousiest job of all, as their whipping boys. In the words of Mr Wilson they have tried to "bully their way against the miners".' But the paper also had this message for the coal-face workers: 'They must not hold a sympathetic nation to ransom.'

Heath

warned: 'The situation in Ulster is not just ugly. It is also extremely grave. The violence has increased and unless people come quickly to their senses it could get worse.' When British troops were sent in in August of that year, they were welcomed by the Catholic community and the *Mirror*. 'Cheers in Bogside as the British troops arrive,' said one headline and the paper stated: 'The decision to put British troops on to the riot-torn streets of Ulster is the right one. Vastly regrettable, but regrettably unavoidable.' The day the troops went in saw the first death of the troubles – a man shot during a battle which broke out after a civil rights meeting. There were to be 3,000 more deaths before an uneasy peace came to Northern Ireland. Back then, the battle lines were unclear. Protestant extremists fought

Leaders of the march insisted it was a massacre without provocation

Tension on the streets of Northern Ireland had flared into violence often before but Sunday, January 30, 1972, was different. On Bloody Sunday, paratroopers fired on a civil rights march in the Catholic Bogside, killing thirteen men and wounding another twelve. The repercussions of that afternoon are still being felt. The soldiers claimed they had been forced to open fire when they came under sniper attack. But leaders of the march insisted it had been a massacre without provocation, and that peaceful demonstrators had been mercilessly gunned down. British troops had been sent into Northern Ireland three years earlier to protect Catholic communities which had come under attack when civil rights protests began. Not that there was no violence on their side. The peaceful marches had quickly turned into riots. The streets of Londonderrry became a nightly battlefield as youths hurled petrol bombs at the police before retreating behind barricades. In the summer of 1969 the *Mirror* had

the police, sometimes with guns. 'Baton-swinging riot police responded by charging in, banging their shields.' In the months that followed, it became clear that the true battle was between the IRA and the army and police. After Bloody Sunday in particular, it was war. The bloodshed and terror escalated with politicians incapable of producing a solution to end the violence. The *Daily Mirror* believed it knew how it could be done, though. It produced its five-point plan on 'How to end the killing.' The first thing, it insisted, was to bring back the British troops. 'In the judgment of this newspaper, events since they were sent in make it imperative to end this military presence. Like it or not, it is believed throughout Ireland that the soldiers are there simply to bolster the Protestant majority against the Catholic minority. Bloody Sunday irrevocably hardened that belief.' The *Mirror* wanted United Nations peacekeepers sent in instead. Had that happened, many lives might have been saved.

16 August The British government introduces internment in Northern Ireland

16 August The IRA begins a mainland bombing campaign

28 October British MPs vote in favour of joining the Common Market

31 October India defeats Pakistan after a two-week border war

16 February A national miners' strike leads to black-outs and a three-day week

Daily Mirror

BRITAIN'S BIGGEST DAILY SALE

3p   Monday, January 31, 1972   No. 21,167

ULSTER'S BLOODY SUNDAY

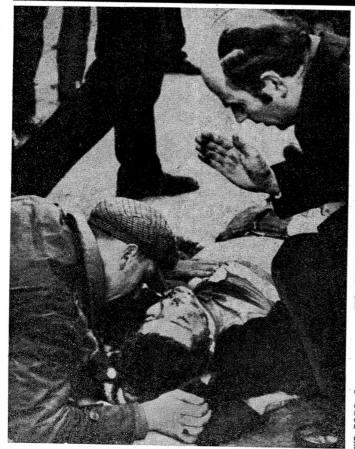

THE LAST RITES

Kneeling in the road, a priest gives the last rites to a dying demonstrator . . . Picture by Stanley Matchett. More of his dramatic pictures—See Centre Pages.

From JOE GORROD in Londonderry

THIRTEEN men were killed yesterday as Army paratroopers broke up a banned Civil Rights march in Londonderry.

Another twelve people—including two women and a child—were wounded by bullets when the Paras stormed into the Catholic Bogside area.

The soldiers claimed last night that they opened fire when they came under sniper attack. They said they were arresting about fifty demonstrators who had been hurling stones at troops behind barricades.

Five soldiers were hurt in the fierce battle—three of them hit by stones and two burned by acid bombs.

March

Eighteen demonstrators were taken to hospital with injuries that were not caused by bullets.

The marchers who died were aged between sixteen and forty.

Last night shocked Civil Rights leaders were calling the incident a massacre.

Bernadette Devlin, the Mid-Ulster M P who took part in the anti-internment march, said: "It was mass murder by the Army.

"This was our Sharpe-ville, and we shall never forget it."

Miss Devlin was referring to the killing of sixty-seven Africans by South African police in 1960.

She claimed: "The troops shot up a peaceful meeting. Then they let loose with bloodthirsty gusto at anything that strayed into their sights.

"Let nobody say that they fired in retaliation."

Mr. John Hume, Londonderry's M P at Stormont, declared: "It was cold-blooded mass murder—another bloody Sunday."

And Mr. Ivan Cooper, M P for Mid-Derry, said: "The soldiers showed no mercy. I was shot at while waving a white flag. People

13 die .. Army accused of 'massacre'

were falling all over the street."

There were immediate threats of revenge from the official I R A in Dublin, and the Provisional I R A in Londonderry.

A spokesman for the provisionals claimed: "At no time did any of our units open fire on the Army prior to the Army opening fire."

The shooting broke out as 12,000 demonstrators who had marched through the Bogside tried to pass barricades put up to stop them getting into the city centre.

Some of the marchers fought a forty-five-minute battle with troops before men of the 1st Battalion of the Parachute Regiment burst through the barricades and charged into the crowd to make arrests.

Bodies

Minutes afterwards the first shots rang out.

The bodies of two men, claimed by the Army to have been firing at them, were recovered by troops.

A public inquiry into the shooting was demanded last night by Cardinal William Conway, Primate of All Ireland.

He said:

"I have received a first-hand account from a priest who was present at the scene, and what I have heard is really shocking.

"An impartial and independent public inquiry is immediately called for, and I have telegraphed the British Prime Minister to this effect."

'SOLDIERS DIDN'T FIRE FIRST SHOT'

THE Army's Ulster chief claimed last night that his men did not "go in shooting" against yesterday's marchers in Londonderry.

"They did not fire until they were fired upon," said Major General Robert Ford, commander of land forces in the province.

He claimed that the dead "might not have been killed by our soldiers."

BBC T V interview that the paratroops' aim was to arrest hooligans who had been attacking them for two hours.

As the soldiers went in, acid bombs were dropped from a block of flats and two of them were injured — one seriously.

At the same time gun-

Continued on Page Two

1973

'Today is The Day of the Great Happening,' the *Mirror* proclaimed. 'January the first, 1973, begins one of the significant New Years in the history of our nation. At last the British are members of the European Economic Community, so modestly called the Common Market.' The *Daily Mirror* never had the slightest doubt about this huge step into the future: 'This is more than the most elaborate trading agreement in the history of nation states. It is more than the greatest trading bloc in the entire world. It is a community of nations who will grow ever closer as the years pass. And one day, perhaps a long time from now, will achieve the persistent dream of a United States of Europe. We should, every one of us, be brimful of rejoicing and hope. The spirit of adventure should be coursing through our veins.' To enter the spirit completely, *Mirror* reporters were sent all over Europe to file on what life was like for our new partners and the paper was edited for a day from Paris – the editorial conference being held in a TV studio with the editor and other executives waving self-consciously to the newsroom in London. The UK had waited a long time to get into the Common Market. Ten years earlier, Britain's efforts to enter had been blocked by French leader General de Gaulle, still smarting at what he thought were snubs to him during the wartime years. The *Mirror* savaged de Gaulle: 'He walks alone. He wishes to walk alone. His desire is that France, regardless of the harsh manner in which the 20th century has reduced her significance and stature, shall dominate the remnants of European power. Never has pride been based upon such folly.' Now de Gaulle had gone and the last remnant of opposition to British entry had disappeared. So on this first day of 1973, the *Mirror* spoke of 'All Our Tomorrows' and the

REFLECTIONS

These were the bad old days of football, when matches were remembered more for pitch invasions and running battles among rival fans than the skills of players gracing the grounds. Manchester United was the first high-profile club to tackle the issue head-on. It announced a crackdown on thugs and targeted the away-match football train specials, the main source of trouble. It banned booze in the carriages and all away tickets had to be applied for in advance. 'Anyone found jumping trains will be handed over to police'. Club chairman David Smith told the *Mirror*: 'Once Manchester United meant Denis Law, Bobby Charlton and George Best. Now it means hooliganism. The time has come for the talking to stop and action to be taken.'

A sombre front-page picture of rescue workers carrying a body from the wreckage of an airliner in France greeted readers on the morning after what was then the world's worst-ever plane crash. The headline read: 'One Of The 344.' Among those killed on the London-bound Turkish Airlines jet which had just taken off from Paris was a group of UK rugby fans who had been at the France versus England game the previous day. They were only there because a strike by engineers at Heathrow had grounded the British Airways flight they should have caught. No one survived. There was 160 Britons on board. Some were returning from winter sunshine breaks in Turkey. The *Mirror* reported: 'Rescuers wept as they gathered up scattered belongings, passports and letters.'

We should, every one of us, be brimful of rejoicing and hope

bright and prosperous future that lay ahead as part of the new Europe. 'We are all a bit more European,' the paper said. 'And we rather fancy some aspects of the Continental way of life - with typical British reserve, of course.' An opinion poll showed that Britons favoured a number of Continental ways of life, including teaching children a foreign language, playing sport on Sundays and drinking wine with meals. They also favoured holding

referendums to decide big political issues. Ironically, the first referendum to be held – two years later – was to ask the British people if they wanted to pull out of the Common Market. By an overwhelming majority of two-to-one they said they wanted to stay in.

27 April Five Oxford University Colleges plan to admit women for the first time

29 May Nixon and Brezhnev sign the Moscow Pact for nuclear non-proliferation

18 June 118 are killed near Heathrow in Britain's worst ever aviation disaster

6 August Idi Amin expels 50,000 Ugandan Asians to Britain

11 August US ground troops withdraw from South Vietnam

Daily Mirror

EUROPE'S BIGGEST DAILY SALE

3p Monday, January 1, 1973 ◆ No. 21,449

JANUARY 1, 1973

A DAY IN HISTORY

GREAT BRITAIN goes into GREATER EUROPE

What does it mean to YOU? Please turn to Page 2

---

5 September Arab guerrillas kill 11 hostages in the Israeli compound at the Munich Olympics

26 November The British government introduces the Race Relations Act

29 December Survivors of a plane crash in the Andes are forced to eat the remains of fellow passengers

1973

23 January The Paris Peace Treaty ends the Vietnam War

30 January Two White House aides are found guilty of conspiracy to spy on the Democratic Party headquarters

1973

REFLECTIONS

Margaret Thatcher was considered a bit of a joke, though a tough one. She was best known for her extremely unpopular policy of ending free school milk when she was Education Secretary - she was known for many years as 'Thatcher the Milk Snatcher'. No one expected her to become Tory leader, especially when she had said only a few years earlier that she did not think there would be a woman

Prime Minister in her lifetime. But within two years, after Ted Heath suffered two election defeats, Mrs Thatcher was the only MP with the guts to run against him. And so the greengrocer's daughter from Grantham, Lincs, took over as Opposition leader. The *Mirror*, while gracious in its praise of the 49-year-old's determination, warned: 'She belongs to the hard-line school of Tories. Their emphasis is on low taxes, low social services, selective education, private medicine and the acceptance of mass unemployment as sometimes a cruel necessity. Will she try to remould the party in her image?' She did. *Mirror* agony aunt Marje Proops said of her: 'I warn her opponents she will not be easily deflected from her chosen course.' How prophetic those words were.

Communism. The *Daily Mirror* was always a harsh critic of America's Vietnamese policy. When Prime Minister Harold Wilson flew to Washington in 1965, it sent with him a front page attacking the 'barbarous mess' of Vietnam, which Wilson showed to President Johnson. It did no good. The 180,000 troops the US had already sent had become 540,000 by 1969. The scale of death and violence was mind-numbing. More than a million people were

The American withdrawal from Vietnam

The most powerful nation the world had known took on a peasant army and lost

'This was a war like no other in that its horror was not diluted by the fact that it was taking place in some obscure land on the backside of the world. Death in Vietnam was fed to us in living, breathing colour. Television saw to that. And the newspapers fleshed out the details. We got everything but the stink of blood and burning flesh in our comfortable homes, the sight and the sound pumped into our cosy, secure existence. The war was not there. It was here.' That was the *Daily Mirror*'s epitaph for the Vietnam war. Thirty years of bloody and brutal conflict which saw the most powerful nation the world had ever known take on a peasant army and lose. It began with the French trying to hold on to part of their former colonial empire. Then America moved in, seeing the situation not as the struggle of the Vietnamese for self-government but the focus of the battle to prevent the spread of

killed and three million injured, 90 per cent of them civilians. American aircraft dropped million tons of bombs, three times the amount dropped by US bombers throughout World War Two. More than a third of South Vietnam's population fled as refugees. America admitted losing 3,248 aircraft and 4,318 helicopters – though the Vietnamese claimed the figures were much higher. Of the 2,300,000 Americans who fought the war, 55,000 lost their lives and well over 300,000 were wounded. At least 165,000 South Vietnamese troops were killed. And it was all in vain. Finally, beaten and humiliated, the end could no longer be delayed. Reporter Anthony Delano wrote: 'America's long and costly involvement in the Vietnam war ended in a frantic scramble for survival on the rooftops of Saigon. Eighty-three Marine and airforce helicopters plucked the last 900 Americans into the air and ferried them out to an armada of nearly 50 ships gathered offshore. Nine years earlier the *Mirror* had called it 'The War That Makes No Sense'. It still didn't, but at last it was over.

---

1 February Women are allowed on the floor of the London Stock Exchange for the first time

3 March The IRA target Whitehall and the Old Bailey in a new mainland bombing campaign

8 April Reclusive artist Pablo Picasso dies in France

29 May The engagement of Princess Anne to Mark Philips is announced

11 September The President of Chile, Salvador Allende is assassinated in a military coup

Daily Mirror

EUROPE'S BIGGEST DAILY SALE

3p   Wednesday, January 24, 1973   No. 21,469

3 am NEWS

Nixon tells the world

YES! IT'S PEACE

By GORDON JEFFERY
Mirror Foreign Editor

THE war between America and the Communists in Vietnam is over.

President Nixon early today announced "peace with honour."

The historic settlement was finally reached at the peace talks in Paris yesterday.

The long-awaited agreement was completed after a final four-hour session between President Nixon's chief negotiator, Dr. Henry Kis-

America's long, long war in Vietnam is over at last

singer, and the leader of North Vietnam's delegation, Le Duc Tho.

The two envoys ended their long bargaining with warm handshakes and big smiles. The picture above

showing an American soldier holding a white dove symbolises the mood of peace in the United States.

In a nationwide broadcast,

President Nixon said that the peace pact would be formally signed on Saturday.

He announced that within sixty days of the ceasefire, all American prisoners of war would be returned and all American forces would be withdrawn from Vietnam.

Nixon's speech —see Back Page

THE BLOODY ROAD TO PEACE — Mirrorscope on the centre pages

---

15 September For the first time, Japanese cars outsell those manufactured in Britain

17 October Egyptian and Israeli soldiers clash in the Sinai desert during the Yom Kippur war

17 October Arab states announce a seventy per cent rise in the price of oil in protest at American support of Israel

24 November Australian Aborigines are granted the vote

25 November A military coup in Greece ousts the President and establishes a dictatorship

1974

1974 saw two elections fought on the issue of 'who governs Britain?' Strikes were plunging the country into chaos, aided by the Conservative Government declaring a three-day working week and cutting off power to factories, offices and homes. But what worried the *Mirror* most was soaring inflation, fuelled by huge rises in the price of oil. A shock issue asked: 'Is Britain going broke? The signs are ominous: a Stock Exchange slump ... a balance of payments crisis ... a wages and prices explosion. These are symptoms of an ugly sickness which threatens to destroy not just our economy but the economies of most of the western world – inflation. It is no stranger to Britain. Ever since the end of World War Two this country has lived on borrowed cash – and borrowed time. Now time appears to be running out.' It concluded: 'We are not broke – yet. But we are getting perilously close to it.' A decade earlier there were concerns if the rate of inflation reached 2 per cent. Now it was up to 16 – and rising. Unemployment stood at 553,000 with dire predictions that it could reach 800,000. At the

REFLECTIONS

In a letters special on broke Britain on Monday July 8, readers were given their say on the economic crisis gripping the nation in a letters page special under the headline 'Crisis Britain: What You Think'. Mrs Ross, of Devon, wrote: 'England has a lot of grit and guts left. We'd all pull our weight to get the country on top again if only the Government would pull its finger out and give people more help.' D. Terry from Birmingham said: 'It would help if there weren't so many people trying to keep up with the Joneses. They get into debt and start crying for more wages.' And an 88-year-old declared: 'I used to work a 60-hour week for a pittance. My remedy for the crisis is to increase the present 40-hour week to 48 hours to boost our exports.'

'This Can't Go On' declared a despairing front page *Mirror* leader after 19 people died and 200 were hurt in IRA bomb attacks on two Birmingham pubs in 1974. The previous year one man was killed and 174 people were injured when four Provo bombs went off outside the Old Bailey and Government offices near Whitehall, marking the start of a renewed IRA bombing campaign. The *Mirror* commented on Home Secretary Roy Jenkins' pledge to introduce tough emergency measures: 'They had better be tough. Very tough. And quick. And effective.' But the awful reality was that the random slaughter could go on, and did go on, for another 21 years leaving in its wake countless broken victims and families who carry scars to this day.

parties of the left and right, as it had done in Germany in the 1930s. It said: 'What the country doesn't need is political extremist.' Five years later the country voted in Margaret Thatcher. There were riots on the streets and unemployment hit three million.

Symptoms of an ugly sickness which threatens to destroy our econom

same time the value of shares had plummeted as investors sold up fearing that companies would go bust. Top names in British industry, the paper reported, were worth less than they had been 15 years earlier. The giant British Leyland car firm, on which a million people depended for work, had seen its shares drop from 90p to 10p. Woolworth's, which owned a thousand High Street shops, was worth less than a third of its value two years earlier. The *Mirror* warned of a looming trade war in which Britain stood to lose more than most other Western countries. It also forecast a switch to smaller cars, a cut in cigarette smoking and dining out, and more families going on holiday in the UK rather than abroad. But the paper insisted that Britain did not have to go broke. 'Walking up the primrose path will be harder than walking down into an inflationary pit,' it said. 'But it is possible and much more profitable. Britain can be saved but only by accepting that, as a nation, we cannot hope to raise our living standards until we are out of the red.' The paper was also worried that the worsening economic situation could lead to a rise of extremist political

Would you be more careful if it was you that got pregnant?

It's a lot easier for a man to have a baby than for a woman. She's the one who has to hump it around for nine months. She's the one who has to grin and bear it. Backache, morning sickness and all. It's not a lot of fun being pregnant, if you don't want the baby it's not a lot of fun being an unwanted baby either. Anyone else interested in this, get advice on contraception from their nearest family planning clinic.

The Health Education Council

Men are encouraged to take responsibility

17 December Britain is struck by economic crisis, leading to a three-day week

23 January Critics blame childcare expert Dr Spock for the rise of a 'permissive society'

14 February Russian author Alexander Solzhenitsyn is exiled after his exposure of life in Soviet labour camps

22 February Heiress Patty Hearst is kidnapped by the Symbionese Liberation Army

20 March A kidnap attempt is made on Princess Anne in the M

Daily Mirror

EUROPE'S BIGGEST DAILY SALE

4p   Tuesday, July 2, 1974   No. 21,910

BANK OF ENGLAND

Y84H 282223

Y84H 282223

One Pound

1

IS BRITAIN REALLY GOING BROKE ?

A Daily Mirror Special Report .. please turn to Page 2

18 May India becomes the sixth nation to hold nuclear weapons

28 May Striking Protestant workers in Northern Ireland topple the power-sharing executive

17 July A bomb explosion at the Tower of London kills one

1 October Britain's first McDonalds opens in London

12 November The sudden disappearance of Lord Lucan is linked to the murder of his nanny

1974

President Richard Milhaus Nixon was called Tricky Dicky as a fledgling politician, and in the summer of 1974 the world saw he hadn't changed. He was not content with being the most powerful man on Earth. In 1972 he had not just wanted to be re-elected, but to wipe out his rivals. So the dodgy people around him in the White House arranged for the Democrat headquarters in the Watergate buildings to be bugged. But they bungled it and were caught by a caretaker. Nixon naturally insisted that their activities were nothing to do with the White House – and especially with him. But gradually the lies were exposed and their astonishing web of deceit and corruption unwound in the most

REFLECTIONS

An editorial under the headline 'Wanted – A Miracle For Britain's Sake' accused the miners of stretching the 'already fragile social contract to snapping point' when they received pay rises of 28 per cent. While accepting coal-face workers deserved their increase 'Britain does depend on them and the coal they dig' – it warned other trade unions who had been waiting in the wings to see what the miners got. The piece went on: 'The railwaymen? The power workers? And all the other unions with industrial power? Will they rashly set out to prove the truth of Chancellor Denis Healy's warning that pay rises on this scale will spell national bankruptcy?'

The referendum campaign to decide whether Britain should remain in the Common Market began on May 1, 1975, with the Government delivering three pamphlets to every household. One explained what it was all about, one put the case for voting Yes and the third for saying No. Anti-Marketeers criticised the Government for trying to scare people. But it was a very one-sided campaign. Every national newspaper except the *Communist Morning Star* urged its readers to vote Yes. So did most members of the Labour Government and the Tory Opposition. Only the extreme Left and Right backed the No campaign. No wonder the referendum was won by a two-to-one majority. Since then, the *Daily Mirror* has maintained its pro-European stance while most other newspapers have turned against the EU.

Whenever the story went quiet, something even more dramatic would happen

astonishing political drama of modern times. The finger of suspicion pointed at people ever closer to Nixon. And one by one, he disowned them. Including his Vice-President, Spiro Agnew. Whenever the story went quiet, something even more dramatic happened. A plane carrying a Nixon aide crashed and a suitcase containing millions of dollars was found. It was clearly intended as a bribe. The dogged *Washington Post* reporters Bob Woodward and Carl Bernstein, aided by their secret source 'Deep Throat', pursued the President relentlessly. When the burglars appeared in court they pleaded guilty but refused to say anything. They had been paid to keep their mouths shut. So Judge John Sirica, acting in the highest principles of American justice, threatened to throw them in jail for a long, long time – and they started singing. More White House aides were caught but Nixon still denied everything. He seemed to be in the clear. Nothing could be proved against him. And then came the most incredible twist of all. A White House engineer revealed that the President taped absolutely everything spoken in the Oval Office. The tapes were ordered to be produced – and turned out to have convenient blanks where Nixon had said something incriminating. Impeachment proceedings were started against him. It was the end. Nixon realised he was finished. In his farewell address to the American people he arrogantly proclaimed: 'I have never been a quitter. But the

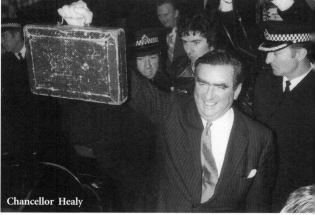

Chancellor Healy

interests of the nation must come first.' The *Mirror* said: 'Today the American people breathe a purer air. They can make a fresh start.' Nixon was replaced by Gerald Ford, the only person in American history to become President without being elected as either President or Vice-President, a man accused of being too stupid to chew gum and walk at the same time. His first act on reaching the White House was to pardon his predecessor so he would never have to face a criminal trial.

---

24 December Former labour minister John Stonehouse is arrested in Australia suspected of fraud

31 December Spiralling inflation causes British wages to rise twenty per cent in a year

20 January The British government abandons the channel tunnel

28 February An Underground crash at Moorgate kills 34

17 April Communist Khmer Rouge forces take Cambodia

DAILY Mirror

EUROPE'S BIGGEST DAILY SALE

4p Saturday, August 10, 1974 • No. 21,944

Washington, August 9, 1974

Nixon's defiant farewell

GOODBYE AMERICA!

From ANTHONY DELANO
in Washington
and GORDON GREGOR
in San Clemente

DEFIANT to the end, Richard Milhous Nixon heads for private life and the sun of California.

This was the final unrepentant gesture of the disgraced President as he left the White House by helicopter.

He was on his way with his wife Pat, daughter Tricia and her husband Edward Cox, to the Nixon estate in San Clemente.

And true to his "Tricky Dicky" image to the last he bummed a free ride.

Nixon said he wanted to leave the White House as President.

And he was still President when he took off from Andrews Air Force base just outside Washington in the presi-

● Continued on Page Two

● Continued on Page Two

BOUVERIE'S FIVE-OUT-OF-SIX BONANZA — Back Page

---

24 April Three die when Baader-Meinhof terrorists blow up the West German Embassy

12 June Indian premier Indira Gandhi is found guilty of electoral corruption

26 September Civil war erupts between Christians and Moslems in Beirut

3 November The Queen opens the North Sea pipeline

22 November The monarchy returns to Spain after the death of General Franco

1975

EQUAL PAY It isn't easy for a newspaper to think of an attention-grabbing way to illustrate a story on the introduction of a new law. But the *Mirror* had no problem the day in December 1975 that the Sex Discrimination and Equal Pay Acts came into force. It printed a male pin-up on the front page, saying 'Girls, it's your turn now.' Equal rights for women had taken 109 years to achieve. It had, said the paper, been a long, hard battle punctuated by the fighting spirit of suffragette Emmeline Pankhurst and the bra-burning antics of the women's libbers. The *Mirror* warned: 'Equality won't suddenly break out overnight. It will still be difficult for women to get to the top. They will still have to fight for better pay, But at least the most blatant forms of discrimination can now be challenged in the courts. And that's worth having.' The new Act meant the end of adverts like: 'Secretary, must be attractive, to work for two dynamic young men.' A personnel chief warned: 'Gone are the days of the dolly bird adverts or the vacancy for a senior male executive.' With the passing of the Act, women were officially the equal of men. Of course, in reality, as the *Mirror* foresaw, they still had a very long way to go before they could claim true equality between the sexes.

A third of babies conceived in Britain are unplanned and unwanted

Marje Proops

SEX The Sixties may have been Swingin' but it wasn't until the Seventies that a new, open and adult attitude to sex was seen. Once again the *Daily Mirror* led the way with a ground-breaking and – for the time – shocking special issue on sexual knowledge. A quarter of a century later, it is the almost daily fare of the media but in 1975 it was so different that it carried a warning to parents on the front page. Legendary agony aunt Marje Proops edited this detailed explanation of sex, which explained about contraception – including drawings of various methods – intercourse, sex for the elderly, sexual problems and the awakenings of adolescence. Marje wrote: 'Ignorance, irresponsibility, apathy: these are the main reasons why more than a third of the 600,000 babies which will be conceived in Britain this year will be unplanned and unwanted. *It is shocking* that between three and four million couples take no contraceptive precautions when they make love. *It is shocking* that adolescents as young as 12 and 13 engage in sex without knowledge of the act of love or its consequences. *It is shocking* that even mature men and women know so little about the facts of life that they are unable to teach their children how they came into the world. Only knowledge and understanding can reduce the appalling statistics.'

1975

24 November Civil war breaks out in Angola two weeks after independence

22 December Pro-Palestinian terrorists seize eighty hostages at the OPEC headquarters in Vienna

1976

7 June The IMF lends the British government £3 billion to prop up falling sterling

20 July The US Viking spacecraft lands on Mars

3 August A severe drought is caused by the record British summer

Daily Mirror

EUROPE'S BIGGEST DAILY SALE

5p Tuesday, August 12, 1975 No. 22,252

PARENTS PLEASE NOTE:
This issue of the Daily Mirror contains a guide to sexual knowledge: allow your children to read it at your discretion

IGNORANCE, irresponsibility, apathy: these are the main reasons why more than a third of the 600,000 babies which will be conceived this year will be unplanned and unwanted.

● IT IS SHOCKING that between three and four million couples take no contraceptive precautions when they make love.

● IT IS SHOCKING that adolescents as young as 12 and 13, engage in sex without knowledge of the act of love, or its consequences; that some teenagers regard the use of a contraceptive as "chicken."

● IT IS SHOCKING that even mature men and women know so little about the facts of life that they are unable to teach their children how they came into the world.

Irresponsibility and ignorance resulted, last year alone, in 220,000 unwanted pregnancies. Out of this number, there were 110,000 abortions and 64,617 illegitimate births.

THESE FIGURES ADD UP TO A DEVASTATING TOTAL OF HUMAN MISERY.

Today and tomorrow we publish a no-nonsense guide to sex. Only knowledge and understanding can reduce the appalling statistics.

THE MIRROR GUIDE TO SEXUAL KNOWLEDGE

EDITED by MARJORIE PROOPS

PLEASE TURN TO PAGE 5

---

8 August The women's peace movement begins in Ulster

24 September Rhodesia announces a two-year transition to black majority rule

9 September Chinese Communist Chairman Mao Tse-Tung dies

1977

3 February The British government announces referenda on Scottish and Welsh independence

27 March Two airliners collide in the Canary Islands, killing 574

1978

Mankind had achieved many things since its prehistoric ancestors crawled out of the primeval swamp. But this was probably the greatest. The creation of life itself. The birth of the first test-tube baby on July 25, 1978 was hailed as a miracle. Louise Brown arrived in the world at Oldham district general hospital in Lancashire. It was a crowning triumph for gynaecologist Patrick Steptoe whose insistence that in vitro fertilisation was possible was as crucial as his skill in achieving this medical breakthrough. He had spent ten years on the experiment. But it didn't come to fruition until they took an egg from a 32-year-old Bristol housewife, Lesley Brown, and fertilised it in a test tube with sperm from her lorry-driver husband. Then they returned it to Lesley's womb. Long before the baby's arrival, her financial future

This medical miracle gave overnight hope to countless thousands of couples

was assured. Payments worth more than £300,000 were made by newspapers desperate to get exclusive rights to pictures. Other newspapers, including the *Mirror*, were furious at this example of chequebook journalism. But the furore over the payment could not diminish the importance of this medical miracle which overnight gave hope to countless thousands of couples who were unable to have children naturally. Mrs Brown's problem was a malfunction of the fallopian tubes which channel the eggs into the womb. Mr Steptoe and his partner, physiologist Robert Edwards, had been waiting for a human guinea pig. In the mid-Sixties Dr Edwards had succeeded in fertilising the eggs of hamsters in his Cambridge laboratory. But when he sought human ovaries the medical profession didn't want to know. 'They thought I was barmy,' he said. But up in Oldham one gynaecologist wanted to help ... Mr Steptoe. In the years that followed he often drove from Oldham to Cambridge with a rabbit as his passenger. Inside the rabbit's warm womb were eggs taken from a woman. Dr Edwards was convinced that it would be only a matter of time before a human baby was produced. Louise's birth proved him right. When she arrived, her father went wild with delight. He flung his arms round his wife, smothered her with kisses and danced a jig of joy. 'It's fantastic, it's fantastic,' he yelled. So it was. Every birth is, but this one really was very, very special.

REFLECTIONS

A special anniversary edition had this message to the nation: 'Go out and party.' 1977 was the Queen's Silver Jubilee year and an editorial on June 6 began: 'England expects ... every man, woman and child to enjoy the celebrations of a lifetime. The Queen's Jubilee will see her subjects cavorting in carnivals, play-acting in pageants, having fun at fetes and fairs.' The paper had a round-up of where the fun was happening. It told how Jubilee fever had gripped the country and had taken manufacturers of 'anything red, white and blue by surprise'. 'Have you tried buying a Union Jack this week? Or a Jubilee crown? And where are our mugs?' There were street parties everywhere in the greatest community celebration since the end of the war.

In a gloomy editorial on Wednesday June 22 under the headline 'Punk Future' the *Mirror* responded to the latest jobless figure, which was perilously close to the 1.5 million mark. School leavers were mainly responsible for the sharp rise, it said. The editorial declared: 'It's not much fun to be young these days. In a month 104,000 school leavers have gone straight from their classrooms to an idle and purposeless life on the dole. Is it any wonder youngsters feel disillusioned? Is it any wonder they turn to anarchic heroes like Johnny Rotten, the punk rocker? Punk rock is tailor-made for those who feel they only have a punk future. Those who work hard and pass exams are just as likely to be denied work as those who don't. A new generation of talent is turning sour before our eyes.'

---

2 April Red Rum wins the Grand National for the third time

June George Lucas' *Star Wars* is released in the UK

15 June Free elections take place in Spain for the first time in 41 years

20 June Strikers and the police come to blows at the Grunwick processing plant

5 July The military oust Pakistan's Premier Bhutto after months of unrest

Daily Mirror

Wednesday, July 26, 1978   8p

STEEL: Inquiry.

STEEL IS QUIZZED ON SCOTT

By MARK DOWDNEY
Political Correspondent

LIBERAL leader David Steel was questioned yesterday by police probing the Norman Scott affair.

Mr. Steel was asked to cast his mind back to 1971, when he and his party's MPs held a secret inquiry into allegations made by Scott.

The male model claimed he had a homosexual relationship with former Liberal leader Jeremy Thorpe —who strenuously denies the allegation.

Mr. Steel, Chief Whip in 1971, was deeply involved in the inquiry.

He was questioned at Westminster yesterday by two detectives from the Somerset and Avon force.

Turn to Page Two

SCOTT: Letters

TEST-TUBE BABY GIRL

The little miracle arrives

MIRACLE MAKERS: Lesley and Gilbert. An extra special baby.

THE miracle baby the world has waited for was born just after midnight. And it's a girl.

The first test-tube baby in history was ushered into the world at Oldham District General Hospital in Lancashire.

She is likely to be named Patricia.

The condition of the baby was said to be "excellent".

She weighed 5lb. 12oz. And mum was doing fine too.

Triumph

The birth, by Caesarian operation, took place amid massive security arrangements.

And it was a crowning triumph for gynaecologist Patrick Steptoe, who made it all possible.

By MIRROR REPORTERS

Mr. Steptoe and co-researcher Robert Edwards, have spent ten years on their experiments.

But their work didn't come to fruition until a few months ago, when they took an egg from 33-year-old Bristol housewife Lesley Brown and fertilised it in a test tube with sperm from her husband, lorry driver Gilbert Brown.

Then they returned it to Lesley's womb.

Long before the birth, the baby's financial future was guaranteed by huge cash payments for syndication rights. They are said to total more than £300,000.

Gilbert planned a move for his wife and baby from their three-bedroom council house in Hassall Drive, Bristol, to a new detached home.

Apart from the blaze of publicity, the birth will bring fresh hope to many women who have been barred from motherhood by infertility.

Mrs. Brown's problem was a malfunction of the fallopian tubes, which channel the eggs into the womb.

Jim gives Maggie pre-election blues—Page Two

26 July Israel sanctions three new settlements in the occupied West Bank

26 September The 'no-frills' Skytrain is launched by Freddie Laker

3 December An exodus of refugees begins from South Vietnam

24 March An accident involving the supertanker Amoco Cadiz causes a huge oil slick off the Brittany coast

10 May Buckingham Palace announce that Princess Margaret and Lord Snowden will divorce

1979

REFLECTIONS

The late 1970s witnessed a number of violent clashes between the racist National Front and anti-Nazis. There had been growing demands for provocative marches to be banned from areas with large ethnic-minority communities. It seemed only a matter of time before someone got killed. Sure enough, on April 23, 1979, a protestor died from head injuries. Blair Peach was a young teacher from New Zealand who had joined a demonstration in Southall, West London. A *Mirror* reporter was prevented from entering the NF rally by stewards who told him: 'The *Daily Mirror* supports these niggers and is a Labour rag.' The bloody clash outside turned really nasty, with 5,000 protestors hurling smoke bombs, bottles and rocks. Blair Peach's death led to a massive outcry when it was revealed that after being arrested he had been beaten by the hated police Special Patrol Group.

He was known simply as The King. As a young man he invented rock and roll and became the greatest teen idol of all time. Now, at the age of 42, he was dead. Millions of fans went into mourning. The *Mirror* switchboard was jammed with sobbing girls pouring out their grief. After his amazing early years, Elvis's life had been a descent into tragedy. He died a bloated, drug-addicted recluse in the bathroom of his Memphis mansion, Graceland. The *Mirror*'s Chris Hutchins told how he once heard Tom Jones warn Elvis in a Las Vegas dressing room that drugs would kill him. Jones, said Hutchins, had told him: 'One day you'll overdo it with those drugs and none of us will be around to help you.'

droves to the new Tory leader, Margaret Thatcher. Mr Callaghan didn't help himself by jetting off to the sunny Caribbean and saying when he returned that he did not see any chaos – often misquoted as: 'Crisis? What crisis?' The *Mirror* chronicled the problems: 'Schools are closing down because there is no heating oil. Buses are off the road. Farm animals face slaughter because feed is not being delivered to them. Supermarket shelves are being emptied by housewives stocking up for a siege as though war had broken out. A million council workers are threatening

The election campaign featured photos of her washing up and pruning the roses

As the winter of 1978 approached, the discontent of millions of trade unionists with government pay restrictions reached breaking point. Workers' standards of living had slipped as inflation took off but pay had to be held down to meet the tough orders of the International Monetary Fund, to which the Labour government had gone with a begging bowl two years earlier. Public sector workers led the stoppages. Rubbish piled up on street corners and there were even places where bodies were not buried. The strikes spread to the private sector. Lorry drivers stopped work, leaving shops short of food. Rail workers set dates for strikes. The country was grinding to a halt in what came to be called the Winter of Discontent. And to make matters worse for Labour Prime Minister Jim Callaghan, a general election was looming. He had to call one by the spring of 1979 and voters, convinced the government had lost control, were switching in

to strike; civil servants want an extra 30 per cent; and there may soon be no trains running in some regions.' It warned: 'Unless the present insanity is ended, the outcome is inevitable: higher prices, higher unemployment and a lower standard of living.' All that was to come true. But the *Mirror* missed out one result of the Winter of Discontent – the return of a Conservative government led by the most right-wing Prime Minister of the century – and the first ever woman Prime Minister. Margaret Hilda Thatcher swept to power after an election campaign which featured benign photo opportunities of her doing the washing up and pruning the roses. On May 4, 1979, she was pictured smiling and waving as she headed for Downing Street. 'I feel wonderful,' she said. 'Absolutely superb.' The country didn't realise what was about to hit it.

8 July Björn Borg is the first modern player to win the Wimbledon Singles title for the third time

18 September President Carter hosts an Israeli-Egyptian summit at Camp David

29 September Bulgarian defector Georgi Markov is killed by a poisoned umbrella on Waterloo Bridge

16 October John Paul II becomes the first non-Italian Pope for over 400 years

1 January A revolution in Iran forces the Shah into exile

DAILY Mirror

Friday, May 4, 1979   8p   F

4 a.m. Thorpe is ousted in the topsy-turvy poll

MAGGIE'S MADE IT!

Now for No 10.. 'it's wonderful!'

Maggie looks confident of success early this morning as the Tory gains pour in.

By JOHN DESBOROUGH

TORY leader Margaret Thatcher is on her way into No. 10 Downing Street.

Early today she was all set to become Britain's first woman Prime Minister.

The Tory majority in the Commons looked like being between 40 and 55 seats, according to computer predictions.

As Mrs. Thatcher left her Finchley constituency after doubling her majority, she said: "I feel wonderful — absolutely superb."

Jim Callaghan's hopes of putting Labour back in power were dashed in a topsy-turvy poll.

There were big swings to the Tories in London and the South; a definite swing to Labour in Scotland and a much less marked swing to the Tories from Labour in the North of England.

Labour-held marginal seats were falling fast.

Just before 4 a.m. the Tories had notched up twenty-seven gains from Labour and four from the Scottish National Party.

Labour had gained two seats from the breakaway Scottish Labour Party and wiped them out in Parliament.

They had also snatched four seats from the Tories, ousting Shadow Scottish Secretary Teddy Taylor from a Glasgow seat.

A sensational blow for the Liberals was the defeat of former party leader Jeremy Thorpe by the Tory at North Devon.

The Liberals were generally struggling. But party leader David Steel was home with an increased majority in his Scottish border seat.

While a woman moved towards the Premiership, it was a black night for several women M.Ps.

OUT were Junior Education Minister Margaret Jackson, defeated by the Tory at Lincoln; Left-winger Audrey Wise, rejected by her Coventry constituency; Helene Hayman, beaten at Welwyn and Hatfield; Maureen Colquhoun, who had been in trouble with her local Labour party in Northampton; and Winnie Ewing, pioneer Scottish Nationalist MP.

● Turn to Back Page

STATE OF THE PARTIES			
LABOUR	10 Gains	37 Losses	221 Seats
TORIES	42 Gains	6 Losses	218 Seats
LIBERALS	0 Gains	1 Loss	6 Seats
OTHERS	0 Gains	8 Losses	5 Seats

The computer forecasts

1979

Four years after the Vietnam war ended, John Pilger reported on its appalling aftermath in a remarkable shock issue. 'Death of a Nation' chronicled the disaster which had struck the beautiful country of Cambodia. Pilger wrote: 'An incredible human disaster has happened in Cambodia, a once peaceful and gentle land in South East Asia. Perhaps more than two million people – a third of the population – have been killed by a fanatical regime whose apparent aim was to wipe out anyone and anything connected with the modern world and to return a whole nation to "Year Zero": the dawn of an age of slavery, without families and sentiment, without machines, schools, books, medicine, music.'

Not only the family has been abolished but all expressions of joy, love and grief

Pilger, accompanied by photographer Eric Piper, described what it was like to fly over Cambodia: 'There is nobody, no movement, not even an animal, as if the great population of Asia stopped at the border. Whole towns and villages on the river bank stand empty: the doors of houses flapping open, cars on their sides, mangled bicycles in a heap, chairs and beds in the street. Beside tangled power lines there is the lone shadow of a child, lying or sitting. It does not move. Nothing appears to grow except the forest and tall, wild grass that follows straight lines, as if planned; it is fertilised, we later see, by human compost, by the remains of tens of thousands of men, women and children. What has happened here has no parallel in modern times. Coming here is like happening on something unimaginable: a human catastrophe and crime without measure. It involved the enslavement of the entire population and the systematic slaughter of all those "touched and corrupted by the twentieth century". All learning, music and song have been banned, and not only the family has been abolished but all expressions of joy, love and grief as well as machines. Anybody with any education was killed: doctors, teachers, technicians, skilled workers, even schoolchildren; anybody who knew foreigners.' John Pilger had no doubt how this

REFLECTIONS

He had reached the political heights but now former Liberal leader Jeremy Thorpe was up before the Old Bailey accused of plotting to murder former model Norman Scott who claimed they'd had a gay affair. Scott made extraordinary allegations against the North Devon MP whose private life was dragged out for public scrutiny. It was said that a hit man had been hired to shoot Scott but instead he had killed a dog, Rinka. Brilliant defence barrister George Carmen claimed Scott had exploited the relationship to make money. Thorpe and his three co-accused were cleared. But he was left a broken man, his political career finished.

The microchip had arrived and it was going to revolutionise our lives. Headlined 'Your Obedient Servant', a *Mirror* report by Michael Helicar on May 29 predicted wild and wonderful things such as Micro Mum and a robot Mrs Mop. Micro Mum, said experts, would be a push-button brain linked to a TV that would be able to 'wake the family with an alarm, open the curtains, make the tea, run the bath and cook bacon just the way you like it'. Mrs Mop, a 3ft 2in robot, would wash the kitchen floor, clean the carpet and mow the lawn. Micro Mum and Mrs Mop never quite made it into our homes, but other predictions in the Helicar report are now in every day use – videophones and flat, wide-screen TVs.

Jeremy Thorpe

had started. Cambodia's misfortune was to border Vietnam and in the spring of 1970 US planes had subjected it to the greatest saturation bombing in history to destroy an alleged Vietcong base. This was a secret war, all details of which were hidden from the public for years. President Nixon's aim was to show the Vietnamese how tough he could be – the 'madman theory of warfare'. But all he achieved was to help bring to power the fanatic Pol Pot and his evil Khmer Rouge regime.

1979

1 April Ayatollah Khomeini declares an Islamic republic in Iran

18 June Brezhnev and Carter sign the SALT-2 arms limitation treaty

20 July Sandinista rebels in Nicaragua oust President Samoza after a long civil war

15 August British athletes Seb Coe and Steve Ovett are world athletic champions

27 August Lord Mountbatten is killed by an IRA bomb

DAILY Mirror

Wednesday, September 12, 1979   8p

WORLD EXCLUSIVE

Report by **JOHN PILGER**

Pictures by **ERIC PIPER**

Death of a Nation

The £11 million ransom mistake

TYCOON Rolf Schild declared last night that the kidnappers holding his wife and daughter were demanding £11 million.

He hinted that the ransom was nearer £1 million.

Mr. Schild dropped his multi-million pound bombshell in a television interview.

The London businessman was asking for the first time since he was released by Sardinian bandits a week to raise the ransom for his wife Daphne, 51, and daughter Annabel, 15.

During the BBC news interview, he said: "The demand is not £11

It may be £1m says tycoon

million. It is nearer the amount mentioned in the papers as being average for this type of kidnap in Sardinia.

That would put the ransom at around £1 million.

Mr. Schild, 55, did not explain why the £11 million figure emerged. It was first reported by Reuters agency in Sardinia but last night

● Turn to Page Two

SCHILD: A TV bombshell

AN INCREDIBLE human disaster has happened in Cambodia, a once peaceful and gentle land in South East Asia. Perhaps more than two million people—a third of the population—have been killed by a fanatical regime whose apparent aim was to wipe out anyone and anything connected with the modern world and to return a whole nation to "Year Zero": the dawn of an age of slavery, without families and sentiment, without machines, schools, books, medicine, music.

The evidence of murder is plentiful. Like the cracked skulls, above, which were dug out from mass graves near Angkor Wat by villagers who had lost relatives.

For four years there has been almost no contact with people inside Cambodia; its borders were sealed. JOHN PILGER, in Cambodia, sends the first of two world exclusive reports.

PLEASE TURN TO PAGE 3

4 November Iranian terrorists take American Embassy staff hostage in Tehran

21 November The Queen's art adviser Anthony Blunt is named as a Russian spy

27 December The Soviet Union invades Afghanistan

21 December A deal for peace in Rhodesia-Zimbabwe is signed in London

1980

22 January Prominent Soviet dissident Dr Andrei Sakharov is exiled to Gorky

1980

Reagan and royal visitor

REFLECTIONS

The landslide election of former B-movie actor Ronald Reagan as US President surprised even the old ham himself. His tearful opponent, sitting President Jimmy Carter, knew he was doomed before polling ended. Carter's ageing but indomitable mother, Miss Lillian, said as he prepared to leave power: 'I just want him home to clean up the garden.' Hardline Republican Reagan, at 69 the oldest man to enter the White House, served two terms during which he launched an arms build-up which the creaking Soviet Union could not match. At first, this raised Cold War tensions. Ultimately it forced the Russians to negotiate smaller nuclear forces. The easy-going President, who forged a close bond with British Premier Margaret Thatcher, made up for his tenuous grasp of international relations and his natural indolence by being an unparalleled communicator with the US public.

A year after coming to power, Margaret Thatcher's government cut social security rises. Those who would suffer were 9 million pensioners, 7 million mothers, 13 million children, 600,000 long-term sick and disabled, and 2.5 million people on supplementary benefit. New rules stopped payments for clothing and shoes for poor children. The *Mirror* wrote: 'Britain's welfare state was born from a conviction that the miseries of the 1930s must never return. Whatever their other differences, politicians of all parties have united to protect the needy. Until today. This attack on the weakest members of society is a cowardly way to try to solve the nation's problems.'

They crashed through the windows and there were sounds of explosions

Television viewers watching on the afternoon of May 5, 1980, witnessed the most incredible live broadcast. Cameras were filming the outside of the Iranian embassy in palatial Prince's Gate in London when suddenly a team of masked men, dressed from head to toe in black, began to swarm down ropes from the roof. They crashed through the windows and there were the sounds of explosions and gunfire. Smoke billowed out from the grand windows. There were shouts. More shots. And then people began to emerge from the front door, some dragged, some with their hands held high. The siege of the Iranian embassy was over. It had begun six days earlier when a group of armed dissidents had taken over the embassy, holding everyone in it prisoner. The hostages included three Britons, one of them a policeman on duty there, PC Trevor Lock. A huge cordon was thrown around the building but, with the eyes of the world on them, they dared not move against the terrorists for fear of harming the hostages. But Margaret Thatcher, only a year after becoming Prime Minister, was not willing to let the kidnappers win. When the gunmen killed two Iranian hostages and threatened to kill others unless prisoners in Iran were released she ordered the crack SAS to move in. Two massive blasts rocked the embassy as they went into action. The explosions were caused by powerful 'thunderflash' stun grenades designed to blind and deafen the terrorists. At the same time the highly-trained troops slithered down ropes fixed to points on the embassy roof. They kicked in the windows and exchanged shots with the terrorists. As smoke and flames billowed from the building, a white flag was seen at a first-floor window. Then the hostages began to file out to safety. All the terrorists were killed. There were charges later that they had been shot rather than risk having them as prisoners. Afterwards it was revealed that when one of the SAS men crashed through the window, he had been confronted by a terrorist armed with a machine-gun. But PC Lock wrestled the gunman to the floor. He was hailed as the hero of the siege and the SAS became famous for their courage, daring and unrivalled skill. The *Mirror* cheered: 'It was daring. Dramatic. Brilliantly planned. And chillingly executed. But best of all, the storming of the Iranian embassy by SAS commandos was a complete success. The SAS – motto "Who Dares Wins" – knocked John Wayne off peak-hour television. And for the first time the world had a ringside seat as Britain's anti-terrorist experts went into action.'

4 March Robert Mugabe is elected Premier of Zimbabwe

25 April A mission to rescue the American hostages in Iran ends in fiasco

29 April British film director Alfred Hitchcock dies aged 80

8 May Yugoslavia's President Tito dies

12 June A terrible famine and refugee crisis threatens East Africa

DAILY Mirror

Tuesday, May 6, 1980   10p

SAS to the rescue in heart of London

- # 19 set free
- # 3 gunmen die

CRACK Special Air Services troops stormed the Iranian embassy in London last night as the six-day siege came to a bloody end.

They were ordered into action when the embassy gunmen shot and killed two Iranian hostages.

Three gunmen died in the battle that followed and two were captured. But nineteen hostages, including the three Britons, were rescued.

BBC technician Sim Harris walked from an ambulance into the casualty department of a nearby hospital waving to BBC colleagues filming his first moments of freedom.

Hostage police constable Trevor Locke, seized when the Arab gunmen took over the embassy last Wednesday, was driven in triumph to Scotland Yard. Embassy clerk Ron Morris also came through the fiery climax to the siege unscathed.

Explosions

Senior officers hailed Pc Locke as a hero. He grappled with one of the Arab gunmen who was trying to hurl a grenade at the SAS men. The two had a furious struggle, and Pc Locke managed to overpower the terrorist.

The dramatic operation to crack the siege was set in motion after gunfire erupted at the embassy.

A body was brought out and the gunmen threatened to kill another hostage every half hour unless their demands for the release of prisoners in Iran were met.

Two massive blasts rocked the embassy as the SAS men went into action. The explosions were caused by powerful thunderflash "stun" grenades designed to simultaneously blind and deafen the gunmen.

At the same time the highly-trained troops slithered down ropes fixed to points on the embassy roof from the start of the siege.

The troops kicked in front and rear windows. Once inside, they exchanged a number of shots with the terrorists.

As smoke and flames billowed from the building, a white flag was seen at a first-floor window. Then the hostages began to file out to safety.

Last night the Army clamped a news blackout on details of the SAS attack.

HOODED HEROES: Two heavily-armed SAS men go into action on the embassy balcony.

THE SIEGE BUSTERS

Operation Thunderflash—Pages 2 & 3.   Leap for life—Page 5.   Free at last.—Back page

---

12 June Tear gas is fired at rioting English soccer fans at the European championship in Turin

17 June NATO announces that cruise missiles will be based at Greenham Common, Berkshire

July America boycotts the Moscow Olympics over the Soviet invasion of Afghanistan

15 August The shipwrecked Titanic is located on the sea bed

22 September Lech Walesa forms the 'Solidarity' union for democratic reform in Poland

1980

REFLECTIONS

In the spring of 1980 one question above all others gripped and tormented the nation: Who shot JR? The US soap *Dallas* may have been as corny as they come, but the characters got a hold on the British people. And when it was leaked that 'slick, slimy, scheming JR' – as the *Mirror* described the boss of the Ewing clan – was going to get what was coming to him, it became the number one topic of conversation. On the night he was shot, 22 million tuned in. But for those who missed it, the BBC's *Nine O'Clock News* showed an action replay. Viewers rushed to betting shops to back their hunches on who was responsible. A William Hill employee said: 'It's a madhouse. We've taken more money on who shot JR than on most of the holiday races.' Larry Hagman, who played JR, was the world's highest-paid TV actor, earning £35,000 an episode. (PS. It was Kristen who did it.)

Mad or bad? That was the question for the jury when 34-year-old lorry driver Peter Sutcliffe, the Yorkshire Ripper, stood accused of butchering 13 women and trying to kill seven more. For five years Sutcliffe terrorised the north of England, bludgeoning his victims with a hammer then stabbing them with a screwdriver. Although he was interviewed by police, he was only caught after a routine check. When he appeared at the Old Bailey the *Mirror* reported: 'There was an ordinariness about him as he stood in the dock and he seemed to worry about where to place his hands.' The jury rejected his plea of manslaughter through diminished responsibility and convicted him of murder. He was jailed for a minimum 30 years but sent to Broadmoor hospital after persuading psychiatrists he heard voices in his head.

Peter Sutcliffe

as he stepped out of his apartment, a fame-seeking youth shot him dead. Earlier that morning, a smirking Mark Chapman had got Lennon to autograph one of his albums. After the killing he boasted: 'Yeah, I just shot John Lennon.' The world was stunned by the senseless slaughter of this brilliant, gentle and peaceful artist. His song-writing partner Paul McCartney said: 'I can't take it in. John is going to be missed by the whole world.' George Harrison said: 'I am shocked and stunned. It's such a terrible waste. I have great love and respect for John.' Ringo Starr was too shocked to say anything. The *Mirror* spoke for all John's fans when it said: 'Like many other men of peace, John Lennon was the victim of the gun, of the violence that sickens and perverts today's society. The Beatles were more

They spent their honeymoon in bed declaring peace was all that mattered

John Lennon wasn't just another Beatle. He was the true rebel in the band which changed the world, a wonderful song-writing talent and an idol not only for his music but for his unashamed and unshakeable conflict with the Establishment. Having proclaimed that the Beatles were more famous than Jesus Christ – a statement of fact in those heady Sixties days – he then shocked everyone by marrying Yoko Ono. They spent their honeymoon in bed with only the world's media for company, declaring that peace was all that mattered. He moved to New York and became a virtual house husband, looking after their young son Sean. In the late 1970s, John began recording again. His great creative talent was about to be unleashed once more. But on a cold December morning in 1980

than just pop minstrels and Lennon was more than just their leader. They changed styles of dress and behaviour as well as music. They symbolised the end of dutiful respect for authority, whether of parents or of governments. They were classless and almost ageless. Everyone bought their records or sang and danced to their music. But they meant something special to the young, especially Lennon, because he reached out beyond entertainment to offer a gentle philosophy of life. He preached love where other and lesser musicians incited death. He offered hope where they exploited death. Until, for some crazed reason, he was instantly destroyed.' John Lennon could not have had a finer epitaph.

1980

24 September Iraq and Iran clash over their border

10 October Margaret Thatcher declares she is 'not for turning' on her economic policies

11 October Two giant earthquakes in Algeria leave more than 20,000 dead

27 October Prisoners in Northern Ireland's the Maze go on hunger strike

1981

21 January Iran releases the American Embassy hostages after 444 days in captivity

DAILY Mirror

SPECIAL ISSUE

Wednesday, December 10, 1980   12p

JOHN LENNON shot dead in New York Dec 8 1980 DEATH OF A HERO

MURDERED SUPERSTAR: One of the last pictures of ex-Beatle John Lennon, taken in New York three weeks ago.

18 February The government promises more money to the coal mines in order to avert a strike

26 March The 'gang of four' launch the breakaway SDP

30 March An assassination attempt is made on President Reagan

5 May Republican hunger striker Bobby Sands dies in the Maze

13 May Pope John Paul II is shot as he tours St Peter's Square

1981

He was the world's most eligible bachelor. She was the shy young beauty who captivated hearts around the world. Their courtship and marriage were just what the nation needed – romantic, glamorous yet traditional. In those heady days, no one could have foreseen how it would end. Nor did anyone take particularly seriously Charles's fledgling relationship with the coy 19-year-old Lady Diana Spencer when she was first pictured on the front page of the *Daily Mirror*. She was holding a toddler at the London kindergarten where she worked, her legs clearly visible through her skirt. 'I never thought I'd be standing with the light right behind me,' she said later. 'I don't want to be remembered for not having a petticoat.' She wasn't. The *Mirror* enthusiastically urged Prince Charles to put the nation out of its misery and make Diana his bride, ungallantly listing 12 former girlfriends. This time it was different. They had known each other since childhood and holidayed together at Balmoral. Soon

She walked to her Prince and the people gasped in the wake of her beauty

the press were in hot pursuit of her – hotter, probably, than Charles was. Their engagement produced a national gasp of pleasure. But there were warning signs. She was clearly besotted yet when he was asked if he was in love he replied hesitatingly: 'Yes, whatever that is.' Their wedding was eagerly anticipated by a country struggling to escape the tag of 'The sick man of Europe'. If there was one thing left that we did well, it was royalty. And nothing better than a royal wedding. Every detail was planned meticulously and slavishly previewed by the media. The ceremony

was watched by tens of millions around the world. In the *Mirror* John Edwards wrote: 'Diana was a silhouette at the West Door of St Paul's, covered in the white mystery of her veil. Over her head the frosty sparkle of diamonds was a glinting halo and the trumpets laid down a barrage. She walked to her Prince and the people who were there gasped in the wake of her beauty. Her eyes danced with light like the diamonds of her tiara. She was gorgeous.' On the morning of the wedding, the *Mirror*'s editorial had said: 'It has the magic of a prince finding his true princess. It has the charm of a boy falling in love with the girl next door (which, of course, Di once was). It has the power to unite the disunited across the nation and through television the world. Just for today. It is the stuff of which fairy tales are made.' At the wedding ceremony, the Archbishop of Canterbury began his sermon with the words: 'This is the stuff of which fairy tales are made.' He had obviously been reading the *Mirror* for inspiration.

REFLECTIONS

Fifteen years earlier women visited their hairdresser about once a week. Now a hairdresser was lucky to see his regular customers every six weeks, the *Mirror* reported. One High Street hairdresser said: 'I used to know exactly which day it was – and even what time – just by looking at the regular clients in my salon. Not any more.' The reason for the change was the 'natural look' promoted during the hairdressing boom of the 1970s. Complicated back-combing and too much lacquer went out and in came styles that women could easily blow-dry themselves, with hairdressers preaching the virtue of shiny, healthy hair. A beauty expert said: 'Too many women have suffered at the hands of stylists who get carried away and think they are creating a work of art. It may have looked wonderful in the salon but was decidedly out of place in the supermarket later.'

As the Labour Party tore itself apart with internal battles in the early 1980s, the *Mirror* begged, pleaded and raged at it to heal the wounds and fight the Tories instead. A full-page editorial in September 1981, written by chief leader writer Joe Haines, said: 'Tony Benn isn't the answer to Margaret Thatcher. They are both extremists. It's no use replacing an Iron Lady with a Plastic Man. Since the war the *Daily Mirror* has been Labour's staunchest supporter. The party is more than a label on a political organisation. For millions it has been the way to a better life. But it is in danger of losing touch with the people.' Despite the *Mirror*'s best endeavours, things were to get even worse for Labour before its revival under Tony Blair 15 years later.

30 June Shots are fired at the Queen in the Mall

17 September London's role as a major world port ends with the closure of the Royal Docks

21 September The *Mirror* launches its first Bingo game, with a jackpot of £30,000

6 October Egyptian statesman Mohammed Anwar el-Sadat is assassinated

12 November The Church of England's General Synod votes in favour of women priests

SO TENDER: The remembered kiss of a Princess in love on a palace's balcony of kings.

Picture: ALISDAIR MACDONALD

My Princess!

14 December Israel announces plans to annex Syria's Golan Heights, captured in 1973

1982

8 January Spain ends its twelve-year siege of Gibraltar

26 February Unemployment in Britain exceeds three million for the first time since the 1930s

28 February The English cricket team defy a sports boycott of South Africa

28 March Heavy fighting takes place between Iran and Iraq in the Gulf War

1982

It began as a bit of a joke. A group of scrap-metal merchants had landed on the faraway island of South Georgia, it was reported. But it soon became clear this wasn't funny. It was the prelude to a full-scale invasion of the nearby Falkland Islands on April 2 by the military junta which ran Argentina. For many years the Argentines had insisted that the islands, which they called the Malvinas, belonged to their country. As Britain would not give them up, they had seized them by force. Margaret Thatcher, suffering enormous unpopularity after little more than a year in office, had to decide whether to accept the situation or fight back. She chose to fight. Surrender was not in her nature. She ordered the greatest task

The greatest task force assembled since the Second World War set sail

force assembled since the Second World War, to set sail for the islands on the other side of the world – stung as much as anything by knowing that her government knew nine days before the invasion that the Argentines planned to invade the Falklands. The small enemy garrison on South Georgia was soon retaken by Royal Marines. Mrs Thatcher appeared outside Downing Street exclaiming: 'Rejoice! Rejoice!' But this had been the easy part. The battle to reclaim the Falklands was going to be much harder and bloodier. As the *Mirror* said: 'If a major war breaks out it will be over the future of the people of the Falklands – not the penguins of South Georgia.' The paper wanted negotiation not war, fearing that there might be huge loss of life once military action began. Its fears were realised when the Argentine cruiser the *General Belgrano* was sunk by a torpedo from a British submarine. The *Belgrano* had been sailing away from the exclusion zone declared by the British but Mrs Thatcher insisted it had been a danger to our ships. The following day the Argentines struck back. The destroyer HMS *Sheffield* was sunk after being hit by a missile. The *Mirror* said: 'One tragedy begets another. The loss of life is beginning to mount. How much higher will it have to go? It is time to prove that peace through diplomacy is the only policy that pays.' But it was too late. Neither Mrs Thatcher nor General Galtieri was in a mood to compromise.

Eight thousand British troops were landed on the Falklands and fought their way across the islands. When they reached the capital, Port Stanley, the Argentines surrendered. If the fighting had gone on much longer, the British forces would have run out of ammunition. Then Mrs Thatcher would have had to resign and British history would have been very different.

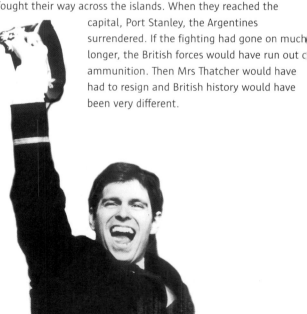

Prince Andrew returns from war

REFLECTIONS

A new breed of people was hailed by the *Mirror* – the Walkmen. 'They never walk alone . . . or skate alone . . . or even cycle alone. They are the people who have hopped on an international craze and now roam the streets wired up to the earphones of Walkman stereo sets.' The craze had astounded experts since the first personal hi-fi was produced in July 1979. Millions had already been sold. But that was not the main pleasure it gave its inventor 'pint-sized Akio Morita, to whom it is a machine to get the world dancing.' Morita, Sony's co-founder, 'believes that it makes people happier and he dreams of his invention spreading everywhere – he even wants disco parties in the jungles.'

'It's a grown-up thing to happen t you,' was Prince Charles's commen when his son and heir was born. Prince William arrived in the worl at 9.03pm on June 21, 1982. Diana had been in labour for 16 hours. A announcement said both were well and the baby 'cried lustily' at birth. The Queen, said to be 'smiling at everyone', heard the news at Buckingham Palace. More than a thousand well-wishers had waited outside St Mary's hospital, Paddington, since early morning. They cheered loudly when they heard the news, waving Union Jack singing 'It's a boy, it's a boy' and shouting 'We want Charlie.' Eventually he stepped out of the hospital, looking rather dazed and with a lipstick smear on his right cheek. He said: 'I can't really say wh he looks like. He's blond, sort of fairish, with blue eyes.' When the crowd yelled 'Give us another one' Charles replied: 'Bloody hell - give us a chance.'

1982

7 July An intruder breaks into the Queen's bedroom at Buckingham Palace

18 September Israel attacks the Palestinian refugee camps of Sabra and Chatila in Beirut

11 October King Henry VIII's ship the *Mary Rose* is lifted from the sea bed after 400 years

29 October Australian Lindy Chamberlain, who claimed her baby was abducted by dingos, is jailed for murder

2 November Channel Four goes on air

DAILY Mirror

Monday, April 26, 1982   14p   ★

TRAINING: Special Boat Squadron men practise a canoe landing.

●Britain takes South Georgia

CRIPPLED: The Argentine submarine Santa Fe which was attacked

●Helicopters hit Argentine sub

●Thatcher talks with the Queen

QUEEN: Seeing Mrs. Thatcher

IT'S WAR
says Argentina

THE ISLAND of South Georgia was back in British hands last night. It was recaptured by Royal Marines who overwhelmed the small Argentine garrison there.

The storming of the South Atlantic island followed an attack by British helicopters on the Argentine submarine Santa Fe.

There were no British casualties, but several of the submarine's crew were wounded and put ashore on South Georgia. Argentina said it had lost three men. Premier

Margaret Thatcher went to Windsor to tell the Queen of the British military action. She will make a Commons statement today.

She does not see the British action as a declaration of war, but Argentine Foreign Minister Costa Mendez yesterday maintained that the country was now "technically at war" with Britain.

The official announcement of the recapture

of South Georgia was given by Defence Secretary John Nott, who emerged from 10 Downing Street with Premier Margaret Thatcher last night to talk to newsmen.

Mrs Thatcher said: "Ladies and gentlemen, the Secretary of State for Defence has just come over to give you some very good news, and I think you'd like to have it at once."

Mr. Nott, looking tired but confident, said:

"British troops landed on South Georgia this afternoon. They have now successfully taken control of Grytviken.

"At 6 pm the white flag was hoisted in Grytviken beside the Argentine flag. Shortly after, the Argentine forces surrendered.

"During the first phase of this operation our helicopters engaged an Argentine submarine, the Santa Fe, off South Georgia.

"The commander of the operation has sent the following message: 'Be pleased to inform Her Majesty that the White Ensign flies alongside the Union Jack in South Georgia. God Save the Queen'."

MIRROR COMMENT and SPECIAL REPORTS: Pages 2, 3, 7, 14 and 15

1984

REFLECTIONS

The battle to allow shops to open on Sundays raged for years. The *Mirror* supported those who wanted to change the law. 'The arguments about whether all shops should be allowed to open on Sundays boil down to one simple question,' it said. 'Is it what the customers want? The answer is equally simple. Yes, it is. There is no rational or spiritual reason why the shops shouldn't open when they want to. Britain is no longer a country which religiously observes the Sabbath. It hasn't done for decades. Small shopkeepers should accept the challenge of Sunday opening, not try to frustrate it. Because the change is now inevitable.' It was almost another decade, though, before the law was changed.

The election of Neil Kinnock as Labour leader in succession to Michael Foot was cautiously welcomed by the *Mirror*. It urged him to end the party's internal divisions and make it electable. Before the party conference in 1984 it said: 'It is time for Labour to face the future again. Its task this week in Blackpool is to start winning the next election. Not to repeat the mistakes which lost the last. Mr Kinnock is determined to present a real alternative to Mrs Thatcher. And he can do it. But only if his party will face the future and not retreat into the past.' Mr Kinnock bravely succeeded in starting the process which led to Tony Blair's unprecedented triumph more than a decade later.

Neil Kinnock

Pickets found themselves faced by row upon row of police in riot gear

Mrs Thatcher had won her war in the Falklands. Now she turned her sights to an enemy closer to home – the unions. The miners had always been the elite of trade unionism and a decade earlier had inflicted humiliating defeat on a former Conservative Prime Minister, Ted Heath. But now Mrs Thatcher had introduced new laws which swung the balance of power away from workers and she was prepared when the miners' militant leader, Arthur Scargill, called a strike, relying on a ballot taken weeks earlier that called for industrial action to prevent pit closures. The union hoped to repeat its tactics of 1972 when mass picketing prevented coal lorries leaving pits. Now pickets found themselves faced by row upon row of police wearing riot gear and determined to get the lorries out. Thatcher had also outlawed secondary picketing – workers in other industries taking action to support strikers – so the miners found themselves alone. The battle was vicious and often bloody, and the *Daily Mirror* found itself disagreeing with both pig-headed leaders. It said: 'The miners' strike is deteriorating into a violence whose scars will be with us for a generation. When Mr Arthur Scargill talks about the miners bringing down the Government he has lost his sense of direction. When the Prime Minister tries to bring down Mr Scargill she is not acting for the benefit of the whole nation. Both are deeply in the wrong.' As the strikers became more frustrated the level of violence increased. The Orgreave coke works near Sheffield saw day after day of pitched battles between 3,000 pickets and 2,000 police. Trip wires were strung across roads to bring down mounted police and telegraph poles cut down to use as battering rams. Booby traps made of barbed wire, steel girders, broken glass and wood studded with nails were set for the police. By the end of 1984, there was only one way the dispute could end yet an NUM special conference voted to carry on the fight. The *Mirror* warned: 'With all the courage and the stupidity of the commanders of the Light Brigade, the leaders of the mineworkers sent the union into the Valley of Death last night. They are on the path to certain disaster. They cannot beat the big guns of the law. Because the law is all of us ... The Light Brigade were gallant beyond measure. But when the dust cleared most of them were dead.' The strike struggled on for another three months. Then, exactly a year after it began, the brave men and the even braver women who had supported them through the bitterest industrial action of the century, marched defiantly together for the last time. Then they went back to work. Scargill had called the strike to prevent the closure of many of the 169 pits. He had warned that the Coal Board's plan was to get the number of pits down to 100. No one believed him. It couldn't happen in a country built on massive coal deposits. But within twenty years there were less than thirty coal pits remaining. The UK mining industry had been utterly destroyed

DAILY Mirror

Wednesday, May 30, 1984   17p   ★

Bloodiest day yet in the pit dispute

ENGLAND, 1984

TWO SIDES Arthur Scargill walks towards a line of riot police. Picture ROY SABINE.

INJURED An ambulanceman in riot gear (right) helps an injured policeman.

A UNION leader faces a line of policemen dressed in riot gear and carrying shields. This is the face of industrial relations in Britain today.

Riot police were used for the first time yesterday against 7,000 striking miners and their president Arthur Scargill.

The pickets were trying to stop coke being taken from the Orgreave plant near Sheffield to British Steel's works at Scunthorpe.

They were met by 1,700 police from 13 forces. Their job was to uphold the law and make sure the lorries got through.

The result was a battle that lasted more than an hour. Forty-one police and 28 pickets were hurt. Eighty-one miners were arrested. Even the ambulance men wore riot gear for the first time as smoke bombs, missiles and nails were thrown.

It was a savage day, a bloody day . . . but as the miners become more determined and the police better equipped to stop them, there were few signs that yesterday's bitter battle was the last.

.. now even ambulance men have to wear riot gear

SEE PAGE TWO

---

14 February Ice skaters Jayne Torvill and Christopher Dean are Olympic Gold medallists

5 March Scientists warn of a 'Greenhouse Effect' caused by carbon monoxide pollution

22 April PC Yvonne Fletcher is shot dead outside the Libyan Embassy in London

23 April The discovery of the AIDS virus is announced in Washington

19 May Poet Laureate Sir John Betjeman dies

1984

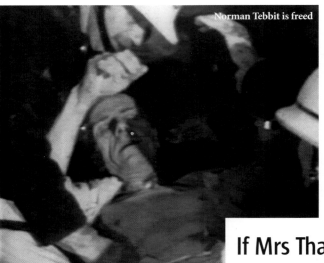

Norman Tebbit is freed

REFLECTIONS

On July 13, 1984 – Friday the thirteenth – Robert Maxwell bought the *Mirror*. The flamboyant publisher and former Labour MP took the paper by storm, appearing in TV adverts himself and insisting that his picture and stories about himself should regularly appear on the front page. In his first months he tried to solve the miners' strike and boasted that he had sorted out the union problems which bedevilled Fleet Street. He jetted around the world hob-nobbing with international leaders, some of them deeply unsavoury. After seven turbulent years, Maxwell died mysteriously off his yacht. He was buried on the Mount of Olives and Israel's President gave his funeral oration. Days later it was discovered that Maxwell had plundered £526 million from his employees' pension funds.

Robert Maxwell

If Mrs Thatcher had been in her bathroom she might have been killed

It was just before three o'clock in the morning. Margaret Thatcher was alone in the sitting room of her suite in Brighton's luxurious Grand Hotel, putting the finishing touches to the speech she would deliver in a few hours to the Tory conference. Then came the blast that was designed to commit the greatest atrocity there had ever been against a British government. A bomb tore through the hotel, bringing part of it crashing down from the roof through the six-storey building. If Mrs Thatcher had been in her bathroom, she might have been killed. The bomb had been planted by the IRA in an attempt to kill the Prime Minister and as many of her Cabinet as possible. They failed in that, although four people, including one MP, died in the most audacious terrorist attack this country had seen. Mrs Thatcher was quickly taken out of the hotel as rescuers struggled to save those trapped in the rubble. Breakfast television viewers saw her close ally, Norman Tebbit, being pulled out on a stretcher. His wife was paralysed in the atrocity. The conference somehow still managed to open precisely on time at 9.30am. Ironically, the first debate was on Northern Ireland. Then Mrs Thatcher made her speech. In it she said: 'The bomb attack was an attempt to cripple Her Majesty's democratically elected government. That is the scale of the outrage in which we have all shared. And the fact that we are gathered here now, shocked but composed and determined, is a sign not only that this attack has failed, but that all attempts to destroy democracy by terrorism will fail.' The IRA's cynical message to the government was: 'Today we were unlucky but you will have to be lucky always.' After delivering her speech, Mrs Thatcher visited the wounded in hospital. She later wrote: 'Norman Tebbit regained consciousness while I was at the hospital and we managed a few words. His face was bloated as a result of being trapped for so long under the rubble. I scarcely recognised him. I also talked to Margaret Tebbit who was in the intensive care unit. She told me she had no feeling below the neck. As a former nurse, she knew well enough what that meant.' The *Mirror* lamented the lack of security at the conference. Anyone could walk into the hotel and searches of bags were lax, it said. That was a lesson the police were quick to learn. Ever since, party conferences have been surrounded by the tightest security.

1984

9 July York Minster is devastated by fire after being struck by lightning

20 September Forty die when an Islamic suicide bomber attacks the US Embassy in Beirut

31 October Indian Prime Minister Indira Gandhi is assassinated by her bodyguards

10 December A gas leak at Bhopal, India kills 2,000 people

1985

6 March The miners return to work after a year on strike

MURDER

DAILY Mirror

FORWARD WITH BRITAIN

Saturday, October 13, 1984

★ 16p

A DEVASTATED building, a wounded policeman and a grieving Prime Minister...three images of an outrage that shocked the nation yesterday.

An IRA bomb, which went off without warning, wrecked Brighton's Grand Hotel where leading Tories were staying for their conference. The explosion killed two people and injured thirty. Two others were still missing last night. Mrs. Thatcher

escaped unhurt but looked shaken as she stood, eyes closed, for two minutes' silence at the conference. And during a debate on Northern Ireland she seemed near to tears.

The Provisional IRA admitted responsibility for the bombing. They said they wanted to wipe out the British Cabinet and added: "Today we were unlucky but YOU will have to be lucky always."

THE IRA SAID YESTERDAY:
❛Today we were unlucky, but remember we have only to be lucky once❜

---

11 March Mikhail Gorbachev is elected head of the Soviet Communist Party

11 May Forty die when a fire breaks out at Bradford City football ground

28 May Tens of thousands are killed by a tidal wave and cyclone in Bangladesh

10 July The Greenpeace ship *Rainbow Warrior* is bombed in New Zealand

15 November The governments of Britain and Ireland sign a historic Agreement over Ulster

1985

It began with a report by the BBC's Michael Buerk into the starving millions in Ethiopia. It turned into the greatest rock event the world has ever seen. The plight of the Ethiopians fired the nation's sympathy – and the imagination of Bob Geldof. First he persuaded a phalanx of stars to record 'Don't They Know It's Christmas', the most successful British single of all time. Not content with that, he began to plan two massive, simultaneous concerts, one on each side of the Atlantic. It was to be called Live Aid. The list of stars who performed was the ultimate Who's Who of rock. The tens of thousands lucky enough to see the gigs live on a perfect July night were dwarfed by the countless millions who watched on television, exhorted by Geldof between acts to 'Give us your f****** money!' They did. £40 million was raised that night. The *Mirror*'s John Blake wrote of the Wembley concert: 'So often tawdry greed and silly tantrums tend to mar huge rock events. But here, for the first time, were most of rock's aristocrats singing their hearts out with just one motive – to help to save a nation from hideous and ugly death. There were many special moments. But for me the most extraordinary point came when all 72,000 people at Wembley started dancing and singing along to the Beach Boys as their show was beamed in via satellite from Philadelphia. It was a spine-tingling and eerie moment, two nations in perfect harmony via the miracle of modern technology. To realise that at that moment they were almost certainly dancing to "California Girls" in Australia, Russia and just about everywhere else in the world was awesome.' The *Mirror*'s editorial said: 'It deserved to be called the Greatest Show on Earth because it was. Yet it was not so much the spectacle that mattered but the purpose. Hundreds of musicians from a profession too often rocked by scandal were united in the most exhilarating and moving act of

REFLECTIONS

Under the headline 'The Final Shame', The *Mirror* told how 42 football fans, mostly Italians, died during a riot at the Heysel stadium in Brussels before the European Cup final between Liverpool and Juventus. The supporters were killed when a wall collapsed as thugs went on the rampage attacking each other with iron bars and hurling molotov cocktails. An editorial called for British clubs to be banned from European competitions. It added: 'We gave football to the world. Now the so-called Liverpool fans give it our national disgrace. No excuses can wipe away the blood that was spilled last night.' The violence was largely blamed on National Front yobs from London who had hijacked the event and whipped Liverpool fans into a vicious frenzy. A Belgian fire chief branded the thugs murderers. English clubs were later banned from Europe.

The terrible scourge of Aids presented newspapers with a real challenge. They needed to play their part in warning people of the danger while not causing blind panic. The news in July 1985 that Hollywood heart-throb Rock Hudson had Aids was a double shock, as his fans didn't realise he was gay. The following year the *Mirror* ran the moving diary of actor Douglas Lambert's fight against the 'plague of the eighties.' It was, said the paper, a grim warning to the world about the countless lives yet to be lost. Lambert said: 'It is touching everybody. It's just going to be horrific. I'm truly glad I'm not going to be around because I could not face one after another of my friends going through what I'm going through.'

Geldof pleads for your money

Singing their hearts out with just one motive – to save a nation from hideous death

charity we have ever seen. Nightly TV bulletins have shown the horror of dying children, bundles of skin and bone covered in flies. Those puny bodies touched the conscience of the world. Live Aid rose above governments. It was a declaration by young people everywhere that something has to be done. Live Aid has shown the way. If governments will now act with the same generosity and enthusiasm, there may be a happy future, after all, for the victims of famine.'

1985

19 November Presidents Reagan and Gorbachev hold a summit in Geneva

1986

14 January Cabinet Minister Michael Heseltine resigns over the 'Westland Affair'

25 February President Ferdinand Marcos is overthrown in the Philippines

31 March The Greater London Council is abolished

15 April America launches an air strike against Libya

THE Mirror

Monday, July 15, 1985   **FORWARD WITH BRITAIN**

★ 18p
CHANNEL ISLANDS 19p

SOUVENIR ISSUE

LIVE AID

ROCKED WITH LOVE

30 April A fire breaks out at the Chernobyl nuclear reactor in the USSR

3 May Tamil separatists escalate their campaign of violence in Sri Lanka

29 June Diego Maradona's 'hand of god' helps Argentina to beat England in the Mexican World Cup

11 July The British government attempts to ban the publication of the memoirs of former MI5 officer Peter Wright

23 July Prince Andrew and Sarah Ferguson are married

1986

The flight of the space shuttle Challenger on January 28, 1986, was considered to be routine, so frequent were these voyages out of the Earth's orbit. The only unusual element was that on board was the first civilian to travel into space, teacher Christa McAuliffe. But 72 seconds after lift-off Challenger exploded in a gigantic fireball, killing all seven astronauts instantly. These were the first space fatalities suffered by the Americans and the shock to the nation was intense. Around the world, millions watched countless reruns of those 72 seconds, the small streak heading higher and higher, and then disintegrating 'into a spiky ball of flame, rolling around the skies forming bizarre jagged shapes, the vast white cloud finally turning itself into a caricature that looked like some tragic, dying swan etched vividly against the brilliant blue,' as the Mirror's Paul Callan wrote. In a school room in New Hampshire, Christa McAuliffe's pupils had been watching Challenger's take-off on TV. There were gasps when they realised something had gone wrong. A teacher said: 'There was silence and shock. Then came the tears.' In an emotional broadcast to the American people, President Reagan said of the astronauts: 'They touched the face of God. Nancy and I are pained to the core. But it is part of taking a chance on expanding man's frontiers. Exploration belongs to the brave.' Challenger had been six days late in blasting off from Cape Canaveral after a series of hitches. Overnight temperatures had plunged to minus 4C and the wind chill at the top of the launch tower had reached minus 23C. Icicles formed on the launch pad. There was electrical trouble with key safety equipment. Yet when she did launch, all seemed to be going well. Mission control sent the message: 'Challenger, go with throttle up,' the order to switch to full power. Commander Dick Scobee, the craft's captain, replied: 'Roger, go with throttle up.' They were his last words. Christa McAuliffe's parents were watching from a VIP site near the launch pad. They hugged each other and sobbed as the fireball turned into vapour streams streaking through the sky as debris fell back to earth and into the Atlantic. White House spokesman Larry Speakes, pale with emotion, said: 'This will not deter the United States from continuing their exploration in space.' But there was mounting concern that the shuttle programme was under considerable pressure. When Challenger blew up, there were 13 other shuttle ready to go. NASA had to keep the programme moving fast to persuade the politicians who held the purse strings that the huge funds needed for space exploration should continue to roll in.

REFLECTIONS

The Car ferry the *Herald of Free Enterprise* capsized as it left Zeebrugge port in Belgium. The *Mirror* reported: 'Twenty-nine people were killed and hopes were fading fast for 240 more missing after a British ferry sank off the Belgian coast. At least 40 divers were still searching for any survivors trapped in pockets of air beneath the waves. Coastguards said there was a slim possibility there might be enough air inside the ship for people to survive, but it was a slim one.' It was indeed – 189 people lost their lives that day. Most of the passengers were Britons on a day trip to Belgium. The Townsend Thoresen ferry had set sail with its bow doors open and when it hit a pier and turned over, water was allowed to gush into the lower decks which contained the vehicles.

One summer morning in the quiet Berkshire town of Hungerford, madman Michael Ryan went on a gun rampage, shooting anything that moved. The loner killed 14 people and injured 16 before shooting himself dead in the grounds of a school. A front-page picture showed a stunned policeman cradling in his arms a distraught young girl whose father had just been killed by Ryan. The *Mirror* said: 'This was the tragic aftermath of yesterday's Hungerford massacre.'

A spiky ball of flame rolling around the skies forming bizarre jagged shapes

Astronaut Christa

NASA CHRISTA

27 August South African police fire on rioting crowds in Soweto

17 September An Arab terrorist attack on a Parisian shopping centre shocks France

21 December Chinese students demonstrate for democratic reforms

29 January President Gorbachev begins reforms named 'Perestroika' and 'Glasnost'

12 June Mrs Thatcher wins a third term in power with a huge majority

1986

1987

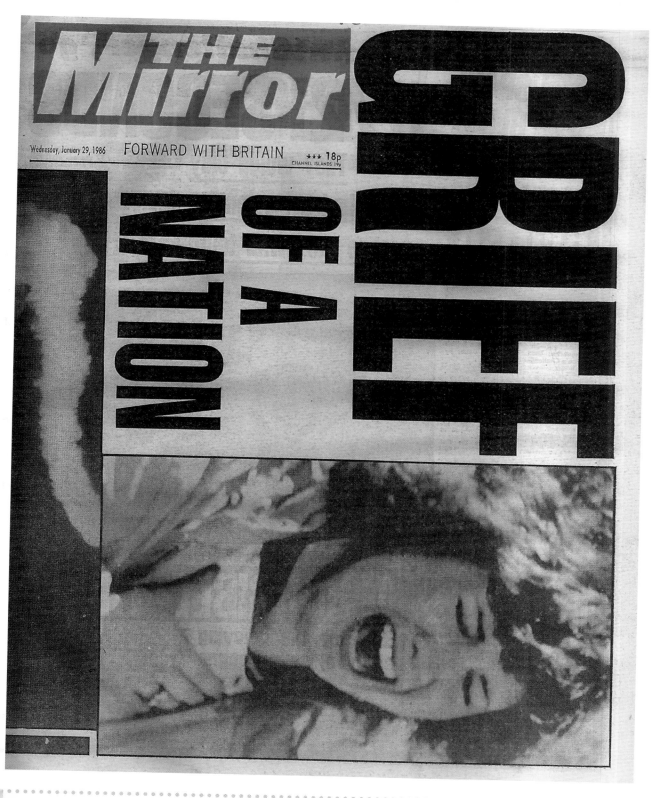

THE Mirror

Wednesday, January 29, 1986   FORWARD WITH BRITAIN   ★★★ 18p
CHANNEL ISLANDS 19p

GRIEF OF A NATION

---

17 July National Security Adviser John Poindexter reveals that money from arms sales to Iran was used to support Nicaraguan rebels

16 September An international agreement is signed to protect the ozone layer

16 October Britain suffers its worst storm of the century

18 November Thirty are killed by a fire at King's Cross station

1988

5 February The first Comic Relief Red Nose day raises millions for charity

1989

For 28 years it had stood as a symbol of division and oppression. The Berlin Wall had been built when the Cold War was at its height, an ugly, brutal landmark keeping apart the people of East and West of the former German capital, and a constant reminder of the threat of war between the Communist bloc and America and its European allies. When any of the Soviet satellite states had attempted to move towards freedom, their efforts had been ruthlessly suppressed. But now a wind of change was blowing, and the election of Mikhail Gorbachev as Russian leader turned it to a storm. The few reforms which were offered started a stampede. Then, on November 10, East Berliners took their future into their hands. They climbed on the hated wall and began to tear it down. They were joined by West Berliners, united in their determination to rid their city of the wall that had kept them apart for so long. The East German authorities, realising resistance was hopeless, sent in bulldozers to smash great holes in the wall. And the people of the East poured through joyously to the West. The *Mirror* said: 'There's been no joy like it in Europe since VE-Day. The faces of the East Berliners crossing into the

The faces of the East Berliners tell the whole story

REFLECTIONS

The image of a solitary student halting a line of tanks in Beijing's Tiananmen Square as the Chinese People's Army moved in to crush mass protests against the government was described by US President George Bush Snr as a 'symbol of defiance the world will never forget.' Hundreds of students are believed to have been killed in the massacre. Raging at the 'rape of Peking', the *Mirror* reported that up to 7,000 more pro-democracy protesters died in Shanghai and other cities with children as young as three slaughtered mercilessly and corpses burned with flame-throwers. Damned by the world, China was unrepentant and crushed all dissent. But in the years to come more freedoms were introduced. The sacrifice of Tiananmen Square was not totally in vain.

Margaret Thatcher had a clever way of making the privatisation of state industries widely popular. She encouraged small investors to take a stake in the new firms, with the enticing prospect of big profits. It worked. In November 1986 the *Mirror*, which opposed privatisation, reported: 'Six million people want to get in on the great British Gas sale. They have asked for information about the £6,000 million worth of shares to go on offer. Small investors will be able to get in on the ground floor with an investment of only £50. All 16 million British Gas customers will be treated as priority applicants and will receive at least 200 shares if they apply for them.' The privatisation was enormously successful, making a fortune for the Government and its City advisers – but not for the small investors.

Ceaucescu

West tell the whole story. The end of the Berlin Wall could be the end of the fear which has haunted our continent for more than 40 years.' The paper had no doubt that the destruction of the wall would lead to the re-unification of Germany – 'though how soon that will take place is anyone's guess. It might be ten years or more.' The Russians were quick to insist that, despite the end of the Berlin Wall, they would not allow a reunited Germany: 'The Soviet Union would not tolerate the elimination of the border between the two. It would not suit any government in Europe – it would not be in anyone's interests.' Margaret Thatcher, while delighted that the wall had been torn down, warned that the idea of German reunification was 'going much too fast.' But the rush to freedom could not be held back. Two weeks later, the Communist chains which had bound the people of Czechoslovakia for 22 years were sundered and their former leader Alexander Dubcek swept to power. A month after that, the hated Romanian dictator, Nicolae Ceaucescu, 'the Butcher of Bucharest', was shot by a firing squad and his country was set free. Within weeks, Germany was reunited and the days of the Soviet Empire were over.

---

7 March Three members of the IRA are shot dead by the SAS in Gibraltar

19 March Two British soldiers are murdered at an IRA funeral

6 July An explosion and fire erupt at the Piper Alpha oil rig in the North Sea

8 August The Iran-Iraq War ends after eight years

13 October The Turin Shroud is revealed as a fake

DAILY Mirror

Saturday, November 11, 1989 **COLOUR NEWSPAPER OF THE YEAR** (INCORPORATING THE DAILY RECORD) National Sale: 3,880,547 22p

REUNITED: Joy of two women no longer separated by the Berlin Wall

TOGETHER AT LAST

West helps East to freedom over the Berlin Wall. . .and last night bulldozers were opening up more crossings in it.

on the day the world became a better, braver, place . .

FREEDOM HOLES BULLDOZED IN THE WALL - Pages 2, 3, 6 and 7

1990

Tony Blair

REFLECTIONS

'**Floods, hurricanes and droughts** plague Britain as global warming increases', the *Mirror* warned. At the time, few of the general public were aware of the threat posed by the build-up of greenhouse gases, principally carbon dioxide, and the damage to the ozone layer which protects Earth from damaging ultra-violet rays. 'A one degree temperature rise would be a major catastrophe,' said the paper. Since then the country has indeed been ravaged by downpours, gales and droughts but more alarming forecasts of melting polar ice caps, London under water and plagues of mosquitoes have yet, thankfully, to take place. Some things never change; the *Mirror* noted that President George Bush was refusing to take action to cut emissions for a decade just as his son, when President, refused to abide by the Kyoto agreement.

Gordon Brown

'**Labour's Young Guns took the** party conference by storm yesterday,' wrote political editor Alastair Campbell in October 1990. He singled out three rising stars from Labour's front bench – employment spokesman Tony Blair; Gordon Brown, trade; and Jack Straw, education. 'Their speeches showed off the emerging A-team of young Shadow ministers Labour leader Neil Kinnock hopes to present as an exciting alternative to the current Tory Cabinet. Mr Blair is just 36, Mr Brown is 38 and Mr Straw is 44.' Little more thab six years later, these three would hold the highest offices of state.

Nelson Mandela was a different kind of revolutionary. Like Gandhi India half a century before, he got his strength from peaceful persuasion. He was locked up by South Africa's apartheid government because they claimed he was a danger. But that mad him a far greater threat to their violent, racist regime. He became symbol throughout the world for those who fought for South Afric to become a democratic state, with a vote for every black and an end to their humiliation by the white minority. Throughout his 27 years in captivity, Mandela never complained, never begged to be released. His inner peace and strength was an inspiration. When the level of protest against apartheid reached fever pitch early in 1990, the authorities took a gamble and decided to release Mande by then 71 years old, hoping he might stop the demonstrations. (February 11, with the world watching on television, Nelson Mande emerged into the sweet air of freedom . . . and raised his fist in triumph. As he came out into the blazing 90-degree heat, he blinke at the battery of cameras waiting to show the world its first glimp

I stand here before you not as a prophet but as a humble servant

of Mandela as a free man. Hand in hand with his wife Winnie, he walked among the waiting crowd, many of whom were not born when he was first imprisoned. If the government thought he wou now disappear from public sight, they could not have been more wrong. Twenty-seven years in jail had changed nothing. He immediately repeated the plea he had made at his trial, for a free society: 'It is an ideal which I hope to live for and to achieve. But needs be, it is an ideal for which I am prepared to die.' He pledged that the armed struggle to end apartheid would go on and said that the economic sanctions imposed against the apartheid regim should not be lifted. As he was driven in triumph to Cape Town, tens of thousands lined the dusty roads through the Cape vineyar When he arrived he addressed the cheering crowds: 'I stand here before you not as a prophet but as a humble servant of you, the people. Your heroic sacrifices have made it possible for me to be here today. The majority of South Africans, black and white, recognise that apartheid has no future. There must be an end to white monopoly and political power. We can no longer wait.' His release signalled that the waiting was almost over. Democracy soc came to South Africa and its first black President was elected. His name, of course, was Nelson Mandela.

1989

15 April 95 football fans die at the Hillsborough stadium in Liverpool

19 October The Guildford Four are freed after fourteen years

3 December The Superpowers declare an end to the Cold War

31 December Romania's leader Ceaucescu is executed by firing squad

1990

22 January The Soviet army crushes a separati rebellion in Azerbaijan

DAILY Mirror

Monday, February 12, 1990   COLOUR NEWSPAPER OF THE YEAR

Saturday's est. sale: 3,935,129
(INCORPORATING THE DAILY RECORD)   22p

DOWN AND OUT

WHERE AM I? Tyson hits the canvas after his sensational KO

MOMENT OF TRIUMPH: Mandela leaves prison yesterday. He vowed that the armed struggle would go on

Tyson is knocked cold – but who's the world champ?

THIS was the moment when "invincible" Mike Tyson's world turned upside down.

The dazed heavyweight champ crawls around on all fours, gumshield hanging out, after being sensationally knocked out by James "Buster" Douglas.

But Tyson caused an even bigger upset when he got to his feet in Tokyo yesterday.

Iron Mike, who gave Nelson Mandela a pair of boxing gloves for his 70th birthday, bounced back with a political KO. He had Douglas stripped of the title, claiming the referee had robbed him of a knockout two rounds earlier.

Tyson, who floored the challenger in the eighth, maintained that Douglas was down longer than 10 seconds because the referee started the count four seconds late.

Yesterday, with no-one holding the title, both boxers were awaiting the outcome of an inquiry.

● Fight Special: Pages 26 – 28

DEFIANT MANDELA'S SALUTE TO FREEDOM

NELSON Mandela emerged into the sweet air of freedom after 27 years yesterday ... and raised his fist in triumph.

He was due to leave his prison outside Cape Town at 1pm our time. But he kept history waiting for an extra 75 minutes as he shared tender private moments with his family.

Then Mandela, 71, and 55-year-old wife Winnie walked hand in hand among the waiting crowd. The man who had become a symbol of hope to his people, most of whom had never

From JOHN JACKSON in Cape Town

even seen him before, was ready to play his part in reshaping the destiny of South Africa.

First he had to face the chilling reality of his country today. Within hours police opened fire on a section of the 200,000-strong crowd waiting to welcome him in Cape Town.

One youth was reported killed and

up to 200 were wounded. But many have given their lives or freedom in the long struggle to free Mandela. He paid tribute to them all when he addressed the crowd. And he repeated the plea for a free society he made at his trial 27 years ago: "It is an ideal which I hope to live for and to achieve. But if needs be, it is an ideal for which I am prepared to die."

Mandela also sounded this ominous warning: "We have no option but to continue the armed struggle which we began in 1960."

INTO THE CAULDRON — See Pages 2, 3 and 4

---

14 February British mortgage rates rise to 15.4%

23 February British ambulance workers end a six-month long dispute

1 April Inmates at Strangeways, in Manchester, run riot over prison conditions

9 April The first free elections in Hungary end years of Communist rule

11 April A 'supergun' headed for Iraq is seized by British customs officials

1990

REFLECTIONS

As the winds of freedom swept through Eastern Europe in 1990 following the collapse of the Berlin Wall 200,000 Russians marched on the Kremlin demanding an end to more than 70 years of Communist rule. Amazingly, their demo had the full backing of Russian reformist leader Mikhail Gorbachev. Six years earlier, shortly before 'Gorby' succeeded ailing President Chernenko, the *Mirror* said: 'He is different. He is urbane, bright and even witty. And where most Soviet leaders can barely muster an evening class diploma he has two university degrees.' For five years Gorbachev piloted the Soviet Union through the Glasnost (Openness) Revolution, struggling to transform its monolithic economic and political structures and smoothing relationships with the West. In 1991 Gorbachev survived a right-wing coup but was later forced to stand down in the face of demands for even further reform.

Gorbachev with wife Raisa

This was the picture even her most bitter enemies thought they would never see: Margaret Thatcher, the Iron Lady, leaving No. Downing Street for the last time after 11 years as Prime Ministe She had not only been the first female Premier; she had change the country forever. She was a woman on a mission, determine to force through her vision of how things ought to be. She had won almost every battle she fought. She would never take 'No' an answer and never accept defeat; certainly not gracefully. So her reign went on and on, opposition to her within her own Cabinet grew. She got rid of the mercurial Michael Heseltine. Sh got rid of her successful Chancellor Nigel Lawson. Finally she go rid of her deputy prime minister, Sir Geoffrey Howe. It was a humiliation too far. To a stunned House of Commons, the mild-

The photographers lining Downing Street put down their cameras and applauded

mannered Sir Geoffrey made the most brutal resignation speech completely undermining Mrs Thatcher. Describing how she had treated Mr Lawson and himself before a vital European conference, he said: 'It's rather like sending in your opening batsmen only for them to find that their bats have been broken the team captain.' That was the starting pistol for a leadership challenge by Michael Heseltine. Mrs Thatcher won the first rour but not by enough votes to give her outright victory. She heard the result while at the British Embassy in Paris, storming down the steps and brushing aside the BBC's John Sargeant to declare 'We fight on.' It had gone too far for that. The next day, back at Westminster, she called each member of her Cabinet in one by one. And one by one they told her it was time to go. The Iron La was finally beaten. Only her devoted husband Denis raged at the 'traitors' and urged her to stay. But on November 22, 1990, Margaret Thatcher announced to a stunned nation that she wou be standing down. Her exit from Downing Street was a tearful affair. But only the *Daily Mirror* captured the historic moment. A her car moved away from No. 10, the photographers lining the road put down their cameras and applauded. With one exception the *Mirror*'s Ken Lennox, who captured one of the most famous and poignant images of the late 20th century.

---

30 May France bans British beef in fears over BSE

26 June European Commission President Jacques Delors promises a single currency

19 July Two British teenage girls are arrested in Thailand for drug smuggling

30 July Conservative MP Ian Gow is murdered by an IRA car bomb

28 August Three Guinness executives are found guilty of massive fraud and jailed

DAILY Mirror

Thursday, November 29, 1990 BRITAIN'S TOP COLOUR NEWSPAPER Sale w/e November 10: 3,820,329 (INCORPORATING THE DAILY RECORD) 25p

Sad Thatcher's final farewell to No 10

TEARS IN THE BACK SEAT

MARGARET Thatcher weeps as she leaves the base of all her power – the "flat over the shop" at No 10 Downing Street. The Iron Lady's eyes filled with tears, and she bit her lip, as she hunched forward in her car yesterday for one last look at home.

Then, with faithful Denis at her side, she settled down to her new role as a back seat driver. The outgoing Premier had kept her composure as she spoke outside No 10 of "11½ wonderfully happy years." But the bitter ending quickly followed.

EXCLUSIVE picture by KEN LENNOX

● Hello, No 11 — Page 4

● **JOBS FOR THE BOYS** Page 2 ● **THE NEW BOY** Pages 3, 4, 5, 6 and 7

---

14 September Inflation rises to 10.6% as the British economy slides into recession

5 October Germany is united

12 November Japan enthrones its new Emperor Akihito

1991

7 February A mortar bomb hits Downing Street

14 March The Appeal Court quashes the convictions of the Birmingham Six

1991

For ten years Saddam Hussein's Iraq had been backed by the West as it fought with Iran. But that support disappeared the moment Iraqi forces invaded neighbouring Kuwait in the autumn of 1990. The United Nations ordered Saddam to get out. He refused. President George Bush, spurred on by Mrs Thatcher, who was then still Prime Minister, began to assemble a remarkable international coalition pledged to drive

THE NATIONAL LOTTERY

THE ESTIMATED JACKPOT FOR
SAT 12AUG2000 IS £7 MILLION

222-08291838-08568

A. 01 02 03 04 05 06

SAT12 AUG.00
FOR 01 SAT DRAW
828385   £ 1.00
RET NO. 209956
222-08291838-08568
FILL BOX TO VOID

REFLECTIONS

In November 1994, lottery fever swept the country as the first draw in the great new national game approached. The jackpot could hit £10 million, the *Mirror* reported, with sales expected to reach £70 million. 'Queues at the 10,000 outlets could leave many disappointed customers with no tickets,' the paper warned. Camelot communications boss David Rigg enthused: 'The response has been astonishing.' The draw was expected to pull in Britain's biggest-ever TV audience of 30 million. The *Mirror* was desperate to find the winner of the first jackpot and offered a £10,000 reward to anyone who would reveal his name. There were seven jackpot winners the first week, each picking up £839,254. One of them was retired miner George Snell, from North London, who celebrated by having his normal Sunday night pint.

The poll tax - officially called the Community Charge - was introduced by Margaret Thatcher a new tax on every home. It was attacked for its unfairness and led the biggest riots in Britain since the Peasants' Revolt of 1381 - which was also over a poll tax, as the *Mirror* helpfully pointed out. The idea behind the charge was that if everyone had to pay equally towards local government, they would insist that councils spent their money wisely. But the opposite happened. Councils used the abolition of the rates to wildly increase their expenditure. Tens of thousands rebelled and refused to pay. Its unpopularity provided a focus for ministers determined to bring down Mrs Thatcher. After she went, one John Major's first moves was to announce that the hated tax would be abolished.

A multi-pronged offensive rocked the Iraqis with its speed and ferocity

out the Iraqis if they did not leave voluntarily. An ultimatum was given and when Saddam ignored the deadline, as he had ignored every plea and threat, war began. On the night of January 17, 1991, 600 warplanes, including British Tornadoes, launched Operation Desert Storm, a ferocious attack on Baghdad and Kuwait. Hundreds of bombs fell around the Iraqi capital in a few hours. The Allies' main targets were airfields as well as nuclear, chemical and biological plants. Oil refineries and gas stations were hit by cruise missiles and bombs from high-flying B-52 bombers. In this most modern war, four giant air-to-air tankers refuelled US fighter jets guarding the B-52s. This massive aerial bombardment went on for a month – and then the troops moved in. The *Mirror* reported on February 25: 'Allied forces were fighting for Kuwait City last night after Saddam Hussein's Iraqi invaders were taken by storm in a devastating ground attack. A multi-pronged offensive rocked the Iraqis with its speed and ferocity. As US and Arab tanks thundered north from the Saudi border, marines swept along the coast towards Kuwait City and paratroopers dropped from the sky to back them up. To the west, Britain's Desert Rats joined the US

Cavalry and French Foreign Legion in a push to battle Saddam's elite Republican Guard. A fleet of 300 helicopters – the biggest in history – airlifted 2,000 soldiers and howitzers deep into Iraq to cut their supply lines. John Major, who had taken over from Mrs Thatcher, said with typical understatement: 'Things seem to be going very well indeed.' Fifteen hours after the Allied ground attack began, it was all over. 'Saddam Hussein caved in last night and ordered his troops to withdraw from Kuwait. His once mighty army was on the run after being humiliated by devastating Allied attacks. Large numbers of Iraqi tanks, trucks and equipment were seen heading north out of Kuwait reported CNN, quoting aides of President Bush. Saddam's prized Republican Guard were also fleeing toward Basra, Iraq's second city, after breaking off a battle with Britain's Desert Rats.' But as a legacy of his invasion Saddam ordered all the oil fields to be torched. The triumphant Allies could have pursued the Iraqi despot and finally disposed of him and the threat he continued to pose. But President Bush and Mr Major, without Mrs Thatcher's bulldog belligerence, called a halt to the military action. The consequences of that decision were still being felt twelve years later, not least by Mr Bush's son, President George W. Bush.

1991

29 June Serbia tries to suppress bids for independence in Slovenia and Croatia

8 August British hostage John McCarthy is released after 5 years in Beirut

31 December An attempted coup against Mikhail Gorbachev fails, but the Soviet Union disintegrates

1992

28 April Rebel Moslem leader Ahmed Shah Masood occupies Kabul, Afghanistan

2 May The acquittal of the policemen accused of assaulting Rodney King sparks riots across Los Angeles

DAILY Mirror

Thursday, January 17, 1991   NEWSPAPER FOR THE NINETIES   Average November sale 3,820,577 (INCORPORATING THE DAILY RECORD)   25p

600 jets attack Saddam

WAR

AIR STRIKE: America unleashed its fighter-bombers and cruise missiles for a devastating attack on Iraq last night. RAF jets were also involved

Bombers hit Baghdad in Operation Desert Storm

WAR with Iraq erupted last night with repeated air raids on Baghdad and Kuwait.

Six hundred warplanes, including British Tornadoes, launched a ferocious attack on the Iraqi capital and other key targets.

The Allied offensive to kick Sad-

From BILL AKASS in Saudi, STEWART DICKSON in Washington and DAVID LEIGH in London

dam Hussein out of Kuwait was under way with a vengeance.

Hundreds of bombs fell around Baghdad during the first few hours of the attack.

The Allies main targets were airfields as well as the nuclear, chemical and biological plants around Iraq which the allies were always determined to smash.

Oil refineries, gas stations and targets were also hit by cruise missiles and bombs from high-flying B-52 bombers.

Above Iraq four giant

US air-to-air fuel tankers re-fuelled the US fighter jets guarding the giant B-52s and other US planes as they dropped their massive loads of bombs.

Iraqi anti-aircraft guns blasted the skies as the first wave of bombings rained down on the city.

A White House spokesman said: "I can tell you it was a swift and massive attack."

An American TV reporter in Baghdad added: "There was a sound of gunfire as bullets fired into the air.

"The initial attack

■ **Turn to Page 2**

1992

By any standards, 1992 was a horrible year for the Windsors – or, in the Queen's own words, it had been an 'annus horribilis'. Hardly a month went by when the royal family was not torn by heartbreak or scandal. James Whitaker wrote: 'In 25 years as a royal reporter I have never known anything like it.' It began when intimate photos of the Duchess of York with a Texan millionaire were found. Two months later, the Palace announced that Fergie and Andrew were to separate. Within weeks, the marriage of Princess Anne and Captain Mark Philips ended in divorce. Through these difficult months, there was growing speculation about Charles and Diana. It was obvious that their marriage was no longer a fairytale. In June

Fire devastated Windsor Castle

In 25 years as a royal reporter I have never known anything like it

the book *Diana: Her True Story* came out, revealing the devastating truth about their relationship. Although at first the Palace tried to ridicule it, later it was learned that Diana herself had collaborated with author Andrew Morton. In August the *Mirror* published extraordinary photos of Fergie frolicking in the South of France with her financial adviser, John Bryan, in what came to be called the 'toe-sucking' pictures. Then came a series of revelations about Charles and Diana. There were the 'Squidgy' tapes of a late-night phone call between the Princess and James Gilbey. These were quickly followed

by the *Mirror*'s sensational revelation that Charles and Camilla Parker-Bowles had been having an affair for a decade, with the release of another tape: this one revealing one of their highly embarrassing late-night conversations. Far from being a fairytale, the relationship between the Princ and Princess of Wales had been exposed as a sham. As if all that wasn't enough for one woman to bear, on November 20 the Queen's beloved Windsor Castle was engulfed by fire. She watched in tears as Prince Andrew led rescue attempting to salvage art treasures. No wonder Her Majesty called her 'annus horribilis' in a speech a few days later. But the year was not over yet. Before it was out, Diana and Charles announced that they were separating. Soon, the Queen was making arrangements to pay tax for the first time in response to public demands. Not just the royal family but the monarchy itself had been rocked to its roots by the events of this year. This was no longer a story about relationships, it had become a critical constitutional issue. And the crisis was going to get even worse.

---

9 December US Marines land in Somalia

22 February Two boys are charged with the murder of James Bulger

26 February A bomb at New York's World Trade Center kills five

19 April A 51-day siege at the Branch Dividian cult in Waco ends in a huge fire

15 October South Africa's Nelson Mandel and FW de Klerk are awarded the Nobel Pea Prize

DAILY Mirror

Wednesday, November 25, 1992 **NEWSPAPER FOR THE NINETIES** Last month's daily sale: 3,505,251 **27p**
(INCORPORATING THE DAILY RECORD)

ONE IS DOING ONE'S BEST

But nobody's perfect, says croaky Queen

By JAMES WHITAKER

THE Queen opened her heart yesterday to tell the nation: I'm not perfect . . . but I'm doing my best.

She talked about what she called the Royal Family's "horrible year" of scandal and turmoil.

And in an amazingly candid speech, she accepted the monarchy should not be above criticism – but called at the same time for tolerance and understanding.

She said: "No section of the community has all the virtues. Neither does any have all the vices.

"I can quite sure that most people try to do their jobs as best they can, even if the result is not always successful."

She added: "He who has never failed to reach perfection has a right to be the harshest critic."

The Queen, her voice croaky as she fought a heavy cold, was speaking at a sumptuous lunch given by the Corporation of London to celebrate her 40 years on the throne. She was well aware the

● Turn to Page 4

ROYAL PLEA A plaintive-looking Queen yesterday as she told of her "horrible year" and asked Britain for understanding Picture: KENT GAVIN

'Happy' Mandy settles for just £100,000 a night

By RONALD RICKETTS and TINA WEAVER

POP bride Mandy Smith won more than half a million pounds from Bill Wyman yesterday – then celebrated with a mince pasty.

Mandy's £580,000 settlement works out at just over £100,000 for each of the five nights she spent with the Rolling Stone after their marriage.

Her mum Patsy said after the deal was announced: "Mandy's happy. I just thank God it's all over."

Mandy, 22, who divorced Wyman last year for his admitted adultery, was allowed to keep her £250,000 house at Muswell Hill, North London.

But mega-rich Wyman,

HOUSE: Mandy

56, still has a £2 million mansion in Suffolk, a villa at St Tropez, and three other homes in London.

Mandy lied in court, it was revealed last night.

She claimed she had received no payment for an interview with the magazine Hello.

But Wyman's lawyers produced evidence she received a substantial sum.

Wyman – said to be worth £24 million – agreed to give Mandy a lump sum of £130,000.

The rocker, who made

■ Turn to Page 2

INSIDE TODAY MIRROR *Woman* **12 PAGES** JUST FOR YOU

10 March Fred West is charged with multiple murder at 25 Cromwell Road

22 April 100,000 Tutsis are massacred by Hutus in Rwanda

29 April Elections take place in South Africa

8 July Kim Il Sung, the longest dictator of the twentieth century dies

19 October A suicide bomber kills 21 in Tel Aviv – the bloodiest attack for 16 years

1997

The last time a Labour Government had been elected, Tony Blair was still a student. Now, on May 1, 1997, he swept to power as the youngest Prime Minister of the century with the biggest landslide in modern polical history. The Tories had been a busted flush within months of John Major's defeat of Neil Kinnock in 1992 but success is never guaranteed in politics – certainly not on the scale of Mr Blair's triumph. Since becoming leader three years earlier on the death of John Smith, he had shown himself to have not just a good public image but a toughness and vision that inspired the British people after the long Tory years of decline. The *Daily Mirror* threw itself wholeheartedly behind the New Labour campaign. 'Margaret Thatcher promised to bring harmony, truth, faith and hope to Britain,' it said. 'Instead we have had discord, deceit, doubt and despair. Our health service has been all but destroyed, our manufacturing industry wrecked, our education system undermined. The old, the young, the sick, the poor, the disabled and the disadvantaged have suffered. A few have grown rich and powerful at the expense of the many.' The *Mirror* believed that with Mr Blair at No. 10, Britain would have the strong leadership it desperately needed. To the sound of D:Ream's 'Things Can Only Get Better', the Labour leader swept around the country at the head of the most efficient election machine Britain had ever seen. But even he could not have foreseen the scale of

REFLECTIONS

John Smith

John Smith was a rare politician – a man respected and admired by everyone. After two years as Labour leader he was confidently expected to became Prime Minister at the next election. But on May 12, 1994, he died from a massive heart attack. The sense of shock and loss extended far beyond Westminster and the Labour Party. The *Mirror* hailed him as 'The Best Prime Minister We Never Had' and said of him: 'He was honourable and honest. Decent and compassionate. Courageous and determined. He stood like a giant at Westminster. His integrity shone like a beacon.' The night before he died, John Smith made a magnificent speech at a gala dinner sponsored by the *Mirror*. His final words were: 'The chance to serve. That is all we ask.' Fate robbed him of that chance and the nation of an outstanding leader.

Bill Clinton was one of America's most popular presidents. He presided over the longest period of economic stability and prosperity enjoyed by the American people. But he was almost brought down by his affair with a young intern, Monica Lewinsky. When word leaked out that he had been involved with her, he completely denied it. 'I want you to listen to me. I'm going to say this again, I did not have sexual relations with that woman – Miss Lewinsky,'

Monica Lewinsky

he told a Grand Jury before TV viewers. When it was proved that he had lied, he was impeached, the first President to suffer that ignomy. But he narrowly fought off the threat and left office recognised throughout the world as a great politician and communicator.

'It is the start of a new dawn,' he told ecstatic party workers

victory. Dozens of Tories lost their seats, including a string of Cabinet ministers and, most spectacularly, Conservative golden boy Michael Portillo, who was trounced by the young – and bemused-looking – Labour hopeful, Stephen Twigg. As a new day broke, Mr Blair and his wife Cherie arrived at Labour's headquarters at Millbank to a rapturous welcome. 'It is the start of a new dawn,' he told ecstatic party workers. Later that day he moved with his family into 10 Downing Street, the first Prime Minister to live there with young children for a century. But the *Mirror*, having got its man elected, was not going to let him rest on his laurels. 'Now prove you're as great as we think you are,' it urged the new Prime Minister as he settled in to run the country.

REFLECTIONS

The Year One children at Dunblane primary school started their day in the gym on the morning of March 13, 1996. Minutes later 16 of them and their teacher were dead. Thomas Hamilton, a loner with a fixation about children and firearms, walked into the gym with four handguns and just started firing. The horror of those five- and six-year olds as they tried to get away can hardly be imagined. Twelve other children and two teachers were wounded, one of them dying later. Only one child escaped unscathed. When the slaughter was over, Hamilton turned a gun on himself. As parents rushed to the school, not knowing the fate of their children, they were directed into two lines. *Mirror* reporter Allan Rennie, who had a child at the school, explained what that meant: 'This way your child is alive. That way your child is dead.'

1994

11 December Russian troops invade Chechnya

1995

17 January An earthquake devastates Kobe, Japan, killing thousands

2 March Nick Leeson, the man accused of breaking Barings Bank is arrested

21 April 167 die when a bomb explodes at FBI headquarters in Oklahoma

28 May The Ebola virus spreads in Zaire

SOUVENIR

Mirror

Saturday May 3 1997

30p

1 O

IT'S TIME TO DO

Prime Minister Tony Blair is hugged by ecstatic wife Cherie at No10 Downing St yesterday. The triumphant Labour leader said: "We are charged with the deep responsibility of government. Today, enough of talking – it is time now to do."

PICTURE: ARNOLD SLATER

1995

14 June France resumes atomic tests in the Pacific

30 August NATO bombs Serbia

3 October Baseball star OJ Simpson is found not guilty of murder

4 November Israeli Prime Minister Yitzak Rabin is assassinated

1996

10 February A bomb explodes in London's docklands, ending the IRA ceasefire

1997

For 17 years Diana was part of our lives. Now where she was there is a void.

There never was anyone quite like Diana. From the moment she was first seen as a coy 19-year-old, she captured and captivated the world's heart. In a media age, she was the greatest icon there has ever been and probably ever will be. The breakdown of her marriage only increased public interest. So there was enormous interest when it was revealed that she had a new man – playboy Dodi Fayed, son of the owner of Harrod's. Their romantic Mediterranean cruise was reported in lavish detail and there was intense speculation about where this relationship might lead. At the end of their holiday they stayed in the Paris Ritz, owned by Dodi's father. Shortly after midnight on September 1 they left with a driver and bodyguard, their movements forever recorded on the hotel's CCTV cameras. Minutes later their limousine crashed in an underpass. Dodi and the driver were killed instantly. Diana died shortly after arriving in hospital. The world awoke to the unbelievable news that she was dead. As with the death of President Kennedy, everyone can remember where they were when they heard. The emotions of the nation were articulated on that Sunday morning by Tony Blair. On his way to church he said: 'She was the People's Princess.' The Voice of the *Mirror* said: 'It hardly seems possible that she is gone. For 17 years Diana was part of our lives. Now where she was there is a void. We will miss the brightness, gaiety and glamour she brought to us. We will miss the controversy she created and the fascination she held for untold millions. We will miss the love she showed to the sick, poor and desperate around the world. Her life is over and our lives have changed. For ever.' That sense of grief engulfed the nation. Thousands paid their respects, leaving an ocean of flowers, standing in silent vigil, weeping openly. Yet the royal family failed to react. The Queen stayed at Balmoral and soon the sorrow turned to anger. The *Mirror* spoke for the nation when it pleaded: 'Your people are suffering . . . Speak to us, Ma'am'. The following day, the Queen made an unprecedented live broadcast. Then came the funeral, with her young sons walking courageously behind her coffin. And her brother, Earl Spencer, making a remarkable, passionate funeral oration. The *Mirror* ran 338 pages on her death and funeral. Its final epitaph was: 'Diana will be remembered for many things. For the love she gave. For the courage she showed. For the brightness she brought to our lives. But most of all she will be remembered for her devotion to children. She was not just the People's Princess. She was the Children's Princess.'

The Mirror

Monday September 1 1997

30p

1961–1997

30 June A huge volcanic eruption in Montserrat buries the island in ash

30 July British rule in Hong Kong comes to an end

17 September In Oslo, ninety countries sign a treaty banning landmines

15 November Saddam Hussein expels six UN weapons inspectors from Iraq

17 November 58 tourists are murdered in a terrorist attack in Luxor, Egypt

1998

For 30 years Northern Ireland had been torn apart by violence, bloodshed and terror. Since the civil rights demonstrations of the sixties exploded into sectarian warfare and the British army moved in, the death toll had reached 3,249. Tony Blair came to power determined to put an end to 'the Troubles'. He appointed Mo Mowlam, a politician with remarkable human qualities, as his Northern Ireland Secretary, and talks began. As the spring of 1998 approached, the Prime Minister decided a deadline must be set to bring matters to a head. All parties met in Belfast in the week before Easter. Their task seemed impossible. Mr Blair was trying to reconcile the irreconcilable, to break down barriers of hatred which stretched back more than 300 years and to bring together people who loathed each other in every way. It needed the

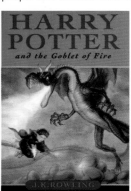

greatest imaginable leap of faith but Tony Blair and Mo Mowlam had it. The key players were the Irish Republic's Premier, Bertie Ahern; the leader of the Ulster Unionists, David Trimble; John Hume, inspirational head of the moderate SDLP; and Gerry Adams, once a key figure in the IRA, now leader of its political wing, Sinn Fein. They met – in separate rooms, since the Unionists would not even sit with the

When one party tried to walk out, Mr Blair stood in front of the door to stop them

Republicans – for four days. It was remorseless. Time after time the talks seemed to have collapsed but they stumbled on. When things looked hopeless, Mr Blair flew into Belfast, saying: 'I feel the hand of history upon our shoulders. I think we need to respond to it.' He forced the talks to continue. No one slept for more than a few hours. At one stage, when one party tried to walk out, Mr Blair stood in front of the door to stop them. During one crisis, President Clinton rang from Washington and eased the stalemate. The talks were supposed to end on Maundy Thursday but still no

deal had been done. So they stayed, still talking, still arguing, through another night until finally the breakthrough was made. Peace had come to Northern Ireland on Good Friday. Tony Blair, without sleep for 35 hours, said: 'Now we have the chance to raise children out of the shadows of fear.' The Good Friday Agreement set up a power-sharing Assembly on which Unionists and Republicans would work together. And most paramilitary groups, including the IRA, called a ceasefire. It was not perfect peace. But it was a great deal better than anything the people of Northern Ireland had known for a long time.

Posh and Becks

1 March 250,000 countryside protestors march in London, the largest UK demonstration for 15 years

22 June MPs vote to lower the homosexual age of consent from 18 to 16

7 August Terrorists bomb the American Embassy in Kenya

13 August Financial crises in Russia and the Far East rock the international economy

16 August The Real IRA explode a car bomb in Omagh, killing 29

Saturday April 11 1998

Mirror

www.mirror.co.uk

20p

THANK GOD

History as peace is declared in Ireland

By KEVIN MAGUIRE
Political Editor

THIS is the handshake that clinches the future of Northern Ireland after 30 years of blood and carnage.

Prime Minister Tony Blair and his Irish counterpart Bertie Ahern warmly clasp each other's hands after brokering an historic peace deal for Ulster following 60 hours of tortuous negotiations.

Minutes after the deal was announced last night, Mr Blair appeared on the steps of Stormont Castle to describe the settlement as "the beginning, not the end".

His voice choked with emotion as he said: "Today we have just the sense of the prize that is before us. The work to win that prize goes on.

"We must not let that slip from our grasp."

Mr Blair flew to Belfast on Tuesday to rescue the deal.

And it took the last minute intervention of US President Bill Clinton to convince the parties to end the wrangling — leaving Northern Ireland celebrating its happiest day in 30 years.

FULL STORY: Pages 2, 3, 4, 5, 6, 7 & 9

TRIUMPHANT: Irish Premier Bertie Ahern and Tony Blair shake hands at Stormont yesterday after announcing the historic deal

IT'S ALL OVER

---

18 August Bill Clinton testifies to a Grand Jury about his relationship with Monica Lewinsky

21 August America attacks Afghanistan and Sudan in retaliation for the African embassy bombings

24 November The Queen announces the end of hereditary peers in the House of Lords

17 December America and Great Britain launch air-strikes against Iraq

1999

1 January The European Single Currency is launched

2000

The past century had been the most wonderful yet terrible hundred years

'Good morning. Welcome to the 21st century and the third millennium.' It was January 1, 2000, and the _Daily Mirror_ was looking with bleary eyes but a clear vision on the prospect facing Britain and the world. Some readers had questioned the great fuss made over the new millennium. It was just another date, they said. But there was a real sense of something ending and something beginning. Looking back was the easy part. The past century had been 'the most wonderful yet terrible hundred years.' If you had to choose one word to sum them up it would be 'more': 'More people, more happiness, more suffering, more comfort, more inventions, more speed, more stress, more knowledge, more crime, more wars, more travel, more killing, more compassion, more culture, more brutality. It has been the most amazing period ever for mankind.' 'So are we better off on this last day of the century than our ancestors were on the first?' the _Mirror_ asked and answered: 'Of course we are. We live longer, in far greater comfort and better health, and are better educated. Most of all,

there is a hunger for knowledge that is pushing back the boundaries ever faster as mankind strides into the next century.' The _Mirror_ looked forward with eager antici-pation, lots of wonder and a little concern as to what the next hundred years would bring. Saying goodbye to the 1900s was rather like moving from a beloved home or throwing out a comfy old suit. But there was a wonderful, exciting new century ahead. Trying to prophesy what would happen in it was beyond any power on Earth, the paper said: 'If you don't believe that, imagine it is January 1, 1900. Could you even start to visualise what your life would be like today?' Then the _Mirror_ asked readers to go back to the start of the millennium just ending – to January 1, 1000, when William the Conqueror hadn't been born and British history had barely started. Considering what had happened in the thousand years since then and the current pace of change 'trying to guess what life will be like on January 1, 3000, is beyond imagination. Our descendants might be living on a still-undiscovered planet – or back in crude huts.' The _Mirror_'s final word on the new century was: 'On this momentous New Year's Day, there are many thoughts and hopes for the future. But the most important of all should be the same as the one of 2,000 years ago. May there be peace on Earth and goodwill to all.' How soon that dream was dashed.

12 February The attempted impeachment of President Clinton fails

24 February A report into the death of Stephen Lawrence condemns racism in the British police force

14 April India and Pakistan test long-range nuclear weapons

21 April 15 American teenagers die in a gun attack at Columbine High School, USA

25 April NATO begins to airlift Kosovan refugees to safety

The Mirror

SOUVENIR EDITION · www.mirror.co.uk · 35p

JAN 1st 2000
WELCOME TO THE NEW MILLENNIUM

THE first sunrise of the 21st century at Pitt Island in the Pacific yesterday. Around the globe billions celebrated a new beginning

---

7 May Elections take place to new Executives in Scotland and Wales

11 August The first total eclipse of the sun since 1927 takes place over Britain

20 September UN peace keepers enter East Timor to quell violence after a referendum on independence

5 October Two high-speed trains collide near Paddington, killing 27

2000

1 March Floods from the swollen Zambezi river displace millions in Mozambique

2000

REFLECTIONS

A devastating outbreak of foot-and-mouth disease threatened to wreck not only the farming industry but thousands of businesses. 'Don't panic' the *Mirror* pleaded on its front page on February 22, 2001, but the Government did. It ordered people to stay away from the countryside with terrible economic consequences. It also insisted on slaughtering 6 million cattle in areas where there was any outbreak of the fast-spreading disease. The daily sight of huge funeral pyres of blazing animals shocked the nation. This policy was roundly condemned by the *Mirror* as an over-reaction, a view later supported by official reports into the foot-and-mouth outbreak, which cost the country £8 billion.

The last years of the 20th century saw an astonishing rise in the development of new technology and gadgets, including the internet and e-mail which transformed the way people worked. But nothing had an impact like the mobile phone. A survey of young people at the end of the century voted it the greatest invention of the previous hundred years. In the three months running up to the millennium alone, 4.5 million mobiles were sold in the UK. Thirty million were in use by the end of that year, despite British users having to pay the highest tariffs in the world.

'The most important, the most wondrous map ever produced by mankind'

The greatest scientific discoveries often don't receive much attention in the press. It is only with hindsight that it is realised how important they are. But on June 27, 2000, the *Mirror* revealed 'the greatest scientific leap forward since man landed on the moon' – in fact, it was arguably even greater than that. Scientists had cracked the DNA code of human life, paving the way for dramatic breakthroughs in the treatment of cancer and other terrible diseases. For the first time they had mapped the body's blueprint, known as the human genome. Understanding the complex make-up of the human being means that within a few years many serious medical conditions could be treatable. One leading scientist hailed the 'book of life' breakthrough as greater even than the invention of the wheel. He said: 'This is the outstanding achievement not only of our lifetime but in terms of human history. This code is the essence of mankind. As long as humans exist it is going to be important and will be used.' What

had been discovered was the genetic map of the DNA that makes us what we are, governs our biological functions and determines our susceptibility to illnesses. The aim of the project was to decode the three billion molecular 'letters' that form the human DNA and provide all the instructions for making a person. The Anglo-US team led by Britain's Dr John Sulston and America's Dr Craig Venter had made it possible for future generations to banish inherited disorders, screen for vulnerability to disease, tailor treatment to genetic make-up, create thousands of new drugs, repair faulty genes and extend lifespan. Within a few years, people could in effect be barcoded at birth to provide doctors with an invaluable database. The discovery of the human genome was announced simultaneously in London and Washington by Tony Blair and President Clinton via a satellite link. Mr Blair said: 'I am proud that Britain has played with others a pioneering role.' Mr Clinton said: 'This is the most important, the most wondrous map ever produced by mankind.' Professor Richard Dawkins of Oxford said: 'Along with Bach's music, Shakespeare's sonnets and the Apollo space programme, the Human Genome Project is one of those achievements of the human spirit that makes me proud to be human.'

Foot-and-mouth pyre

---

20 May Prime Minister's wife Cherie Booth gives birth to a baby boy

29 June Cuban refugee Elian Gonzalez is returned home from America

25 July A burst tyre causes Concorde to crash on take-off from Paris, killing 113

August British oarsman Steve Redgrave wins his fifth Olympic gold medal

14 August 198 Russian crew are fatally trapped in the *Kursk* submarine

The Mirror

Tuesday June 27 2000

www.mirror.co.uk

32p

Inside: Our brilliant M mag

IT'S ONE GIANT LEAP FOR WOMANKIND

IT'S ONE SMALL PIECE OF MAN..
ONE GIANT LEAP FOR MANKIND

Joy as scientists crack DNA code of life

TRIUMPH: John Sulston

By JILL PALMER and LUCY ROCK

THE greatest scientific leap forward since man landed on the moon was announced yesterday.

Scientists — led by Britain's John Sulston and America's Craig Venter — have finally cracked the DNA code of human life, paving the way for dramatic breakthroughs in the treatment of cancer and other killer diseases.

Mapping the body's blueprint, known as the human genome, was hailed last night as a turning point in history. The new understanding of the complex make-up of the human being means that within 25 years heart disease and many cancers could be curable.

Tony Blair called it a "revolution in medical science, the first great techno-logical triumph of the 21st century".

FULL STORY: PAGES 4,5,6 & 7

TRIUMPH: Craig Venter

---

1 October A second intifada by the Palestinians begins in the Middle East

17 October Speed restrictions are placed on 1,000 miles of Britain's railways

11 December George W Bush wins the American Presidential Election following a Supreme Court ruling

2001

1 May Anti-capitalist demonstrators hold a May Day protest in London

7 June Tony Blair becomes the first Labour leader to secure a full second term in office

2001

New York was just waking up on a beautiful morning when out of the clear blue sky came mass murder and terror. At 8.58am local time on September 11, 2001, American Airlines Boeing 767 Flight 11 with 92 passengers and crew on board sliced into the World Trade Centre's Tower One where thousands of office workers had just started their day. Fire engulfed the upper ten storeys. Bodies and debris rained down on the Manhattan streets below. Before anyone realised it was not an accident, a second plane had ploughed into WTC's Tower Two, this time in view of a live television audience. Less than half an hour later, another hijacked aircraft smashed into the Pentagon. A fourth plane, probably headed for the White House, crashed when its

REFLECTIONS

Britain had been threatened before by strikes but not for well over a century had there been such an anarchic attempt to bring down the government. And it was all over the price of fuel. It began in a small way with a protest at the high tax on diesel and petrol. Somehow it escalated out of control until oil depots were blockaded and garage pumps ran dry. Supermarkets and shops warned they would have to close. The country was grinding to a halt. Public opinion, which had backed the action, now turned against the motley band leading it, and the blockades were lifted. But it was the only time since Tony Blair became leader of the Labour Party that the Tories managed to edge ahead in opinion polls.

Drugs had become an increasing problem with growing demands for the law to be strengthened. The *Mirror* tried to remove the hysteria from the debate in a shock issue, pointing out that an estimated 2 million young people took Ecstacy every week. 'Simply preaching to youngsters about the dangers of Ecstasy will not prevent them taking it. Solemn warnings on TV by fuddy-duddy MPs won't stop them. Young people do it because their friends do it. They see it as a harmless pleasure.' What was needed was sensible education about the risks, the paper argued.

The second tower, then the first, collapsed in horrible slow motion

incredibly brave passengers fought with the hijackers. It was, as the *Mirror* said, a declaration of war. But the worst was to come. The second tower, then the first, collapsed in horrible slow motion, killing anyone still inside or nearby. Original estimates were that 10,000 died, although the figure miraculously came down to less than a third of that, including hundreds of firefighters and police officers. The news of the atrocities was broken to President George W. Bush, only in office a few months, as he attended a conference. The look of panic in his eyes said everything. The stories of heroism and suffering were extraordinary. US Editor Andy Lines wrote: 'People jumped from windows of the 110-storey buildings – some from as high as the 80th floor. A couple plunged to the ground hand-in-hand as fireball explosions ripped through the symbol of America's financial might. Dozens more clamoured for help from behind the glass as entire storeys were torn apart.' It was soon clear that the attacks were organised by al-Qaeda. Their leader, Osama bin Laden, became the world's most wanted man. America mobilised for a war on terror. Tony Blair played a leading role in the days that followed by helping to assemble a united international response. Within weeks US and British forces moved into Afghanistan, where the cruel Taliban regime played host to al-Qaeda. On the day after 9/11, the *Mirror* said: 'This was not just the worst terrorist atrocity there has ever been. It has changed the world for ever just as surely as it has changed the Manhattan skyline. It might seem as if nothing could be worse than what we witnessed yesterday, but it could be.'

THE Mirror   Friday September 14 2001 32

Astonishing photos moments before collapse

INSIDE THE TOWER

SEE PAGES 15, 16, 17, 18 & 19

---

28 June Slobodan Milosevic is flown to the Hague to be tried for 'crimes against humanity'

19 July Conservative peer Lord Archer is jailed for four years for perjury

29 January President Bush describes Iraq, Iran and North Korea as an 'axis of evil'

9 February Princess Margaret dies in her sleep

13 March President Mugabe is re-elected in Zimbabwe amid accusations of intimidation and fraud

THE Mirror

Wednesday September 12 2001

32p

WAR ON THE WORLD

29 April Diane Pretty loses an appeal to allow her husband to help her die

10 May Seven die when a train is derailed at Potters Bar, Hertfordshire

27 August The World Summit for Sustainable Development opens in Johannesburg

12 October A bomb explodes in a disco in Kuta, Bali, killing 192

26 October A siege in the Moscow Theatre ends with the death of 118 hostages from gas poisoning

2002-3

WAR The beginning of the 21st century had started, like the 20th, with great hopes for peace and a new world order. It had taken 14 years for those hopes to be dashed then. Now they vanished in less than two. The terrible events of 9/11 led to a united international response against terrorism but President George W. Bush and his White House associates were determined to go further. The *Daily Mirror*, while grieving with the American people for their losses and supporting action to rid the world of terrorism, became uneasy at the use of military might. Particularly as Tony Blair joined with the US first in Afghanistan, where al-Qaeda had been based, and then in an unpopular war on Iraq. The paper worried about what would replace the tyrannical and cruel Taliban regime in Afghanistan and feared an open-ended commitment for British forces. The assault on Afghanistan achieved its immediate objectives swiftly, although Osama bin Laden, the mastermind of the September 11 atrocities, was not captured. Yet months later British troops were still there. 'What the hell is going on?' the

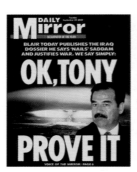

Mirror demanded in one memorable edition. Worse was to come. President Bush was determined to wage war on Iraq to remove Saddam Hussein. Tony Blair, while attempting to steer him down a United Nations route, agreed that British troops would join US forces. Mr Blair claimed that the Iraqi despot had weapons of mass destruction. The *Mirror* demanded see the evidence. When Downing Street produced what they claimed was a dossier of killer facts, it was rejected by the paper and its readers as failing to provide any genuine evidence. Public opinion was overwhelmingly against war and the *Mirror* played a crucial role in providing a focus for opposition, including backing the biggest mass demonstration ever seen in Britain. But on March 20, 2003, the war began.

'She was quite simply the most magical grandmother you could have

ROYALS She was not just the Queen Mother, she was the nation's granny. She had helped the people of Britain through the dark days of war, seen her husband die tragically young yet had created a unique role for herself. Even after she turned 100, the Queen Mother still insisted on performing official duties. On February 11, 2002, her younger daughter, Margaret, died. True to form, the Queen Mother insisted on going to the funeral. Six weeks later, she was dead herself. The most moving tribute came from her grandson Charles. Clearly distraught, he said: 'She was quite simply the most magical grandmother you could have and I was utterly devoted to her. Her departure has left an irreplaceable chasm in countless lives but, thank God, we are all the richer for the sheer joy of her presence and everything she stood for.' At first there was little public reaction and the *Mirror* apologised on its front page: 'Sorry, ma'am, that so many of us are showing you so little respect.' The response was extraordinary. More than 400,000 paid their respects when her coffin was moved to lie in state in

Westminster Hall. Queues formed four miles long and people waited for more than 12 hours to file past the coffin. It had been a ghastly time for the Queen but her subjects turned out in their millions two months later to celebrate her Golden Jubilee. But the joy of those happy days was not to last. In October, former royal butler Paul Burrell went on trial accused of stealing a number of items which had belonged to Princess Diana. The case collapsed in a fiasco and Burrell told his incredible story in the *Mirror*. It included the amazing warning which the Queen had once given him: 'Be careful, Paul. There are powers at work in this country about which we have no knowledge.'

2 January Two teenage girls are shot dead in a gangland feud in Birmingham	**14 January** A police officer is stabbed to death during an anti-terrorist raid in Manchester	**1 February** Africa is gripped by an AIDS epidemic. Two million deaths are recorded in a year	**1 February** The American space shuttle Columbia explodes on re-entry	**17 February** A congestion charge scheme is introduced in central London

THE Mirror

Tuesday March 19 2002

NEWSPAPER OF THE YEAR 32p

M's OSCAR FASHION SECRETS SEE PULLOUT

Four months ago, Tony Blair said the war in Afghanistan was as good as over.. now 1,700 British troops are being sent in and we're told to expect casualties

WHAT THE HELL IS GOING ON?

FULL STORY AND ANALYSIS: PAGES 4 AND 5

DAILY Mirror

Thursday June 13 2002

NEWSPAPER OF THE YEAR

ARGENTINA TRAGEDY

DON'T FORGET TO PACK YOUR HANDBAGS, DEARS

PS: AS WE SAID YESTERDAY .. WE'RE THROUGH

DAILY Mirror

Wednesday November 6 2002

NEWSPAPER OF THE YEAR 20p

WORLD Exclusive

WHAT THE QUEEN TOLD THE BUTLER AT THAT MEETING:

“ Be careful Paul, nobody has ever been closer to a member of my family than you were to Diana. There are powers at work in this country about which we have no knowledge ”

REVELATIONS: Paul Burrell yesterday

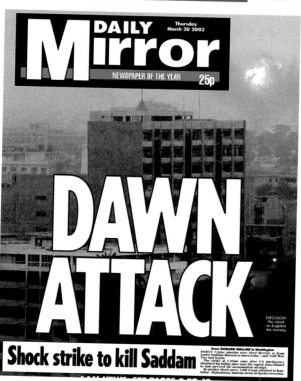

DAILY Mirror

Thursday March 20 2003

NEWSPAPER OF THE YEAR 25p

DAWN ATTACK

EXPLOSION: The attack on Baghdad this morning

Shock strike to kill Saddam

From RICHARD WALLACE in Washington

LOOKING FORWARD

By David Seymour
Readers' Editor

Newspapers are a record of the past but occasionally they attempt to predict the future. It is not a safe pastime. Predictions can be disproved swiftly while it takes much longer for them to be proved true. Yet as the *Daily Mirror* celebrates its centenary, it is worth trying to forecast what the next hundred years will bring. Fascination with the media is stronger today than ever. There are many competing vehicles for providing information and the speed of change is dizzying. Can we even be sure there will be newspapers at the end of this century? As much as anything is certain, yes we can. The *Mirror*'s editor, Piers Morgan, wrote recently: "If newspapers didn't exist, someone would invent them." Electronic media provide a fantastic alternative, not a substitute. As this book has shown, the story of the *Daily Mirror* is a history of the changing face of the media. Not just newspapers, either. The *Mirror* has recorded the launch and growth of radio, television and electronic methods of communication. Naturally we have no idea of what will be invented in the next few years, let alone the next hundred. Nor can we do more than imagine what techniques of news and picture gathering there will be. Though you can be sure human ingenuity will continue to play as great a part in the future as it has in the past. The one thing for certain about ever more sophisticated technology is that it will fail to work at crucial moments. Journalists don't. On the contrary, when the pressure is on, they are at their best. The war in Iraq has shown that ingenuity, bravery and professionalism are as vital today as they were when the *Mirror* covered the Balkans war in 1912 and the two world wars. And as necessary. For the demand for swift, detailed and accurate news is escalating. We have a good idea of the sort of stories which will fill our pages in the years ahead. The royals will continue to provide romance, pageantry and outrage, as they have done so often. There will be tales of heroism and tragedy. Disasters and crimes. Marriages and divorces. Wars and famines. Compassion and scandal. Yes, it will be the same fare which has gripped the public throughout the first tabloid century though with new generations of journalists providing them for new generations of readers. But the actual stories will remain a mystery until the moment they break. Part of the thrill of journalism is not knowing what the day will bring. The *Daily Mirror*'s first hundred years were full of excitement. But there is nothing more exciting than not knowing what tomorrow will bring. As the *Mirror*'s founder, Alfred Harmsworth, wrote a century ago, the possibilities for the future are infinite.